HUMANISM, READING, AND ENGLISH LITERATURE
1430–1530

Humanism, Reading, and English Literature 1430–1530

DANIEL WAKELIN

OXFORD
UNIVERSITY PRESS

OXFORD

UNIVERSITY PRESS

Great Clarendon Street, Oxford OX2 6DP

Oxford University Press is a department of the University of Oxford.
It furthers the University's objective of excellence in research, scholarship,
and education by publishing worldwide in

Oxford New York

Auckland Cape Town Dar es Salaam Hong Kong Karachi
Kuala Lumpur Madrid Melbourne Mexico City Nairobi
New Delhi Shanghai Taipei Toronto

With offices in

Argentina Austria Brazil Chile Czech Republic France Greece
Guatemala Hungary Italy Japan Poland Portugal Singapore
South Korea Switzerland Thailand Turkey Ukraine Vietnam

Oxford is a registered trade mark of Oxford University Press
in the UK and in certain other countries

Published in the United States
by Oxford University Press Inc., New York

British Library Cataloguing in Publication Data

Data available

Library of Congress Cataloging in Publication Data

Data available

Typeset by Laserwords Private Limited, Chennai, India
Printed in Great Britain
on acid-free paper by
Biddles Ltd., King's Lynn, Norfolk

ISBN 978–0–19–921588–1

Acknowledgements

This book began under the guidance of Richard Beadle, a supervisor whose learning is matched only by his prudence and patience. Derek Pearsall and James Simpson examined what became about half of this book and made crucial suggestions for the other half. A. S. G. Edwards gave me bibliographical advice to get me started. Many other people passed on references and unpublished work or commented on my unpublished work: Julia Boffey, Sarah Cain, Alexandra Gillespie, Penny Granger, George Keiser, Lucy Lewis, Linne Mooney, Catherine Nall, Suzanne Reynolds, David Rundle, Fred Schurink, and Christopher Tilmouth. In the final stages Mark Hall and Ruth Roberts helped me to check things. I gladly thank these people for any improvements which they have prompted and apologize for any faults which they would have avoided.

Support for this project firstly came from a three-year doctoral research grant from the Arts and Humanities Research Council and then from the Master and Fellows of St Catharine's College and of Christ's College, Cambridge, who were kind enough to give me employment. Support for travel came from the graduate research fund at Trinity Hall, Cambridge, and from the Huntington Library, San Marino. I am very grateful to all of these organizations.

For allowing me to consult their books, often at their inconvenience, I must thank the librarians and archivists of Corpus Christi College, Emmanuel College, Gonville and Caius College, Pembroke College, St John's College, Trinity College, and the University Library in Cambridge; the University Library in Chicago; the University Library in Glasgow; the Brotherton Library in Leeds; the British Library, the College of Arms, Lambeth Palace Library and the National Archives in London; Chetham's Library and the John Rylands Library, Manchester; Balliol College, the Bodleian Library, Corpus Christi College, Exeter College, Magdalen College, Merton College, the Queen's College, and Wadham College in Oxford; Salisbury Cathedral Library; and the Huntington Library in San Marino.

I could not have made so many trips to Oxford without a kind welcome from my late and sadly missed aunt, Polly Brockall, nor to other cities without the friends on whose cat-ridden sofas I have tried to sleep. My parents, Roger and Jenny, have encouraged me in too many ways to list. And the most supportive was Joel who, though incredulous that anyone would write a book about a load of old books, helped me to do so.

Contents

List of Abbreviations and References

In quotations from manuscripts or early printed books, I expand all abbreviations silently. Similarly, in quoting from modern printed editions, I remove the italics or diacritics which marked abbreviations and expand ampersands. I cite incunables from specific copies, with the library and the classmark in parentheses after the place, publisher, and date. I cite fifteenth- and sixteenth-century translations by the translators rather than by the original authors, or by their editor if they are anonymous. All translations into modern English are my own unless stated. I translate *res publica* as *commonweal*, which is vague and archaic enough not to pre-empt fifteenth-century definitions with the connotations of any current phrase. I use the following abbreviations for books, journals, or libraries cited in more than two chapters:

Anstey (ed.), *Epistolae*	Henry Anstey (ed.), *Epistolae Academicae Oxon.*, Oxford Historical Society, 35–6, 2 vols. (Oxford Clarendon Press, 1898)
Bekynton Correspondence	George Williams (ed.), *Official Correspondence of Thomas Bekynton*, RS 56, 2 vols. (London: Longman and Trübner, 1872)
BL	London, British Library
BJRL	*Bulletin of the John Rylands Library*
BLR	*Bodleian Library Record*
BodL	Oxford, Bodleian Library
Boethius, *De Consolatione*	Boethius, *De Consolatione philosophiae*, in his *De Consolatione philosophiae; Opuscula theologica*, ed. Claudio Moreschini (Munich: Teubner, 2000)
BRUC	A. B. Emden, *A Biographical Register of the University of Cambridge to 1500* (Cambridge: Cambridge University Press, 1963)
BRUO	A. B. Emden, *A Biographical Register of the University of Oxford to A.D. 1500*, 3 vols. (Oxford: Clarendon Press, 1957–9)
Carlson, *English Humanist Books*	David R. Carlson, *English Humanist Books: Writers and Patrons, Manuscript and Print, 1475–1525* (Toronto: University of Toronto Press, 1993)
Caxton's Own Prose	*Caxton's Own Prose*, ed. N. F. Blake (London: Deutsch, 1973), with references to section numbers and line numbers
CCCC	Cambridge, Corpus Christi College Library
CHBB: III	Lotte Hellinga and J. B. Trapp (eds.), *The Cambridge History of the Book in Britain. Volume III: 1400–1557* (Cambridge: Cambridge University Press, 1999)

CUL	Cambridge, University Library
DNB	H. C. G. Matthew and others (eds.), *The Oxford Dictionary of National Biography* (Oxford: Oxford University Press, 2004); <http://www.oxforddnb.com/subscribed/>
EETS	Early English Text Society
os	original series
es	extra series
EHR	*English Historical Review*
Grafton and Jardine, *Humanism*	Anthony Grafton and Lisa Jardine, *From Humanism to the Humanities: Education and the Liberal Arts in Fifteenth- and Sixteenth-Century Europe* (London: Duckworth, 1986)
GUL	Glasgow, University Library
HEHL	San Marino, CA, Henry E. Huntington Library
HL	*Humanistica Lovaniensia*
Humfrey 1970	[A. C. de la Mare and Richard Hunt], *Duke Humfrey and English Humanism in the Fifteenth Century* (Oxford: Bodleian Library, 1970)
Humfrey 1988	[A. C. de la Mare and Stanley Gillam], *Duke Humfrey's Library and the Divinity School 1488–1988* (Oxford: Bodleian Library, 1988)
JMH	*Journal of Medieval History*
JRL	Manchester, John Rylands Library
Kekewich and others (eds.), *Vale's Book*	Margaret Lucille Kekewich and others (eds.), *The Politics of Fifteenth-Century England: John Vale's Book* (Stroud: Sutton, 1995)
LPL	London, Lambeth Palace Library
Lydgate, *Fall*	John Lydgate, *The Fall of Princes*, ed. Henry Bergen, EETS es 121–4, 4 vols. (London: Oxford University Press, 1924–7), with reference to book numbers and line numbers
Lydgate, *Minor Poems*	John Lydgate, *Minor Poems*, ed. Henry Noble MacCracken, EETS es 107, os 192, 2 vols. (London: Kegan Paul, Trench, Trübner, 1911–34)
MED	Hans Kurath and others (eds.), *The Middle English Dictionary* (Ann Arbor, MI: University of Michigan Press, 1952–2001); <http://ets.umdl.umich.edu/m/med/>
MP	*Modern Philology*
Myers (ed.), *Household*	A. R. Myers (ed.), *The Household of Edward IV: The Black Book and the Ordinance of 1478* (Manchester: Manchester University Press, 1959)
NA	London, National Archives
NML	*New Medieval Literatures*
OBC	Oxford, Balliol College Library
OED	James A. H. Murray and others (eds.), *The Oxford English Dictionary*, ed. John A. Simpson and E. S. C. Weiner,

	2nd edn. 20 vols. (Oxford: Clarendon Press, 1989); <http://dictionary.oed.com/entrance.dtl>
OMC	Oxford, Magdalen College Library
Ovid, *Metamorphoses*	Publius Ovidius Naso, *Metamorphoses*, ed. William S. Anderson (Stuttgart: Teubner, 1977)
Rundle, 'Republics and Tyrants'	David Rundle, 'Of Republics and Tyrants: Aspects of *quattrocento* humanist writings and their reception in England, *c*.1400–*c*. 1460' (unpublished D.Phil. thesis, University of Oxford, 1997)
RS	Rolls Series
Simpson, *Reform*	James Simpson, *The Oxford English Literary History: Volume 2: 1350–1547: Reform and Cultural Revolution* (Oxford: Oxford University Press, 2002)
SJC	Cambridge, St John's College Library
STC	A. W. Pollard and G. R. Redgrave, *A Short Title Catalogue of Books Printed in England, Scotland, and Ireland, and of English Books Printed Abroad, 1475–1640*, ed. W. A. Jackson, F. S. Ferguson, and Katherine F. Pantzer, 2nd edn., 3 vols. (London: Bibliographical Society, 1976–91)
Strohm, *Politique*	Paul Strohm, *Politique: Languages of Statecraft between Chaucer and Shakespeare* (Notre Dame, IN: University of Notre Dame Press, 2005)
TCBS	*Transactions of the Cambridge Bibliographical Society*
TCC	Cambridge, Trinity College Library
Wars in France	Joseph Stevenson (ed.), *Letters and Papers Illustrative of the Wars of the English in France during the Reign of Henry the Sixth*, RS 22, 2 vols. (London: HMSO, 1861–4)
Watts, *Henry VI*	John Watts, *Henry VI and the Politics of Kingship* (Cambridge: Cambridge University Press, 1996)
Weiss, *Humanism*	Roberto Weiss, *Humanism in England During the Fifteenth Century*, 3rd edn. (1941; Oxford: Blackwell, 1967)
Wilson and Fenlon (ed.), *Winchester*	Edward Wilson and Iain Fenlon (ed.), *The Winchester Anthology* (Cambridge: Brewer, 1981)
[Worcester], *Noblesse*	[William Worcester], *The Boke of Noblesse*, ed. John Gough Nichols (London: Roxburghe Club, 1860)
[Worcester] (trans.), *Tullius de senectute*	[William Worcester] (trans.), *Tullius de senectute* (Westminster: Caxton, 1481; STC 5293; CUL, classmark Inc.3.J.1.1. [3497])
Worcestre, *Itineraries*	William Worcestre [*sic*], *Itineraries*, ed. John H. Harvey (Oxford: Clarendon Press, 1969)

All quotations from the work of Chaucer come from *The Riverside Chaucer*, ed. Larry D. Benson (1987; Oxford: Oxford University Press, 1988).

1

Introduction: humanism as reading

Tuam ob humanitatem humanissime in me non paucis quidem temporibus collatam
tibi gracias ago maximas : necnon tui propter assiduam illamque gratissimam conuer-
sacionem qua tecum sum fructus : quum illis finibus illive commitatui siue teritorio
proxime interfui. quibus etsi vires ad gracias condignas referendas minime valent siue
valide constant : precibus attamen vtar. Quod preterea ad me scribis ut interludia
siue commedias anglicanas vulgaresve tibi nanciscerer siue adquirerem summo quidem conatus labore tandem acquisiui. Adeo namque raro existunt possessoresque
eorundem ita varij ut circa talia conari siue niti labor merito frustratorius appellari
nuncuparive potest. Quare ut tuis votis satisfacerem : assiduo labore conatus adulatorijsque verbis possessorum animos tandem mitigaui eaque lege acquisiui ut quam
primum transferas exemplar deinde mihi restituas ut tradam possessori. vale. Tuus
singulis in rebus prout vires suppetunt

I thank you for the kindness you have so warmly shown me, on not a few occasions
indeed, and also for the constant and most pleasant visits I have enjoyed in your
company, when I was present in that place, or in that county or neighbouring country.
Although my powers by no means avail nor suffice to offer fit praise, nevertheless I
will offer prayers. Besides which, you write to ask me to obtain or get for you the
interludes or comedies in English or in the vulgar tongue. And indeed I've striven with
the greatest effort and at last I've got them. Until now they've rarely been available
and the owners of them have been so fickle that you might well call or pronounce it a
fruitless task to strive or aim for them. Therefore, so that I could answer your prayers, I
strove with diligent labour and I have softened the hearts of the owners with flattering
words. And I've got a copy, with the stipulation that as soon as you transcribe the
exemplar then you'll return it to me so that I can return it to the owner. Farewell,
yours in all things, as far as strength allows him.

At the very beginning of the sixteenth century some schoolmaster or pupil
copied this letter into a small collection of letters. The letters mostly come
from a network of boys and old boys of Magdalen College School in Oxford.[1]
Why were the letters collected? They exemplify good Latin, one of the goals of
the school in Oxford, and good correspondence, a transferable skill for a keen

---

[1] BL, MS Arundel 249, f.82v; transcribed wrongly in Ewald Flügel (ed.), 'Kleinere Mitteilungen
aus Handschriften', *Anglia*, 14 (1892), 463–501 (498).

young man to learn. A few of the letters are by Bernard André or Thomas More, not members of the school but admirable models of style, and thus these letters suggest the influence of humanism on the young schoolboys. The handwriting is unexceptional, but someone has added to it some curving 'brackets' or *lunulae*, a punctuation mark then rare in England, commoner in humanist milieux in Italy. The rest of the manuscript has verses with glosses, composed by Stanbridge, the famous master at the school, and Latin verse by Stefano Surigone, an Italian poet who had visited England.[2] In all of the letters, as in this one, men worry whether they are eloquent enough to address their friends, cultivating the fine manner of the humanists. They are in training for the sixteenth century, for the English Renaissance.

But if there are signs of humanism in these letters, then something surprising appears. What does this particular letter discuss? The writer has been hunting for 'interludes or comedies in English or in the vulgar tongue'. These men cultivate not only Latin style but English drama and they cultivate it with 'persistent work' ('assiduo labore'), hunting out rare copies from the friends of friends. This 'work' was normally found among the great bibliophiles and normally applied to lost letters of Cicero or recondite classical verse. Here the humanists seem interested in English literature. The interest recurs in another letter in this book of model letters: in one letter, the writer discusses 'the parts which I added to the comedy of Solomon' ('eas partes quas in comediam illam que de salamone est adiecimus'). A play about Solomon is mentioned too in some phrases for translation practice from Magdalen College School. Who knows which language the play of Solomon was in? But it is intriguing, if it might be English, that the addressee of this other letter is John Holt, a master at Magdalen College School, and that the writer is Thomas More.[3] More, Holt, and the men of Magdalen are familiar as pioneers of humanist studies in England in the sixteenth century. What is less familiar is their interest in 'the vulgar tongue' both for grammar and even in reading plays for pleasure. There is no shame about that. These men were trained to use their letters to advertise their erudition; yet they could advertise their reading English in these letters too, it seems, as part of their literary lives.

The trace of 'the vulgar tongue' is slender though: the plays have rarely been available in the past ('Adeo namque raro existunt'). Yet we can pursue that trace into the past, beyond the letter. We know a lot about one play

---

[2] David Thomson, *A Descriptive Catalogue of Middle English Grammatical Texts* (New York: Garland, 1979), 233–8. For *lunulae*, see BL, MS Arundel 249, ff.81v–82r.

[3] BL, MS Arundel 249, f.85v, discussed by William Nelson (ed.), *A Fifteenth Century School Book* (Oxford: Clarendon Press, 1956), pp. xxvii–xxix, 27. Carole Weinberg, 'Thomas More and the Use of English in Early Tudor Education', *Moreana*, 15 (1978), 21–30 (23–5), describes the context.

which More and Holt quite likely knew. Both spent time in the household where was performed *Fulgens and Lucres*, the earliest secular play in English. (Chapter 6 returns to *Fulgens and Lucres*.) But when we read *Fulgens and Lucres*, we can pursue the traces further backwards still. It may be the first in a sequence of plays, but it is just one more in an already distinguished line of other works 'in the vulgar tongue' written and read by the humanists of the century beforehand. *Fulgens and Lucres* was based upon a neo-Latin, Florentine debate translated into English by a famous humanist nobleman. The debate was printed in translation in London in 1481 alongside translations of Cicero's dialogues. One of the dialogues had been dedicated in 1472 to the founder of Magdalen College School. The founder, a bishop, had employed as his chaplain a priest who translated Vegetius into rime royal in 1460, imitating the style of a translation made in 1441 for Humfrey, Duke of Gloucester. And so we can trace backwards from a scholar collecting English plays to the father of English humanism, good Duke Humfrey, commissioning translations from the classics. What we find is a longstanding humanist interest in English literature during the fifteenth century, long before Medwall and More. It is the first and simpler task of this book to trace this 'vernacular humanism' during the fifteenth century.

HUMANISM IN ENGLISH LITERATURE DURING THE FIFTEENTH CENTURY

To link humanism with the literature of those years perhaps seems surprising. It is often said that there was little humanism in fifteenth-century England—in any language. When Roberto Weiss wrote, over sixty years ago, a book called *Humanism in England During the Fifteenth Century*, he hinted in his opening lines that it was indeed *during* those years that humanism transformed English intellectual life. However, in the rest of his book he was more grudging, belittling what he found, and his grudging has been echoed by most historians since. Recent books have continued to cite him as proving that there was *no* humanism in England *during* the fifteenth century.[4] Yet since the 1960s several people have begun to suggest areas in which humanism did flourish in England then. Some have recognized the new class of lay administrators of the Yorkist and early Tudor years—the graduates of Magdalen College School among them—while others have catalogued the large number of humanist books in monasteries, universities, and occasionally at court. Thanks to palaeography

---

[4] Weiss, *Humanism*, 1.

and prosopography, we can now survey a small but fertile field of humanist activity in England during the fifteenth century.[5]

However, even the heartiest defenders of humanism in Latin still write—sometimes with the classicist's hauteur with which Weiss wrote—that literature 'in the vulgar tongue' was not influenced by humanism. There has been little exploration of the links between fifteenth-century English literature and English or Italian humanism.[6] The consensus is that although humanism might have affected the Latin culture of England during the fifteenth century, it had no effect upon English literature. For example, a recent one-volume history of 'medieval' English literature mentions no humanist writing beyond a translation placed inaccurately in a chronological table.[7] However, in fact, humanism did influence some—and only some—English literature during the fifteenth century. This book, then, notes for the first time the place of humanism in English literature between the 1430s, when Humfrey, Duke of Gloucester, was collecting his famous Latin books and translations, and the early sixteenth century. The English plays collected by scholars of Magdalen College School, or *Fulgens and Lucres* performed in the household where the young Thomas More lived, are just some examples among many.

Yet there is no need to repeat this conclusion continually: it is found implicit in the examples throughout this book. The implications are what matter more. To observe humanism within fifteenth-century literature challenges not only the history of humanism but the history of our literature in general. Within that history, the place of the fifteenth century seems unsure: it currently appears in two apparently different guises, exemplified in two brilliant recent books. David Wallace, the editor of *The Cambridge History of Medieval English Literature*, has pronounced the beginning of the fifteenth century 'a historiographical watershed of prime importance': the innovativeness of

[5] For example, Denys Hay, 'The Early Renaissance in England' (1965), in his *Renaissance Essays* (London: Hambledon, 1988), 151–67 (158–9); *Humfrey 1970* and *Humfrey 1988* (based upon A. C. de la Mare's research); David Rundle, 'On the Difference between Virtue and Weiss: Humanist Texts in England during the Fifteenth Century', in *Courts, Counties and the Capital in the Later Middle Ages*, ed. Diana E. S. Dunn, Fifteenth Century Series, 4 (Stroud: Sutton, 1996), 181–203 (181–4). See also now Michael Wyatt, *The Italian Encounter with Tudor England: A Cultural Politics of Translation* (Cambridge: Cambridge University Press, 2005), 19–32, on fifteenth-century Italian travellers in England.

[6] Denys Hay, 'England and the Humanities in the Fifteenth Century' (1975), in his *Renaissance Essays* (London: Hambledon, 1988), 169–231 (213–14).

[7] Clare Carroll, 'Humanism and English literature in the fifteenth and sixteenth centuries', in *The Cambridge Companion to Renaissance Humanism*, ed. Jill Kraye (Cambridge: Cambridge University Press, 1996), 246–68 (246–8); A. C. Spearing, *Medieval to Renaissance in English Poetry* (Cambridge: Cambridge University Press, 1985), 89–90; David Wallace (ed.), *The Cambridge History of Medieval English Literature* (Cambridge: Cambridge University Press, 1999), 872, misdating *Knyghthode and Bataile*.

fourteenth-century literature 'ends abruptly after 1400'. Wallace follows several recent critics who have sought to explain the apparent mediocrity of fifteenth-century writing, in comparison with that of Chaucer and Langland. They suggest that after Chaucer's death the readership for English poetry became broader in compass but shallower in taste. They give as the causes the limitations on public debate under the jittery Lancastrians or the repression of religious writing in response to heresy. For the study of humanism, most problematic is the accompanying suggestion that the Lancastrian age 'adumbrated' the restrictions on political, religious, and literary freedom under Henry VIII.[8] On the one hand, then, the fifteenth century is a dark age because it is like the Renaissance. A contrary view appears in *The Oxford English Literary History* for these years. There James Simpson criticizes English culture during the sixteenth century for its narrowness, particularly in humanist writing, and for its annihilation of what preceded it. But unlike Wallace and others, he praises fifteenth-century culture for its diversity and richness, free from the narrowness of humanism and Reformation.[9] How do we reconcile these two dissimilar histories of a century? In fact, these two histories—and I simplify them and others for brevity—are similar. Both praise the 'medieval' or 'pre-modern' years before 1400 and both compare those years to the demonized 'Renaissance' or 'early modern' years of Henry VIII's reign. Both blame humanism, and certain religious changes, for the decay.

Yet what remains difficult to reconcile are not their histories of decay but their chronologies. Laying these two stories side-by-side, it is unclear how to judge the 1400s. Wallace portrays the first rot, Simpson the last blush of brilliance. To read fifteenth-century writing, then, is to test the two prevailing histories of medieval literature. In particular, to read humanist writing of that century is to test that against which medieval literature has been defined, praised or vilified. Where does the century fall? And how do we evaluate humanism as a result? What emerges is not simple and reveals the flaws in any grand narrative about the century and about the movement. Humanism ushers in an age neither of gold nor of iron but something more various and complex.

---

[8] Wallace (ed.), *Cambridge History*, pp. xxi–xxii, 637–9, summarizing the most important studies by Fisher, Strohm, and Watson; David Wallace, 'Dante in Somerset: Ghosts, Historiography, Periodization', *NML*, 3 (1999), 9–38 (33, 36); David Wallace, *Chaucerian Polity: Absolutist Lineages and Associational Forms in England and Italy* (Stanford, CA: Stanford University Press, 1997), 61.

[9] Simpson, *Reform*, 32–33, 45–52, 558–61, with 68–77, 121–8, 229–43 on humanism. For analysis of this remarkable book, see the special issue of *Journal of Medieval and Early Modern Studies*, 35 (2005).

OTHER HUMANISMS

So why have people lately rejected humanism? Because in the past people often instead eulogized it, through its connection with the loaded word *human*. In the letter copied at Magdalen College School, the word *humanitas* appears, and is repeated with the insistence of a catchphrase ('humanitatem humanissime'), and it seems a good thing: it seems to mean *kindness*. But in other letters in that collection *humanitas* seems to have another meaning, something like *literary taste*. One correspondent praises his reader for having '*humanissimas* ears' which might be offended by such an uncultivated writer ('aures humanissimas'). Throughout these letters the scholars worry over their style, over whether they will be eloquent enough and so on ('rudis incultusque stilus').[10] So which is humanism? An eternal verity or a passing and superficial style? The double meaning of *humanitas* requires us to take up partisan positions for or against humanism—and for the Renaissance or for the Middle Ages. For many people, the term *humanism* defines a great leap forward in the very soul and fabric of the human. It was Hegel who punned on the *humaneness* of the humanities which flourished in the 1400s and 1500s. His pun in turn influenced the secret Hegelian, Jacob Burckhardt, when he defined the spirit of the Renaissance by the birth of modern man in his rationality, individuality, and energy.[11] Burckhardt's definitions still shape our view of the Renaissance as the birth of the truly human. Therefore, some literary critics who have sought to praise earlier writers have formed a new, hybrid category of *medieval humanism* identified by signs of rationality, secularism, and optimism in the Middle Ages. Into this category they have slotted Alain de Lille, Chaucer, Gower, Christine de Pizan, and others. However, this category brings all the troubles of the terms *medieval* and *Renaissance*: it is because humanism is understood as a phenomenon of the wider Renaissance of man, that any early humanism must be explained away as a paradoxically medieval trend.[12] What is it that needs this label? Qualities which could be better described as *humane*,

[10] BL, MS Arundel 249, f.82v, and also f.81v, f.83v.
[11] Wallace K. Ferguson, *The Renaissance in Historical Thought: Five Centuries of Interpretation* (Boston, MA: Houghton Mifflin, 1948), 154–61, 185–6, 190–1.
[12] Douglas Gray, 'Some Pre-Elizabethan Examples of an Elizabethan Art', in *England and the Continental Renaissance: Essays in Honour of J. B. Trapp*, ed. Edward Chaney and Peter Mack (Woodbridge: Boydell, 1990), 23–36 (27–34); Douglas Gray, 'Humanism and Humanisms in the Literature of Late Medieval England', in *Italy and the English Renaissance*, ed. Sergio Rossi and Dianella Savoia (Milan: Unicopli, 1989), 25–44 (38–42); James Simpson, *Sciences and the Self in Medieval Poetry: Alan of Lille's* Anticlaudianus *and John Gower's* Confessio Amantis (Cambridge: Cambridge University Press, 1995), 18–19; R. W. Southern, *Medieval Humanism* (New York, NY: Harper and Row, 1970), 32, 42–52. Nevertheless, Douglas Gray (ed.), *The Oxford Book of Late*

anthropocentric, or *secular*. Yet these qualities were surely available to thinkers at many times before and after the Renaissance, and we therefore do not need a countervailing category, an oxymoron, of *medieval humanism*.

To avoid such labels, we must define these terms more precisely—as others, beyond our letter-writers, did in the sixteenth century. As far as we know, the earliest English use of the noun *humanist* dates from 1589 and it refers to someone practising the literary studies known as the humanities and particularly a classical scholar or someone teaching Latin. Only in the 1830s did the abstract noun *humanism* emerge, and that word did specify certain anthropocentric philosophies developed in Germany at that time. The confusion between the *human being* and earlier *humanism* is sealed then.[13] To stop the confusion, for the fifteenth and sixteenth centuries *humanism* is best glossed by the most similar phrase then in use: the *studia humanitatis*. In those centuries people grouped together certain studies—grammar, rhetoric, poetry, history, and moral philosophy—and linked them to the study of classical sources, Greek and Latin. The groupings appear in the lectures arranged in Italian universities. For example, Carlo Marsuppini in 1431 was hired to lecture on poetry, rhetoric, philosophy, Greek, and ethics, while his rival Francesco Filelfo in 1434 was hired to lecture on the rhetoric and literature of the Greeks and Latins ('Poesiam, Rethoricam, Phylosofiam, Grecum et Eticam', 'ad lecturam oratorie gregarum et latinarum' [*sic*]). As these studies grew more established, people referred to them together as the *studia humanitatis* and, in universities, to the lecturer in them as the *humanista*.[14] To define *humanism* as the study and imitation of classical antiquity best reflects how writers and scholars in fifteenth-century England used similar terms. For example, in 1440 a papal servant in England praised Humfrey, Duke of Gloucester, for cultivating the sweet 'humanitatis studia' by patronizing scholars. In the 1480s the master at Magdalen College School, again, was contracted to teach grammar, poetry, and 'alias humanitates'. A

Medieval Verse and Prose (Oxford: Clarendon Press, 1985), was the essential starting point for this book.

[13] *OED*, *humanist* and *humanism*. Vito R. Giustiniani, 'Homo, Humanus, and the meanings of "Humanism"', *Journal of the History of Ideas*, 46 (1985), 167–95 (171, 175–83), distinguishes the different senses.

[14] Paul Oskar Kristeller, 'Humanism and Scholasticism in the Italian Renaissance', *Byzantion*, 17 (1944–5), 346–74 (350, 356, 365–6); Paul F. Grendler, *The Universities of the Italian Renaissance* (Baltimore, MD: Johns Hopkins University Press, 2002), 212–13 (*n.* 65), 226 (*n.* 113), and generally 207–12, 230–2; Augusto Campana, 'The Origin of the Word "Humanist"', *Journal of the Warburg and Courtauld Institutes*, 9 (1946), 60–73 (60–6); Giuseppe Billanovich, 'Auctorista, humanista, orator', *Rivista di cultura classica e medioevale*, 7 (1965), 143–63 (158–60); Rino Avesani, 'La professione dell' ≪umanista≫ nel Cinquecento', *Italia medioevale e umanistica*, 13 (1970), 205–32; Benjamin G. Kohl, 'The Changing Concept of the *studia humanitatis* in the Early Renaissance', *Renaissance Studies*, 6 (1992), 185–209 (185–6).

document about the schooling of Edward V and then a prologue by William Caxton use the English word *humanity* to define some programme of study in 1473 and 1483 respectively. The word continued to be used for the cultivation of classical Latin: Skelton refers to Cicero's 'faculte called humanyte' or the work of 'Retoricyons and oratours in freshe humanyte'.[15]

Besides being endorsed by these early uses, most historians now follow this definition of *humanism* as a range of scholarly practices applied to classical culture. The standard definition comes from Paul Oskar Kristeller:

that broad concern with the study and imitation of classical antiquity which was characteristic of the period and found its expression in scholarship and education and in many other areas, including the arts and sciences.[16]

Humanism, then, is a self-conscious commitment to return to the classics, or *ad fontes*, as did the advocates and teachers of the *studia humanitatis*. Such a definition serves in this book as a heuristic tool by which to identify English writing which might be moulded by humanism: literature which studies or imitates classical literature in this self-conscious way. A slight blurring may be necessary: Kristeller sometimes refers more strictly to educational institutions, and fifteenth-century universities seldom did official business in English. Nevertheless, he also includes translation as an important part of the humanists' endeavours.[17] It is also clear that even the best students of *humanitas* used the vernacular sometimes. For example, some glosses 'vulgariter' or 'anglice', as they put it, appear in copies of Roman satires annotated by John Gunthorpe, cleric and ambassador, or a copy of a recent controversy about the merits of Scipio and Caesar. Even erudite men thought that Roman pirates were like 'robynhode' or frankly glossed the 'clunem' as the 'buttok'.[18] The vulgar tongue was heard in the university and schoolroom too: in Chapter 2 there is a letter in English from the University of Oxford about the inspiration of the *studia humanitatis* and in Chapter 5 there are some schoolboys who used English to unravel Cicero and Terence.

In such cases, though, humanism appears less as a philosophical-*ism* or world-view than as a range of activities: David Carlson has spoken of

[15] *OED, humanity, n.*, 4[a] and 4b, and *n*. 8 in Chapter 2 and *n*. 62 in Chapter 5 below; John Skelton, *Speke Parott* and *Why Come Ye Nat to Courte?*, in *The Complete English Poems*, ed. V. J. Scattergood (New Haven, CT: Yale University Press, 1983), 230–46 (line 194), 278–311 (lines 528–9); *MED, humanite* omits this sense.

[16] Paul Oskar Kristeller, 'Humanism', in *The Cambridge History of Renaissance Philosophy*, ed. Charles B. Schmitt and others (Cambridge: Cambridge University Press, 1988), 113–37 (113).

[17] Kristeller, 'Humanism', 121.

[18] LPL, MS 425 (Gunthorpe's Horace), f.76v, f.83v, f.86r, f.89r, f.101r, f.107r, and HEHL, MS Ellesmere 34.B.6 (Gunthorpe's Juvenal), f.22r ('buttok'), f.26v, f.41r-v, on which see *Humfrey 1970*, nos. 91–5; TCC, MS O.9.8 (the controversy), f.22r, f.26r-v, f.27v, f.35v ('robynhode'), f.38r.

'humanist gestures', a phrase which usefully implies that humanism is a practice.[19] Activities and not ideas are what we can trace in the manuscripts and printed books which survive. Englishmen compose and correct Latinate verse; read or pretend to read translations of Claudian; reconstruct Cicero's lost works from classical dictionaries; add indexes, marginalia and glosses to the works of Chaucer; sell phoney books which they claim are by Cato the Elder as textbooks for government; tell the bourgeoisie what not to read. In a circular sense, then, this opening definition of humanism captures the conclusion of this book; it reflects what will emerge in English poems, tracts, and documents from 1430 to 1530. Yet it also opens our eyes in the first place to see what is emerging. If we attend to humanism as a practice, we can see the practice unfolding, even fleetingly, in the margins, or in other fugitive, curious places, such as prologues, *ex libris* notes, or military memoranda. If we look at this more microscopic level, then we will see humanist activity in English literature during the fifteenth century.

CHAUCER AND WALTON FROM MEDIEVAL TO RENAISSANCE

Yet do the 'humanist gestures' or activities really offer something new? To study and imitate antiquity is obviously not the prerogative of the humanists alone, nor some novelty in the fifteenth and sixteenth centuries. Antiquity existed long before the Italians studied its remains in the 1400s: in just the previous century, the English friars and the courtiers of Charles V of France had studied some classical texts, for example. So what distinguishes fifteenth-century English humanism? What occurs is not a complete transformation in the surface of literary works or in the object of intellectual enquiry; what shifts is the deeper 'dispersal', the relationship and use, of these elements.[20] Different people in different times and disciplines get something different from the past, especially when the past in question is a millennium of recorded antiquity. So the republican Rome praised by Florentines in 1400 differs from the imperial Rome praised by some Lancastrians in 1460 (as noted in Chapter 3 below). These visions differ again from Samuel Johnson's use of Juvenal or, more recently, Brendan Kennelly's of Martial. English-speaking writers have seen a diverse

---

[19] Carlson, *English Humanist Books*, 5.
[20] The historical models come from Michel Foucault, *The Archaeology of Knowledge*, trans. A. M. Sheridan Smith (1969; London: Tavistock, 1972), 148, 158, 172–3, and Régine Pernoud, *Pour en finir avec le Moyen Âge* (Paris: Seuil, 1977), 18–20, 39.

spectrum of antiquities over the years and, if we wish to enjoy their works, we need to be a little relativistic; none has the best purchase on antiquity as each uses it to different ends. In the fifteenth and sixteenth centuries, humanists in English do use some of the same materials as earlier scholars, but as they do so they distinguish their work from that of earlier ones. How they do so will emerge if we consider some precedents for their work and their responses. Perhaps the most obvious precedents for humanist studies in English are the English translations of Boethius's *De Consolatione philosophiae* made by Geoffrey Chaucer and John Walton between 1380 and 1410 and the translation of Vegetius' *Epitoma rei militaris* dated to 1408, possibly also by Walton. By seeing how humanists read, gloss, translate, annotate, or rewrite those works, we can see how they distinguish their studies from Chaucer's and Walton's.

Of course, Chaucer's relationship to humanism is a vexed question: he certainly knew some of the Italian works of Boccaccio and Petrarch, but was he influenced by their classical scholarship? Both Chaucer and Walton wrote their translations when humanist scholarship was still rare in Italy and almost unknown in England. Their translations are not really attempts to study and imitate classical antiquity in the humanist vein. Firstly, Boethius, a sixth-century Christian servant of the Goths, does not quite count as a 'classic' in the strict sense. However, even if we overlook that quibble, Chaucer's *Boece* is not an attempt to sip from wells of pure Latin. Chaucer consulted not only Boethius's text but also heavily a thirteenth-century French version of it and Nicholas Trevet's commentary, and sometimes another tradition of commentary. It has been said that *Boece* belongs to a specific genre of 'late-medieval' translation, which was designed to aid understanding by accretion rather than by stripping to the bare original.[21] For Chaucer, writing *Boece* seems to have prompted a revolution not in classical scholarship but in the philosophy of love in *Troilus and Criseyde*—a great achievement, but one with mixed feelings about the cursed pagans.

John Walton's translation seems similarly unconcerned with returning *ad fontes*: Walton did use the Latin text but also borrowed from Trevet's commentary and from Chaucer's *Boece*. Yet in his prologue Walton distances himself from Chaucer. He seems humble when he claims to be 'vnmete' to Chaucer and Gower; but of Chaucer he adds:

> This wot I wel, no þing may I do like,
> Þogh so þat I of makyng entirmete;

---

[21] A. J. Minnis and Tim William Machan, 'The *Boece* as Late-Medieval Translation', in *Chaucer's* Boece *and the Medieval Tradition of Boethius*, ed. A. J. Minnis (Cambridge: Brewer, 1993), 167–88 (168, 178–9, 184). Tim William Machan (ed.), *Sources of the* Boece (Athens, GA: University of Georgia Press, 2005), 1–11, has most recently traced the sources.

His purpose is quite different from Chaucer's anyway:

> Noght liketh me to labour ne to muse
> Upon þese olde poysees derk,
> For Cristes feith suche þing[es] schulde refuse;
> Witnes upon Ierom þe holy clerk.
> Hit schulde not ben a Cristen mannes werk
> Tho false goddes names to renewe [...]

He *is not allowed to* or 'may' not compete with Chaucer. He presents himself as a godly sage refusing to imitate the matter of classical pagan poetry; the poetry is 'derk': hard to understand and wicked.[22] This might be the requisite humility. But Walton prepared for his translation a commentary in which he does discuss some of the classical allusions, and even cites the myth of Orpheus as told by 'Ouyde in his boke of Metamorphoseos'. But in his commentary he allegorizes the myth of Orpheus and other classical myths and he warns that the 'lytteral' level of each fable is only a 'lesyng' (*lie*).[23]

The translator of Vegetius' *Epitoma rei militaris* into prose—whoever he is, perhaps Walton again—shows no interest in his colophon in the dangerous glitter of antiquity, even if he is not outspokenly hostile to it. Instead, he tells us that this work was made because it is relevant to present pastimes and policy:

[...] to grete disport and daliaunce of lordes and alle worþi werrioures þat ben apassed by wey of age al labour and trauaillyng, and to greet informacioun and lernynge of ӡonge lordes and knyghtes þat ben lusty and loueþ to here and see and to vse dedes of armes and chyualrie.

The motive for writing here omits the ideas of fidelity, reproduction and revival that later translations give. The text is useful and might as well be recent as classical; indeed, the other books translated for Walton's patron, Lord Berkeley, were recent; they were by Ranulph Higden and Giles of Rome.[24] These earlier translations are not deferential to old books for their oldness, but for their new science; the intention is not to study antiquity.

---

[22] John Walton (trans.), *Boethius: De Consolatione Philosophiae*, ed. Mark Science, EETS os 170 (London: Oxford University Press, 1927), stanzas 5–6.

[23] 'Appendix', in Walton (trans.), *Boethius*, 365–6, 368, 371–8, discussed by Brian Donaghey, Irma Taavitsainen, and Erik Miller, 'Walton's Boethius: From Manuscript to Print', *English Studies*, 80 (1999), 398–407.

[24] Geoffrey Lester (ed.), *The Earliest English Translation of Vegetius'* De Re Militari, Middle English Texts, 21 (Heidelberg: Winter, 1988), 189:33–190:5. Walton's authorship of the translation of Vegetius' *Epitoma* is uncertain and rests on a rebus that may represent Walton, Bannerton, or even Clifton (Lester (ed.), *The Earliest English Translation*, 23–8); but see *n*. 30 below for another clue that it might be Walton.

However, these claims about intention are finicky and controvertible. And indeed, Chaucer's and Walton's intentions were hidden from fifteenth-century readers with neither the library nor the time to study their works in depth. These works remained popular throughout the fifteenth century. What is the implication of their survival alongside the humanist translations which will be discussed in later chapters? We cannot divide earlier, 'late-medieval' works from later, humanist ones so neatly. As Bruno Latour has remarked, in the history of technology the boundaries between periods cannot be tidily told: different tools or skills, invented in different ages, persist in use side-by-side; it is false to label things sequentially as pre-modern and modern, say, or as 'out-of-date'.[25] Books are perhaps the paradigmatic 'technology' for this model of time: although a work may be written in one century, it can outlive its author and be copied, printed, and read centuries hence. It is important to register firstly, then, that humanism does not erase previous methods of classicism; the humanists could still read Chaucer. Secondly, the fingerprints of fifteenth-century readers reveal that a humanist thirst for antiquity was in fact sated by *Boece* and by Walton's translations. Walton's preface suggests that he did not want 'Tho false goddes names to renewe': but some manuscripts omit his grumpy preface.[26] For although books can endure across time, books do not remain the same: fifteenth-century scribes and readers dressed up these earlier books. Chaucer and Walton will influence the translations that emerge later (and in later chapters): but the influence flows both ways. If Chaucer and Walton seem reasonable precedents for classical translation—so that we ask: what's so special about humanism?—it is partly because the humanists changed how people read them. These changes let us see how humanist practices differ from earlier uses of antiquity.

Firstly, although Chaucer and Walton drifted far from the ancient text, some readers were fascinated by returning to it. The presentation of the translations invited a look at the source. Many copies of both translations from Boethius give the first few words of each section in Latin, so that one can use the original with the English readily, and two copies list these Latin *incipits* in a table at the front.[27] Two manuscripts of Chaucer's version gave the whole

---

[25] Bruno Latour, *We Have Never Been Modern*, trans. Catherine Porter (1991; Hemel Hempstead: Harvester Wheatsheaf, 1993), 72–5.

[26] Walton (trans.), *Boethius*, stanza 6. The preface is missing in two of the parallel-text copies: BL, MS Harley 43 and a copy described by R. A. Dwyer, 'The Newberry's Unknown Revision of Walton's Boethius', *Manuscripta*, 17 (1973), 27–30 (28).

[27] For Latin incipits, see BL, MS Additional 16165, f.4r–94r (*Boece*); CUL, MS Gg.IV.18, Oxford, Balliol College, MS 316 A and MS 316 B (Walton's Boethius); for a *tabula*, see BL, MS Additional 10340, f.3r, and Salisbury, Cathedral Library, MS 113, f.1r–v (*Boece*). The scribe of BL, MS Harley 44 (Walton's Boethius), f.13r–v, f.17v, f.24v, sometimes omits or misplaces the Latin, as if he does not understand its purpose. M. C. Seymour, *A Catalogue of*

Latin in alternation with the English, section by section. Three manuscripts of Walton's version have the Latin text in parallel with the English, and in one of Chaucer's a reader started adding the Latin but, forgivably, gave up.[28] Some readers could, then, have used these loose translations to read the original text like a humanist schoolboy with his bilingual textbook. And what did people read in the translations themselves? In most manuscripts, there are only a few marginalia, but the few are classicizing. Some help the budding classical rhetorician by noting the tropes such as hypallage, antithesis and irony; some help the critic or historian by noting some Roman military equipment or a few ancient heroes such as Cato and Pompey. In two manuscripts of Vegetius' *Epitoma* in English, the scribes provide a few red marginalia, which explain the English words for outdated military equipment by noting the original Latin; the scribes also note the labyrinth as the 'domo dedali' ('house of Daedalus').[29] What is odd is that these references to Daedalus, Cato and Pompey are in fact Walton's additions to his sources, some touches of further classical colour. Yet these are his only additions; and it is these exceptional and inessential things onto which later annotators batten.[30] The page design and marginalia emphasize the classical pedigree of the book rather than any relevant 'informacioun'. Between the writers and their readers, priorities have changed.

Yet who made these parallel texts and glosses? Were they in the earliest exemplars by Chaucer and Walton—suggesting a philological habit of mind earlier on—or were they added later? For *Boece*, it has been observed that there are Latin glosses tightly squeezed into even the early manuscripts after

Chaucer Manuscripts, 2 vols. (Aldershot: Scolar, 1995–7), I.43–53, describes *Boece* manuscripts in collaboration with R. Hanna.

[28] Respectively CUL, MS Ii.III.21 (alternate languages), and another fragmentary copy like this described by George B. Pace and Linda E. Voigts, 'A "Boece" Fragment', *Studies in the Age of Chaucer*, 1 (1979), 143–50 (148–9); SJC, MS G.29; BL, MS Harley 43; and a copy described by Dwyer, 'The Newberry's Unknown Revision', 28 (Walton in parallel); Salisbury, Cathedral Library, MS 113, ff.1v–2v (*Boece* with added Latin).

[29] Respectively, BL, MS Additional 10340, f.3v, f.5r ('ypalage', 'ironice'); Salisbury, Cathedral Library, MS 113, f.1v ('ypalage', 'antetesis'); CUL MS Ii.III.21, for example f.51v (Ovid and military equipment in *Boece*, II.m.5); BL, MS Harley 44, f.78r, f.97v (Cato, Pompey, Julius, and Plato in Walton (trans.), *Boethius*, stanza 763, added by Walton to his source; see 340*n*.); OMC, MS lat. 30, f.35v, f.45r, f.47r, f.54r, f.56v (Lester (ed.), *Earliest English Translation*, 90:30, 102:7, 105:7, 113:32–6, 116:18–30); CUL, MS Additional 8706, f.30v (Lester (ed.), *Earliest English Translation*, 90:30). The use of *hypallage* predates *OED*'s first citation by 150 years.

[30] That the translator from Vegetius adds a reference to the labyrinth, called in some MSS the 'domo dedali', further suggests some link with Walton, who adds a reference to the 'hous of Dydalus' to Boethius (Walton (trans.), *Boethius*, 339*n*.; Lester (ed.), *The Earliest English Translation*, 203*n*.; Chaucer, *Boece*, II.pr.12.156 and 1014*n*.); yet the phrases could come from Isidore of Seville, Nicholas Trevet, or Chaucer, *House of Fame*, 1920.

copying has finished, as if they were not authorial but a scribal afterthought.[31] In the two manuscripts which alternate *Boece* and the Latin, the arrangement was necessarily scribal and these are early copies too. But in one copy of *Boece* and one of Walton's Boethius the Latin added in parallel is visibly added later, to judge by its appearance squashed round the English in discomfort or with interruptions.[32] Who were the readers of such books? The copy of *Boece* with the Latin added has been in a cathedral library since the fifteenth century, a bilingual copy in a university library as long. Other copies of *Boece*, with glosses, circulated in academic or clerical milieux: one was early on bound with works by Leonardo Bruni, and another owned by John Bury of Clare Priory, a man who knew some humanists.[33] The link between the learned reader and the learned page design emerges most clearly in the parallel text of Walton's Boethius copied by Thomas Chaundler, a distinguished teacher. He gave to his patron, the humanist Thomas Bekynton, a second manuscript of Boethius with what he called a line-by-line gloss ('linearis glosæ').[34] By the mid-fifteenth century English translations have intruded into scholarly libraries and scholars have retrospectively intruded their classical passions into the English translations.

It is in this manner that William Caxton printed *Boece* in 1478. Caxton's edition of *Boece* pretends to links with humanism for it ends with Latin verses by the teacher Stefano Surigone, whom Caxton perhaps met when they both lived in Cologne in the early 1470s.[35] The printer himself returned *ad fontes*, to a Latin manuscript more accurate than Chaucer's, to gather long excerpts of the Latin for headings in each section, long enough to provide full texts of a

---

[31] Tim William Machan, 'Scribal Role, Authorial Intention, and Chaucer's *Boece*', *Chaucer Review*, 24 (1989), 150–62 (156–7); Tim William Machan, 'Glosses in the Manuscripts of Chaucer's *Boece*', in *The Medieval Boethius: Studies in the Vernacular Translations of* De Consolatione Philosophiae, ed. A. J. Minnis (Cambridge: Brewer, 1987), 125–38 (130).

[32] Salisbury, Cathedral Library, MS 113, ff.1v–2v (*Boece*); SJC, MS G.29, ff.29v–30r (Walton's Boethius). However, in the latter, the Latin was added before rubrication, as the same styles adorn both languages in parallel (for example ff.11r–14r).

[33] Respectively Salisbury, Cathedral Library, MS, 113, f.iii^v, on which see *BRUO*, I.531–2, under Thomas Crycetur; CUL, MS Ii.III.21, on which see *BRUC*, 170, under John Crowcher, and J. C. T. Oates, *Cambridge University Library: A History: From the Beginnings to the Copyright Act of Queen Anne* (Cambridge: Cambridge University Press, 1986), 12; CUL, MS Ii.I.38 (*Boece* and Bruni), on which see Oates, *Cambridge University Library*, 337; BodL, MS Bodley 797, on which see *BRUO*, I.323, under John Bury.

[34] BL, MS Harley 43. Chaundler gave his glossed copy to Bekynton in 1452 (*Bekynton Correspondence*, I.274) but signed BL, MS Harley 43 as Chancellor of Oxford and therefore after 1457: see M. R. James, *The Chaundler MSS* (London: Nichols, 1916), 57; *Humfrey 1970*, no. 34(c).

[35] Seth Lerer, *Chaucer and his Readers: Imagining the Author in Late-Medieval England* (Princeton, NJ: Princeton University Press, 1993), 155–60; Sergio Rossi, *Ricerche sull'Umanesimo e sul Rinascimento in Inghilterra* (Milan: Vita e Pensiero, 1969), 9–10 (*n.* 13).

few of Boethius' verses. He might have included this Latin merely to help him be flexible in typesetting.[36] However, he makes a virtue of practicality when, in his epilogue, he links the translation to the humanist study of Latin itself:

And for as moche as the stile of it is harde and difficile to be understonde of simple persones, therfor the worshipful fader and first foundeur and enbelissher of ornate eloquence in our Englissh, I mene Maister Geffrey Chaucer, hath translated this sayd werke oute of Latyn into oure usual and moder tonge, folowyng the Latyn as neygh as is possible to be understande.

Then he notes the wisdom of the book and adds:

Thenne for as moche as this sayd boke so translated is rare and not spred ne knowen, as it is digne and worthy, for the erudicion and lernyng of suche as ben ignoraunt and not knowyng of it, atte requeste of a singuler frende and gossib of myne I, William Caxton, have done my debuoir and payne t'enprynte it [...][37]

Instead he claims to preserve an ancient text: he claims, as he will of other dodgy translations, that the English follows the Latin 'as neygh as is possible to be understande'. This is almost an infraction of the trades' description act. Moreover, this closeness to antiquity wins Chaucer a crown for 'ornate eloquence' and a hard 'stile'—the literary style over the sentence. Caxton offers the book for 'erudicion', which sounds more bookish than the social 'informacioun' offered in the prose Vegetius in 1408. Some of his readers did indeed use it for erudition, getting close to the Latin. Three readers added to their copies of the printed *Boece* more of Boethius' Latin in the margins, obviously using the translation to navigate the original work. Two readers sometimes corrected the Latin which Caxton had already given them. Another got the book bound with a Latin edition of Boethius' work, two others into volumes with versions of Cato's *Disticha*.[38]

---

[36] *Chaucer According to William Caxton: Minor Poems and* Boece *1478*, ed. Beverly Boyd (Lawrence, KA: Allen Press, 1978), p. xvi and *metra* III.m.4, III.m.5, III.m.7 and IV.m.2; Brian Donaghey, 'Caxton's Printing of Chaucer's *Boece*', in *Chaucer in Perspective: Middle English Essays in Honour of Norman Blake*, ed. Geoffrey Lester (Sheffield: Sheffield Academic Press, 1999), 73–99 (90). See also the account of the Latin text in James E. Blodgett, 'Some Printer's Copy for William Thynne's 1532 Edition of Chaucer', *The Library*, 6th series, 1 (1979), 97–113 (107–11).

[37] *Caxton's Own Prose*, 7:20–7, 7:32–7.

[38] Leeds, Brotherton Library, classmark Ripon Cathedral XVI.E.20q, sig. a5r (Latin added, and probably the margin now cut from sig. a6r, as there is the same *signe de renvoie*); HEHL, classmark 82740, sigs. a2r, b6v, b8v–c1v, c4v, d2v–d3r, f1r, d8v, e7r, h2r–h2v (Latin added; sig. b4 is mislabelled b3 in this copy; sigs. a7, a8 and b1 are misbound after b8); LPL, classmark Sion College, arc. L.40.4/72, sigs. a2r–a7r (text added), sigs. a2v–a3r (corrections); Oxford, Exeter College, classmark 9.M.4815 (3), sig. a2v (corrections), on which see *n.* 83 in Chapter 5 below; OMC, classmark Arch. B.III.2.12 (2), bound with a printed edition of the Latin, which a reader has sometimes corrected (sigs. a2r-v, b8v, d5r), on which see Alexandra Gillespie, *Print*

So we can sometimes contrast older scholarship with humanist scholarship. Unlike Chaucer or Walton, working at second hand or nervous of pagan poetry, later fifteenth-century readers blend in the glosses and parallel texts which highlight the original or sniff out the features of classical culture which interest them: antithesis and hypallage, Cato and Pompey. Yet these things were in Chaucer's or Walton's work already: it is older writing about antiquity which allows the readers to study and imitate antiquity. So the claims to novelty look meretricious. Caxton claims that *Boece* is 'rare and not spred ne knowen' and hard to find, just like the schoolboy who was hunting for English comedies: but there were manuscripts available. Yet if there is not too much new knowledge here, there is a new use of this knowledge, and a self-consciousness of the novelty. It is this new interest in the original, and the sense of its novelty, which distinguishes humanism.

THE FREEDOM OF CHAUCER'S READERS

Yet is this reading as erudite as Caxton's words would suggest? It does not seem so. This reading remains at the level of textual practices or mere 'gestures', as people crib their way through the grammar or lift a few showy figures or factlets from their original senses or contexts. So if we look at humanism primarily under a microscopic focus as 'humanist gestures', we belittle it. We reduce its novelty, yet we also reduce its remit or depth, from the formation of man to erudition in Latin *minutiae*. So humanism has seemed of late. By limiting the term *humanism* to the curriculum of the *studia humanitatis*, the most rigorous historians and most hostile critics have recently seen the humanist not as the saviour of civic life, but as a banal grammarian. This first element of the recent picture of the humanist seems exemplified in the later reading of *Boece* or of Walton's translations: this is superficial reading. Yet the second element of the recent picture of the humanist is that, as a grammarian, he is the self-promoting defender of an arcane elite, who initiates the student into his cult by obedience and subservience. Moreover, this humanist reader, drilled in grammar and rhetoric, is perfectly drilled for submission to the absolutist princes of Renaissance Europe, with the flashy Latin needed to please those rulers. His textual corrections were analogous to his psychosocial repressions, his schoolroom discipline to political oppression, and so on. The

Culture and the Medieval Author: Chaucer, Lydgate, and their Books 1473–1557 (Oxford: Oxford University Press, 2006), 67–72.

most powerful statement of this critique comes from Anthony Grafton and Lisa Jardine, and it filters into studies of English literature and humanism, by medievalists and critics of early modern culture alike.[39] We might recall that in the letter quoted above, the shared love of English interludes presses the writer into obsequiousness: he has worked with 'diligent labour' at flattering the owners of the interludes so that they might allow others to enjoy them ('assiduo labore conatus adulatorijsque verbis'). Culture is an elite treasure to be won by self-abasement and toadying. And what are these letters copied for? To teach other young men to write stylishly and flatteringly for 'aures humanissimas'—ears attuned to discriminate and judge.

These are important arguments and it is with them that any study of humanism must engage. However, some questions occur about the superficiality of humanist study, and these questions prompt further ones about the politics of it. Firstly, how superficial was this humanism? There is some difficulty with evidence. In copies of Chaucer's and Walton's translations, much of the apparatus of humanist reading was in fact added by *scribes*: so were the limited studies of style or grammar what *readers* actually did when they used these books? Even when the glosses and so on were the work of readers, still they do not *record actual* reading but seem designed to *prompt future* reading and thought, whether by the same person or someone else. That is what a 'nota' or a parallel text is for. But did anyone ever follow the prompts? And did they *only* follow those prompts? Even if the glosses and so on prompted or recorded some intended or noteworthy responses, they did not exhaustively record all possible or actual readings. We find only narrow, bookish behaviour because we have used only narrow, bookish evidence; the thoughts which fit into margins are small ones.[40] There is a problem with the evidence.

Yet the problem also brings opportunities. The humanists, studying antiquity from a thousand years' distance, depended on the act of reading, on the basic movement of eyes over a page, and on comprehending and explaining words. But is that all they did? After all, in recent decades, the theory of reading has emphasized the essential freedom of the reader: his or her mind generates meaning; he can interpret or misinterpret a work quite contrary to

---

[39] Grafton and Jardine, *Humanism*, pp. xii–xiii, 9–25, 136–45; Wallace, *Chaucerian Polity*, 261–98, and Simpson, *Reform*, 68–77, 230 (*n.* 79); Robert Black, *Humanism and Education in Medieval and Renaissance Italy: Tradition and Innovation in Latin Schools from the Twelfth to the Fifteenth Century* (Cambridge: Cambridge University Press, 2001), 22–30; Stephanie H. Jed, *Chaste Thinking: The Rape of Lucretia and the Birth of Humanism* (Bloomington, IN: Indiana University Press, 1989), 4 (*n.* 2), 18–32.

[40] Peter Mack, 'Rhetoric, Ethics and Reading in the Renaissance', *Renaissance Studies*, 19 (2005), 1–21, lucidly explores these issues.

the will of the author, in various ways.[41] To seek humanism (as this book does) in the activities of readers will not reveal its limits so much as reveal its possibilities; it will reveal only the process of humanism and leave the purpose of it still open for discovery. We must be careful not to dismiss philological or stylistic reading. From antiquity onwards, pedagogues have imagined a hierarchy between the study of the textual 'surface' and 'deep' reading, by which they mean something more philosophical. Therefore, as Rita Copeland notes, simple education and cognition have been associated with children and so have too often been used as signs of political infancy and disempowerment. Indeed, this chapter has so far be*little*d humanism for remaining at the *low level* of glossing.[42] Copeland's warning reveals the assumptions within the standards by which we currently attack humanism. It is not that humanist reading or philology *is in itself* demeaning or oppressive, as it is now often shown to be: rather, the presumptions of certain schoolmasters or canny, authoritarian princes *made it so*—and academics today, a group promoted for their ability to read deeply, still *see it so*. It depends how people used it. Humanist reading may begin with the deadening routine of classical philology or rhetorical elaboration but it does not need to remain there.

In fact, the superficiality of humanist reading seems more liberating than the more elaborated methods of reading available to Chaucer and Walton, the procedures of allegorical commentary. Walton wrote a commentary on his translation of Boethius and there is also a fifteenth-century commentary on book I of Chaucer's *Boece*, both of which try to limit our responses by expounding certain Christian allegories from the works. Walton's commentary is (as noted above) fearful of the 'lytteral' meaning of classical myth because there is something still for us to do, something still to be expounded: 'a fable lackyng lytteral truthe vnexponed is noght elles but a lesyng'.[43] By contrast, if humanist notes record readings which seem sometimes unexpounded or over-literal, then these notes reveal a reader freer to interpret. For example, the readers of Caxton's print of *Boece* wrote only a few notes engaging with the philosophy of it in their copies (in the thirteen copies that I have seen); however, perhaps the most notes engaging with the philosophy appear in a

---

[41] Kevin Sharpe, *Reading Revolutions: The Politics of Reading in Early Modern England* (New Haven, CT: Yale University Press, 2000), 27–62, summarizes the developments.

[42] Rita Copeland, *Pedagogy, Intellectuals and Dissent in the Later Middle Ages: Lollardy and Ideas of Learning* (Cambridge: Cambridge University Press, 2001), 23, 57–62, 84–8, 140.

[43] Walton (trans.), *Boethius*, 378. See also the allegorizing commentary on *Boece* in BodL, MS Auct. F.3.5, ff.198r–220v, printed in Noel Harold Kaylor Jr, Jason Edward Streed, and William H. Watts (eds.), 'The Boke of Coumfort of Bois', *Carmina Philosophiae*, 2 (1993), 55 –104.

copy in which there are also the most passages of the Latin added in the margins, all by one reader of the fifteenth or early sixteenth century. Indeed, the reader seems to navigate the original Latin while he navigates the ideas which most concern him, some moving ideas about public service and about the essential liberty of the soul, beyond the reach of tyrants.[44] For him, returning to antiquity, with the help of English, and noting bold ideas went together. But who knows which legitimated which? If we look for humanism in the notes or parallel texts which emphasize the textual surface—notes or parallel texts which are themselves writings needing to be read—we do not limit what kind of humanism we will see there. There is still a lot to discover.

The unlimitedness of this reading emerges in the work of one final reader of Chaucer's *Boece*. William Worcester (1415–*c*.1483) was the author of a translation from Cicero and of a Ciceronian political treatise known as *The Boke of Noblesse* (discussed in Chapter 4 below). He also annotated a manuscript of Chaucer's *Boece* which still survives. Although he could read Latin, Worcester seems to have used the book, with its few lines of the Latin before each prose and metre, to help him work through the original. He copied into one of his notebooks from a Latin manuscript of Boethius some classical myths which he also highlighted in the English *Boece*.[45] This seems superficial reading. Moreover, Worcester used it for rhetorical posing: he took one reference, to the 'proude beestis clepid Centaurus, that be of halfe man and halfe best', out of context and with it he padded his own work, *The Boke of Noblesse*, quite needlessly. Ironically, the line follows Chaucer's phrase which includes elements from Trevet's commentary.[46] Yet Worcester not only took from *Boece* some fancy allusions for his own work; he also took from it some political lessons. He wrote four of his eight marginalia and a pointing finger beside book I, prose 4, on lines about Boethius' service of the 'comune profit' or what Worcester's marginalia call his 'officium rei publice'. This theme was Worcester's own: so Boethius the civic hero reappears in *The Boke of Noblesse* in these terms, and perhaps in echo of the phrasing of Chaucer: 'the said juge Boecius loved rightwisnesse to be kept, and the pore

---

[44] HEHL, classmark 82740; for the Latin see *n*. 38 above.

[45] Cambridge, Pembroke College, MS 215, f.66r–v; Chaucer, *Boece*, IV.pr.3.79, IV.m.3.1; Worcestre, *Itineraries*, 391; Boethius, *De Consolatione*, IV.pr.3.15, IV.m.3.1–2. See Daniel Wakelin, 'William Worcester Reads Chaucer's *Boece*', *Journal of the Early Book Society*, 5 (2002), 182–5, for palaeographical detail.

[46] [Worcester], *Noblesse*, 21; Chaucer, *Boece*, IV.m.7.29–30, with Trevet's contribution described by A. J. Minnis, 'Chaucer's Commentator: Nicholas Trevet and the *Boece*', in *Chaucer's* Boece *and the Medieval Tradition of Boethius*, ed. A. J. Minnis (Cambridge: Brewer, 1993), 83–166 (151). Cambridge, Pembroke College, MS 215, has lost all leaves after *Boece*, IV.pr.5, so we cannot know whether Worcester annotated this line.

comyns of Rome in that susteyned and maynteyned' and so on.[47] Although *Boece* was not originally an exercise in classical scholarship, it trains Worcester and other readers in a loose method of classical imitation and allusion. Moreover, it gives Worcester an inspiring model of selfless service of the commonweal.

How do we explain this outcrop of interest in the 'comune profit' or *res publica*? How does it relate to the study of grammar, rhetoric, mythology, and so on by readers of Chaucer and Walton? Is there a link between reading about antiquity and thinking about the commonweal? David Starkey, in particular, has mooted a humanist influence on such thinking.[48] Yet the politics may be general fifteenth-century ones rather than humanist ones: English writers in the fifteenth century use words such as *commonweal, common profit*, and other echoes of the Latin *res publica* with increasing frequency. The sincerity of these terms and their effects on real reform have been doubted: but those doubts are, to some extent, irrelevant in this study, not of political institutions, but of what people read and wrote. Moreover, as we know, what one can publicly say does to some extent delimit what one can publicly do.[49] The commonweal does appear in the pamphlets and speeches made between the 1440s and 1480s and in the chronicles which record the disturbances of those years.[50] Most recently, Paul Strohm has noted this new vocabulary for political discussion in the fifteenth century which, he has argued, is largely a secular, rational vocabulary which enshrined the idea that one could reason about political life.[51] Is this vocabulary connected to humanism at all? Strohm stresses the 'mixed' heritage of the reason of state and David Rundle argues that we cannot call *commonweal* a humanist term.[52] Indeed, some critics of Florentine humanism now see that movement as one which obscured the

---

[47] Cambridge, Pembroke College, MS 215, ff.6r–9r; *Boece*, I.pr.4.89, I.pr.4.106; [Worcester], *Noblesse*, 52–3; Chaucer, *Boece*, I.pr.4.103–8.

[48] 48 David Starkey, 'Which Age of Reform?', in *Revolution Reassessed: Revisions in the History of Tudor Government and Administration*, ed. Christopher Coleman and David Starkey (Oxford: Clarendon Press, 1986), 13–27 (19–25); David Starkey, 'England', in *The Renaissance in National Context*, ed. Roy Porter and Mikuláš Teich (Cambridge: Cambridge University Press, 1992), 146–63 (149–51). For doubts, see G. R. Elton, 'A New Age of Reform?', *Historical Journal*, 30 (1987), 709–16 (710–11, 715–16).

[49] John L. Watts, 'Ideals, Principles and Politics', in *The Wars of the Roses*, ed. A. J. Pollard (London: Macmillan, 1995), 110–33 (119–23).

[50] For example, see Kekewich and others (eds.), *Vale's Book*, 195–202, 208–10, 215–18; William Marx (ed.), *An English Chronicle 1377–1461: A New Edition* (Woodbridge: Boydell, 2003), 19:4–5, 67:32, 68:4, 80:36, 83:11, 83:28.

[51] Strohm, *Politique*, 4, 8.

[52] Strohm, *Politique*, 17; David Rundle, 'Was There a Renaissance Style of Politics in Fifteenth-Century England?', in *Authority and Consent in Tudor England: Essays presented to C. S. L. Davies*, ed. G. W. Bernard and S. J. Gunn (Aldershot: Ashgate, 2002), 15–32 (23 –4).

realities of politics, of class conflict, of guild-based society, and of despotism.[53] The interest in the commonweal in fifteenth- and sixteenth-century England, then, may stem from some root quite different from humanism.

Yet because it is only a discursive practice—a way of reading, a set of allusions, a style—humanism does not *necessarily* prompt a concern for the commonweal: but it *possibly* could prompt that. The possibility is followed in Worcester's reading of *Boece* and in other readings. Caxton in his epilogue also notes in passing Boethius' 'exile for the comynn and publick wele', and in one copy of Caxton's print somebody noted the passage on Plato's theory that kings should be philosophers.[54] This passage which refers to Plato was also excerpted from Walton's version of Boethius, and one scribe who copied it copied too the Latin passage from Boethius in support.[55] Others copied a stanza of political maxims from Walton's poem and ascribed them simply to 'Boicius de consolacione'; John Shirley added this stanza to Hoccleve's *The Regiment of Princes* and to a French translation of Vegetius' *Epitoma*.[56] One reader of Vegetius' *Epitoma* in English prose noted some maxims which praised the 'bonum commune' above private needs; he ascribed them to Aristotle and Valerius Maximus.[57] These political ideas may be known to, or even unconsciously held by, these men already; these more widely known ideas influence their reading or copying of Chaucer and Walton's works. However, despite being widely known, these ideas seemed to require some citation or support from antiquity to lend authority and expression to them. The commonweal was not so secure that it did not need endorsement from Boethius, Plato, or others. This may be showing off one's erudition, the worst use of the *studia humanitatis*; but reading is so unpredictable or free that even this use of the *studia humanitatis* could introduce some inspiring ideas.

The second, more complex task of this book is to gauge exactly where this reading led humanist English literature during the fifteenth and early sixteenth centuries. We must not begin by assuming that humanism was more humane, for few people, least of all the humanists and their disputatious historians, are both humane and scholarly: but nor must we begin by assuming the opposite. The readers of humanist literature were unpredictable. They

[53] John Najemy, 'Civic Humanism and Florentine Politics', in *Renaissance Civic Humanism: Reappraisals and Reflections*, ed. James Hankins (Cambridge: Cambridge University Press, 2000), 75–104 (80–1, 100–1).

[54] *Caxton's Own Prose*, 7:3–4; HEHL, classmark 82740, sigs. a6v, a7r (Chaucer (trans.), *Boece*, I.m4.15-I.pr4.48); note that sigs. a7, a8, and b1r are misbound after sig. b8v.

[55] Curt F. Bühler, 'A Middle-English Stanza on "The Commonwealth and the Need for Wisdom"', *English Language Notes*, 2 (1964), 4–5.

[56] BL, MS Royal 20.B.xv, f.1v; HEHL, MS Ellesmere 26.A.13, f.iii^r.

[57] BL, MS Additional 4713, f.93r.

stripped poems of their patrons, spotted the *memento mori* in celebrations of civic life, taught grammar from books of policy and policy from books of grammar. To mix the history of humanism or of English literature with the history of reading—the practices of glossing, translating, adapting, editing, printing—blends an unpredictable compound. In it, all of these histories dissolve and we must begin concocting them afresh.

2

Duke Humfrey and other imaginary readers

Although we must be cautious about the novelty of the *studia humanitatis*, nevertheless there were some changes in the cultural life of the fifteenth century. The English nobility had always taught their younger members the arts of courtly and military life, but for centuries those arts were learned within the household by osmosis rather than formally in schools and colleges. However, in the 1430s and 1440s, the nobility increasingly were schooled in grammar and other bookish subjects and began their slow conquest of the universities. Previously only younger sons intended to become prelates had attended university, but in these years a few more senior noblemen attended too. Then, several noblemen and distinguished clerics at court founded colleges in the second quarter of the fifteenth century, and Henry VI dispensed his favours on the universities and other learned institutions, most famously Eton College at Windsor and King's College at Cambridge. Several of his most prominent noblemen supported, or even engineered, this patronage. There may have been a political motive to such support for education in the 1430s. From this time lay noblemen displaced clerics on the governing council and, whatever the exact power of the councillors, it may be that claims to learning bolstered the influence of individual members.[1] Yet certainly the increasing bookishness of the English nobility is reflected in the increasing number of educational tracts and 'mirrors for princes' produced for them in the fifteenth century, after few in the preceding centuries.[2]

---

[1] In general, see Nicholas Orme, *From Childhood to Chivalry: The Education of the English Kings and Aristocracy 1066–1530* (London: Methuen, 1984), 24–5, 66–7, 71, 147–53, 214–16; Joel T. Rosenthal, 'The Universities and the Medieval English Nobility', *History of Education Quarterly*, 9 (1969), 415–37 (416–20, 429). On the 1430s, Ralph A. Griffiths, *The Reign of King Henry VI: The Exercise of Royal Authority, 1422–1461* (London: Benn, 1981), 239–48, 268 (*n.* 77), 278–9; Watts, *Henry VI*, 132–3, 167–71; Barrie Dobson, 'Henry VI and the University of Cambridge', in *The Lancastrian Court*, ed. Jenny Stratford, Harlaxton Medieval Studies, 13 (Donington: Tyas, 2003), 53–67 (54, 56, 66).

[2] Orme, *From Childhood to Chivalry*, 95–7, 100–3. Of course, we know more about fifteenth-century books in general than about those of preceding centuries, so this judgement must be made warily.

Yet if it is hard to quantify this engagement precisely, the bookish nature of this learning emerges in several written reports of noble reading and study. Even within the household, the informal sphere of lifelong learning, plans for education were more frequently being formalized and written down.[3] For example, in 1428 the Privy Council appointed Richard, Earl of Warwick, as tutor to Henry VI, who was now seven years old and ready for formal education. The commission explains the reasoning behind the appointment:

Pource quen nostre joefnesse il est expedient et covenable que nous soions endoctrinez et apris des bons meures lettrure langage norture et courtoisie et autres vertues et enseignementz au persone roial covenientz au fin que par ce puissons le mieulx nous avoir et gouverner en conservacion de nostre honoure et estat quant nous vendrons : moienant la grace de Dieu a greindre eage.[4]

Because in our youth it is expedient and fitting that we be educated and informed of good manners, literature, language, nurture and courtesy and other virtues and teachings appropriate to a royal person, so that thereby we might be better able to hold and govern in preserving our honour and estate when we come, by the grace of God, to greater age.

The importance of education is today a self-evident piety repeated everywhere, whatever our financial and practical support of it. Yet this document from 1428 must take time to protest that learning is 'covenable' or fitting, and the protest was not a needless preamble; eight years later some men allegedly wanted to distract the king from his studies. And note what kind of learning is considered fit: not only the traditional 'nurture' but also the literary and linguistic arts of 'lettrure', as an English digest of this document says. The tutor will teach 'nurture lettrure langage and oþer manere of cunnyng [...] suche as it fitteth so greet a prince to be lerned of': scholarship fit for a king.[5] History sounds especially important: the king should read:

mirrours and examples of tymes passed of þe good grace and ure prosperite and wele þat have fallen to vertuous Kynges and to here landes and subgittes of þat oo part and of þe contrair fortune þat hath ensued to Kynges and to here landes and subgittes of þe contrarie disposicion on þat oþer part.[6]

These 'mirrours' for princes are not theoretical ones like those of Aquinas or Giles of Rome, but narrative histories; they are conflated in this document with 'examples of the tymes passed'. Might this document about Henry VI,

---

[3] Noted by Nicholas Orme (ed.), 'The Education of Edward V', in his *Education and Society in Medieval and Renaissance England* (London: Hambledon, 1989), 177–88 (177–8).

[4] Harris Nicolas (ed.), *Proceedings and Ordinances of the Privy Council of England*, 7 vols. (London: Commissioners on the Public Records, 1834–7), III.296–7.

[5] Nicolas (ed.), *Privy Council*, III.299. On the distractions, see IV.135–6.

[6] Nicolas (ed.), *Privy Council*, III.299. IV.329–30 also refers to exemplary histories.

written in 1428, also be inspired by the *studia humanitatis*, the study of the classical past?

It is hard to speak clearly about this early document, but it is easier to speak of the wider trend at the English court to extend the usual process of courtly information into a keener pursuit of academic erudition—the difference between the reading imagined by Walton and by Caxton (in Chapter 1). The trend continued throughout the century. For example, in 1457 the University of Oxford enjoined Henry VI's newborn son to study classical history in order to learn to govern, and because they are in Latin the familiar slogans now sound more like Italian humanist slogans about the memory of antiquity, the commonweal, letters and liberal arts ('antiquitatis memoria', 'rempublicam', 'litteris ac liberalibus artibus').[7] When the royal household changed hands, the humanism continued. The Yorkist princes and noblemen were also set to study poetry or 'grammar, musicke and other cuninge and excercises of humanyte'—the earliest reference I have found in English to the *studia humanitatis* or humanities—and again the important 'noble storyes'.[8] It remains unclear whether the broader display of learning prompted a turn to humanism, or vice versa. More important is to stress that the wider civilizing process among the royalty and nobility was the backdrop to their more narrowly humanist studies and to the story of 'humanyte' in English.

In fact, most humanists who use the mother tongue begin their works with a nod to some royal or noble patron. The most esteemed patron was not Henry VI himself but was his uncle and protector of the realm for part of his boyhood, Humfrey, Duke of Gloucester (1390–1447). From the 1430s onwards the good Duke Humfrey became quite famous for his support of scholarship in the University of Oxford; he fits that wider fashion among his peers for dabbling in academia. However, his patronage was more extensive and took a more sharply humanist turn. He employed Italian scholars as secretaries and orators, and he received numerous manuscripts and dedications to new works from Italians overseas. Then (the focus here) he commissioned two works in English which respond to his Latin humanist concerns: *The Fall of Princes* (1431–8) by John Lydgate (*c.*1370–1449/50?) and *On Husbondrie* (1441–3) by an anonymous poet of great skill. How is his humanist reading presented in the Latin letters of his secretaries and correspondents and as an implied reader of these English poems? And did he really read these books or did they have other readers?

---

[7] Anstey (ed.), *Epistolae*, II.340.

[8] Myers (ed.), *Household*, 126–7, 137–8 (grammar and 'poetica'); Orme (ed.), 'Education of Edward V', 186, with 'humanyte' used in 1473, predating *OED*, *humanity*, *n.*, II.4. See *n.* 15 in Chapter 1 above. *Cunning* also usually denotes specialized erudition (*OED*, *cunning*, *n.*, 1–4; *MED*, *conning* (ppl.), 2), whereas *nurture* denotes the social arts of courtly life (*OED*, *nurture*, I.1.a; and *MED*, *norture* (n.), 3).

Humfrey's own humanist reading in the vernacular had great value as a princely image; but as an image it was less substantial than it seems. In fact, the real readers were humbler men who read about the princely humanist reader and, in the process, did some real humanist reading for themselves. *The Fall of Princes*, composed only three years after the commission to educate Henry VI, has been proposed as a possible attempt to educate the king.[9] After all, it teaches what Henry's tutor should: that fortune smites the ill-disposed. But although it suggests the flavour of the royal education which we can sense behind these documents, it and the other poem, *On Husbondrie*, are not only for royal readers. John Watts has argued that in the fifteenth century courtly culture and politics were 'democratized' to some extent.[10] In the long run, something similar happened to humanist reading.

IMAGINING DUKE HUMFREY

If the fifteenth century saw a growth of formal education among the nobility and royalty, then Humfrey was not quite so unique a figure. Nor even within the history of humanism was he as unique as has been said: the important research of David Rundle has reminded us of the duke's precursors. He calls the tendency to credit the duke with the coming of humanism 'magnate attraction', that is, the tendency to credit everything to some glamorous nobleman.[11] These are important warnings. Yet there is something notable in the duke's patronage. Between 1439 and 1444 he gave to the University of Oxford some 274 books, which were notable because at least 81 contained classical works, including some rare rediscoveries, or works by Italians modelled closely upon antique literature. This proportion contrasts, for example, with a similarly large, contemporary donation to All Souls' College, Oxford, which included only seven works by pagan authors and no recent secular writing.[12]

[9] Susanne Saygin, *Humphrey, Duke of Gloucester (1390–1447) and the Italian Humanists* (Leiden: Brill, 2002), 58–9, 63. For a convincing rebuttal, see Alessandra Petrina, *Cultural Politics in Fifteenth-Century England: The Case of Humphrey Duke of Gloucester* (Leiden: Brill, 2004), 115, 128–9.

[10] John Watts, 'Was there a Lancastrian Court?', in *The Lancastrian Court*, ed. Jenny Stratford, Harlaxton Medieval Studies, 13 (Donington: Tyas, 2003), 253–71 (267–8).

[11] David Rundle, 'Humanism before the Tudors: On Nobility and the Reception of the *studia humanitatis* in Fifteenth-Century England', in *Reassessing Tudor Humanism*, ed. Jonathan Woolfson (Basingstoke: Palgrave Macmillan, 2002), 22–42 (23); Rundle, 'Republics and Tyrants', 49.

[12] Alfonso Sammut (ed.), *Unfredo duca di Gloucester e gli umanisti italiani*, Medioevo e Umanesimo, 40 (Padua: Antenore, 1980), 60–84; *Humfrey 1988*, plate 25.d; A. C. de la Mare,

Moreover, whoever wrote the inventories of the duke's gifts—especially in 1444—recognized that these classical or classicizing works were a distinct object of study: he gathered as a group the Roman grammarians, philologists, and historians, alongside Boccaccio and Petrarch, only after the traditional academic authors. As one author swooned, Humfrey had given 'volumina rara insolita ac necessaria', both the standard curriculum and something unusual.[13] We may want to recall his precursors and his interests beyond humanism, but his contemporaries did distinguish his books as a special field of the study and imitation of classical antiquity.

We only know so much about Humfrey's gifts, now that most of them have perished, because the scholars in the fifteenth century—and curators in the twentieth century—commend them.[14] With the duke long since dead, we can see his humanist patronage primarily as other men catalogue and report it. The same limitations apply if we try to assess not the duke's donations but his own scholarship. Was he a princely humanist, a royal reader? There is room for debate: three biographers have written with optimism about his scholarship while others have sharply separated the duke's impressive patronage from his own underwhelming intellectual gifts.[15] However, rather than settle the intriguing biographical debate, we can concede that a history of his personal reading must also rest upon written reports. Indeed, with Humfrey's reading the public reports seem to be just as important as the private act itself. The princely reader *himself* does not have to read classical literature to be *known* as a humanist; for that knowledge or impression to spread, it is more important that *other people* see or read or hear about the books that are supposedly his. His own fame as a reader rests upon the books he gave away for other people to read. Did he himself ever read them? He did borrow back from Oxford a work of Plato in 1445—but we only have someone else's word for this too.[16] Of course, in an age when reading was often

'Manuscripts Given to the University of Oxford by Humfrey, Duke of Gloucester', *BLR*, 13 (1988–9), 30–51, 112–21 (34, 118). Contrast Chichele's inventory in E. F. Jacob, 'Two Lives of Archbishop Chichele', *BJRL*, 16 (1932), 428–81 (469–81), with classical texts on 471, 476, 479–80.

[13] 'Capgrave's Preface Dedicating his Commentary *In Exodum* to Humfrey Duke of Gloucester', ed. Peter J. Lucas and Rita Dalton, *BLR*, 11 (1982), 20–5 (21).

[14] David Rundle, 'Habits of Manuscript-Collecting: The Dispersals of the Library of Humfrey, Duke of Gloucester', in *Lost Libraries: The Destruction of Great Book Collections since Antiquity*, ed. James Raven (Basingstoke: Palgrave, 2004), 106–24 (112).

[15] A positive view: Petrina, *Cultural Politics*, 214–24; Sammut (ed.), *Unfredo*, 47–9; K. H. Vickers, *Humphrey Duke of Gloucester: A Biography* (London: Constable, 1907), 341, 419–20. A sceptical view: Rundle, 'Republics and Tyrants', 101, 142–7, 152–8; Walter F. Schirmer, *Der Englische Frühhumanismus: Ein Beitrag zur Englischen Literaturgeschichte des 15. Jahrhunderts*, 2nd edn. (1931; Tübingen: Niemeyer, 1963), 31, 50; Weiss, *Humanism*, 40–1, 67–8.

[16] Anstey (ed.), *Epistolae*, I.246.

aural, communal, or ceremonial, then the public dimensions were integral to it. But with Duke Humfrey, this point is especially true: in the written reports which stand as a public testimony to his scholarship it is the public nature of the testimony that matters.

The sharpest testimony appears in Latin letters and letter prefaces from, to or about the duke. These letters not only publicize his reading; they often pause to describe its public effect. Perhaps the most striking letter is the dedicatory preface to a Latin version of Boccaccio's *Corbaccio*, composed by his secretary Antonio Beccaria. The secretary betrays the private reading of the duke:

[...] non solum quicquid latina lingua dici potuit, tu solus qui princeps es, et quidem praestantissimus, ingenii tui magnitudine amplectaris, verum etiam si quid est quod alieno sermone aliqua cum dignitate confectum sit, id etiam studere ac cognoscere non desistis. Omitto nunc ga[l]licas historias aut potius romanas eo sermone conscriptas, quas ita memoriter tenes, ut caeteros te audientes in tui admirationem atque stuporem saepius converteris, cum nulla res sit ex suis ac caeterarum nationum rebus gestis, quam non tibi notiorem esse constet quam vigilantibus lyncis oculis orientem solem.[17]

[...] you alone among princes, and indeed the most distinguished, with the greatness of your wit do not only embrace whatever can be said in the Latin language; but also you do not cease to study and learn about whatever there is which has been accomplished with some dignity in another language. I omit now the French histories or rather romances composed in that language, which you retain in memory so well that you have converted those who hear you to admiration and indeed more often to amazement, since there is no event from their own histories or from those of other nations, which is not certain to be better known to you than the rising sun to the watchful eyes of the lynx.

The letter seems to betray that the duke often in fact reads vernacular books, or what sound like French *romans*.[18] Yet Beccaria's modest *occupatio*, his favourite rhetorical device, does not hide Humfrey's preference for the vernacular, but subtly boasts about it. In another letter Humfrey—or probably Beccaria, again, writing for him—even offers to an Italian king as a fine gift Livy's history in French.[19] The provenances of the duke's books suggest that French

---

[17] Sammut (ed.), *Unfredo*, letter 9:8–17.

[18] No dictionary of medieval Latin lists *romana* as a noun (although many have not reached *r*); R. E. Latham, *Revised Medieval Latin Word-List from British and Irish Sources* (London: British Academy, 1965), defines *rom/ancia* as a 'romance' or 'story'. Beccaria's 'romanas' could perhaps be an adjective (Latham, *Word-List*, *[Rom]anus* for 'in French', listed under *Rom/escotum*) in chiastic opposition to *gallicas* ('about the French nation') but that renders the phrase 'eo sermone conscriptas' tautological.

[19] Sammut (ed.), *Unfredo*, letter 44:42–8. Jenny Stratford, 'The Manuscripts of John, Duke of Bedford: Library and Chapel', in *England in the Fifteenth Century: Proceedings of the 1986 Harlaxton Symposium*, ed. Daniel Williams (Woodbridge: Boydell, 1987), 329–50 (339–40, 350), describes Humfrey's own French Livy.

was the language of choice for books exchanged among the governing ranks, whereas only clerical donors or receivers required Latin. Humfrey owned several classical or humanist works in French or English versions, but then gave the original Latin to the University of Oxford.[20] He even signs his *ex libris* note in French: a public declaration of ownership. He and others were proud to report his favour for a language which might seem anathema to a classicist.

Why were they so? Perhaps Humfrey was not a great Latinist really, whatever his patronage of others. Yet the vernacular languages are useful because they allow him to disseminate his unusual learning among other laymen. English and French were the languages of propaganda: most of Humfrey's political manifestos and declarations use these tongues.[21] So the preface of Beccaria seems to tell us that after reading the *romanas* the duke can communicate with foreign visitors in a vernacular and thereby impress them. And the preface tells us that the duke's studies, whatever their language, are used to impress his visitors: he memorizes passages with which to amaze them. Elsewhere, his reading is not private but always due-to-be-public, each book almost a script for future discussion. Moreover, the letters about him do not only report that Humfrey's reading impresses people; by reporting the reading, the letters themselves are designed to impress other audiences in turn. The letters boast about his boasting about his reading.

Yet what underpins such boasting is a presumption that it is good for a nobleman to be a scholar, a growing presumption in the fifteenth century, here in a specifically humanist form. A fine example is the preface by Pietro del Monte to his *De Vitiorum inter se differencia et comparatione*, sent to the duke. David Rundle has made the important observation that this book is in fact a work of plagiarism, and that del Monte cannot have thought too highly of the duke to give it to him.[22] And del Monte compounds his dishonesty by describing the duke's great memory, even remembering every chapter and verse, as Beccaria did, and takes care to praise scholarship in general terms. He asks which of Humfrey's virtues makes him 'equal to the princes of an earlier

---

[20] Sammut (ed.), *Unfredo*, 98–132: manuscripts nos. 10, 13, 24, 28, 30–1, and 38 (in Latin, from clerics) and nos. 1, 5, 36, and 37 (in French, from laymen); for duplicated Latin and vernacular works see manuscripts nos. 5, 21, and 35; and in the inventories nos. 206–9, 216, 232, 240, and 271; and *The Fall of Princes* and *On Husbondrie* below.

[21] *Wars in France*, II.ii.440–51; Anstey (ed.), *Epistolae*, I.184; Thomas Rymer (ed.), *Foedera, conventiones, literæ, Et cujuscunque generis acta publica*, 10 vols. (The Hague: Neaulme, 1739–45), V.i.76–7; S. B. Chrimes (ed.), 'The Pretensions of the Duke of Gloucester in 1422', *EHR*, 45 (1930), 101–3.

[22] David Rundle, 'On the Difference between Virtue and Weiss: Humanist Texts in England during the Fifteenth Century', in *Courts, Counties and the Capital in the Later Middle Ages*, ed. Diana E. S. Dunn, Fifteenth Century Series, 4 (Stroud: Sutton, 1996), 181–203 (194–9).

age' and better than his peers ('superioris aetatis principis te aequalem'). It is
his skill in the liberal arts fit for a prince:

Quae res, cum in privato in magnis efferri laudibus soleat, in principe tamen numquam
satis digne extolli aut praedicari solet. Is enim quem de bello, de pace, de sociis, de
subditis, de annona, de armis, de ductando exercitu deque omni reipublicae statu ingens
cura sollicitat, perraro ad videndos, nedum legendos libros otium sibi videtur posse
vindicare; quod qui fecerit, neque minus publicae utilitati animum accomodaverit, is
vere princeps maximis in caelum praeconiis est efferendus, is omnium linguis, omnium
litteris perpetuae posterorum memoriae commendandus. Hinc apud clarissimos
antiquitatis scriptores, Caesaris virtus ac diligentia plurimum commendatur, quod
cum exercitu proficiscens eos libros diserte atque eleganter inscripserit, quos vulgo
Commentarios appellamus; Augustus quoque fertur in Mutinensi bello quotidie legere,
scribere aut declamare consuevisse; Theodosius vero mirum in modum extollitur, quo
die quidem exercebatur in armis, vel subditorum causis ius dicebat, nocte autem libris
ad lucernam incumbebat. Felices medius fidius hi fuere, et quavis humana laude ac
gloria dignissimi; felix quoque et tu, qui et in negotio et in otio negotium facile reperire
consuevisti [...][23]

However, even though we tend to exalt with great praise a private citizen for this
activity, it can never be sufficiently exalted or fanfared in a prince. For the man
harassed by great cares of war, peace, followers, subjects, crops, arms, leading the
army and the state of the whole commonweal—he most rarely seems able to find
leisure to glance at, let alone to read, books. Whenever he does find time, and yet
does not think any less about public affairs, that prince really should be praised to
the skies with the highest commendations; he should be commended to the perpetual
memory of our descendents in the mouths and writings of all men. For this reason
the most famous writers of antiquity praised greatly the virtue and diligence of Caesar,
for while setting out with the army he composed with elegance and eloquence those
books which we usually call *Commentarii*. It is also said that Augustus was in the habit
of reading, writing, or practising oratory daily during the war with Modena. Indeed,
they extol Theodosius to a remarkable degree because by day he practised arms or
gave judgement in his subjects' cases, but by night he huddled under the lamp with
his books. By Jove, they were happy and most deserving of all mortal praise and glory;
and you are happy too, for you have managed to find occupations in both business
and at rest [...]

This preface uses several rhetorical devices that recur in other descriptions
of Duke Humfrey. Firstly, there is an excitable and incredulous tone which
suggests that there is still something remarkable in the princely reader or
humanist: the writer uses phrases such as 'perraro' and 'mirum in modum' and
piles up the competing duties of each prince in bewildering lists. Secondly, what
makes the prince's studies remarkable are those competing duties. The duke's

---

[23] Sammut (ed.), *Unfredo*, letter 3:10–28.

reading is not the reading of a recluse or contemplative; it is reading wedged tightly into the active life. From classical times to the seventeenth century, European scholars express ambivalence towards leisure and retirement and dream of blending the active life and scholarship. The dream reappears in other letters to Duke Humfrey or by other English scholars in the fifteenth century.[24] Thirdly, the princely reader is described in a very imperial tone. The classical studies they idealize supply that praise, in allusions to Roman emperors, taken from Suetonius' work—hardly an unambiguous source.[25] The imperial comparisons become common in describing the duke, especially after he donates books to Oxford: Caesar also founded a library which, we hear, outlasted his controversial political reputation. So the duke is blithely equated with the Caesars: 'and you are happy too' ('felix quoque et tu').[26] Finally, if we read the preface by del Monte with care, the prevailing theme is not in fact the learning of princes but the acclaim it wins: so many of the words describe reputation and commendation ('efferi', 'extollere', 'laus', 'praedicare', 'videtur', 'praeconia', 'linguae', 'litterae', 'memoria', 'commendere', 'fertur', 'clarissimus', 'gloria', 'dignissimus'). Now he may, again, betray that his portrait is inaccurate or tendentious. Such tendentiousness might well arise from the writer's precarious finances and career as he, like other humanists, advertises his services to a patron. Such tendentiousness might betray that the fashion for education among the aristocracy in England was still not secure; they needed to see the 'pay-off'. Whoever's the motive is, though, there is a cynical concern with reputation in this encomium: Pietro del Monte is not praising the princely humanist but describing the praise due to him. Whether it is accurate or not about the duke's studies, this letter suggests that those humanist studies were important as publicity or image-making.

THE PRINCELY READER IN *THE FALL OF PRINCES*

These letters, then, corroborate the recent criticism that the humanists peddled classical learning as an ornament for social climbers, whether princes or the scholars themselves (as sketched in Chapter 1). However, if we turn from these

---

[24] Sammut (ed.), *Unfredo*, letters 3:27–35, and 39:16–23, 41:12–35, 43:15–35, 43:43–53, which introduce, and seem influenced by, Plato's *Republic*; Anstey (ed.), *Epistolae*, I.53–4; *Bekynton Correspondence*, II.311–13. See in general Brian Vickers, 'Leisure and Idleness in the Renaissance: The Ambivalence of *otium*', *Renaissance Studies*, 4 (1990), 1–37, 107–54 (8–15, 141, 153).

[25] Sammut (ed.), *Unfredo*, 152.

[26] Sammut (ed.), *Unfredo*, letter 16:30–5; Anstey (ed.), *Epistolae*, I.178, I.204.

Latin prefaces to poems in English, does the assessment hold true? It sounds
as though Duke Humfrey would flaunt his erudition in the French vernacular;
so why not in two English works? Besides collecting Latin manuscripts and
texts, he commissioned Lydgate's *The Fall of Princes* and the anonymous *On
Husbondrie*. *The Fall of Princes* is a translation of Boccaccio's *De Casibus
virorum illustrium*, although it is in fact based on a French translation made
by Laurent de Premierfait in 1409. In prologues to various books and in the
final envoy, Lydgate informs us that Duke Humfrey commissioned the poem
in 1431. But the duke's interest may have waxed and waned. There may have
fallen pauses, for lack of payment or for other projects, after books II and VII.
Yet in the poem the duke usually sounds solicitous for the book: we hear his
request that Lydgate add further moral envoys to his work and that he insert
a speech by Collucio Salutati (episodes discussed below). Lydgate may have
presented the poem in stages with various begging letters and envoys, before it
was completed in 1438/9.[27] The short discussion here will not do justice to so
lengthy and complex a work, but it will consider solely how Lydgate imagines
his princely reader. As a humanist, as the Italians do? In a flurry of flattery, as
the Italians do?

The duke first appears in the prologue. At first here Lydgate follows his
French guide, Laurent de Premierfait, in defending free translation and in
rebuking the ignorance of princes.[28] Then, in some original verses, he portrays
a prince who is not so ignorant:

> For in the tyme off Cesar Iulius,
> Whan the tryumphe he wan in Rome toun,
> He entre wolde the scoole off Tullius
> And heere his lecture off gret affeccioun;
> And natwithstandyng his conquest and renoun,
> Vnto bookis he gaff gret attendaunce
> And hadde in stories ioie and gret plesaunce.
>
> Eek in this land, I dar afferme a thyng:
> There is a prynce ful myhti off puissaunce. [...]

Then we hear about the political duties of this new prince, and then of his
pastimes:

---

[27] For the composition, see Derek Pearsall, *John Lydgate (1371–1449): A Bio-bibliography*,
English literary studies monograph series, 71 (Victoria, BC: University of Victoria, 1997), 32–3;
Walter F. Schirmer, *John Lydgate: A Study in the Culture of the XVth Century*, trans. Ann.
E. Keep (1952; London: Methuen, 1961), 215–16. All quotations, with parenthetical book and
line numbers, come from Lydgate, *Fall*.

[28] Compare Laurent de Premierfait, *Des Cas des Nobles Hommes et Femmes: Book I*, ed.
Patricia May Gathercole, Studies in the Romance Languages and Literatures, 74 (Chapel Hill,
NC: University of North Carolina Press, 1968), 90.

[…] Off hih lettrure, I dar eek off hym telle,
And treuli deeme that he doth excelle

In vndirstondyng alle othir off his age,
And hath gret ioie with clerkis to comune:
And no man is mor expert off language,
Stable in study alwey he doth contune,
Settyng a-side alle chaungis of Fortune;
And wher he loueth, yiff I shal nat tarie,
Withoute cause ful loth he is to varie.

Duc off Gloucestre men this prynce calle,
And natwithstandyng his staat and dignite,
His corage neuer doth appalle
To studie in bookis off antiquite,
Therin he hath so gret felicite
Vertuously hymsilff to ocupie,
Off vicious slouthe to haue the maistrie.   (I.365–99)

Does Lydgate present the duke's reading as a taste for the *studia humanitatis*? In several ways he does: the duke has a taste for 'language', 'antiquite', and 'hih lettrure'—perhaps the first distinction of high art in English—which is echoed in an emphasis upon 'lettrure' elsewhere in the poem (II.25, IV.225). These words make the duke's reading sound bookish and scholarly, like the studies dictated for the Lancastrian and Yorkist princes. Yet Lydgate does still hint how remarkable it is that a prince will study like a clerk 'natwithstandyng his staat and dignite'. That 'natwithstandyng' expresses surprise at finding a scholar-prince. And although being different is seldom in the fifteenth century a good thing, here it is excellent: the prince 'doth excelle' in his wisdom 'alle othir of his age', praise which runs parallel to comments in Latin letters that the duke is more like the ancients than the moderns.[29] But what are Lydgate's criteria of excellence? They echo the criteria of humanists in Latin. Firstly, the Italians make it commonplace that the duke's reading fits tightly into an active public life. Lydgate too interweaves these lines with others about governing with the vigilance of Argus and about pursuing the Lollards.[30] Secondly, the humanists emphasize the grandeur of bookishness by comparing Humfrey to Julius Caesar. Lydgate also introduces Caesar as a precedent or standard, making the comparison casually as if it were obvious ('Eek in this land'). This prologue suggests that the implied reader is the duke and that his reading befits a prince. These suggestions would confirm the recent view of Lydgate as a sort of propagandist, trying to develop for the duke a 'persona as a

---

[29] Compare Sammut (ed.), *Unfredo*, letter 3:7–10.
[30] Lydgate, *Fall*, I.372–83, I.400–13. Lydgate forgets that Argus finally nodded off: see Ovid, *Metamorphoses*, I.713–14, and *n.* 21 in Chapter 3 below.

learned statesman' in 'cultural politics'.[31] Humanist erudition is here part of
the treatment of knowledge as power once thought common in the sixteenth
century, now thought so in the fifteenth too.

Yet we must be wary, for prologues and epilogues, like humanist letters,
were usually obsequious in their quest for employment or earnings, as are
the prefaces to academic books today. We must be wary, too, for it is hard
to tell whether princes ever read the books of prince-pleasers; we must not
assume it. Did Duke Humfrey have a real interest in Lydgate's work? There
is some evidence that the duke was scholarly enough at least to tinker with
it. His most likely intervention is noted in book II, when he asks Lydgate
to interpolate a humanist declamation into Boccaccio's work (II.967–1344).
Boccaccio is listing the later Roman kings, and very briefly mentions Tarquin,
the rapist of Lucretia. Lydgate initially promises not to digress into the tale
of Lucretia, because Chaucer has already told it, but he changes his mind
because:

> Also my lord bad I sholde abide,
> By good auys at leiser to translate
> The doolful processe off hir pitous fate.
> Folwyng the tracis off Collucyus,
> Which wrot off hir a declamacioun [...][32]

As it happens Boccaccio tells the story in a later book and Lydgate there
apologizes for having prematurely translated 'Pierius' at the 'biddyng off my
lord' (III.981–7). What did the lord bid? It seems that Duke Humfrey bid
Lydgate to translate the *Declamatio Lucretiae*, a pair of speeches by Lucretia
and her husband, composed by Collucio Salutati, Chancellor of Florence
(1331–1406). The claim that the duke did so is plausible, because he did
own a manuscript of Salutati's work which still survives; it is entitled there
'Colucii Pyeri Salutati Declamacio quedam', which possibly explains Lydgate's
'Pierius' for Salutati. Interestingly, in the duke's manuscript this work is again
an addition—not necessarily made at his command—slotted onto some
blank leaves and an extra bifolium.[33] It may be that he favoured this work

---

[31] Jennifer Summit, '"Stable in Study": Lydgate's *Fall of Princes* and Duke Humphrey's
Library', in *John Lydgate: Poetry, Culture, and Lancastrian England*, ed. Larry Scanlon and James
Simpson (Notre Dame, IN: University of Notre Dame Press, 2006), 207–31 (212); Petrina,
Cultural Politics, 261.

[32] Lydgate, *Fall*, II.1006–10, and the Boccaccian passage on II.974–1001, rendering six lines
of French (printed in Lydgate, *Fall*, vol. IV, 174–5). Lydgate often worries about repeating stories
already available in English: I.3018–20, I.3723–5, I.5944–57, VI.3220–1, VIII.670–9.

[33] Eleanor Prescott Hammond, 'Lydgate and Coluccio Salutati', *MP*, 25 (1927), 49–57;
Manchester, Chetham's Library, MS Mun. A.3.131 (27929), ff.200v–203r; on which see Rundle,
'Republics and Tyrants', 424–6; *Humfrey 1970*, no. 17; Sammut (ed.), *Unfredo*, manuscript no.

highly enough to have it added both to a Latin book and an English poem; and the coincidence suggests if not that the duke really read his books then certainly that he was consistent in his humanist patronage.

But what was the significance of adding the myth of Lucretia, a myth infamously malleable in different hands? It has been argued that Salutati composed his version in order to defend the liberty of Florence. But the story can be told in various ways: Chaucer, for example, dodges the republicanism and emphasizes womanly faithfulness.[34] Lydgate does not say why the duke asked him to translate it, but he himself salts the tale with less republicanism than moralism. He translates the speeches loosely into a domestic homily by repeatedly adding the words *true wife, clean, virtue, wifely, clear, cleanness.* Lucretia is called 'a merour' or 'good exaumple' to others—like an exemplum from a sermon on chastity.[35] Have not some important political ideas been lost from the homily? Lydgate now attacks desire, delectation, lust, lechery, and adultery. He twice removes words suggesting Tarquin's royalty, which would highlight the constitutional conflict, and instead calls him a 'knyht'.[36] Does he soften the republicanism of his Florentine source, in order to please the English prince? After all, elsewhere in *The Fall of Princes* he does reveal his wholehearted monarchism and his fear of social upheaval, and he often dulls the criticisms of Boccaccio.[37] With a duke reading, who wouldn't? But the story of Lucretia is too dark for such whitewashing. How could one tell it without talking of the exile of the Tarquins? Indeed, Lydgate neglects to purge from Salutati all the civic bile and he retains words such as *common profit, oppressed, tyrant, tyranny,* and the decision 'alle kynges to exile'.[38] Lydgate is a diffuse writer, not always consistent in his argument, especially across

21. Humfrey added an *ex libris* to the front of the two texts originally in the book but a different *ex libris* at the end of the added text (f.2r, f.91, f.205r).

[34] Stephanie H. Jed, *Chaste Thinking: The Rape of Lucretia and the Birth of Humanism* (Bloomington, IN: Indiana University Press, 1989), 38–9; Nigel Mortimer, *John Lydgate's* Fall of Princes: *Narrative Tragedy in its Literary and Political Contexts* (Oxford: Clarendon Press, 2005), 63–6, 76–8; Chaucer, *Legend of Good Women,* lines 1680–93, 1674–85.

[35] Lydgate, *Fall,* II.974, II.1042, II.1059–60, II.1069–71, II.1073, II.1081, II.1084–5, II.1089, II.1092, II.1112, II.1196, II.1207, II.1210, II.1259–60.

[36] Lydgate, *Fall,* II.1019, II.1124, do not translate 'regis' and 'regia' from the Latin: compare *Coluccio Salutati: Editi e inediti Latini dal Ms. 53 della Biblioteca Comunale di Todi,* ed. Enrico Menestò, Res Tudertinæ, 12 (Todi: Tipografica Porziuncola, 1971), 35–43 (35, lines 2, 10, and 12).

[37] Rita Copeland, 'Lydgate, Hawes and the Science of Rhetoric in the Late Middle Ages', in *John Lydgate: Poetry, Culture, and Lancastrian England,* ed. Larry Scanlon and James Simpson (Notre Dame, IN: University of Notre Dame Press, 2006), 232–58 (243–5, 252); Derek Pearsall, *John Lydgate* (London: Routledge and Kegan Paul, 1970), 249.

[38] Lydgate, *Fall,* II.970, II.1020, II.1181, II.1190, II.1343, and II.1323. Compare the French printed by Bergen in Lydgate, *Fall,* vol. IV, 174–5 ('roys', 'peuple', 'seigneurs', 'seruitude').

this vast poem, and it is his inconsistency which prevents him from being a complete toady.

Nevertheless, any criticism of princes is softened, because we have already heard that this section was commissioned by a prince. Yet to commission a poem is not the same as to read one. The story honours the patron, for it seems designed not to teach him—he already knows these lessons, Lydgate would rush to say if pressed or whipped—but to teach other men. This is the essential feature of *The Fall of Princes*: Humfrey is not a pupil but a teacher. This is confirmed in the other quite convincing sign of his patronage. Lydgate adds to the poem some sixty-nine envoys which emphasize the already emphatic lessons and he does so, he says, at the duke's express command. He:

> Gaff me charge in his prudent auys,
>
> That I sholde in eueri tragedie,
> Afftir the processe made mencioun,
> At the eende sette a remedie,
> With a lenvoie conueied be resoun
> And afftir that, with humble affeccioun,
> To noble pryncis lowli it directe,
> Bi othres fallyng [thei myht] themsilff correcte.   (II.147–54)

This is not a moment of counsel for Humfrey, with him imagined to need the 'remedie' in this book. The readers are the other 'noble pryncis', who—unless the poet dares to teach the king—are probably men below Humfrey in rank but still prominent in the realm. There is a broader imagined readership than the mere heir to the throne. This is confirmed in the envoy (IX.3553–76) and in the prologue:

> It is almesse to correct and a-mende
> The vicious folk off euery comounte,
> And bi exaumplis which that notable be
> Off pryncis olde, that whilom dede fall,
> The lowere peeple from ther errour call.   (I.206–10)

The poem teaches the whole 'comounte', which suggests the enfranchised men in any county. Some of these phrases come from the French version of Boccaccio's prologue ('charitable a la communauté'), but Lydgate expands them. He mentions the 'lowere peeple', for example, and he repeats elsewhere in the poem that it is a poem for all the community or estates.[39] A happy accident shaped this turn: the French version, Lydgate's source, begins with an obsequious letter to a lord; but this letter appears in only a few manuscripts

---

[39] Compare de Premierfait, *Des Cas*, ed. Gathercole, 92, paragraph 4; *MED*, *communite* (n.). See also Lydgate, *Fall*, I.51, I.155–9, II.22–6, II.970, IV.224–5, IX.3582–4.

and Lydgate has not seen it or has not used it. What he does use is Boccaccio's own prologue, which also appears in the French, where Boccaccio dedicates the work to a familiar friend of his own rank and says that he hopes to teach the whole commonweal. It is a poem *about* princes, but *for* humbler men to read.

THE REAL READING OF *THE FALL OF PRINCES*

Sure enough, the evidence from surviving manuscripts confirms that *The Fall of Princes* was read by a wider range of noblemen and others below them in rank. This is in fact common to most fifteenth-century mirrors for princes, as the bibliographical evidence suggests. No matter to whom the mirror for princes was first dedicated, there is only occasionally a copy extant that was given to the dedicatee and even if there is such a copy then it is rarely the sole copy in existence. For example, Ashby's *The Active Policy of a Prince* survives in a scruffy booklet that was surely never given to the Prince Edward whom Ashby professes to teach; Hoccleve's *The Regiment of Princes* survives in over forty manuscripts which were not all read by Henry V or even by noblemen; and so on for other works of the genre.[40] The same general pattern emerges in the copies of *The Fall of Princes*. At most only two of the thirty-nine complete copies—some now fragmentary—seem to have been owned by the English royal family, by real princes, before the Reformation.[41] Among the other readers were princes in the broader sense, men prominent in the commonweal and often, we might note with ghoulish irony, men who fell from grace too, such as Sir John Tiptoft, Constable of England, or Edmund Dudley, two famous casualties of regime change.[42] Further readers of it came from the ranks of civil society: gentry, lawyers, scholars and monastic houses; it was unusual among English poems in that it also appears in inventories

[40] CUL, MS Mm. IV.42 (Ashby); Nicholas Perkins, *Hoccleve's* The Regiment of Princes: *Counsel and Constraint* (Cambridge: Brewer, 2001), 161–2, 177; Orme, *From Childhood to Chivalry*, 89, 95–8 (in general).

[41] Mortimer, *John Lydgate's* Fall of Princes, 253, suggests that BodL, MS Hatton 2, was owned by Henry VIII and Princeton, University Library, MS Taylor 2, by Edward IV. In BodL, MS Hatton 2 the formal inscription looks like a pen-trial; I have not seen the Princeton manuscript.

[42] A. S. G. Edwards, 'The Influence of Lydgate's *Fall of Princes* c.1440–1559: A Survey', *Mediaeval Studies*, 39 (1977), 424–39 (429); and, for example, BL, MS Royal 18.D.iv (Tiptoft, on whom see Chapter 6 below), and BL, MS Additional 21410 (Dudley, on whom see *DNB*, Dudley, Edmund, <http://www.oxforddnb.com/view/article/8147>, accessed 28 August 2005).

of academic libraries.[43] The prince who is the implied reader is not the only real reader; the real readers are the wider 'comounte' of political society. We should bear this in mind when we consider the purpose of any mirror for princes.

Taken together, the poem's imagined readers and its real readers suggest that Lydgate wrote not only as part of a 'cultural politics' to glorify the Lancastrian kings. He also imagined and found a wider range of readers, who were encouraged to prudential reflection by his poem. And as some other critics say of his work in general, he finds time to criticize princes, not just to praise them.[44] In this democracy of readers and of sympathies does Lydgate's poem diverge from the princely humanism of Humfrey? The Latin letters esteem the duke for being a connoisseur of rarefied learning, distinguished from others; the English poem esteems him as an advisor in political matters and to the wider 'comounte'. Is there a division between princely humanism and the vernacular politics of this book? For James Simpson, Lydgate often offers an unsettled treatment of authority because he comes from an unsettled culture, and is not a smug 'Renaissance' humanist: he does not defer to authorities, of the present or of antiquity; he is typical of 'medieval' learning, syncretic and catholic and questioning. However, for other critics, Lydgate is sceptical of authority exactly because he is humanist in his taste.[45] Which is true? Does *The Fall of Princes* escape the politics of Duke Humfrey as it escapes the *studia humanitatis* he loved?

The poem is inconsistent about the link between knowledge and power: for example, it rebukes Nero that his fine education cannot compensate for his misgovernance (VII.614–20, VII.640–73), but it praises the liberal arts which are so called because only men born free (*liber*) or born in 'lyneal hih noblesse' should study them (I.4257–63). Throughout, though, the poem does bear some traces of the humanist keenness for antiquity, in which Boccaccio and Laurent de Premierfait were forerunners. In expanding the translation, Lydgate also drew on Boccaccio's other great work of scholarship, his *De*

[43] Edwards, 'Influence of Lydgate's *Fall of Princes*', 428–30, and A. S. G. Edwards, 'Lydgate Manuscripts: Some Directions for Future Research', in *Manuscripts and Readers in Fifteenth-Century England: The Literary Implications of Manuscript Study*, ed. Derek Pearsall (Cambridge: Brewer, 1983), 15–26 (21–2). For another copy in an academic library, see Peter D. Clarke, with R. Lovatt (eds.), *The University and College Libraries of Cambridge*, Corpus of British Medieval Library Catalogues, 10 (London: British Academy, 2002), 601 (UC53.76).

[44] Simpson, *Reform*, 55–62; Maura Nolan, ' "Now Wo, Now Gladnesse": Ovidianism in the *Fall of Princes*', *ELH*, 71 (2004), 531–58 (552–3).

[45] Simpson, *Reform*, 50–2. Contrast the older studies by Friedrich Brie, 'Mittelalter und Antike bei Lydgate', *Englische Studien*, 64 (1929), 261–301 (262); Schirmer, *Lydgate*, 207, 227; Alain Renoir, *The Poetry of John Lydgate* (London: Routledge and Kegan Paul, 1967), p. viii, 31, 110, 142–3.

Genealogia deorum gentilium. Besides the *Declamatio Lucretiae* he drew on Salutati's *De Laboribus Herculis*, a rare book which Duke Humfrey owned. He drew too on classical texts themselves, Ovid frequently, but also Aulus Gellius, Justinus, Josephus, Lucan, and Valerius Maximus, albeit all of them briefly rather than in depth. What is most important is that Lydgate alerts the reader to these sources: whereas Laurent de Premierfait expanded many stories silently, Lydgate names his authorities in many lines, citing 'the writyng off Ouidius' especially often (I.2666).[46] The writing style of *The Fall of Princes* does seem to reflect from time to time the humanist preference for ancient literature.

And who was this humanist literature for? There is one cluster of clues to answer the question. Just as Lydgate took care to note the classical sources he had been reading, so a few scribes took care to mark them too. In lots of copies there are Latin marginalia by the scribe, usually as a sort of finding-aid, summarizing the gloomy catalogue. But in a few copies some of the marginalia draw the eye to biblical, classical, or humanist sources.[47] Who thought that the sources were noteworthy? With so many copies surviving, the evidence is copious and contradictory, but a hypothesis can be made—if not squarely proven. The hypothesis is technical and fiddly to explain. Certain clues in two of the copies raise the possibility that the Latin scholarly notes were part of the original design of the poem, presumably for Duke Humfrey. One manuscript, Harley 1766, is a shorter version of the poem, largely complete for book I and parts of book II but thereafter only a patchy witness to the full text; and in this book many scholarly notes appear in books I and II, few thereafter. Another manuscript, Harley 4203, is a full text and contains many scholarly notes for books II–IX; but sadly it lost its first three quires, with all of book I, as early as the fifteenth century. Where both manuscripts overlap in having the full text, in book II, the Latin notes often correspond, and they might have corresponded once in the parts of book I lost in one copy.[48] But do these

[46] Emil Koeppel, *Laurents de Premierfait und John Lydgates Bearbeitungen von Boccaccios De Casibus Virorum Illustrium: Ein Beitrag zur Litteraturgeschichte des 15. Jahrhunderts* (Munich: Oldenbourg, 1885), 50–72, identifies many classical and other sources; for others, see Susan Schibanoff, 'Avarice and Cerberus in Salutati's *De Laboribus Herculis* and Lydgate's *Fall of Princes*', MP, 71 (1974), 390–2; Patricia M. Gathercole, 'Lydgate's «Fall of Princes» and the French Version of Boccaccio's «De Casibus»', in *Miscellanea di Studi e Ricerche sul Quattrocento Francese*, ed. Franco Simone (Turin: Giappichelli, 1967), 167–78 (174–5).

[47] Nine citations in BL, MS Harley 1766; thirteen in BL, MS Harley 4197; twenty-three in BL, MS Harley 4203.

[48] In BL, MS Harley 1766, seven of nine source citations appear in books I-II, as do all six other notes longer than a mere 'nota' and/or character's name. In BL, MS Harley 4203 in books II-IX there are twenty source citations and sixty-one other notes longer than a mere 'nota' and/or character's name. The manuscripts overlap for three notes in book II (BL, MS Harley 1766, f.98r x 2, f.103v; BL, MS Harley 4203, f.39v x 2, f.42r). In BL, MS Harley 4203, ff.1r–36v, are

two manuscripts have any textual authority? It has been plausibly suggested that Harley 1766 reflects the special involvement of Lydgate, because it has an odd shorter text, which would require considerable editorial intervention, and because the scribe and illuminator were connected with his town of Bury St Edmunds and with other copies of his poems, perhaps dedicatory copies.[49] And it is possible that Harley 4203 is closely linked to Lydgate's own exemplars, for it ends with the colophon of his French source, otherwise found only in one other copy, and surely a chore for a scribe to interpolate if it were not already in an exemplar which preserved carefully a text close to Lydgate's own.[50] The marginalia in Harley 4203 are also not unique, but often reappear in another copy.[51]

The fact that these marginalia recur in scattered fragments suggests the wider diffusion of them once, at least in lost exemplars; but their scattered, fragmentary nature also suggests that they must have seemed inessential. The evidence from copies of other works suggests that including such marginalia, often needing rubric and fiddly layouts, was a chore gladly abandoned: for example, the Latin commentary to Gower's poetry was so fiddly that the scribes cut corners or cut it altogether; some similar fate befell the sources placed in the margins of the early copies of *The Canterbury Tales* but dismissed by most of the later scribes.[52] Despite the exigencies of book production, we can hypothesize that Lydgate prepared *The Fall of Princes* with Latin marginalia which noted some of its sources—but that many scribes ignored them.

There are objections to this hypothesis; but before we consider them (below) what would such authorial marginalia be for? They would link Lydgate's great work with the works of Gower and Chaucer, of course; the marginalia in them

replacements, as is evident from the squashed layout where the replacements dovetail on f.36v, and from the new hand and use of parchment on f.37r. There are four source citations on the replacement leaves (f.19v, f.24r x 3) which correspond instead with four in JRL, MS Eng. 2 (f.20v, f.25r x3). The notes in JRL, MS Eng. 2 seem a separate textual tradition, and only correspond with those shared by other manuscripts once (f.30v; compare BL, MS Harley 1766, f.76r).

   [49] Kathleen L. Scott, *Later Gothic Manuscripts, 1390–1490*, 2 vols. (London: Harvey Miller, 1996), II.302–4; Edwards, 'Lydgate Manuscripts', 17–18, 22; A. S. G. Edwards, 'The McGill Fragment of Lydgate's "Fall of Princes"', *Scriptorium*, 28 (1974), 75–7.

   [50] BL, MS Harley 4203, f.181v. BL, MS Additional 21410, f.168r, also has the French colophon and, on f.164r, the final Latin scribal note as in BL, MS Harley 4203, f.180r (IX.3029).

   [51] BL, MS Harley 4197, with nineteen notes also found in BL, MS Harley 4203, but seven of them abbreviated.

   [52] Derek Pearsall, 'The Organization of the Latin Apparatus in Gower's *Confessio Amantis*: The Scribes and their Problems', in *The Medieval Book and a Modern Collector: Essays in Honour of Toshiyuki Takamiya*, ed. Takami Matsuda, Richard A. Linenthal, and John Scahill (Cambridge: Brewer, 2004), 99–112 (103–12); Derek Pearsall, 'The Ellesmere Chaucer and Contemporary English Literary Manuscripts', in *The Ellesmere Chaucer: Essays in Interpretation*, ed. Daniel Woodward and Martin Stevens (San Marino, CA: Huntington Library, and Tokyo: Yushodo, 1995), 263–80 (271).

are surely the immediate models. Yet the marginalia in *The Fall of Princes* turn the Chaucerian game of source-spotting into a humanist game. Of the forty-five marginalia about the sources in the related series, only a quarter cite the Bible; most of them cite classical sources, especially Ovid, who is often cited in the verse itself. The humanist study of antiquity emerges most clearly in two passages where the marginalia are copious in manuscript Harley 4203. Some sixteen marginalia highlight the story of Lucretia in book II, and five of them turn out to be word-for-word snippets from the Latin *Declamatio Lucretiae* by Coluccio Salutati, the work which the duke wanted Lydgate to translate.[53] Then in book IV there is an antiquarian description of Roman triumphs, during the life of Marcus Manlius Torquatus. The marginalia here highlight Aulus Gellius as the source and give seven rough excerpts from Aulus Gellius's *Noctes Atticae*. In the poem itself, Lydgate takes care to record that he interpolated this passage from Aulus Gellius (IV.239).[54] Both sets of marginalia, then, preserve traces of the study and imitation of antiquity undertaken by Lydgate—if not by Duke Humfrey—and they advertise his quite recondite reading very publicly in red. Yet what is this reading for? The notes from Aulus Gellius suggest a humanism that is mere antiquarianism, and an antiquarianism about the ceremonies for honouring a leader. Other humanists in England annotated descriptions of the triumphs, and other works in English such as *The Serpent of Division* and *De Consulatu Stilichonis* translated accounts of Roman ceremonies of honour.[55] However, the source citations in *The Fall of Princes* also add something to the moral lessons which rebuke princes. The marginalia about triumphs might add pathos to the fall which follows glory, and the triumph here glorifies not a prince but a republican who fought for 'the comoun' of Rome and '*pro Re Publica*' or 'For comoun proffit', as Lydgate repeatedly says (IV.218, IV.304, IV.310). Then the marginalia from Salutati's work on Lucretia may reflect the duke's commission but they also rebuke princes, as this story always threatens to; the final Latin note reminds us that the rape led to the exile of kings ('Causa mortis lucrecie reges erant extra Roman. totaliter expulsi').[56] Even beyond these two

---

[53] BL, MS Harley 4203, ff.41r–42v (at II.974–1345): 'Brutus pater lucrecie', misinterpreting the text (printed in *Salutati: Editi e inediti*, 39, line 31); 'Sanctate matronalee thronos' (39, line 40); 'que mulier erit tutu violata lucrecia' (39, line 43); 'fatebur occultum' (41, line 9); and 'Parce pater perce coniunx' (41, line 9).

[54] BL, MS Harley 4203, f.86r-v; BL Harley 4197, f.79r-v; Aulus Gellius, *Noctes Atticae*, ed. P. K. Marshall, 2 vols. (Oxford: Clarendon Press, 1968), V.vi.2, 5–6, 8–9, 16, 18, 17, 20, the source for Lydgate, *Fall*, IV.239–302.

[55] TCC, MS O.9.8, f.26v (humanist note on Aulus Gellius and triumphs); John Lydgate, *The Serpent of Division*, ed. Henry Noble MacCracken (New Haven, CT: Yale University Press, 1911), 20–2, 53; *De Consulatu Stilichonis* in Chapter 3 below.

[56] BL, MS Harley 4203, f.42v; the phrase is not from Salutati.

episodes, the source citations, whether from classical literature, scripture, or proverbs, often sharpen the rebuke of princes or effuse civic feeling.[57] So if they are remnants of the duke's library, they seem hostile to his kind: they seem more congenial to the humbler readers, observing the folly of princes, whom the poet aimed to teach.

However, can we really hypothesize that Lydgate, with or without the duke, planned the page design in order to educate a wider readership in humanism or even in politics? The fragments of the planned design are, unfortunately, too fragmentary to make the hypothesis secure. The red marginalia could stem not from the poet or the imagined reader, Humfrey, but from the other later scribes and readers of the work. For example, the notes from Salutati's *Declamatio* could come from the other copy owned by an Englishman, by the humanist William Gray, or from another lost copy.[58] Moreover, other classicizing notes were added by other readers far from Humfrey. In one copy a few notes on Ovid adorn book I. Somebody who corrected another copy also noted a citation of Ovid and glossed a few references to the muses, Charon, and so on. Somebody who corrected another copy attended to the spelling of classical names.[59] In many copies the fifteenth- and sixteenth-century readers spotted the names of the characters, often classical of course, and of the authors whom Lydgate claims to cite, especially in the prologue to book IV about famous poets.[60] Across these various books, the humanist study of antiquity in Lydgate's work does not seem to be the prince's prerogative; it comes independently from the other readers beyond him.

[57] BL, MS Harley 4203, f.19v, and JRL, MS Eng. 2, f.20v (Luke 11: 17); BL, MS Harley 1766, f.82v (Judges 14: 18); BL, MS Harley 4203, f.37r, and BL, MS Harley 4197, f.36v ('Pauper virtuosus est generosus'); BL, MS Harley 4203, f.39v, BL, MS Harley 1766, f.98r, and BL, MS Harley 4197, f.38r ('Cum malis operibus principum corumpitur conuersacio subiectorum'); BL, MS Harley 4203, f.79r, and BL, MS Harley 4197, f.73r ('Parcere prostratis est nobilis ira leonis'); BL, MS Harley 4203, f.125r ('Virtus et generositas heredibus hereditarijs non incubunt'); BL, MS Harley 4203, f.172r, and BL, MS Harley 1766, f.235v (Psalm 103: 15).

[58] R. A. B. Mynors, *Catalogue of the Manuscripts of Balliol College* (Oxford: Clarendon Press, 1963), p. xliv, notes Gray's copy; Clarke, with Lovatt (eds.), *University and College Libraries of Cambridge*, 586 (UC52.12), lists another, now lost. One marginal phrase in BL, MS Harley 4203, f.42r, includes a variant ('fatebur occultum') found in Humfrey's copy (Manchester, Chetham's Library, MS Mun. A.3.131 (27929), f.202v) and William Gray's (BL, MS Royal 8.E.xii, f.156r) but not in all manuscripts: compare the one edited by Jed, *Chaste Thinking*, 147, line 25.

[59] JRL, MS Eng. 2, f.25r (Ovid), f.29r (Ovid); classical annotations in BodL, MS Rawlinson C.448, f.14r (Ovid), f.60v (muses and Ovid), f.78v (Styx glossed), f.81r (Charon glossed); Oxford, Corpus Christi College, MS 242, f.22r ('yuoee' into 'ynoee', 'Agve' into 'Agave', 'Semellis' into 'Semeles').

[60] For example, BL, MS Harley 1245, f.42v (Livy), f.53r (Ovid), f.86r (Juvenal and others), f.86v (Aulus Gellius's 'names of crownes'), f.108v (Livy) including a reference to Criseyde on f.30v; Chicago, University Library, MS 565, for example f.6v (Caesar), f.8r (muses), f.71r (Juno), f.220v (Cato), f.283r (indexing Lucretia).

Yet whether the apparatus were originally for Duke Humfrey but ignored by most scribes, or were only added by a few readers, the same point emerges. The study of antiquity is not essential to the poem. That confirms what else we know of its reception: people usually copy excerpts from 'Bochas', or annotate it, for lugubrious morals about the vanity of the world or the dangers of women.[61] While the humanist duke commissions *The Fall of Princes*, the poem follows his humanist tendencies only fitfully, and the other readers follow them even less. This response is unlike the response by scribes and readers of Chaucer's *Boece*, say, who dressed old works with new scholarly apparatus, rather than removing it (as Chapter 1 showed). But the result is a similarly untidy history, rather than some neat 'periodization'. Humanist reading develops haphazardly, or sometimes does not develop at all, contingent upon personal taste or even error, and regardless of the prince, his posing, and his politics. This work—like all works perhaps—is too big and bewildering to be read one way and, however the poet or the duke read it or wanted it read, the readers did their own thing.

WRITING FOR THE HUMANIST IN *ON HUSBONDRIE*

It is the other English poem composed for Duke Humfrey which reveals the powerful influence which Duke Humfrey and his humanism could have on a writer *and* on other readers. Soon after Lydgate finished *The Fall of Princes* Duke Humfrey received a second English verse translation, usually called *On Husbondrie*. While Lydgate imagined a wide readership, who responded diversely, the other poet fits the style, matter and page design for one implied reader, who is imagined to be quite simply Duke Humfrey. So, unlike Lydgate, whose classical study is intermittent and often second-hand, the poet of *On Husbondrie* follows a classical source in Latin with the rigour of a philologist, in quest of literary excellence. *On Husbondrie* is a close translation of the prose agricultural treatise *De Re rustica*, composed by Palladius around 300 AD.[62]

---

[61] Mortimer, *John Lydgate's* Fall of Princes, 224–9, 231–3, 244; Edwards, 'Influence of Lydgate's *Fall of Princes*', 431–9. See, for example the marginalia in JRL, MS Eng. 2, f.15r-v, f.16v, f.24r, f.25r, f.30v, f.38v, f.40v; GUL, MS Hunter 5 (S.1.5), f.25v, f.29v, f.31v, f.33v, f.36v.

[62] *On Husbondrie* survives in three manuscripts, here cited by abbreviations: BodL, MS Duke Humfrey d.2 = Du; GUL, MS Hunter 104 (T.5.6) = Gw; BodL, MS Additional A.369 = Bo. They are described later in this chapter. Quotations, with book numbers and line numbers in parenthetical Arabic numerals, come from Mark Liddell (ed.), *The Middle-English Translation of Palladius De Re Rustica* (Berlin: Ebering, 1896). Latin quotations, with book, chapter, and sentence numbers in parenthetical Roman numerals, come from Palladius Rutilius Taurus Aemilianus, *Opera*, ed. Robert H. Rodgers (Leipzig: Teubner, 1975). Barton Lodge

Given the topic of Palladius' work, it has been suggested that Duke Humfrey commissioned this version not as 'a mere humanist exercise in style' but as 'a useful manual' for the men who managed his estate.[63] This is possible, for the Roman agrarian authors had been usefully read for centuries; but utility is not the only possible reason to read an agricultural treatise. The choice of a classical text might mark it as a work in the humanist fashion; the Italian humanists, especially in Bologna, especially favoured the classical agricultural works.[64] The Roman agrarian authors also appeared among the classical texts which Duke Humfrey imported from Italy around 1440.[65] That is the shelf on which we can imagine this poem and, if we read it closely, it clearly appears to be an exercise in classical scholarship rather than a useful manual. Moreover, its scholarship has an implied reader who is not a farmhand but a scholar-prince.

Of course, one could read *On Husbondrie* for advice on bee-keeping and muck-spreading; readers are unpredictable. The surviving copies have twenty marginalia about agricultural tips, for example that 'fennel is similar to dill' ('fferula similis est aneto'). Moreover, every copy of the poem is foliated carefully and the stanzas are lettered from *a* to *h* and these marks serve an alphabetical index at the front of all three copies, which might prompt practical reading.[66] Alphabetical lists, sequential tables of contents, and foliation, some added by later hands, appear in other English works of practical science or other copies of Palladius.[67] It has been suggested that Duke Humfrey was retiring from public life about the time that this poem was written, and that the agricultural poem signals 'a retreat from the active life to one focused on rural concerns'. He certainly commissioned grand projects on his estate at Greenwich in the 1430s and 1440s.[68] Yet we must remember that agricultural expertise also had a powerful cultural charge in this period as a signal of political expertise: political theorists from Aristotle onwards describe expertise in agriculture as the equivalent of expertise in statecraft.

(ed.), *Palladius On Husbondrie*, EETS os 52, 72 (London: Trübner, 1873–9), is an inaccurate transcription of the incomplete manuscript Bo.

[63] Petrina, *Cultural Politics*, 268, 275.

[64] R. H. Rodgers, *An Introduction to Palladius*, Bulletin of the Institute of Classical Studies: Supplement, 35 (London: Institute of Classical Studies, 1975), 9; Karl Brunner, 'Continuity and Discontinuity of Roman Agricultural Knowledge in the Early Middle Ages', in *Agriculture in the Middle Ages: Technology, Practice, and Representation*, ed. Del Sweeney (Philadelphia, PA: University of Pennsylvania Press, 1995), 21–40 (31).

[65] Sammut (ed.), *Unfredo*, letters 25:20–1, 32:25–6, 33:5–6.

[66] Du ff.x^r-xviii^v, Gw ff.1r-6v, Bo ff.1r-8v (indexes); Du f.58v (dill).

[67] For example, CUL, MS Ee.I.13, ff.1r-91v; GUL, MS Hunter 185 (T.8.7), ff.1r-6v; BL, MS Sloane 686, f.1r-v, ff.19r-20v; CUL, MS Ll.I.18, f.1r, f.19r-v; BL, MS Additional 44922, f.76r; BL, MS Sloane 2945, ff.200r-207r; SJC, MS B.3, f.184r; BL, MS Sloane 372, ff.2r–12r.

[68] A. S. G. Edwards, 'Duke Humfrey's Middle English Palladius', in *The Lancastrian Court*, ed. Jenny Stratford, Harlaxton Medieval Studies, 13 (Donington: Tyas, 2003), 68–77 (75–6); Vickers, *Humphrey*, 234, 444–5.

Fifteenth-century poems often use husbandry as a symbol for governance, as does William Worcester's *The Boke of Noblesse* in 1475 (discussed in Chapter 4 below).[69] Perhaps the commission of *On Husbondrie* was rather a sign that Humfrey was fit to govern. It must be said, though, that there are few explicit hints in the poem itself of such symbolism. The scribe entitles the first book on management as 'Gouernaunce', a notable mistranslation of the Latin 'industria' (I.ii.1); but *govern, governance,* and *rule* are used in other English agricultural writing as words for estate management.[70] The bees are described in anthropomorphic terms, but so they were in Latin, and the poet makes no more of the allegory even when he translates 'cosyn', 'regne', and 'oost' (VII.vii.6–9; 7.169–78).[71] A political reading of husbandry is possible, and may be worth exploring further. But what is more prominent is the implication that Humfrey is reading not as a husbandman but as a humanist.

Unlike many previous translations into English, this poem emphasizes its classical source. It has been well demonstrated that translations before the fifteenth century did not seek unadulterated access to the past: they undertook a form of exegesis, which was directed to certain contemporary needs.[72] Now, fifteenth-century translations of religious and scientific texts were often crabbedly close, through incompetence as much as design.[73] But, by contrast, the poet of *On Husbondrie* really is a skilful faithful translator and he highlights his fidelity to the source as if it were deliberate. At one point, after a spirited description of some hens, he concludes:

> [...] But these arayis
> To speke of heere, for nought but myrth and play is;
> Yet as myn auctor spak so wold I speke,
> Sith I translate, and looth am from hym breke.   (1.732–5)

---

[69] Aristotle, *Politics*, ed. and trans. H. Rackham (Cambridge, MA: Harvard University Press, 1932), I.i.9–10. For example, George Ashby, *Dicta et opiniones diversorum philosophorum*, in his *Poems*, ed. Mary Bateson, EETS es 76 (London: Kegan Paul, Trench, Trübner, 1899), 42–100 (lines 589–93); Rossell Hope Robbins (ed.), *Historical Poems of the XIVth and XVth Centuries* (New York, NY: Columbia University Press, 1959), 222–6 (lines 73–6); John Lydgate and Benedict Burgh, *Secrees of Old Philisoffres*, ed. Robert Steele, EETS es 66 (London: Kegan Paul, Trench, Trübner, 1894), lines 2367–80.

[70] Du f.4r. One copyist mistakes the changing page headings for chapter headings (Bo ff.9v–12r). *MED*, *governaunce* (n.), 6.(a), notes a rare sense meaning *regimen*, found in, for example, BL, MS Sloane 686, f.1r (Walter of Henley).

[71] Two leaves are missing after Bo f.86v (7.126) and thus in Lodge's edition.

[72] Rita Copeland, *Rhetoric, Hermeneutics, and Translation in the Middle Ages: Academic Traditions and Vernacular Texts* (Cambridge: Cambridge University Press, 1991), 175–8.

[73] Samuel K. Workman, *Fifteenth-Century Translation as an Influence on English Prose*, Princeton Studies in English, 18 (Princeton, NJ: Princeton University Press, 1940), 15, 20.

This is one of only two places where the translator speaks in his own voice, and even here he stresses how keen he is to speak *not* with his own voice but 'as myn auctor spak'. In fact, in the manuscript which the author had prepared (as discussed below), the scribe highlights these lines with the marginal comment 'the author speaks' ('Auctor loquitur'); one reader of another copy highlighted the declaration by underlining it.[74] Yet the poet not only reveals that his translation is an unadulterated record of his author; he fanfares the noteworthiness of being unadulterated.

There is some irony in this claim to accuracy because, in pausing to make it, the poet has in fact interrupted his source and even omitted the last seven words of Palladius' chapter I.xxx.4. Moreover, he has just described the 'myrth and play' of the hens and chicks fairly expansively, straying a little from his source.[75] At only one other point does he comment upon his source, when he dissents from some occult beliefs in the book. He was perhaps nervous of the occult, for there were allegations that Humfrey's wife was a witch; other writers also took time to protest that Humfrey knew nothing of such things.[76] By and large, though, the poet offers the duke a translation very loath to break from its source. He preserves almost every tenet and nuance of the Latin prose, even down to phatic idioms which need not have been preserved such as 'ne multa dicamus' or 'And, short to sey' (III.ix.2, 3.64). He only muddles a few passages (X.xi.1–2, 10.113–26; XI.xix.1–2, 11.491–504) and he only cuts one substantial passage, about the sexual exploits of newly castrated bulls (VI.vii.2, 6.92–126). He also keeps Palladius' first-person voice and in places he even heightens it when an impersonal passive verb is personalized. Thus 'tamen mihi usu conpertum est' becomes 'Their plauntes y ha seyn in ytail here' so that the speaker's place in Italy at the heart of Roman culture is clear (III.xxv.20, 3.907; see 4.552). The author is made present, almost as if speaking, and the translator is occluded.

Finally, this act of ventriloquism shapes the poet's English style so that he echoes the foreign tongue closely and vividly. It is sometimes suggested that the style is clear and practical, addressed to plain utility with few Latinisms; in fact the opposite is true.[77] In most stanzas there are some inventive coinages

---

[74] Du f.16r; Gw f.12r. *On Husbondrie* mentions the 'author' again (2.67, 2.441, 3.1141) and translates Palladius' own references to sources (2.404, 4.467).

[75] The Latin I.xxvii-xxx increases in length by almost a third to be the English 1.575–735 (126 Latin lines to 161 English). Elsewhere, on average, one line of Latin prose receives one line of English verse (for example Latin I.1–563 become English 1.1–574).

[76] I.xxxv.2, 1.844–7. See R. A. Griffiths, 'The Trial of Eleanor Cobham: An Episode in the Fall of Duke Humfrey of Gloucester', *BJRL*, 51 (1969), 381–99 (389), and Robbins (ed.), *Historical Poems*, 180–3 (line 44), where Humfrey worships no 'straunge goddis'.

[77] Petrina, *Cultural Politics*, 275. Contrast the account of the Latinity by Derek Pearsall, *Old English and Middle English Poetry* (London: Routledge Kegan Paul, 1977), 240–1.

borrowed directly from Latin or words chosen from the polysyllabic part of the English language. Some stanzas have many such words:

> And make liquamen castimoniall
> Of peres thus: take peres right mature,
> And with hool salt hem trede, and flesshe and all;
> When they beth resolute, in stondis pure
> Or erthen pottes picched saaf and seure;
> And after monethes iij do hem suspende,
> And righ[t] goode licour of hem wol descende.   (3.827–33)

It seems that *liquamen* and *castimonial* are not otherwise found in English, although *castimony* appears in Caxton's *Eneydos*, a pseudo-classical translation. *Mature* is attested in English here for the first time, while *resolute* may have seemed new as it had only appeared in a couple of scientific translations; *suspend* is used in the etymological Latin sense of 'hang', rather than metaphorically (as also at 12.170).[78] As these lines show, the Latinate words are not only the specialized words but are also the more general words which could have been rendered more plainly. Indeed, so keen is the poet to sound classical, that he adds a few Latinate touches without any prompting cognate word in the source: he uses *adolescents* or *orbicular* without any prompt from Palladius, and seemingly for the first time in English.[79] He adds some mythological allusions too: he often turns the Latin writer's plain *sun* ('sol') into Phoebus or dresses up the astrological calendars in each book. A few changes seem quite clever: the 'facem libidinis' or *torch of desire* becomes 'Cupido', which perhaps echoes Cupid's *fax* or torch in Ovid's poetry.[80] How much credit do such coinages and dressings deserve? They are a mere train of mythological imagery such as college easily supplies. Moreover, the pseudo-classical style is in fact not that classical: when the poet mentions Phoebus or Cupid, he begins to diverge from Palladius' words and to use Chaucerian cliché (a trend discussed in Chapter 3 below). Nor were all of his Latinate words borrowings of course, and nor were all from Latin, as so many Latinate words reach English through French. The words *liquor* and *descend* evoke the flowery parts of Chaucer and the borrowings which end with —*al*, —*ure*, and —*end* recall Lydgate's favourite suffixes. Placing these words at the line endings also recalls the way that Lydgate displays his aureate words. And the decision to turn Palladius' prose into rime royal misrepresents the Latin but aligns the poem with Chaucer's Trojan history, Walton's version of Boethius, or Lydgate's *The*

---

[78] *OED*, *liquamen*, n.; *MED*, *liquamen* (n.); *OED*, *castimony*, n.; *OED*, *mature*, a.; *MED*, *mature* (adj.); *OED*, *resolute*, a.; *MED*, *resolute* (adj.); *OED*, *suspend*, v., II.8.a; *MED*, *suspenden* (v.).

[79] 4.869, IV.xiii.6; 3.312, III.xiv.1; *OED*, *adolescent*, n; *OED*, *orbicular*, a.

[80] VI.ii.2, 6.28; VIII.v.1, 8.106; VIII.iv.5, 8.102, perhaps recalling Ovid, *Metamorphoses*, I.461.

Fall of Princes. The poem looks classical, but according to English canons of classicism.

In page design, too, *On Husbondrie* recalls English tradition. Marginalia can sometimes be found in copies of Chaucer, Gower, Hoccleve, and others as well as translations of Boethius and sometimes Vegetius (as seen in Chapter 1 above). The red marginalia to *The Fall of Princes* might have been composed for Duke Humfrey, or might not; the evidence is too fragmentary to be sure. But no copy of that poem goes as far as do the copies of *On Husbondrie*. Because the poet elides his own role as reader or interpreter, he must help his reader to undertake the interpretation of antiquity for himself. An elaborate textual apparatus highlights the text's foreignness—like the note that 'Auctor loquitur'—and invites the reader to work on bridging it. Firstly, almost every page has tiny glosses between the lines and the glosses are not in English, with a few exceptions, often on odd words such as 'gemmes' (3.99, 3.177), but in Latin. Such glosses in Latin reveal the source of these English words and make the English poem seem the sort of book that needs scholarly reading; in fact, not all of the Latin is found in Palladius. In other lines which are very arcane or clever, glosses or marginal notes explain and translate the words. For example, when Palladius writes plainly *after two days* ('post biduum') the poet writes the fanciful 'When Phebus chare hath goon aboute hit twye'; but then he has to gloss his line to explain that the phrase means 'post duos dies' and in the margin he writes the label 'circumlocutio' as if to boast of his rhetorical skill in the method of circumlocution.[81] In fact, beside the glosses there are fourteen marginalia which draw the reader's eye to the rhetorical tropes, such as hyperbole, syncope, metaphor, and the hypallage beloved of readers of *Boece*.[82] What do the glosses on language and notes on rhetoric do? The glosses evoke the grammatical exercises of the schoolroom, while the indexes and lettered divisions evoke Latin university books.[83] The training in reading, and in reading Latin, in universities and schools is what the page design of *On Husbondrie* demands. The page design directs the eye to the poem's difficult style and implies that the reader will be a scholar of its style.

The scholarly page design serves one very specific scholar: Duke Humfrey. The scholarly devices slightly resemble—in fact, they exceed—the visible signs of scholarship in some of the humanist books given to Duke Humfrey. For example, linguistic glosses appear in a translation of Plato's *Timaeus* and

---

[81] Du f.18r on I.xxxv.13, 1.957.   [82] Du ff.79r-81v.

[83] They are described well by Suzanne Reynolds, *Medieval Reading: Grammar, Rhetoric and the Classical Text* (Cambridge: Cambridge University Press, 1996), 33–41, 76–9, and throughout Henri-Jean Martin, and Jean Vezin (eds.), *Mise en page et mise en texte du livre manuscrit* ([Paris]: Éditions du Cercle de la Librairie—Promodis, 1990).

in a collection of plays by Humfrey's household poet, Tito Livio Frulovisi. An anthology of texts copied from one of Humfrey's lost gifts to Oxford concludes with an alphabetical glossary with a few translations into English and several etymologies and explanations of classical terms such as *anapaest*, *Argive*, or *Doric*. In works by Piercandido Decembrio or by Antonio Beccaria, Humfrey's secretary, scribes occasionally highlight literary and rhetorical structures like allegory, song, and *similitudines*.[84] Palaeographers have spotted Duke Humfrey's own hand in his other books, noting a 'sententia' in Cicero's *Epistolae ad Atticum* or tinkering with finding-devices in other classical texts.[85] Overall, in *On Husbondrie* the prompts to a scholarly reader evoke the prompts in his other books. The imaginary humanist reader in *On Husbondrie* is Duke Humfrey.

IMAGINING DUKE HUMFREY IN *ON HUSBONDRIE*

Yet the identity of this implied reader is most secure because the poet describes his reading very vividly—as vividly as do the Italian writers. Moreover, much more distinctly than Lydgate, the poet of *On Husbondrie* imagines Humfrey as a reader influenced by humanist studies. Yet what is the purpose of this description of him? Why does he link Humfrey with the study of Phoebus and hypallage? Some clues emerge from another of the vivid descriptions of his humanist reading by an Italian. The most vivid sketch is in a preface composed by Pietro del Monte, a papal protonotary to the English court, in early 1440. Del Monte contributed to the well-known debate between Poggio Bracciolini and Guarino Veronese about whether Scipio or Caesar was the greater man. In the preface to his contribution, he reports that he showed the debate so far to Duke Humfrey, who read it avidly:

Paucis atque post diebus rogatus a me quale ipsius \ esset /de ea disputatione iudicium : responsum paucis ita reddidit heros · Ego inquit poggii et Guarini eloquentiam plurimum admiror et laudo dignos que ob eam immortali honore et gloria censeo ·

Nam hec suauissima humanitatis studia que pene extincta erant : eorum ingenio labore et industria ueterem splendorem decoremque recuperarunt · nostreque etatis hominibus magna horum exempla spes data est ad priscam illam latine lingue elegantiam propius accedendi · Ceterum mordacem illum ac nimis contumeliosum

[84] De la Mare, 'Manuscripts Given', 36–7; SJC, MS C.10, ff.19r-20r; BodL, MS Auct. F.5.26, p. 226, p. 230; Rundle, 'Republics and Tyrants', 255–8, 434–41; BL Harley, MS 1705, f.36r, f.42r; BL, MS Royal 5.F.ii, f.59v.
[85] De la Mare, 'Manuscripts Given', 33, 115–16; Rundle, 'Republics and Tyrants', 415.

50 *Duke Humfrey and other imaginary readers*

scribendi modum quem in nulla sue inpugnationis parte · Guarino pretermisit magna remprehensione dignum iudicio [...] [86]

After a few days, I asked him what his judgement of that debate was, and the hero briefly gave this answer. He said, 'I greatly admire the eloquence of Poggio and Guarino and I praise them and judge them worthy of immortal honour and glory for it.

'For those most sweet humanities, which had almost been extinguished, have recovered their old splendour and honour thanks to their genius, labour, and industry. Hope of more closely resembling that antique elegance of the Latin tongue is given to men of our age by their great example. But the other acerbic and excessively argumentative manner of writing, which Guarino did not neglect to use in any part of his attack, I judge to be worthy of great condemnation.'

This is not the general learning of other Lancastrian noblemen: Humfrey praises the Italian authors specifically for the 'humanitatis studia', the humanities which define humanism. He can even refer to these studies with 'hec' or 'those', as if he addresses the *cognoscenti* who already know which *those* subjects are. Moreover, Humfrey notes the extinction of the humanities in an intervening age, and their rebirth now in our time ('nostreque etatis'), a familiar history of humanism and rebirth, related by other writers such as his secretary Beccaria and others.[87]

Why report this humanist reading? We might think that learning found favour among the Lancastrian noblemen for its utility, or the political cachet of its supposed utility. It is a commonplace in other humanist letters to Duke Humfrey that his studies are not an idle pastime but are—aren't all studies?—a vital training for public life (as we saw above). But Humfrey's learning sounds here less useful than leisurely: Pietro del Monte first describes how he himself was reading when he found some reprieve from papal business, and then how Humfrey too finds a few fleeting moments for just a few words.[88] Moreover, the duke's first concern is literary decorum: he idealizes the ancient elegance of Latin and hopes to recreate it as a language devoid of factionalism and anger; he says that he is sad that Guarino lowered the tone of scholarly debate with harsh uncongenial words. Susanne Saygin has suggested that that the duke is 'sidetracked' into stylistics and ignores the debate's political relevance

---

[86] CUL, MS Gg.I.34 (i), f.92r-v, on which see David Rundle, 'Two Unnoticed Manuscripts from the Collection of Humfrey, Duke of Gloucester', *BLR*, 16 (1998), 211–24, 299–313 (211–24). Contrast the less emphatic later revision in 'Pietro del Monte a Poggio Bracciolini', in Poggio Bracciolini, *Opera Omnia*, ed. Riccardo Fubini, 4 vols. (Turin: Bottega d'Erasmo, 1964–9), IV.615–39 (620).

[87] Compare Sammut (ed.), *Unfredo*, letters 9:30–7, 42:16–23, or, for example, *Bekynton Correspondence*, I.159, I.231. Thomas M. Greene, *The Light in Troy: Imitation and Discovery in Renaissance Poetry* (New Haven, CT: Yale University Press, 1982), 30, 33, describes these tropes, but suggests that they seldom appear in England.

[88] CUL, MS Gg.I.34 (i), f.92r.

to his own troubles. But David Rundle has noted more fully that the exercise in literary debate could have political significance too.[89] Yet another English reader of this debate was especially interested in avoiding bitter style.[90] And in the Latin letters about Duke Humfrey we sense the prestige to be gained from being seen as, primarily, a man of letters.

The political capital in studying humanist niceties is most clear in the English translation of Palladius, *On Husbondrie*. In the poem's lengthy pro-logue, the poet of course mentions Humfrey's political business, routing the heretics, for example, but he presents him more fully as a humanist. By 5 November 1439 the duke had given 129 books to Oxford, and the poet of *On Husbondrie* mentions the one hundred and thirty books given to Oxford and the clerks beavering on them (prol. 89–96).[91] More strikingly, and less verifiably, he mentions a coterie of humanists influenced by the duke:

> For clergie, or knyghthod, or husbondrie,
> That orator, poete, or philosophre
> hath tretid, told, or taught, in memorie
> Vche lef and lyne hath he, as shette in cofre;
> Oon nouelte vnnethe is hym to profre.
> Yit Whethamstede, and also Pers de Mounte,
> Titus, and Anthony, and y laste ofre
> And leest. Our newe is old in hym tacounte
>
> But that his vertu list vs exercise,
> And moo as fele as kan in vertu do.
> He, sapient, is diligent to wise
> Alle ignoraunt, and y am oon of tho.
> He taught me metur make, and y soso
> Hym counturfete, [...]   (prol. 97–110)

The clearest thing that the poet does here is imagine that the English poem belongs to a new type of humanist culture. He describes himself coming last and modestly least among the scholars of the *studia humanitatis* who wrote for or lived with the duke: Pietro del Monte, Tito Livio Frulovisi, Antonio Beccaria and—more intriguingly—the Abbot of St Albans, John Whethamstede. As in

---

[89] Saygin, *Humphrey*, 91–2; David Rundle, 'Carneades' Legacy: The Morality of Eloquence in the Humanist and Papalist Writings of Pietro del Monte', *EHR*, 117 (2002), 284–305 (286–92).

[90] TCC, MS O.9.8, f.46r, and also f.25r-v, f.28r, f.39v.

[91] Sammut (ed.), *Unfredo*, 58, describes the donations. The prologue was likely written before Humfrey donated 135 more books in February 1444, though the round number of 130 might include ten books which Humfrey donated in November 1441. D. R. Howlett, 'The Date and Authorship of the Middle English Verse Translation of Palladius' *De Re Rustica*', *Medium Ævum*, 46 (1977), 245–52, describes the context.

del Monte's letter, their humanism is quite new: there is scarcely one 'nouelte' which could satisfy Humfrey; he is so avant-garde that their new learning is already old and familiar to him. This comment recalls the preface to the play *Eugenius* given to Humfrey by Frulovisi: Frulovisi there fears that his work, which is also new, 'can offer nothing new' to his patron, because he manifests all virtues already ('quod nouus sit', 'Nil ad te noui potest afferre').[92] The poets use their patron to legitimate their novelty, perhaps necessary in an age fearful of newfangledness; yet in so doing they flatter him as a pioneer.

The prologues to *On Husbondrie* also make several other comments found in the Latin letters and prefaces which describe him. One is the comment that Humfrey has an adept memory and holds in it each work as if shut up in a coffer, even down to the leaf and line references, so that he can demonstrate to others what he has read. Another is the combination of the duke's 'vertu' in exercising people and his 'diligent' instruction, as found in letters by Leonardo Bruni or Pietro del Monte where the duke's 'virtus ac diligentia' compels them to write.[93] What is more unusual is that the English poet claims that the duke taught him to compose verse: 'He taught me metur make'. What does he mean? His *taught* could simply mean that Humfrey *commanded* him to make a poem.[94] Yet in the epilogues to books I and II the poet seems to mean that he was actually taught how to write by his prince. When book I is complete, the poet approaches him with his 'incorrect' draft and seeks his judgement. He:

> [...] doon nerre His prince Humfrey.
> This incorrect, aferd lest fuke or wem
> Enfect, y to this duc directe, and sey: [...]
>
> To the these incorrectid versis rude,
> Noot y not why ner how mys metrified,
> Thus ofre y, pra[i]yng thy celcitude
> Do that my wrong and they be iustified.   (1.1183–5, 1.1198–201)

A request for correction of course finds precedents in countless other books of the time. Yet in this book it is not only a humility topos but is an attempt to imagine Duke Humfrey as a skilful reader—and to find some political capital in that imagining. Now, it may well be true that Humfrey did have a rhythmic ear and did mould *On Husbondrie*'s excellent rime royal. Other poets

[92] Tito Livio Frulovisi, *Eugenius*, in *Opera hactenus inedita T. Livii de Frulovisiis de Ferraria*, ed. C. W. Previté-Orton (Cambridge: Cambridge University Press, 1932), 223–84 (224). But David Rundle, 'Tito Livio Frulovisi and the Place of Comedies in the Formation of a Humanist Career', *Studi Umanistici Piceni*, 24 (2004), 193–202 (196–7), shows that Frulovisi probably first composed the play for a different patron.

[93] Sammut (ed.), *Unfredo*, letters 2:26–34, 3:43–52.

[94] See the obsolete sense in *OED*, *teach*, B.I.4, or *MED*, *techen* (v.), 9a.

praised Humfrey for being a keen teacher or for being 'expert in poetrye'.[95] Yet whether it is true or not, the claim that the duke can teach or correct metre may have a distinct political resonance. The prologue has already related Humfrey's correction of heresy and rebellion, and said that he is fit to 'wise' and 'gouerne' the nation due to his virtue (prol. 41–66). His ability to 'wise' and 'exercise' writers also reveals his intellectual fitness to govern. As Stephanie Jed has shown, the humanist terms for textual criticism make a metaphorical link between textual correctness and the punishment of civil disturbance.[96] Writers closer to Duke Humfrey use such metaphors: Pietro del Monte says that the duke exercises his 'iudicio' or 'judgement' on Guarino's improper style, and he sharpens the legal analogy in a letter to Abbot John Whethamstede: Humfrey there 'is a most severe reprover of vices and can wisely and eruditely judge the humanities' ('vitiorum acerrimus vindex est et de hisce humanitatis studiis [...] erudite ac sapienter iudicare potest').[97] Frulovisi's *Vita Henrici Quinti* praises him in parallel as a patron who nurtured writers ('nutriebat') and an uncle who nurtured the young king ('nutrivit') and casts him in one scene as a lawgiver.[98] His critical and textual skills have a clear political resonance in general, then. They have even clearer resonance in *On Husbondrie*, because the poet requests correction not only of his metrical solecisms ('they') but also of some judicial mistreatment or 'wrong'. He has lamented this wrong earlier (prol. 113–20) before he seeks justification here. To be a good reader is analogous to being a good lord.

If these images offer political praise, maybe humanist reading is once again an ornament for princes. However, before we see the image of the princely humanist as 'propaganda' or a 'message', we must ask technically how that image would be transmitted. When we discuss someone's political 'image' we do so metaphorically and sometimes lazily, often treating the fifteenth century as if it were as saturated by visual media and tricks of PR as our own century is. After all, who saw this account of Humfrey as a humanist reader? In *The Fall of Princes* Lydgate made it clear that his dedicatee was not his real reader, and he wrote his moral exemplars about princes for other men to read. But surely *On Husbondrie* is not so public? The style seems sculpted

---

[95] Eleanor Prescott Hammond, 'The Nine-Syllabled Pentameter Line in Some Post-Chaucerian Manuscripts', *MP*, 23 (1925), 129–52 (131–2). Compare Lydgate, *Fall*, IX.3397; John Lydgate, 'On Gloucester's Approaching Marriage', in Lydgate, *Minor Poems*, II.601–8 (line 146); John Russell, *The Book of Nurture*, in *The Babees Book*, ed. F. J. Furnivall, EETS os 32 (London: Trübner, 1868), 113–239 (117, lines 3–4).

[96] Jed, *Chaste Thinking*, 22–3, 29–32.

[97] 'Piero del Monte, John Whethamstede, and the Library of St Albans Abbey', ed. R. Weiss, *EHR*, 60 (1945), 399–406 (405).

[98] Titi Livii Foro-Juliensis, *Vita Henrici Quinti, Regis Angliæ*, ed. Thomas Hearne (Oxford: [no publ.], 1716), 2, 40–1.

to fit Duke Humfrey's imagined tastes and these prologues and epilogues describe his own personal intervention in terms more vivid than Lydgate's. In that epilogue to book I the duke's political 'image', as we say, is actually a more tangible and immediate artistic 'image' or act of mimesis. We are not just told about Humfrey's reading; it is almost acted out around the page we hold, as if the page were a script. The poet decribes 'This' particular 'incorrect' book being interrupted in mid composition and placed in motion within a physical presentation scene ('nerre' here; 'these' very lines). Humfrey himself is addressed in the second-person singular as 'the', that is, as *thee* or *you*. Then, finally, the poet announces that the duke really has corrected the mistakes:

> My bone is graunt and to correctioun
> That half is doon; that other half mot stonde
> In hope as yit vndir protectioun.   (1.1202–4)

If these lines are true, they are curious. Firstly, their praise—if political impact is sought—is rather muted: Humfrey has been so busy scanning the verse that the poet still stands in need of his legal or financial aid in 'that other half' of his request. Secondly, more graphically than del Monte even, he imitates the scene of presentation and reading as if it is currently taking place. The pause while Humfrey corrects is marked on the page with a spatial gap of six lines between the request and the thanks for correction (between the two quotations I have used) although the gap may just reflect the more spacious layout of the epilogues.[99] The humanists often favoured and fetishized autograph copies of their friends' writing, but *On Husbondrie* seems to be a genuine relic of a reader.

Rather than 'propaganda', is there a simple explanation for that imagining of Humfrey? Does the presentation manuscript reveal whether the words held inside it were ever really corrected by him? One manuscript (Du) is likely, given its coat of arms and fine quality, the book presented to the duke himself. Some scholars have found a deliberate mistake later marked with a cross and a marginal gloss in Humfrey's hand.[100] Yet, most strikingly, in this copy the prologue and the first few epilogues appear on separate leaves of parchment tipped in between the translation, which is otherwise copied in complete quires.[101] So the epilogues which describe Humfrey's reading could have been added once each 'book' of Palladius had been presented and read:

---

[99] Du f.22v.

[100] Howlett, 'Date and Authorship', 246; A. C. de la Mare, 'Duke Humfrey's English Palladius (MS. Duke Humfrey d.2)', *BLR*, 12 (1985), 39–51 (49, *n*. 12). The epilogue to book II also describes how Humfrey 'gynnyth crossis make' (2.480–4).

[101] Du f.22r, f.31r, f.35r. De la Mare, 'Duke Humfrey's English Palladius', 44, 50 (*n*. 19), collates it: I^{10} (1 cancelled), II^8-II^8, IV^8 (and one leaf added after 8), V^8 (and one leaf added after 8), VI-VII^8, VIII^6, IX-XVI^8, XVII^2.

that is, after the scenes of reading and correction which are described. Other Latin books produced within the duke's household betray similar copying in stages: the telltale signs are blank leaves, alterations in layout midway, and repetitions of his inscription of ownership.[102] Humfrey may then have been not an imaginary reader but a real one, interrupting the writer of this poem. The image of the princely reader in this manuscript is not a mere chimera; it is more like a fingerprint.

However, Humfrey was not the only person to touch this text. For some reason, having made a presentation copy, the very same scribe deliberately fabricated or, to be generous, recreated this scene of Humfrey's reading in a second manuscript (Gw). His second copy visually duplicates the first line by line, page by page, like a modern printed book, in effect.[103] Unfortunately it is now mutilated and the epilogues have been pulled out, along with many other leaves. However, from extant catchwords, leaf and quire signatures, and the number of lines to a page, one can reconstruct that it did once include those epilogues. However, in the first book the epilogues describing Humfrey's reading were added later on separate sheets, like real reports; in this second book the epilogues were copied within regularly sized, continuous quires, without any sense of history during production.[104] Therefore this book was probably not given to Humfrey, at least not in pieces, for him to correct, but still included lines which claimed to have been interrupted and actually read by him thus. He was a real reader of one copy, but he was only an imaginary reader of this second one. Such duplicates were not unknown: Frulovisi's *Vita Henrici Quinti* exists in twin manuscripts, identical in layout, hand and, remarkably for a text in prose, on leaves which sometimes share the same disposition of words per page. The only difference is that one carries not Humfrey's coat of arms but those of England, so it seems that the duplicate

[102] BL, MS Royal 5.F.ii, f.91v, f.131v (translations from Greek Patristic literature by Beccaria); SJC, MS C.10, f.97r, f.115r-v (Frulovisi's comedies). Henry David Jocelyn, 'The Two Comedies of Tito Livio de' Frulovisi Allegedly Written in England', *Studi umanistici Piceni*, 12 (1992), 135–42 (137–41), warns that piecemeal copying might not truthfully reflect piecemeal composition.

[103] This scribe copies Du ff.x^r-xxi^r, ff.1r-5v, ff.14r-31v, ff.53r-118v and Gw ff.1r-43v, ff.51r-64v. De la Mare, 'English Palladius', 41, suggested that they were 'close in style'. There is one difference: Gw lacks the glosses and marginal notes found in Du, although they were present in Gw's exemplar: when a second scribe takes over for quire IX, he includes some glosses at first, before realizing that he should not and stopping (Gw ff.44r-45v).

[104] On the first leaf of quire V (once signed folio 22, now vanished) and in the middle of quire VI (once folio 31). Gw collates thus: I^{10} (1 cancelled, wants 4–6), II^8 (wants 1–5), III^8 (wants 2–7), IV^8 (wants 8), V^8 (wants 1–2, 7), VI^8 (wants 2–3, 6), VII^8, VIII^8 (wants 8), IX^8 (wants 1), X^8, XI-XII^8 (hypothetical, both completely missing), XIII^8 (wants 3, 7); several other quires have vanished.

was made for his nephew, Henry VI.[105] The king might have received the duplicate of *On Husbondrie* too. But who knows? Whoever did receive it received a vivid image—but now an imaginary one—of Humfrey's reading, erudition, and patronage.

THE REWRITING OF DUKE HUMFREY'S BOOKS

However, to see even the imaginary princely reader as a political image is to see too little. With their liberty to rewrite or misread, the readers of Duke Humfrey's books make him not an idol but an example for their own reading—a less vainglorious role. It has been argued that certain sixteenth-century humanists confected their reputations through publishing their letters and memoirs and even through circulating their marginalia. Yet Lisa Jardine, often a stern judge of them, has defended this confection because it provided examples for others, 'inviting the disciple or follower to emulate, copy, fashion themselves in the image of the great master'.[106] That emulation or copying unfolds in Pietro del Monte's letter (quoted in the last section), where the duke describes how Guarino has salvaged the humanities and inspired others by his 'great example'.[107] Humfrey says that he follows the Italian example but, in this conversation, Humfrey is an example too. The readers of his own copy of this work and of other copies marked the praise for the duke's humanism.[108] With his Latin books, it is easy to confirm his influence. Men were copying and counterfeiting them both before and after he gave many of them to the University of Oxford. In the library in Oxford signs of his ownership were often preserved, and occasionally added.[109] When the university wrote to parliament to commend the duke's gift, the university noted the influence of the duke thus upon other men, 'for the comyn profyte and worshyp of the reme' as well as for 'the lovyng of Godd, encrece of clergy and konnyng men'.[110] The books of the princely reader advance his glory, but they also encourage the whole commonweal to imitate his reading.

---

[105] CCCC, MS 285 and London, College of Arms, MS Arundel 12: for example ff.32r-35v in the former reproduce those foliated ff.29r-32v in the latter. See Rundle, 'Two Unnoticed Manuscripts', 222.

[106] Lisa Jardine, *Erasmus, Man of Letters: The Construction of Charisma in Print* (Princeton, NJ: Princeton University Press, 1993), 4, 58.

[107] CUL, MS Gg.I.34 (i), f.92r-v.

[108] CUL, MS Gg.I.34 (i), f.92r; BodL, MS Bodley 915, ff.170v-171r, on which see *Humfrey 1970*, no. 55; TCC, MS O.9.8, f.46r.

[109] *Humfrey 1988*, 18–49, 87–97; Rundle, 'Republics and Tyrants', 158; Rundle, 'On the Difference between Virtue and Weiss', 199–200; de le Mare, 'Manuscripts Given', 40–2 and plate 3(b); David Rundle, 'Habits of Manuscript-Collecting', 112–14. Rundle notes that the *ex libris* is often erased from books purloined by other scholars, presumably to obscure the theft.

[110] Anstey (ed.), *Epistolae*, I.184.

The same is true of his English commissions. As the poet in *On Husbondrie* says: 'y soso | Hym counturfete' (prol. 109–10). The second copy of *On Husbondrie* counterfeited his presence as reader, perhaps in order to impress the king. But in a third and final manuscript of *On Husbondrie* (Bo), we find that Humfrey's book is not an idol of him; instead, it inspires others to fashion themselves as readers in his image. The orthography of this third book suggests that the scribe worked at some geographical or cultural distance from Humfrey, but a close look shows that he worked from an exemplar visually identical to the duke's presentation copy, fully laid out with glosses, marginalia, and index.[111] The resemblance becomes clear paradoxically through the errors in this third copy, whose scribe did not understand that the index must refer to specific foliated leaves and commenced the text haphazardly part-way down a leaf, instead of starting the first stanza *a* on a new page; he also misplaced the running-titles for book I part-way down the page as if they were marginalia.[112] His errors betray that the learned page design of *On Husbondrie* was a novelty to scribes accustomed to English literary work. Nevertheless, just as his Latin books inspired scholars in Oxford, *On Husbondrie* apparently inspired this person far from Duke Humfrey himself to imitate his book and the reading it invites. Moreover, the spreading interest in humanism did not solely glorify Humfrey himself. In the fifteenth century he enjoyed a volatile political reputation until, in 1447, enemies on the governing council charged him with treason, and possibly speeded his death; in posthumous struggles, scholars and nobles fought for and won his official rehabilitation in 1455.[113] It may be due to the fall from grace, or perhaps to the fall of the whole Lancastrian dynasty in 1461, that the scribe of this third manuscript of *On Husbondrie* deliberately omits the prologue and epilogues where the duke is named.[114] Nevertheless, the form of writing and reading which he inspired still thrived among others, while he himself had disappeared.

Furthermore, other readers further still from the prince counterfeited his books. *On Husbondrie* survives in only three copies, but its importance is clear in the survival of another poem which imitates it closely. That poem is *Knyghthode and Bataile* and the date and milieu of it pull us far from Duke Humfrey. The poem was completed early in 1460 and copied into three manuscripts over the following few decades. It originally appeared under the auspices of

[111] Bo does not copy Du itself: each omits a few lines that the other keeps: Du on f.71r omits lines 4.954–60.

[112] Du f.1r; Bo f.8v; and see also Bo ff.8v-10v. He later copies the headings correctly (Bo ff.12v-15v, f.29v).

[113] Watts, *Henry VI*, 229–31.

[114] Bo f.8r lacks two stanzas of book III which would be on the same leaf as an epilogue in copies which resemble manuscript Du (f.53r); someone removed or ignored a leaf from an exemplar at some stage.

Viscount Beaumont, whose allies had opposed Humfrey's belligerent policies, and who had himself arrested Humfrey in 1447.[115] Nevertheless, the poem clearly imitates the literary form and page design of *On Husbondrie*: it too is a translation into English verse of a late classical work of technical prose, this time of Vegetius' *Epitoma rei militaris*, a work on military affairs. Like the earlier poem, in all three copies each page is foliated and has eight stanzas marked *a* to *h*, and a corresponding index at the back; some small glosses appear between the lines and Latin notes adorn many margins.[116] The copying of the elaborate page design suggests that, twenty years later, the author of *Knyghthode and Bataile* was reading *On Husbondrie*. He chose to imitate a method of translation and scholarly reading in a milieu far removed from the prince who inspired them.

Moreover, the later poet was reading other humanist books. The scribe in the earliest copy emulates other humanist books in his use of round brackets (*lunulae*) in brown or red ink. These marks had been invented by Coluccio Salutati for copying and unteasing the classics in 1398 but remained very unusual in England. Therefore these *lunulae*, the earliest (as far as I know) in an English text, suggest that the poet or scribe was familiar with Italian books and tried to imitate a distinctive punctuation mark in them. [117] Secondly, one can identify the owners of one copy as humanist readers from the surname Hatteclyff which appears there in Greek ('quod αττεχλιφ'). Hatteclyff was probably William Hatteclyff, a physician to Margaret of Anjou and then a secretary and ambassador to Edward IV, who had studied at Padua in the 1440s and knew John Tiptoft, John Gunthorpe, and John Russell, all men of humanist taste, and William Caxton. Or Hatteclyff might just be his son, Edward, who was educated several decades later at Oxford, at John Russell's expense, and perhaps owned a copy of Lactantius copied by the humanist scribe Thomas Candour.[118] So *On Husbondrie* seems to have inspired an imitation by a man of humanist taste which in turn fell into the hands of readers with humanist tastes of their own. However, the mere punctuation marks do not tell us what the *readers* thought; they tell us that the *writer* or scribes had read humanist books and wanted to imitate them. Similarly, even

---

[115] Daniel Wakelin, 'The Occasion, Author and Readers of *Knyghthode and Bataile*', *Medium Ævum*, 73 (2004), 260–72 (263–4), and Chapter 3 below.

[116] Cambridge, Pembroke College, MS 243; BL, MS Cotton Titus A.xxiii; BodL, MS Ashmole 45 (ii).

[117] Cambridge, Pembroke College, MS 243, f.i^r, f.ii^r (x 2), f.5v, f.11r, f.31r, f.36r, f.47v, and BodL, MS Ashmole 45, f.47v, discussed by Daniel Wakelin, 'Scholarly Scribes and the Creation of *Knyghthode and Bataile*', *English Manuscript Studies*, 12 (2005), 26–45 (37–41, 44–5).

[118] Wakelin, 'Occasion, Author and Readers', 266–8, citing BL, MS Cotton Titus A.xxiii, f.56v; f.57r. Edward's signature is similar, but not identical, in a copy of Lactantius: GUL, MS Hunter 274 (U.5.14), flyleaf f.A^v, f.72r.

the signature of Hatteclyff raises doubts: both Hatteclyffs had a more diverse
career than the label *humanist reader* suggests—but it is the decision to write
the flashy Greek signature which intentionally and reductively restyles its user
as a humanist. The humanism here may not be the affectation of a duke; but
even among this wider readership it is still something of an affectation or
'self-fashioning'.

Something similar emerges with the transmission of *The Fall of Princes*. The
poem was not (it was noted above) read only by Duke Humfrey. The work
was dispersed to many readers. And just as in the last copy of *On Husbondrie*
the prince's name was removed, so in copies of *The Fall of Princes* he falls
off the page. For example, one closing envoy of *The Fall of Princes*, which
is 'specially direct to hym that causyd the translacioun' and is only directed
'secundely to alle othir' (IX.3302), appears in only about a third of the copies.
Moreover, a further four copies include the envoy, but without the first few
stanzas in which Lydgate talks of his princely reader, so that the envoy begins
instead by turning more generally 'To alle thoo that shal this book be-holde'
(IX.3394).[119] In one manuscript another closing envoy is no longer 'direct
vnto my lord', as it is in the manuscript with the Latin marginalia, but is
'diret vnto Princys' and in the first three lines the single royal prince with
his noble lineage is expanded into the plural 'Noble princes' who have 'your
lynes conveied doun fro kynges': and they could be the whole English nobility
given the fecundity of Edward III.[120] Another passage about the patronage
needed by poets may have been directed especially to the duke in order to
encourage him to pay up, and it is missing in many manuscripts.[121] Relative
to the number of manuscripts, too, very few readers highlight with notes the
other lines about Duke Humfrey's involvement, although the first printer of it
did.[122] Textual tradition, then, diminished the eulogy of the princely scholar
in a way that contrasts the keenness of humanists to record his presence in

---

[119] Bergen's notes in Lydgate, *Fall*, volume IV, 3–9, reveal that the final envoy appears in full
in (by his sigla) MSS 8118, A, H2, probably H3, H4, H5, R3, Lee, Hat, and probably 4255. It
appears without thirteen stanzas (IX.3303–93) in MSS A2, H, Long and Cor. An odd number
of stanzas is unlikely to vanish because a scribe missed a page of his exemplar: the manuscripts
usually contain two columns of a set number of stanzas, and therefore even numbers of stanzas
per page or per folio.

[120] BL, MS Additional 39659, f.185v (Lydgate, *Fall*, IX.3541–3). Compare for example BL,
MS Harley 4203, f.181v.

[121] Eleanor Prescott Hammond, 'Poet and Patron in the *Fall of Princes*: Lydgate and Humphrey
of Gloucester', *Anglia*, 38 (1914), 121–36 (123–4).

[122] In the manuscripts I have seen, rubrics or marginalia or headings which highlight the
duke appear in only four: Chicago, University Library, MS 565, f.6v; BL, MS Harley 1766, f.1r
(*tabula*), f.9v (I.379); BL, MS Royal 18.B.xxxi, f.3r; JRL, MS Eng. 2, f.3r. Many of them are added
much later. For printers, see Alex Gillespie, 'Framing Lydgate's *Fall of Princes*: The Evidence of
Book History', *Mediaevalia*, 20 (2001), 153–78 (161–3).

Latin books. Yet, the poem's reputation grew: people often referred to *The Fall of Princes* by referring simply to the authority of 'Bochas', as if the English poet was the humanist Boccaccio.[123] And Lydgate sometimes had a humanist reputation of his own. An imaginary epitaph for Lydgate dressed him as a humanist, 'the British Virgil', and John Bale recounted a wholly false humanist career for him; even his aureate style was renowned as 'halff chongyd latyn'.[124] Duke Humfrey is soon forgotten: the humanist scholars are not.

Moreover, *The Fall of Princes* also inspired an imitation: an English translation of selected lives from Boccaccio's *De Mulieribus claris*. The project and poetic form recall Lydgate's, and the poet professes direct inspiration. In his prologue he, or maybe she, says that few have written about famous women, except for:

> John Bokase—so clepyde is his name—,
> That wrote the fall of pryncys stronge and bolde
> (And into Englissh translate is the same).
> An odyre he wrote vnto the laude and fame
> Of ladyes noble, in prayse of all wymen;
> But for the rareness few folke do it ken.[125]

This reading of 'the fall of pryncys' is wholeheartedly humanist. Firstly, the sole manuscript of this English *De Mulieribus claris* has a Latin verse prologue and titles for each short biography written in red in a humanist script. The use of a humanist script in a vernacular book is very rare in England at this time.[126] Secondly, what the translator borrows from *The Fall of Princes* is an interest in classical history: he later says that he is only interested in the women of pagan antiquity, although he includes Eve and often warns against paganism.[127] He also borrows from Lydgate a tendency to make classical allusions, especially to

[123] Edwards, 'Influence', 431–4; Herbert G. Wright, *Boccaccio in England from Chaucer to Tennyson* (London: Athlone, 1957), 3, 21–2.

[124] BL, MS Harley 116, f.170v ('Maro Britanis' or Virgil among the Britons), alluded to in Pearsall, *Lydgate (1371–1449): A Bio-bibliography*, 41; Renoir, *Lydgate*, 1, 3.

[125] Gustav Schleich (ed.), *Die mittelenglische Umdichtung von Boccaccios De claris mulieribus*, Palaestra, 144 (Leipzig: Mayer und Müller, 1924), lines 16–21, on which see Janet Cowen, 'An English Reading of Boccaccio: A Selective Middle English Version of Boccaccio's *De Mulieribus claris* in British Library MS Additional 10304', in *New Perspectives on Middle English Texts: A Festschrift for R. A. Waldron*, ed. Susan Powell and Jeremy J. Smith (Cambridge: Brewer, 2000), 129–40.

[126] BL, MS Additional 10304. Otherwise, see eight English letters in humanist script in an Oxford formulary (CCCC, MS 423, pp. 37–44); some humanist influence in Chaundler's copy of Walton's Boethius in BL, MS Harley 43, described in *Humfrey 1970*, no. 34 (c); some individual humanist graphs in a secretary hand noted in Wilson and Fenlon (eds.), *Winchester*, 4.

[127] Schleich (ed.), *Boccaccios De claris mulieribus*, 169–217, following Giovanni Boccaccio, *Famous Women*, ed. and trans. Virginia Brown (Cambridge: Harvard University Press, 2001), pref. 9, pref. 11.

Ovid, in places where none are made by Boccaccio. He has a nitpicky, scholarly
tone, with the odd 'dygressyon' on points of genealogy or 'dissencion' between
different sources.[128]

In these poems, *Knyghthode and Bataile* and *De Mulieribus claris*, writers
have imitated the method of translation and elaborate page designs of the
books made for the humanist prince Duke Humfrey. They have, though, done
so without immediate reference to the duke; the scholarship survives without
a princely scholar. However, although this tradition of vernacular humanism
has escaped from a prince's circle, this book still glorifies the great. The
translator of *De Mulieribus claris* is less critical of his goddesses, princesses,
and queens than is the preachy Lydgate. He notes that Boccaccio includes the
vicious with virtuous:

> For his intent so streyghtly is not taken
> All to speke of vertue and goodenesse,
> Noon to call noble but thei, that forsaken
> Of vycyous lyvynge the vnthriftynesse,
> Butt ferthermore this name of worthynesse
> Through the goode pacyence of the herersse
> To vndirstond of better and of wersse, [...]

He redefines nobility and worthiness not 'so streyghtly' as 'vertue and good-
enesse' but as fame of any sort. He often uses the word 'notable' of people
quite wicked, in fact.[129] The fascination with pagan history leads to an amoral
interest in anything that is famous or powerful. The fascination with fame and
power proves to be the spirit of much humanist writing during the fifteenth
century.

[128] For allusions, see Schleich (ed.), *Boccaccios De claris mulieribus*, 83–4 (not in Boccaccio,
Famous Women, pref. 3), 134–40 (pref. 6), 141–54 (pref. 6), 358–65 (II.1), 526 (IV.6), 856
(VIII.2), 872–5 (VIII.2), 919, 922–4 (VIII.7), 1257 (XXXVIII.4), 1481 (XXVII); 673 and 852.
[129] Schleich (ed.), *Boccaccios De claris mulieribus*, 120–6 (Boccaccio, *Famous Women*, pref.
6), 137, 191, 743, 751.

3

Allusion, translation, and mistranslation

The Italian scholars and John Lydgate praise Humfrey, Duke of Gloucester, for being a scholar and, as such, they liken him to Julius Caesar. Caesar also wrote books and founded a library during his busy life: 'and you are happy too', they tell the duke ('felix quoque et tu'). Just as some people emulated Humfrey's studies, so the writers of the fifteenth century also emulated this habit of likening people to the heroes of antiquity in order to glorify them. Of course, the habit was not entirely new: earlier orators and chroniclers used comparisons to classical heroes when describing the events of their day: in the early Lancastrian years, Thomas Walsingham did so very fully.[1] But the allusions do acquire a new prominence and prestige as the fifteenth century goes on. For example, a change occurs in writing about Henry V. During his lifetime, the speaker in parliament in 1421 reminded Henry V to follow Julius Caesar, but only in recalling—like Caesar, it seems they thought—how much he owed to God. In a letter Cardinal Beaufort reminded Henry V *not* to follow Alexander the Great: the king could outstrip Alexander if he recalled how much he owed to God.[2] These men conjure up the glory of the ancients but they then dismiss this worldly glory in a penitential vein. In later writing about Henry V, the tone alters. On commission from Humfrey, Duke of Gloucester, Tito Livio Frulovisi composed a chronicle about Henry V in a style of Latin and a historical structure modelled more closely on classical histories. Then in Oxford in 1449, somebody copied, perhaps from a book donated by Duke Humfrey, a Latin version of one of Lucian's 'dialogues of the dead'. Into this classical dialogue, between Alexander, Hannibal, and Scipio, steps Henry V. But now he is not rebuked by the ancient men and their falls; he rebukes them. He at first says that he rejects their worldly fame and empire, but he goes on to

---

[1] [Thomas Walsingham], *The St. Albans Chronicle 1406–1420*, ed. V. H. Galbraith (Oxford: Clarendon Press, 1937), for example 12, 28–9, 86, 88, 90, 94–5, 112–14.

[2] Chris Given-Wilson and others (eds.), *The Parliament Rolls of Medieval England*, 16 vols. (London: National Archives, 2005), IX.265; Cecil Monro (ed.), *Letters of Queen Margaret of Anjou and Bishop Bekington and Others*, Camden Society, os 86 (London: Camden Society, 1863), 4. See also 'The Chronicle of John Strecche for the Reign of Henry V (1414–22)', ed. F. Taylor, *BJRL*, 16 (1932), 137–87 (187).

boast that his own fame and empire are greater. Minos, judging the dialogue, concludes that Henry V wins and praises him for his rhetoric: 'By Jove, Henry, you orated well, as befits a strong and wise prince' ('Per Jouem, Henrice, recte uti fortem prudentem principem decet, perorasti').[3] Now the present prince can outstrip the ancient. Now the present prince can be described even within a wholly pagan setting, boasting to Minos in hell. Now the present prince, speaking in the idiom of a classical dialogue, is speaking as befits a prince.

Throughout the mid and late fifteenth century people seem to have thought that speaking with some classical colour like this did befit the most important moments. English writers during the upheavals and battles of the Wars of the Roses use allusions and classical similes to glorify people, events, and ideas, or just to fatten their own style. It is as if they wrote in togas. These allusions occur in the records of living history by English and Italian writers. Like Walsingham, his predecessor at St Albans, John Whethamstede records recent events with mythographic trimmings, redolent of Chaucerian classicism but in Latin.[4] George Neville sends news of English affairs to Italy in a letter with an allusion to Lucan.[5] Often writers use these allusions in the letters, speeches, and mummings which they addressed to important men, as if to establish the *ethos* of the writer or speaker and his addressees—to set the tone, as it were. Comparisons to Caesar and others recur in the letters of the University of Oxford to Humfrey, Duke of Gloucester, and his peers.[6] William Sellyng greets the worthies of the English church as if they are senators and 'patres conscripti'.[7] Lydgate uses these allusions to address the king or the mayor of London in his mummings—and to acclaim Henry V as one of the 'worthy nyen' like Hector. The scribe John Shirley annotates one of Lydgate's mummings quite fully, explaining the authors and the myths alluded to, so that this piece of occasional verse becomes a work of scholarship.[8]

[3] William O'Sullivan, 'John Manyngham, an Early Oxford Humanist', *BLR*, 7 (1962–7), 28–39 (39).

[4] *Registrum Abbatiæ Johannis Whethamstede*, ed. Henry Thomas Riley, RS, 28, 2 vols. (London: HMSO, 1872–3), for example I.159, I.168, I.174–7, I.290, I.297, I.330, I.338–9, I.346–8; on which see recently David R. Carlson, 'The Civic Poetry of Abbot John Whethamstede of St. Albans († 1465)', *Mediaeval Studies*, 61 (1999), 205–42 (214, 230).

[5] Rawdon Brown (ed.), *Calendar of State Papers and Manuscripts, Relating to English Affairs, Existing in the Archives and Collections of Venice and in Other Libraries of Northern Italy: Volume I. 1202–1509* (London: HMSO, 1864), 100 (no. 370).

[6] Anstey (ed.), *Epistolae*, for example I.123–4, I.178, I.203–4, II.355, II.476.

[7] BL, MS Cotton Cleopatra E.iii, ff.108r–112v, ff.115r–118r, on which see Weiss, *Humanism*, 156.

[8] John Lydgate, 'A Mumming at Eltham', in Lydgate, *Minor Poems*, II.672–4 (lines 1–4, 36–49, 81–4); John Lydgate, 'A Mumming at London', in Lydgate, *Minor Poems*, II.682–91 (lines 24–32, 64–129, 147, 243–68); John Lydgate, 'A Mumming for the Mercers of London', in Lydgate, *Minor Poems*, II.695–8, on which see Aage Brusendorff, *The Chaucer Tradition* (Copenhagen: Pio-Branner, 1925), 466–7.

As well as flattering the listeners directly, a lofty tone is set by comparing the people and events of the fifteenth century to the people and events of antiquity. That happens in formal oratory. Pietro del Monte and Antonio Beccaria, associates of Duke Humfrey, address parliament in humanist Latin or with classical allusions.[9] One of these allusions, to Julia Caesar, recurs among others in the diplomatic speeches of John Gunthorpe.[10] In the 1470s and 1480s further classical allusions appear in some English speeches to parliament by Robert Stillington and by John Russell, Gunthorpe's associate. Whoever copied Russell's speeches underlined the allusions as if they were of note.[11] Other classical comparisons come in other works of epideictic rhetoric, such as an epithalamion by Lydgate for Duke Humfrey,[12] or the poems with which scholars such as Pietro Carmeliano and Giovanni Gigli try to impress the Tudors in the 1480s.[13] It is clear that the allusions seemed impressive, for they appear in political documents and consultations in which people sought to persuade their peers on quite practical matters. They appear in the preamble to some courtly ordinances,[14] in the polemical tract *Somnium Vigilantis* of 1459 (discussed in Chapter 6 below) and on half a dozen occasions in the letters, polemics, and legal theory of Sir John Fortescue.[15]

Yet these similes and allusions invite one criticism often lodged against humanism as a scholarly and literary practice: that these writers make the classical reference a tool of specious flattery for princes and despots.[16] Is the

---

[9] Susanne Saygin, *Humphrey, Duke of Gloucester (1390–1447) and the Italian Humanists* (Leiden: Brill, 2002), 118.

[10] BodL, MS Bodley 587, for example f.84v (Julia Caesar), printed in Pierre Chaplais (ed.), *English Medieval Diplomatic Practice*, 2 vols. (London: HMSO, 1982), I.234–53 (especially I.248); on which MS, see *Humfrey 1970*, nos. 82, 95.

[11] J. Brigstocke Sheppard (ed.), *Literæ Cantuarienses: The Letter Books of the Monastery of Christ Church, Canterbury*, RS 85, 3 vols. (London: HMSO, 1887–9), III.279, III.282–3; 'Bishop Russell's Parliamentary Sermons in 1483', printed in S. B. Chrimes, *English Constitutional Ideas in the Fifteenth Century* (Cambridge: Cambridge University Press, 1936), 167–91 (169–70, 172, 174), from BL, MS Cotton Vitellius E.x, ff.141r–144v, ff.170r–176v, ff.177r–183v. Russell appears in Chapters 5 and 6 below.

[12] John Lydgate, 'On Gloucester's Approaching Marriage', in Lydgate, *Minor Poems*, II.601–8 (lines 32–5, 71–80, 134–55, 176–82).

[13] Gilbert and Godelieve Tournoy-Thoen, 'Giovanni Gigli and the Renaissance of the Classical Epithalamium in England', in *Myricae: Essays on Neo-Latin Literature in Memory of Jozef IJsewijn*, Supplementa Humanistica Lovaniensia, 16 (Leuven: Leuven University Press, 2000), 133–93 (141–5); David Carlson, 'King Arthur and Court Poems for the Birth of Arthur Tudor in 1486', *HL*, 36 (1987), 147–83 (155–62).

[14] Myers (ed.), *Household*, 86, 212.

[15] Sir John Fortescue, *De Laudibus legum Anglie*, ed. S. B. Chrimes (Cambridge: Cambridge University Press, 1942), 10, 32, 137, 211; Sir John Fortescue, *The Governance of England*, ed. Charles Plummer (London: Oxford University Press, 1885), 112, 149–50, 347–8; *The Works of Sir John Fortescue, Knight*, ed. Thomas (Fortescue) Lord Clermont, 2 vols. (London: privately printed, 1869), I.22–3, I.77–8, I.137, and I.151, with a list of sources on I.347*–48*.

[16] Grafton and Jardine, *Humanism*, pp. xiii-xiv.

humanist book, then, if not read by the prince, still in service to him? This depends on whether we count such flimsy allusions as the fruit of humanist reading. For many of the lighter similes and allusions made in fifteenth-century writing do not come from humanist reading; they come from reading Chaucer—albeit through the distorting lens through which readers often saw *Boece* and his other works, under which his glories seemed to be curious allusions and flowery rhetoric. Is this tradition, then, as guilty of prince-pleasing as humanism is? Yet even if we look beyond these brief allusions, it seems that the writers who study and imitate antiquity more fully and lovingly are also guilty of flattering the princes of their own time. That seems true in two works which rely extensively on classical models. One is *De Consulatu Stilichonis*, written in 1445 for the Duke of York, who took over some of Duke Humfrey's political causes. It seems to offer an exemplum for the duke to learn from, but in fact offers scholarship and style which are an ornament for a princely figure, as *On Husbondrie* did. The glory to be won from comparisons to the ancients is explained in another translation, *Knyghthode and Bataile*, written in 1460 for Henry VI, in a form closely modelled upon *On Husbondrie* (as was noted in Chapter 2 above). But the praise offered in a translation becomes more complex than the mere exemplum or comparison; sometimes the act of reading the classics fully and closely leads a writer to richer ideas. This complexity emerges not only when the work escapes from the prince's hand for other readers to adapt, but when the writer himself works at reading or misreading his source.

THE MUSES OF OSBERN BOKENHAM

The allusions to classical mythology and literature made by Lydgate and the poets of *On Husbondrie* and *De Mulieribus claris* are widespread in the English verse of Chaucer and his imitators. Some of the allusions do reflect people truly reading the classics: Phoebus' chariot appears helpfully near the start of Ovid's *Metamorphoses* and so it reappears in lots of English verse. In fact, the allusions usually invoke one or two of the better-known mythical figures: Phoebus drives his chariot across the sky and Venus inflames the heart hundreds of times; only a few poets mention and count the muses.[17] But these limitations and repetitions betray that the allusions are slightly

---

[17] Chadwick-Healey's full-text database *English Poetry, Second Edition* (<http://collections. chadwyck.co.uk/home/home_ep2.jsp>, accessed 22 August 2005), offers a rough gauge: between 1350 and 1500 Phoebus is named 434 times (including Lydgate, *Fall*, VII.1611, VII.2797–800, VIII.1270, 1620, 2330) and Venus 609; the 'muses' as a group are named twenty-three times, in two romances and by Chaucer, Walton, Burgh, Bokenham, and Lydgate (*Fall*, III.63).

used, second-hand. They often come from other English poems rather than from the study of antiquity. Alongside humanist influences, there is another form of classicism in English literature at this time, namely Chaucerian or 'Lydgatean' allusion. Yet the love for these allusions—if *allusion* does not suggest more learning than they have—is apparent in the attention which the readers pay to them. It is visible in copies of *Boece* and Walton's translations (noted in Chapter 1) and is visible in anthologies of Chaucerian poetry too. For example, in one well-known anthology, facing Chaucer's 'The Complaint of Mars' is a wonderful painting of Mars, Venus, and Jupiter; elsewhere in this book, in the margins of *The House of Fame*, the scribe marks Chaucer's sources in Ovid and Virgil, using the 'Vnde Ouidius' phrase, used in Duke Humfrey's note in *On Husbondrie*; and when Chaucer stops following Ovid and Virgil, the scribe stops annotating; he also copies the marginalia to the learned poem *Reson and Sensuallyte*, about half of which give information about the classical references. Another Chaucerian anthology had euhemeristic notes about the gods.[18] These notes typify fifteenth-century concerns: glossing allusions to the gods, especially symbolically or euhemeristically; glossing mythical heroes and heroines, especially with potted biographies; citing the classical encyclopaedists who store this knowledge; spotting the parallels in the work of Ovid and Virgil, and only seldom in the work of other poets. In the prologues and epilogues where fifteenth-century poets sell themselves, the poets wish they could drink from Helicon's well or follow Cicero in eloquence. Lydgate, most inventively, regrets that the liquor of Bacchus does not flow through his Suffolk veins. When people tell literary history in the fifteenth century they do not only list Chaucer, Gower, and Lydgate; they often add Chaucer, Gower, and Lydgate to a longer list of—give or take a name—Homer, Cicero, Virgil, Ovid, Seneca, Dante, and Petrarch.[19] English literary tradition pretended to classical influences.

It is hard to disentangle whether Chaucerian poetry made readers amenable to the humanist fashion for antiquity, or the humanist fashion altered the reading and writing of courtly verse. But what the two trends share are their

---

[18] *Bodleian Library MS Fairfax 16*, ed. John Norton-Smith (London: Scolar Press, 1979), f.155r, ff.156r–157r, ff.158v–159v, f.207r–v, f.216r, f.217r, f.218r, f.220v, f.221v, ff.223v–225r, ff.229r–230v, ff.235r–236r, f.243r, ff.244v–245v, ff.246v–247r, ff.248v–249r, f.252r-v, f.258v, f.267v, f.270r, f.286r, f.299v; *Manuscript Trinity R.3.19: A Facsimile*, ed. Bradford Y. Fletcher (Norman, OK: Pilgrim Books, 1987), f.67v.

[19] For example Lydgate, *Fall*, VIII.193–6, IX.334–41, IX.3437–9; Osbern Bokenham, *Legendys of Hooly Wummen*, ed. Mary S. Serjeantson, EETS os 206 (London: Oxford University Press, 1938), 4043–66. On *English Poetry, Second Edition* (<http://collections.chadwyck.co.uk/home/home_ep2.jsp>, accessed 22 August 2005) between 1350 and 1500: 'Tullius' or 'Cicero' and variants appear eighty times (and 'Tullius Hostilius' twice); 'Bachus' and variants seventy-five times; 'Elicon', 'Parnaso' and variants only six times each, mostly in Chaucer, Lydgate, Burgh, and Bokenham. Compare Lydgate, *Fall*, IV.57–140, IX.3387–414; Bokenham, *Legendys*, 407–18.

prestige and their usefulness in winning prestige for the writer, his patron or his theme. One writer who explains the prestige is Osbern Bokenham, a friar of Clare Priory (1392/3–in or after 1464). Bokenham composed nearly two hundred saints' lives, most of them translated from the *Legenda Aurea*, most in prose and a few in verse. He dedicated nine of the verse lives to local patrons, and they and four others circulated separately. In one of the dedicated lives, he considers the merits of using classicizing rhetoric. This is his life of St Mary Magdalen, which he says, in the prologue or 'Prolocutorye', was commissioned by Isabel Bourgchier on Twelfth Night 1445 (6 January 1446 by our reckoning). She was the neighbour and patron of Bokenham's priory and was the sister of Richard, Duke of York; Richard was the lord of Clare by hereditary right and another patron of the priory there. There was a verse genealogy of him on a bilingual manuscript hung from a dowling rod in the priory, and Bokenham most likely composed that too.[20] In his 'Prolocutorye' to the life of St Mary Magdalen, he reflects upon how to find the style which befits a commission which is both holy and aristocratic. He says that he will begin with a prayer, and in this he follows Plato, even though Plato is a pagan (5117–39). And his prayer ends ostensibly by rejecting pagan style:

> Where-fore, lord, to þe alone I crye
> Wych welle art of mercy and of pyte,
> And neythyr to Clyo ner to Melpomene,
> Nere to noon oþir of þe musys nyne,
> Ner to Pallas Mynerue, ner Lucyne,
> Ner to Apollo, wych, as old poetys seye,
> Of wysdam beryth both lok and keye,
> Of gay speche eek and of eloquencye; [...]   (5214–21)

But we must not be fooled: he protests too much, with seven negatives in four of the lines, and he begins to list the muses anyway—as he will in *De Consulatu Stilichonis* (below). Similarly, he spurns the 'curial' love poets, but concedes their eloquence too:

> Yet not-for-þan is here centens
> So craftyd up, and wyth langwage so gay

[20] Simon Horobin, 'The Angle of Oblivioun: A Lost Medieval Manuscript Discovered in Walter Scott's Collection', *Times Literary Supplement*, 11 November 2005, 12–13, reports the recent discovery of the full collection. On the links between Clare and York, see Bokenham, *Legendys*, 4982–5262; A. S. G. Edwards, 'The Transmission and Audience of Osbern Bokenham's *Legendys of Hooly Wummen*', in *Late-Medieval Religious Texts and their Transmission: Essays in Honour of A. I. Doyle*, ed. A. J. Minnis (Cambridge: Brewer, 1994), 157–67 (166); Christopher Harper-Bill (ed.), *The Cartulary of the Augustinian Friars of Clare*, Suffolk Charters, 11 (Woodbridge: Boydell, 1991), 11, 102–4; [Osbern Bokenham], 'This Dialogue betwix a Seculer asking and a Frere

> Uttryd, þat I trowe þe moneth of may
> Neuere fresshere enbe[l]shyd þe soyl wyth flours [...]
> Was neuere þe tayl gayere of a po,
> Wych þan enherytyd alle Argus eyne
> Whan Marcuryis whystyl hym dede streyne
> To hys deed slepe; of wych language
> The craft to coueyte where grete dotage
> In m[yn] oold dayis and in þat degre
> That I am in; [...]   (5234–46)

The image of rhetoric as a flowery meadow is pseudo-classical, for elsewhere it is used of Cicero's style and likened to Claudian's scene of Proserpina picking flowers (1455–7; see also 1449–64, 4046–8). Bokenham also imagines rhetoric with an image of Argus from Ovid, one never paralleled exactly by other Middle English poets.[21] The curious images betray that Bokenham does not reject the rhetoric of courtly poets. He rejects their morals, he says, 'Yet not-for-þan'—that is, *nevertheless*—they have a splendid style.[22] He says he hardly dares to 'coueyte' their rhetoric from which age and social 'degre' exclude him, but that is only a humility topos. *Humble* and similar words pepper the lines and the other legends too (5118, 5130, 5139, 5247; see 9446, 9833). Two recent critics have argued that Bokenham spurns the classics, which he sees can serve the patriarchy and corrupt the piety of the waning 'Middle Ages'.[23] But Bokenham covets this pseudo-classical rhetoric.

Yet this rhetoric might indeed be criticized, firstly for being dynastic, as those critics have seen. Bokenham employs the fine rhetoric—like the humility topoi—when it is time to address his lofty patroness, the sister of the Duke of York. He makes these little allusions at other high points in the stories, but nowhere does he use them as thickly as in describing a commission from

---

answeryng [...] ', in Osbern Bokenham, *Legenden*, ed. C. Horstmann (Heilbronn: Henninger, 1883), 269–74.

[21] On *English Poetry, Second Edition* (<http://collections.chadwyck.co.uk/home/home_ep2. jsp>, accessed 22 August 2005) between 1350 and 1500: this Argus appears thirty times, in two romances and in Chaucer, Gower, Charles d'Orléans, Bokenham, Lydgate, Metham, and *Reson and Sensuallyte*, sometimes with Mercury but never with the 'po' (peacock), even when in a couplet rhyming in —o. See Gustav Schleich (ed.), *Die mittelenglische Umdichtung von Boccaccios De claris mulieribus*, Palaestra, 144 (Leipzig: Mayer und Müller, 1924), lines 863–75, expanding Giovanni Boccaccio, *Famous Women*, ed. and trans. Virginia Brown (Cambridge: Harvard University Press, 2001), VIII.3. Neither Ovid, *Metamorphoses*, I.722–3, nor the English *De Mulieribus claris* mentions the species of bird.

[22] *Not-for-than* appears in *MED* under *not*, adv., 4(c).

[23] Sheila Delany, *Impolitic Bodies: Poetry, Saints, and Society in Fifteenth-Century England* (Oxford: Oxford University Press, 1998), 45, 65, 202–3; Carroll Hilles, 'Gender and Politics in Osbern Bokenham's Legendary', *NML*, 4 (2001), 189–212 (192, *n*. 8).

Isabel.[24] He opens this prologue on the day when Phoebus entered Capricorn, while Isabel and her sons are dancing in their finest array:

> Was neuyr [wyth] flouris [whyt], blewe and grene,
> Medewe motleyid freshlyere, I wene,
> Than were her garnementys; for as it semyd me
> Mynerue hyr-self, wych hath þe souereynte
> Of gay texture, as declaryth Ouyde,
> Wyth al hire wyt ne coude prouyde
> More goodly aray þow she dede en[cl]os
> Wyth-ynne oo web al methamorphosyos.   (5027–34)

Bokenham has donned his fanciest fashions too. The reference to Minerva as a weaver is a rare one but one he favours in his saints' lives (4059, 5218) and in *De Consulatu Stilichonis*.[25] (It also appears in the English *De Mulieribus claris*. Could this and other correspondences link the English *De Mulieribus claris* to Bokenham's work somehow?)[26] And this glorious humbug dresses up some lines of naked dynastic ambition. In introducing his patroness, he stresses her brother's 'pedegru' to the throne of Castile. In the mid 1440s York had royal ambitions abroad: he sought to marry his son to the princess of France and his followers seem to have been collecting evidence for his claim to the Castilian throne; neither plan flourished.[27] Yet Bokenham expresses a vague hope for success in winning the throne of Castile, 'Wych god hym send, yf it be hys wyl' (5004–19). The poem can only utter vague rumour about the lord and must be evasive: 'But of þis mater no more now spekyn I wyl,' he ends (5020).

In every way these allusions, although cute, are specious. Firstly, the allusions flatter the powerful family for a grandeur that they have not yet achieved. Secondly, the allusions are intellectually pointless. They sit extraneous to the sentence, in syntactic apposition, describing people 'as' something else, or

[24] But see the elaborate prologue in Bokenham, *Legendys*, 1449–68.
[25] Ewald Flügel (ed.), 'Eine Mittelenglische Claudian-Übersetzung (1445)', *Anglia*, 28 (1905), 255–99, 421–38 (lines 249, 375). Delany, *Impolitic Bodies*, 41–2, 56–7, suggests the source as Ovid's *Fasti*. On *English Poetry, Second Edition* (<http://collections.chadwyck.co.uk/home/home_ep2.jsp>, accessed 22 August 2005) between 1350 and 1500 'Minerva' and variants appear seventeen times, but never as the goddess of weaving. Lydgate, *Fall*, IV.92–4, rhymes 'cloos' and 'Methamorphoseos' in a biography of Ovid.
[26] Schleich (ed.), *Boccaccios De claris mulieribus*, 624–37 (Boccaccio, *Famous Women*, VI.3). Schleich (ed.), *Boccaccios De claris mulieribus*, 201–2, praises the lives of St Catharine and St Agnes by 'Saynt Ambrose, which with gode eloquucyon | Wryten hathe her life sufficiently'; Bokenham, *Legendys*, 4037–41, ascribes his life of St Agnes to 'seynt Ambrose, | Wych wyth hey style it doth endyte' and hopes to translate 'suffycyently' (*Legendys*, 4037–41).
[27] Anthony Goodman and David Morgan, 'The Yorkist Claim to the Throne of Castile', *JMH*, 11 (1985), 61–9 (64–5); *Wars in France*, I.80; Richard Beadle and Colin Richmond (eds.), *Paston Letters and Papers of the Fifteenth Century: Part III*, EETS ss 22 (Oxford: Oxford University Press, 2005), no. 956:20–3.

describing often what they are 'not' like. This is true of the allusions used
by other writers: a princess is 'As' Helen and Lucretia are; a duke acts 'With'
Caesar and Pompey; English affairs are described simply 'like as Scipio' or
'Right so it happed in olde daies at the Citee of Rome [...]'.[28] It has been said
that humanist imitation was essentially 'metaphoric' and drew weak analogies
between the past and the present rather than forging any stronger connection.[29]
The weakness inheres in these classical allusions in the political writing of
fifteenth-century England too. Therefore the writer must supplement the
classicism with reference to other legal or historical discourses, such as the
'pedegru', which would truly win the arguments. Finally, the allusions in
Bokenham's 'Prolocutorye' and in other political writing are superficial not
only in their use but also in their learning, for though they reflect the prestige of
antiquity, they do not often reflect the careful humanist study of antiquity. The
ersatz feel is clearest in English works: for example, Bokenham's description
of rhetoric as the 'ethna flowrs' plucked by Proserpina, 'as claudian doþe telle',
echoes either Chaucer's reference to the story 'In Claudyan' or only *De Raptu
Proserpinae*, used in elementary schooling; Lydgate compares his prince to
classical heroes, including Troilus, a more local than classical hero.[30] Even when
genuine classical books are plundered, the allusions are torn from context.
There is humanist fashion here, but there is no full or deep humanist reading.

AN EXEMPLUM FOR THE DUKE OF YORK

Alongside these superficial responses, however, there is a fuller and deeper
reading of the classics by two translators of the mid-fifteenth century. Both of
these translators sometimes respond to antiquity in ways similar to those of
the writers of fleeting allusions. However, both also respond in more complex
ways and, intriguingly, reflect upon their ways of reading and responding. The
earlier work with such reflection is *De Consulatu Stilichonis*, an unrhymed verse
translation of part of a panegyric by the late fourth-century poet Claudian.
In it Claudian praises his patron, the general Stilicho, who had finally been
elected consul after years of power behind the throne of his ward. He describes
Stilicho's virtues and achievements and then relates how the provinces beg

---

[28] Lydgate, 'On Gloucester's Approaching Marriage', lines 71, 134; Brigstocke Sheppard (ed.),
Literæ Cantuarienses, II.282.

[29] Thomas M. Greene, *The Light in Troy: Imitation and Discovery in Renaissance Poetry* (New
Haven, CT: Yale University Press, 1982), 86.

[30] Bokenham, *Legendys*, 1456; Chaucer, *The Merchant's Tale*, IV.2229–32. See also Lydgate,
'On Gloucester's Approaching Marriage', line 136.

Rome to persuade the modest hero to accept the consulate.[31] The unique copy
of the English translation is an intimate book with illuminated initials which
display the arms of Richard, Duke of York (1411–60), and a colophon which
specifies that the poem was 'Translat and wrete at Clare. 1445', that is at Clare
in Suffolk in 1445.[32] From the patron, time, and place, the translator was most
likely Bokenham again. However, in translating the poem, Bokenham—if it
is he—responds to antiquity more fully than in his 'Prolocutorye' and reflects
upon how to respond to the ancients.

In an epilogue the translator addresses his book, in the common topos of *go
little book*, and tells it what to learn from Claudian. As in *On Husbondrie*, the
purpose is apparently to imitate the style of classical verse. This is humanism
as a discursive practice, with an outright denial of ideas or philosophy:

> Thy maystyr Claudyan euyn as hys chyld. þou lytyll tretys swe.
> And wurshypp hym. wyth latyn tunge embelshyd hath with penne.
> Preyse god in hym as in paynemys. whos doctryne whylom crewe
> To good manerys and preconysyd vertu to heuen renne.
> Loue not hys law / love weel hys word. þe thyk chyuse fro þe thenne.
> Oure feyth and hys be not as oon þey goo in dyuers sutys.   (epi. 1–6)

The epilogue initially favours Claudian more for his style than his content: he
is a grammar-school *magister* or 'maystyr' who instructs the 'chyld' or English
poem in Latin poetry and, like Chaucer, his distinctive achievement was to have
'embelshyd' poetic diction. With an odd variation on the customary prayer to
sift the wheat from the chaff, the poem is advised not to love Claudian's 'lawe'
but to 'love weel his word'. That steers away from the dangers of paganism, of
course, but it also surprisingly upends the usual hierarchy of 'superficial' and
'deep' reading. So does *De Consulatu Stilichonis* reduce Claudian's poem to a
textbook, and infantilize the reader as a mere schoolboy studying grammar
and style? This would be one striking offering to a grown man as powerful as
Richard, Duke of York.

If we open the book, though, the appearance and style imply this sort of
reader. Each double page offers not only a translation, but also the original
Latin of *De Consulatu Stilichonis* in a 'parallel text' on the left, with some

---

[31] Quotations, with parenthetical line numbers, come from Flügel (ed.), 'Eine Mittelenglische
Claudian-Übersetzung (1445)'; quotations of the Latin come from Flügel's edition of the parallel
text, but with the line numbers prefixed 'XXII' as in the standard edition of Claudius Claudianus,
Carmina, ed. John Barrie Hall (Leipzig: Teubner, 1985).

[32] BL, MS Additional 11814, f.25r. The main hand resembles one of three which add some
fifteenth-century documents to a cartulary from Clare (BL, MS Harley 4835, f.56r, bottom
document, and f.56v) in a distinctive *g*, *p*, and *w*, and an overall spiky aspect, although the rough
additions to the cartulary are more cursive. Anne F. Sutton and Livia Visser-Fuchs, *Richard III's
Books: Ideals and Reality in the Life and Library of a Medieval Prince* (Stroud: Sutton, 1997),
fig. 16, illustrates ff.18v–19r.

spaces in the Latin so that the slightly longer English can catch up, for easy comparison. What sort of reader is implied by the parallel text? The parallel text appeared in some copies of Walton's and Chaucer's versions of Boethius which evinced very superficial reading. And one model for it might be schoolbooks. Schoolboys often read Claudian's *De Raptu Proserpinae*, alongside Cato's *Disticha* and the other basic authors, in copies with glosses and marginalia which explained unusual words and names.[33] As it happens, a second scribe put into the Clare book some similar marginalia, and the poet wove glosses on a few names into his translation as he went along. The Clare book also has a prose prologue, dividing Claudian's poems into praise and blame, and placing this one 'in wise contrary' to *In Rufinum* within his career; this description of his works may imitate the *accessus ad auctores* found in commentaries in schoolbooks.[34] Moreover, a bilingual layout is, as A. S. G. Edwards has noted, often found in copies of Cato's *Disticha*, the popular school-text, albeit usually with the Latin and English alternating, not in parallel.[35] Benedict Burgh's translation of the *Disticha* was said to have been made 'for the erudicion of my Lord Bousher', that is, for the son of the Bourgchiers, the neighbours and patrons of Clare Priory.[36] A bilingual layout in *De Consulatu Stilichonis* might invite Richard, Duke of York, too to 'erudicion', to the more bookish education then fashionable with the nobility.

Was Richard really a Latinist or a humanist reader like Duke Humfrey? He had a few links through his public duties to Zenone Castiglione, who had led Duke Humfrey to many of his Italian clients, and to Thomas Candour, a humanist scribe.[37] And poets do sometimes eulogize him in a loosely bookish way. One chronicler, writing for York, says that he has 'great intelligence' and

---

[33] For example Cambridge, Peterhouse, MS 215, f.36r, f.61v, ff.72v–78r (Claudian's *De Raptu Proserpinae* and other school-texts), and *The Commentary of Geoffrey of Vitry on Claudian 'De Raptu Proserpinae'*, ed. A. K. Clarke and P. M. Giles, Mittellateinische Studien und Texte, 7 (Leiden: Brill, 1973), plates 1–2, 4 (layout), 16–18, 40–1, 45, 60. For genre, see *Commentary of Geoffrey of Vitry*, 4–5, 125–6.

[34] BL, MS Additional 11814, for example, f.5v, f.20r, f.23r. Although similar, the hand of the colophon, marginalia, and epilogue differs from that of the main text, for example, in the graphs *a* and *g*.

[35] A. S. G. Edwards, 'The Middle English Translation of Claudian's *De Consulatu Stilichonis*', in *Middle English Poetry: Texts and Traditions: Essays in Honour of Derek Pearsall*, ed. A. J. Minnis (York: York Medieval Press, 2001), 267–78 (268–9).

[36] *Caxton's Own Prose*, 15a:4–6; Harper-Bill (ed.), *Cartulary*, 103–5; Edwards, 'Bokenham's Legendys', 166.

[37] On Castiglione: *Wars in France*, II.i.335–7, II.i.371–3; *Bekynton Correspondence*, I.289–95; Saygin, *Humphrey*, 144–71, especially 162. On Candour: P. A. Johnson, *Duke Richard of York 1411–60* (Oxford: Clarendon Press, 1988), 21; Joel T. Rosenthal, 'Richard, Duke of York: A Fifteenth-Century Layman and the Church', *Catholic Historical Review*, 50 (1964–5), 171–87 (182); Margaret Harvey, *England, Rome and the Papacy 1417–1464: The Study of a Relationship* (Manchester: Manchester University Press, 1993), 34–5, 41, 66, 116, 185.

'in Latyn hath good inspeccion'. The verse genealogy of him from Clare Priory makes the oddly precise, if wrong, claim that his forefather had founded the priory because Giles of Rome, a member of this order of friars, composed *De Regimine principum* for him! As it happens, Richard is the only English layman known to have owned *De Regimine principum* in Latin.[38] But these are eulogies, so their reports of his erudite life seem dubiously flattering. So too is it dubious whether he was as erudite as the parallel text of *De Consulatu Stilichonis* invites him to be. As in the elaborate copies of *On Husbondrie*, the humanist reading recorded in *De Consulatu Stilichonis* is not recorded at all; it is implied as a possibility when the scribe offers the Latin—unknowing of whether anyone will use it. After all, the design of a parallel text does allow York to read Claudian's Latin but it does not *compel* him to do so; he has, on the page, a choice of what to read.

Furthermore, the poet is inconsistent about the reading he invites. Later in the epilogue he proposes another way of reading, now a moral way:

> Thys lesson breff and long also. Claudyan now hath tawght.
> In wordys thyrk. in sentens cleer. In whom as in a merour
> Princys may se her outward gestys […]   (epil. 8–10)

Now Claudian's language is said to be 'thyrk', an East Anglian word meaning *murky*,[39] while his moral lesson is as clear as a 'merour' for 'Princys'. And what one should look at in this mirror are the historical 'gestys' or deeds of Stilicho. There is some novelty in this reliance upon one classical history for instruction. Mirrors for princes often used short exemplary tales, but they trimmed the tales to fit a wider ethical framework, as in Hoccleve's or Gower's works. One mirror for princes of the 1430s even warned of the dangers of historical *memoria*, and offered lessons through complex theology and allegory instead.[40] But in his prologue to *De Consulatu Stilichonis* the poet stresses that historical *memoria*, or 'remembraunce' of an exemplary hero, will offer lessons to the duke:

> […] Shew the to his highnes. for this oon entente
> That be thi remembraunce. vertue moote him please

---

[38] John Hardyng, *Chronicle*, ed. Henry Ellis (London: Rivington and others, 1812), 23; [Bokenham], 'This Dialogue', stanza 4; Charles F. Briggs, *Giles of Rome's* De regimine principum: *Reading and Writing Politics at Court and University, c.1275–c.1525* (Cambridge: Cambridge University Press, 1999), 68–70, 142. For other books, see Sutton and Visser-Fuchs, *Richard III's Books*, 21–30.

[39] *OED*, *therk, a.*; *MED*, *therk(e)* (adj.), citing Bokenham, *Legendys*, line 2520.

[40] Jean-Philippe Genêt, 'New Politics or New Language? The Words of Politics in Yorkist and Early Tudor England', in *The End of the Middle Ages? England in the Fifteenth and Sixteenth Centuries*, ed. John L. Watts, Fifteenth Century Series, 6 (Stroud: Sutton, 1998), 23–64 (38); Jean-Philippe Genêt (ed.), *Tractatus de regimine principum ad regem Henricum Sextum*, in his *Four English Political Tracts of the Later Middle Ages*, Camden Society, 4th series, 18 (London: Royal Historical Society, 1977), 40–173 (119–20).

> Aftir whom grace folowith. soon from heven sent
> Which in loonge tymes. makith right sure ease.   (prol. 8–11)[41]

Tellingly, at one point later he mistranslates the verb *you teach* as 'remembir' ('doceas', 74, XXII.70). The trust in the exemplary uses of history seems sensible here: to remember the life of Stilicho as it is told in the poem—not as it really was—could teach virtue. In the first half of the poem, Clemency and Faith preach to Stilicho and then there is a survey of his career structured to show the cardinal virtues. The portrait of Stilicho serves to show or rebuke the virtues and vices familiar from other mirrors for princes: clemency and loyalty, lechery and pride (174–90, XXII.160–72).[42] Claudian's poem will not just be rediscovered through the reader's grammatical study; it will also reform the reader.

Could it truly do so? Could the reader learn from a life so different, a thousand years old? The poet sounds uncertain about this moral reading too. The prince 'may' and 'owyn' (*ought to*) learn from the book, but the words betray that he has not actually done so yet; in the prologue, the poet's 'entente' is that the prince will love virtue, but the intention remains only conditional ('moote'). There may be bibliographical reasons for the uncertainty. After all, as in *On Husbondrie*, the reading *by* the duke is less securely evident than the praise *for* him. So A. S. G. Edwards has convincingly argued that *De Consulatu Stilichonis* was meant to be read not by York but by others, to see if they were responsive to its political hints.[43] The manuscript supports this hypothesis. Firstly, the parallel text allows other people to see what it is that York is imagined to be reading, even if they are not literate in Latin. Secondly, although the only manuscript has his coat of arms, the many names on its flyleaves remind us that the prince is seldom the only reader of the mirror for princes (as we saw in Chapter 2). If York did ever handle it, it escaped his hands and was owned or doodled in by other men in the fifteenth and sixteenth centuries.[44] Finally, because of the topos of *go little book* the prologue and epilogue describe York in the third person as 'this prince', rather than with imperatives (prol. 15–21). If he was reading it, it was with others looking over his shoulder. The poem offers not only an exemplum to teach him but a way to describe him.

[41] There may be an echo of these lines in the Latin text of stanza 12 of Bokenham's genealogical 'Dialogue' about York ('Gratia succurat quod longe tempore vivat').

[42] Compare Genêt (ed.), *Tractatus de regimine principum ad regem Henricum Sextum*, for example 128–33 (clemency or *misericordia*), 108–9 (faith), 106–7 (lechery), 56–8 (pride).

[43] Edwards, 'Claudian's *De Consulatu*', 274–5.

[44] BL, MS Additional 11814, f.3r–3v: George 'wayllie'; Thomas, William, and John 'Astun'. This may be Thomas Astun of Outwell, Cambridgeshire (d. 1493), with a son named William, whose will is NA, MS PROB 11/11, f.68r. In 1525 William 'newman' added verses to the back flyleaves (ff.26v–29r). He may be William Newman of Harlow, Essex (d. 1558), whose will is NA, MS PROB 11/43, ff.47r–48r.

ALLUDING TO STILICHO

The description includes of course much outright praise. No fifteenth-century poet would forget to praise his patron, nor would the friars of Clare Priory, who praised York in their painted windows, genealogical rolls, and cartulary. So in his prologue the poet calls York the prince:

> Which of al Engelonde is namyd the defence
> In loonge labourys. ful like to stilico   (prol. 5–6)

Now Stilicho is not so much an exemplum whom York may imitate in the future, but is a sort of extended simile whom York is 'ful like' already. The likeness is observed further:

> Marke stilicoes life. whom peoplis preysed
> with what labouris. of the regions wide
> And Rome hir selfe. the consulat he vpreised
> ffor now the parlement pierys. wher thei goo or ryde
> Seyen the duke of yorke hath god vpon his side
> Amen. amen. blissed Ihesu make this rumour trewe
> And aftir feele peryles. this prince with Ioie endewe.   (prol. 15–21)

We are told to 'Marke' the life of Stilicho because ('ffor') the life of York is going well. Yet there is more vagueness about why and how to 'Marke' Stilicho. Will marking him help York somehow, when he's already doing quite well? Or will it alert us to how great York is, just as Stilicho was? Some likeness is implied, but it is not sketched clearly. Nor could it be: we learn nothing clear about Stilicho except that people loved him, and nothing more. The English poet only translates part of book two of *De Consulatu Stilichonis* and by so doing he omits the survey in book one of the hard work with which Stilicho earned the consulship; all we see is the adulation. And that suits York, to whom the poet ascribes no special achievements beyond an expectant 'rumour'. The peers are not speaking officially in parliament but are chattering on the hoof as they 'goo or ryde'; they merely 'Seyen' that God supports him and the poet must still pray that the rumour come true. All that Stilicho and York share is popularity. York's other achievements and qualities remain suspiciously vague.

They need to be vague because any similarity to a consul one thousand years dead can only be vague. They also need to be vague because York's achievements were rather vague at this time. What had York achieved that was 'ful like' to running an empire? Three critics have examined *De Consulatu Stilichonis* in the light of York's fortunes in 1445, the year in the colophon.

John Watts, in the most detailed analysis, surprisingly rejects the date in the manuscript because York's career in the 1450s seemed to echo Stilicho's instead. Watts interprets the reference to York's 'defence' of England as a reference to his post as Protector of the Realm in 1454, when Henry VI was ill. In the poem York has no technical appointment but is merely 'namyd' or reputed the 'defence' of England. He had been lieutenant of Normandy, which perhaps seemed like a strategic defence of English concerns.[45] But in fact in 1445 York was soon to relinquish the lieutenancy so perhaps, two critics have sensibly suggested, his power seemed waning.[46] Yet we must beware of too much hindsight. In 1445 York was seeking, and looked set to win, an extension of his lieutenancy, and he had recently received many overdue payments and grants; his stock perhaps seemed rising. Nevertheless, the alternative command of John Beaufort in Maine in 1443 had brought him dishonour. Similarly, in summer 1445 the powerful Duke of Suffolk warned parliament that the truce with France might not last, and so he publicly advised York to take advantage of the lull to restock the garrisons; hindsight here reveals that York did not do so. Finally, by 1446 the Keeper of the Privy Seal had visited Normandy to collect evidence for some accusations of malpractice lodged against York.[47] Overall, then, York's position in 1445 was uncertain: he was being rewarded for his lieutenancy in Normandy, but people were beginning to criticize his lieutenancy too. The uncertainty colours the vague account of his triumph as only 'rumour' and praise—nothing more substantial.

It may even be the uncertainty in 1445 to which *De Consulatu Stilichonis* is addressed. A few bureaucratic documents do record York's official response

---

[45] John Watts, '*De Consulatu Stiliconis*: Texts and Politics in the Reign of Henry VI', *JMH*, 16 (1990), 251–66 (252–3, 256–7). C. T. Allmand, *Lancastrian Normandy 1415–1450: The History of a Mediaeval Occupation* (Oxford: Clarendon Press, 1983), 31, 251–4, reports that Normandy was often seen as a strategic defence of England itself.

[46] Edwards, 'Claudian's *De Consulatu*', 274–5; Delany, *Impolitic Bodies*, 137–8. David Starkey, 'Which Age of Reform?', in *Revolution Reassessed: Revisions in the History of Tudor Government and Administration*, ed. Christopher Coleman and David Starkey (Oxford: Clarendon Press, 1986), 13–27 (25), seems to imply that York commissioned *De Consulatu* in order to celebrate his lieutenancy, and seems to cite NA, MS C 54/288, m.20 in support. I failed to find the reference in this document, which covers 1437–8, or in NA, MS C 54/295 or NA, MS C 54/296, which cover 1444–6.

[47] A positive interpretation: Michael K. Jones, 'Somerset, York and the Wars of the Roses', *EHR*, 104 (1989), 285–307 (291). A negative one: *Wars in France*, II.ii.438, II.ii.605–6; Given-Wilson and others (eds.), *Parliament Rolls*, IX.412, and see IX.506–7; Johnson, *Duke Richard*, 41, 77; Michael Jones, 'John Beaufort, Duke of Somerset and the French Expedition of 1443', in *Patronage, the Crown and the Provinces in Later Medieval England*, ed. Ralph A. Griffiths (Gloucester: Sutton, 1981), 79–102 (79–80, 89, 97); Allmand, *Lancastrian Normandy*, 47, 260. T. B. Pugh, 'Richard Plantagenet (1411–60), Duke of York, as the King's Lieutenant in France and Ireland', in *Aspects of Late Medieval Government and Society: Essays Presented to J. R. Lander*, ed. J. G. Rowe (Toronto: University of Toronto Press, 1986), 107–41 (124–5), dates Moleyns's attack earlier.

to the criticism of his lieutenancy.[48] Might the poem make a further oblique comment? Throughout his stormy fortunes, York's followers conducted a sort of whispering campaign. Sometimes they made polemical verses or bills with forthright opinions. His chamberlain, William Oldhall, a landowner in Clare and constable of Clare Castle, was accused of circulating seditious bills in Suffolk in 1453.[49] Sometimes they were more subtle. The king complained of the treasonous gossip from York's loyal 'townes'. His towns could well include Clare: cases of seditious speech seem to have been frequent in Suffolk in 1445 and 1446.[50] In 1450 the king even writes in a letter to York that it is not his actions which are troublesome but the 'straunge langage' people say about him; people are threatening that 'ye schulde take upon you that ye nothir aught nor as we doutenat ye wole not attempte'. Bizarrely, the king does not fear that York will attempt something, and cannot even say what the something is, but he worries about the rumour anyway. York responds by warning the king to 'considere the grett grutchyng and romore' about his governance. To propagate more rumours, these letters between them were then circulated somehow, and copied more widely, as were other of York's letters.[51] In such a climate, rumour might seem the best way to praise York, even if it is a rather vague way. The prologue of *De Consulatu Stilichonis* evokes the sound of rumour, of the voice of the lords, in order to praise York for not much.

In trying not to say much a poem one thousand years out-of-date proves ideal. The similarity between Stilicho and York is so vague that the poem can pass only limited comment upon York's success in Normandy, and therefore any ambition or pride is as deniable as rumour. And yet one part of *De Consulatu Stilichonis* does offer a closer correspondence—once the poet has mistranslated it. This part of Claudian's poem discusses rumour and what cannot be said, and it is transformed into an allusion to the allegations of York's incompetence and embezzlement in Normandy. In Claudian's poem, the goddess of Rome relates how the Eastern Empire elected the eunuch

---

[48] Printed in Kekewich and others (eds.), *Vale's Book*, 180–3.

[49] Rossell Hope Robbins (ed.), *Historical Poems of the XIVth and XVth Centuries* (New York, NY: Columbia University Press, 1959), 201–3, 207–22; Richard Firth Green (ed.), 'An Epitaph for Richard, Duke of York', *Studies in Bibliography*, 41 (1988), 218–24; J. S. Roskell, 'Sir William Oldhall, Speaker in the Parliament of 1450–51', in his *Parliament and Politics in Late Medieval England*, 3 vols. (London: Hambledon, 1981–3), II.175–200 (II.183–6).

[50] R. A. Griffiths (ed.), 'Duke Richard of York's Intentions in 1450 and the Origins of the Wars of the Roses', *JMH*, 1 (1975), 187–209 (204). I. M. W. Harvey, *Jack Cade's Rebellion of 1450* (Oxford: Clarendon Press, 1991), 31–2, mentions much sedition in Suffolk.

[51] Griffiths (ed.), 'Duke Richard of York's Intentions', 189–90, 204, on which see Michael Hicks, 'From Megaphone to Microscope: The Correspondence of Richard Duke of York with Henry VI in 1450 Revisited', *JMH*, 25 (1999), 243–56 (244, 246–8). For other public letters, see Carole Rawcliffe (ed.), 'Richard, Duke of York, the King's "obeisant liegeman": A New Source for the Protectorates of 1454 and 1455', *Historical Research*, 60 (1987), 232–9 (234, 238).

Eutropius as its consul; in response to the disgrace, Stilicho in the West forbade mention of the eunuch's name:

> [...] polluimur. macula quod reris eois
> Omen erat. quamquam nullis mihi cognita rebus
> ffabula uix tanto. risit de crimine rumor
> Opprobriis stat nulla fides. nec littera venit
> Vulgatura nefas. in quo vel maxima virtus
> Est tua [...]
>
> [...] quisquis eous
> Scribere desierit. fastos portenta gabinos
> Ista latent. propriam labem texisse laborent
> Cur ego quem nunquam didici sensi ve reatum
> Gratuler exemptum [...] (XXII.292–310)
>
> [...] we arn put in blame
> That <u>thou</u> excusist the. and seyst <u>thus</u>; the eest peple of þe worlde
> That Ruffyne servid gode fortune had; oo day and with <u>treson</u>
> Steyned my worshippe. but what for this; I knew nevir þis worde <u>trewe.</u>
> The <u>commoun</u> Rumour of foltysh' people; nevir of this sclaundir gladyd
> In such rebukys no feith <u>is had; of credens</u> nevir cam letter
> <u>The</u> to accuse and in this parte; thi grettest worshippe groweth [...]
>
> [...] Thestirlyngis now may be glad; which cessith to write <u>of the.</u>
> Thise vnkouthe slaundrys were nevir herde; amonge þe gabynys <u>true</u>
> Why sholde I ioye a dede exempte; or <u>pardonnyd</u> either of lawe.
> Which nevir I felte ne nevir was lernyd; þat it trespas myght be.   (319–41)

(I have underlined English words not paralleled in the Latin.) The translator makes two errors here. Firstly, he glosses the Eastern Empire's eunuch consul as Rufinus, which is wrong: the passage is about Eutropius. Claudian's poem *In Rufinum* was better known than his *In Eutropium*, and is mentioned in the prose prologue to the Clare copy; once again, an English poet draws on only limited classical learning. Secondly, more oddly, the letters which are vaguely *about to publicize the crime* of appointing a eunuch elsewhere ('Vulgatura nefas') become in English letters specifically composed 'The to accuse', namely *to accuse thee*; twice more the English poet adds a reference to 'the' or *you* as the object of slander (320, 338). In the Latin the rumour concerns the eunuch, who only serves to contrast the wonderful Stilicho; in the English the rumour concerns Stilicho himself, the hero and addressee of the panegyric. Furthermore, the second scribe spotlights the mistranslation by writing in the margin 'deo gracias Ricardo' ('Thanks be to God for Richard') and 'no treson | no pardon'.[52] The poet is clearly talking about something, connected

---

[52] BL, MS Additional 11814, f.20r, by lines 340–1, XXII.309–10.

to York, which cannot be talked about. The classical poem offers a usefully oblique way of talking at all.

Yet the correspondence is not very precise, and it is the only correspondence found in a book a thousand years old. Usually, *De Consulatu Stilichonis* evokes a vaguer likeness between the glories of antiquity and the present. After all, the vaguest likeness is enough to suggest the humanist project of reviving antiquity. The poet says as much in some other lines he mistranslates. Claudian relates that Stilicho has been prompting men of letters to seek honour; under his generous reign there is an equality of opportunity and 'No vertue is hyd' by humble birth if one has 'noble maners':

> [...] egregios. inuitant premia mores
> Hinc prisce redeunt. artes felicibus inde
> Ingeniis aperitur iter. despecta que muse
> Colla leuant. opibus que fluens et pauper eodem
> Nititur ad fructum studio [...]   (XXII.125–29)

> Thy rewardys calle hem to noble maners; and Jentle condicions to vse
> Be thyn excytyng craftys lefte; þat som tyme were wele knowe
> Be had now newly ageyn in mynde; and gladsom wey is openyd
> To happy wittis which evir reioysen; vertue in pryncis high
> The modrys of eloquence the musys ix; which late durst nat loke vp
> Now lefte her neckys and wisely talke; dytees ful delectable.
> Bothe pore and riche labouryd righte sore; encrese to gete with
>   studye [...]   (133–9)

(Again I have underlined words not paralleled in the Latin.) The new consul is 'excytyng' the practitioners of the liberal arts with his virtue, which poets long to eulogize or 'reioysen'. The English poet rejoices quite a lot: excitement is the defining tone of the translation, even more than of the original, as he adds little effusive words here and elsewhere (*gladsome, glad, high, well,* and *great*) with the energy and vacuity of a PR officer.[53] Claudian often describes a new consul's tenure as a period of renewal; that must have been a common wish in late fourth-century Rome; a very similar passage appears in his *Panegyricus dictus Manlio Theodoro Consuli* (XVII.261–9). Yet the English poet transforms the sense of belatedness into the precise humanist history of a classical age, a middle age, and a rebirth. Claudian tells us that under Stilicho's reign the ancient arts simply 'return' ('prisce redeunt. artes'); the English poet expands and says that the arts once had a flourishing period when they 'were wele knowe' but then were actually 'lefte' or abandoned in some darker age and have only 'newly' or 'late' returned. These lines are, broadly, like the praise of Duke Humfrey, and by him of Guarino, that one man inspired others to revive lost eloquence.

---

[53] *De Consulatu*, lines 49, 166 (*glad*), 13, 176 (*high*), 105, 140, 162 (*well*), 75, 95, 123 (*great*).

Bokenham is himself inspired to revive lost eloquence more fully by Stilicho's life than by the saints' lives. He evokes classical verse by using an unrhymed verse form which seems an imitation of the Latin hexameter in its stateliness. The second scribe also expended philological care on the text: he collated and corrected the Latin in a few places, perhaps using the translation as a guide to errors.[54] However, the poet embroiders his poem with extra classical finery: he glosses who the muses are (quoted above), and what the herbs of Circe and the Elysian Fields are (146, XXII.134; 419, XXII.378). These are common interests in humanist poetry: the English *De Mulieribus claris* added comments about the muses 'nyne in nowmbir' and kept Boccaccio's original mention of Circe's poisoned drinks.[55] In *De Consulatu Stilichonis* the fiery sun's compass becomes all that 'phebus seeth', perhaps taking a phrase from Boethius, and men are teased 'with Venus lust' rather than just with youthful stirrings.[56] Once again, Bokenham adorns his work with more of the lazy classical allusions of the Chaucerian tradition, as does the poet of *On Husbondrie*, and as do the other writers of political ephemera in the fifteenth century. His translation is a form of extended allusion designed not to educate York, but to give him a book in a style befitting his grandeur—even if that grandeur, and so the poem's uses for its style, are vague. It is the activities of translation and allusion which themselves suggest the greatness of the present just by recovering antiquity.

THE TRANSLATION OF POWER IN *KNYGHTHODE AND BATAILE*

Another translator from the middle of the fifteenth century, the poet of *Knyghthode and Bataile*, comments further on the use and processes of translating antiquity to glorify the present. This poet translates Vegetius' *Epitoma*

[54] He changed 'succo' to 'lucro', like the English poem's 'lucre', and 'serena' to 'seuera', like the English poem's 'rigorous' (35, XXII.32; 71, XXII.66). He corrected 'videret' to 'iuberet' but the English was based on the error here (156, XXII.144–5). The Clare text is odd but is closest to a group of seven thirteenth-century manuscripts n₁, g, F₁₇, R, J₃, F and P₂, described by J. B. Hall, *Prolegomena to Claudian*, Bulletin of the Institute of Classical Studies: Supplement, 45 (London: Institute of Classical Studies, 1986), 7, 9, 11–12, 20, 23–4.

[55] Schleich (ed.), *Boccaccios De claris mulieribus*, 1429 (not in Boccaccio, *Famous Women*, XLVII.2), 1230–2 (XXXVIII.3: 'infectis veneno poculis'). On *English Poetry, Second Edition* (<http://collections.chadwyck.co.uk/home/home_ep2.jsp>, accessed 22 August 2005), 'Circe' only otherwise appears in Lydgate and Burgh's *Secrees of Old Philisoffres*.

[56] *De Consulatu*, 64 (XXII.60), 'sol igneus ambit', translated more like Boethius, *De Consolatione*, II.m.6.8–10 (Nero rules all men 'Quos videt [...] Phoebus'); *De Consulatu*, 81 (XXII.75), 'luxuriante iuuenta', perhaps misreading the minims in 'iuuenta' as if cognate with 'uenus'.

rei militaris and, like the poet of *On Husbondrie*, he insists upon his fidelity to his source and invites scholarly reading with the tics of Chaucerian classicism and a fiddly page design. However, this poet presents more precise links between his humanist translation and the moment for which he translated. The translation was supposedly presented to Henry VI by some staunch loyalist on 1 March 1460.[57] In a state of military alert and political entrenchment in 1459–60, there was good reason to portray Henry VI reading Vegetius' *Epitoma rei militaris*, a military manual. That winter others tried to make him seem more bellicose than he was usually thought to be. One chronicler, Abbot John Whethamstede, reports that the king read his Vegetius in autumn 1459 before the Battle of Ludford. Whethamstede had mixed political sympathies, and his image of Henry VI reading is open to different interpretations. In the chronicle, the king reads Vegetius and learns that a small but well-trained army can conquer any foe. But, comically, the advice of Vegetius does not encourage the king; he reflects 'rather' or 'better' ('melius') upon recent history and concludes that as his army is ill-trained, despite his reading, he is scuppered. The image of the king reading Vegetius leads to no new thinking or reform; it simply reminds us that the Romans 'subjugated others to their empire' ('suoque imperio subjugabant').[58] That is, like the comparison of York to Stilicho, it hints rather non-committally that the king marches in the footsteps of the ancients, but does not actually teach him how to do so nor prove that he did so. So too in the poem *Knyghthode and Bataile* it is not Vegetius' particular military teaching that matters; what matters instead is the humanist process of recovering the past.

This distinction—between recovering useful lessons, which happen to be ancient, and recovering antiquity for its own sake—emerges if we first compare one of the several earlier French and English versions of this classical work (one of which was discussed in Chapter 1). Writers had for centuries been willing to steal from Vegetius' *Epitoma* without respect for the age and authority of the book: for example, Giles of Rome takes a few snippets from Vegetius but sometimes speaks with open hostility of Vegetius' secularity; Giles of Rome's own readers in turn cited his Vegetian advice but ascribed it merely to Giles himself, displacing the authority of the ancients for

---

[57] Quotations, with parenthetical line numbers, come from R. Dyboski and Z. M. Arend (eds.), *Knyghthode and Bataile*, EETS os 201 (London: Oxford University Press, 1935), with corresponding references to the Latin text in Vegetius, *Epitoma rei militaris*, ed. M. D. Reeve (Oxford: Clarendon Press, 2004). Daniel Wakelin, 'The Occasion, Author and Readers of *Knyghthode and Bataile*', *Medium Ævum*, 73 (2004), 260–72, sketches the context.

[58] *Registrum Abbatiæ Johannis Whethamstede*, I.338–9, citing Vegetius, *Epitoma*, I.i.2–5; on the campaign, see Given-Wilson and others (eds.), *Parliament Rolls*, XII.458–61; Bertram Wolffe, *Henry VI* (London: Methuen, 1981), 319.

that of the schoolmen.[59] When people did acknowledge Vegetius' influence, they were sometimes ambivalent about it. It is often said that Christine de Pizan translates Vegetius' work into French in *Le livre des fais darmes et de chevalerie* (*c*.1410). But in fact de Pizan only uses parts of Vegetius' work and also uses Frontinus' as well as Honoré Bouvet's *L'Arbre des batailles* for much of books II-IV. Yet most interesting is her explanation of why she does not follow 'thauctor' Vegetius. Vegetius has spoken:

en termes generaulx selon les vsages du temps des preux conquereurs passez / assez suffise aux bons entendeurs des choses darmes

in general termes after the manere and vsage of the preu auncyent conquerours past ynough suffysauntly to goode vndrestanders of the thynges of armes

But de Pizan worries that only the 'goode' reader or listener will understand the words of the old writer Vegetius. We must take more detailed instructions on sieges from knights currently expert in such matters:

Neantmoins pour plus particulierement donner enseignement non pas a ceux qui le sceuent comme besoing ne leur en soit / mais a ceulz qui au temps aduenir le pourront bien lire ou oyr par desir de sauoir comme escripture soit chose au monde sicomme perpetuelle nous semble bon de adiouster a nostre dicte euure plus particulierement des choses bonnes et propices en fait de combatre / cite chasteaulz et villes selon les vsages du temps present pour plus ordonner entendible exemple.

¶ Neuertheles for to gyue a more partyculer vndrestandynge / not to theym that knowe hyt / but to theym that in tyme comynge shal mowe rede and here it desyrynge the knowlege therof / ¶ Where the scrypture in bokes is a thynge perpetual as to the worlde / it semeth me goode to adde in thys oure sayde werke more partyculerly thoo thinges that be goode and propyce to assaylle Cytees Castelles and Townes after the manere and waye of the tyme present for to gyue therof a more Intellygyble example [...][60]

She synthesizes modern knowledge with classical texts. However, she insists that the old texts be comprehensible or 'Intellygyble', ready to be applied to 'a more partyculer vndrestandynge'. Vegetius' antiquity is not a source of reverence but instead renders his counsel too arcane, better suited to men already learned. For de Pizan, all that distinguishes his wisdom is simply that it is written down: if this advantage were transferred to current experience, it too

---

[59] Vegetius is the main influence on *The Governance of Kings and Princes: John Trevisa's Middle English Translation of the* De regimine principum *of Aegidius Romanus*, ed. David C. Fowler, Charles F. Briggs, and Paul G. Remley (New York, NY: Garland, 1997), III.iii; but see the criticism of classical sources in I.i.10, I.ii.23. See the references to Giles of Rome, not Vegetius, in Frank Taylor and John S. Roskell (eds. and trans.), *Gesta Henrici Quinti* (Oxford: Clarendon Press, 1975), 28, 40; and Genêt (ed.), *Tractatus de regimine principum*, 83–5.

[60] Christine de Pizan, *Lart de cheualerie selon Vegece* (Paris: Verard, 1488; classmark BL IB.41088), sig. f6r-v; William Caxton (trans.), *The Book of Fayttes of Armes and of Chyualrye*, ed. A. T. P. Byles, EETS os 189 (London: Oxford University Press, 1932), 152:32–153:22.

would acquire the patina of authority. New science may prove better than old books. In works such as this one, then, the teaching of Vegetius had long been absorbed and conflated in ways which conceal or reject his classical origins.

This amnesia does not afflict the poet of *Knyghthode and Bataile*. This poet advertises his dependence on a source. Firstly, like *On Husbondrie*, this poem conjures the tone of Latin by using a tortuous grammar, with ablative absolutes and gerundives, and a sesquipedalian phraseology. The vocabulary is even more Latin than the Latin is, with some long words used in English when no like words occur in the original: 'apostata', 'coacte', 'evitatioun' (1787, 2464, 3006). Some other words get extended in English with Latin prefixes: the Latin 'vigilantibus' soldiers become 'pervigilaunt' in English and their 'longioribus' fingers become 'elongaunt' (244–6; I.vi.4).[61] Like *On Husbondrie* again, the poem has an index, with numbered pages and lettered stanzas, and marginal notes, all of which invite a scholarly reading. The index sometimes highlights the book's antiquity. Of 129 entries in the index, five gloss the word listed, six direct us to explanations of obsolete equipment like the tortoise, and nineteen direct us to lines where the poet gives glosses or etymologies or comments on the work of translating:

> Antiquytee denamed hem Triayrys,
> In theym, as in the thridde, al to repayre is. (1858–9)

> Cohors the Latyn is, this regioun
> Tenglish it fore, help vs, good Lord! (707–8)

English humanists often glossed the military vocabulary in their classical texts, as if it were especially difficult; and the readers of English and French translations of Vegetius, or Frontinus too, did likewise.[62] Yet the purpose behind the glosses woven into *Knyghthode and Bataile* is not only to elucidate difficulties, but also to highlight the alterity of his text. Is it too fanciful to suggest that the revival of an ancient text offers a hopeful symbol for the revival of the king's power?

---

[61] Derek Pearsall, *Old English and Middle English Poetry* (London: Routledge Kegan Paul, 1977), 240–2, discusses the style. According to *OED, MED*, and Chadwick-Healey's *English Poetry, Second Edition* (<http://collections.chadwyck.co.uk/home/home_ep2.jsp>, accessed 22 August 2005), *evitacioun* appears first here, *elongaunt* only here. *Coact* is rare but does occur in other humanist translations: Lydgate, *Fall*, II.1941; *On Husbondrie*, XII.174 (*coart* but surely meaning *coact*); an English translation of Petrarch's *Secretum*, in Wilson and Fenlon (eds.), *Winchester*, f.19v.

[62] For example, Oxford, Balliol College, MS 121, f.iv^(r-v) (list of Roman officers of state; Valerius Maximus owned by Richard Bole); Oxford, Balliol College, MS 123, ff.159v–167v (glossary, with many military words; Sallust, owned by Richard Bole); BL, MS Additional 12028, f.170v (glossary to Frontinus in French); OMC, MS lat. 30, ff.35v–36r, f.45r, f.47r, f.54r, f.56v, and CUL, MS Additional 8706, f.30v, described in *n.* 29 in Chapter 1 above.

The poet of *Knyghthode and Bataile* says almost as much, when he spells out why one should follow the ancients, in book I. Vegetius notes the dearth of heroes today: whom can one find to teach what has been forgotten?

Quem invenias qui docere possit quod ipse non didicit? De historiis ergo vel libris nobis antiqua consuetudo repetenda est.   (I.viii.7)

Haec necessitas compulit evolutis auctoribus ea me in hoc opusculo fidelissime dicere quae Cato ille Censorius de disciplina militari scripsit, quae Cornelius Celsus, quae Frontinus perstringenda duxerunt, quae Paternus diligentissimus iuris militaris assertor, in libros redegit, quae Augusti et Traiani Adrianique constitutionibus cauta sunt.   (I.viii.10–12)

> How may I lerne of hym that is vnlerned,
> How may a thing informal fourme me?
> Thus I suppose is best to be gouerned:
> Rede vp thistories of auctoritee,
> And how thei faught, in theym it is to se,
> Or better thus: Celsus Cornelius
> Be red, or Caton, or Vegetius.
>
> Vegetius it is, that I entende
> Aftir to goon in lore of exercise, [...]   (306–14)

How could *Knyghthode and Bataile* learn from Vegetius if Vegetius was confessedly 'vnlerned'? Vegetius denies any authority of his own but *Knyghthode and Bataile* builds it up again, by adding references to Vegetius as if he were as learned as his own teachers.[63] Yet the references to Vegetius remind the reader that this book is a translation. This reminder is important, for the poem hinges upon the idea of reviving one's fortunes by turning not to military books especially, but to old books. Vegetius himself explains that wretchedness and internal dissent plague rebels and heretics (1671–77) and that the Lancastrians can shed despair by looking to the past for inspiration:

Unum illud est in hoc opere praedicendum, ut nemo desperet fieri posse quae facta sunt [...]   (III.x.13)

> Oon thinge heryn is wisely to be seyn,
> Of this matier that ther noman dispayre;
> As hath be doon, it may be doon ayeyn; [...]   (1678–80)

This line was one of inspiration to other Lancastrians as their fortunes fell. At the end of Fortescue's *De Laudibus legum Angliae*, the exiled Lancastrian

---

[63] Christopher Allmand, 'The *De re militari* of Vegetius in the Middle Ages and the Renaissance', in *Writing War: Medieval Literary Responses to Warfare*, ed. Corinne Saunders, Françoise Le Saux, and Neil Thomas (Cambridge: Brewer, 2004), 15–28 (15), notes Vegetius' sources.

Prince Edward quotes this line from Vegetius to stir his confidence.[64] The poet of *Knyghthode and Bataile*, reading Vegetius further, can go further. Next Vegetius relates how through centuries of peace and prosperity the Romans have neglected the arts of warfare. The English poet mistranslates these lines to mention the recent Lancastrian defeats at St Albans and at Blore Heath (1685–7). Yet then comes the promise that the defeated army can revive through humanist reading:

Apud veteres ars militaris in oblivionem saepius venit, sed prius a libris repetita est, postea ducum auctoritate firmata.   (III.x.18)

> Seyde ofte it is: the wepon bodeth peax,
> And in the londe is mony a chiualere,
> That ha grete exercise doubtlesse
> And think I wil that daily wil thei lere,
> And of antiquitee the bokys here,
> And that thei here, putte it in deuoyre,
> That desperaunce shal fle comynge espoyre.   (1692–8)

The English poet simplifies the process of imitating the past. Vegetius in fact says that, 'military skill more frequently came to be forgotten among former generations' and was only later 'recovered again from books and afterwards regulated'. By contrast, the translator forgets the forgetfulness of former men and makes them shining models of wisdom. Moreover, his choice of word is telling: he does not talk of the past in general ('Apud ueteres') but of a specific 'antiquitee', a word he uses six more times. By contrast, the 1408 translator of Vegetius never used this word, well established in English, but translated *antiquus* blandly as *old*.[65] The hope that Roman warfare could be studied and then imitated was a common simplification among humanists, as in Leonardo Bruni's *De Militia*, for example.[66]

The poem thus effects a *translatio imperii*. This myth of the 'transfer of power' westwards, from Babylon through Rome and France to England finally, was a familiar trope in fifteenth-century England.[67] Close to the poem in place and personnel is a pageant made for Margaret of Anjou at Coventry in 1456.

[64] Fortescue, *De Laudibus*, 137.
[65] *Knyghthode and Bataile*, 833, 1159, 1263, 1384, 1858, 2743. Compare Geoffrey Lester (ed.), *The Earliest English Translation of Vegetius' De Re Militari*, Middle English Texts, 21 (Heidelberg: Winter, 1988), for example 81:3 (II.iv.3), 88:22 (II.xiii.2), and *MED, antiquite*.
[66] See the introduction to *War and Society in Renaissance Florence: The De Militia of Leonardo Bruni*, ed. C. C. Bayley (Toronto: University of Toronto Press, 1961), 178–81, 202–5, 209.
[67] A. G. Jongkees, 'Translatio studii: les avatars d'un thème médiéval', in *Miscellanea Mediaevalia in memoriam Jan Frederik Niermeyer*, ed. D. P. Blok and others (Groningen: Wolters, 1967), 41–51; with fifteenth-century examples in Anstey (ed.), *Epistolae*, I.53–4; *Bekynton Correspondence*, II.318–19.

Here, the Nine Worthies greet the queen, including Caesar claiming to be 'souerayne of knyghthode | And emperour of mortall men' and claiming that her young son 'Shall succede me yn worship'. The pageant constantly repeats the terms *Emperor, Empress,* and *Empire* to describe the ancient heroes, but also the English king, queen, and their realm.[68] In the pageant the myth of *translatio imperii* imagines a torch passed from realm to realm: in *Knyghthode and Bataile* the torch has been extinguished and must be relit. That is what has been called a 'recursive' turn to the past, patterning the present on what is lost, and it differs from earlier 'exegetical' translations which transformed texts to meet changing needs over time.[69] Yet in fact the recursion is what is needed: by imagining a simple transfer from past to present, and by creating the transfer in a close and Latinate translation, the poet enacts a sort of obedience and fidelity to the past, an obedience which anchors the present.

POLEMICAL AND CIVIL TRANSLATION IN *KNYGHTHODE AND BATAILE*

Yet the process of translation is more complex than that, because the act of reading introduces uncertainty into it. The reader can follow his text or diverge from it; he can intend to use the text for one reading but the text may invite another. There is some of this uncertainty in the poet's reading of Vegetius. Firstly, the stylistic imitation of the source obscures the fact that, unlike *On Husbondrie, Knyghthode and Bataile* is not very faithful to the source in substance; the professed fidelity is a sham. There is very little method to his changes: he does not omit obsolete matter, like that in book II, as Christine de Pizan and other readers of Vegetius did.[70] Instead, the poet conflates different

---

[68] R. W. Ingram (ed.), *Records of Early English Drama: Coventry* (Toronto: University of Toronto Press, 1981), 33:6–34, 30:9, 30:16, 32:11. Actually, after Julius Caesar's conclusion, Godfrey of Bouillon later offers a godly coda to the pageant, urging a crusade.

[69] The terms come from Simpson, *Reform,* 81–6, and Rita Copeland, *Rhetoric, Hermeneutics, and Translation in the Middle Ages: Academic Traditions and Vernacular Texts* (Cambridge: Cambridge University Press, 1991), 61.

[70] For example, *Knyghthode and Bataile* records the obsolete Roman military institutions in book II (642–69, II.i; 705–851, II.vi–II.viii), which other readers little used: compare Josette A. Wisman, 'L'*Epitoma rei militaris* de Végèce et sa fortune au Moyen Âge', *Le Moyen Âge,* 85 (1979), 13–31 (27–31), and the mere 12 of 89 excerpts from book II in [Jean de Rovroy(?) (trans.)], 'Aucuns notables extraitz du livre de Vegece', ed. Leena Löfstedt, *Neuphilologische Mitteilungen,* 83 (1982), 297–312 (301–2, 306–7), or the mere four out of fifty excerpts in the Italian manuscript BodL, MS Auct. F.5.22, ff.1r–3v.

parts of the source and abbreviates or expands it willy-nilly. Most of the changes only appear when one painstakingly analyses *Knyghthode and Bataile* alongside its source. But some misreadings in book IV are immediately visible because they are influenced by the politics of 1460. The pressure of events on the reader makes him mistranslate.

In book IV Vegetius delves into meteorology and lists Greek and Latin names of the winds which vex naval commanders. Other translators took shelter from these obscure names: for example, in a French translation Jean de Meun here made his only divergence from the Latin to admit his bafflement.[71] By contrast, *Knyghthode and Bataile*'s poet faces the cardinal and lateral winds with gusto:

> How thei amonge hem self discorde, is couth.
>
> Theest cardinal is called subsolan,
> And on his lifte hond hath he Sir Vulturne, [...]
>
> Auster is cardinal meridian,
> Nothus ful grymly goth on his right side,
> And Chorus on the [lift] hond forth thei han,
> And Zephirus that cardinal, abide
> Wil in the west, and when him list to ride,
> Grete Affricus shal ride on his right honde,
> And Duk Fauonius on his lift honde.
>
> If ·III· or oon or tweyne of these vp blowe,
> Tethis, of hir nater that is tranquylle,
> Thei lene vppon, oppresse and ouerthrowe,
> And causeth al crye out that wold be stille; [...]
>
> Sum varyaunce of tyme will refreyne
> Her cruelous and feers rebellioun,
> A nothir helpith hem to shake her cheyne
> As all the firmament shuld falle adoun
> And Occian lepe ouer Caleys Toun; [...]   (2671–97)

The poet creates a vivid picture through personifying the classical winds as over-mighty lords who 'oppresse and ouerthrowe' the nymph Tethys. Vegetius' advice about meteorology becomes a political allegory as the plain storms ('turbinum') become 'discorde' whipping the waves into 'feers rebellioun' (IV.xxxviii.1). The poet describes a threat to the sea, shield of an island nation, and to Calais, England's first line of defence. There was a threat: the town of

---

[71] Jean de Meun (trans.), *Li Abregemenz noble honme Vegesce Flave René des establissemenz apartenanz a chevalerie*, ed. Leena Löfstedt, Annales Academiæ Scientiarum Fennicæ, series B, 200 (Helsinki: Suomalainen Tiedeakatemia, 1977), IV.xxxviii:14–20, IV.xxxviii.36–8; there were other additions, made by an early 'editor' (11–13).

Calais had been captured by the Earl of Warwick to serve as a pirate fortress.[72] Under pressure of these events the poet of *Knyghthode and Bataile* has stopped translating Vegetius' practical tips for naval warfare; he uses the classical text merely as a pretext to allude to current events. What is striking is that neither the storm, the personification, the nymph, nor the political puns occur in the Latin. There may be a looser classical allusion, to book I of Virgil's *Aeneid*, where the journey of Aeneas to found the Roman Empire is diverted by an envious goddess and the winds Aeolus, Eurus, and others, until Jupiter quells the storm, angry that the winds have provoked a storm without his command. Many readers have found there echoes of other rebellions, from Richard II's day onwards.[73] Moreover, others described the civil upsets of Warwick in Calais and the Yorkist rebellion in similar terms. Whethamstede described 'Favonius' blowing Warwick's ships to Calais and Neptune blessing his escapades. In 1461, a year later, the Yorkist George Neville ended a letter to Francesco Coppini about the recent civil battles by hoping that the storms would subside and a calmer breeze would waft the Yorkists into harbour at last.[74] So although the poet cuts the real classical text of Vegetius, he adds the pseudo-classical allusions—to Tethys, Duke Favonius, and so on—preferred in other political writing of the time.

Moreover, while the pseudo-classical allusions of the time were used for flattery and insinuation, the ones in this poem get used for worse things still, for vicious hatred and a partisan triumphalism. The metaphor of the kidnap or rape of Tethys is sinister, as is the glee over the Yorkists defeated and tossed overboard 'fisshes forto fede' (2896, IV.xliv.9)—one grisly titbit which does come from the source! But is the translator only showing off to his prince and loyal friends? Is this all he is doing? As a translator, he exploits the freedom of the reader to reinterpret his source for new occasions, yet the 'freedom' cuts both ways. Theoretical thinkers about reading often celebrate the power of the reader to appropriate a text.[75] But they are less vocal about the disruptive power of a text to appropriate the reader, we might say, to infiltrate and surprise the mind. The reader might begin with one intention but find

[72] G. L. Harriss, 'The Struggle for Calais: An Aspect of the Rivalry between Lancaster and York', *EHR*, 75 (1960), 30–53, and Colin F. Richmond, 'The Earl of Warwick's Domination of the Channel and the Naval Dimension to the Wars of the Roses, 1456–1460', *Southern History*, 20 (1999), 1–19, explain the background.

[73] Virgil, *Aeneid*, I.50–156, in *Eclogues, Georgics, Aeneid I–VI*, trans. H. Rushton Fairclough (Cambridge, MA: Harvard University Press, 1974). Compare Christopher Baswell, 'Aeneas in 1381', *NML*, 5 (2002), 7–58 (23–5).

[74] *Registrum Abbatiæ Johannis Whethamstede*, I.330–1, I.345; *Calendar of State Papers [...] of Venice. Volume I*, ed. Brown, 100–1 (no. 370).

[75] For a passionate but one-sided account, see Michel de Certeau, *The Practice of Everyday Life*, trans. Steven Rendall (Berkeley, CA: University of California Press, 1984), 165–76.

that the unpredictable process of reading leads him far from that intention or subverts it, perhaps without his recognition. This is what happens to the writer of *Knyghthode and Bataile*, who reads Vegetius to glorify his king, but finds himself translating quite different material. Even the topos of the sea in rebellion can be interpreted variously. When the battle and storm finally abate, the king appears as a master mariner:

> This Reume in Thoccian of propur kynde
> Withoute wynde hath his commotioun,
> The maryner therof may not be blinde,
> But whenne and where in euery regioun
> It regneth, he moste haue inspectioun; [...]
>
> The Maister Marynere, the gouernour,
> He knoweth euery cooste in his viage
> And port saluz; and forthi grete honour
> He hath, as worthi is, and therto wage. (2777–94)

Like Jupiter, the governor settles the disturbance of 'propur kynde' or natural, hereditary rule. Yet what seems like an absolutist or even imperial allegory also entails some responsibility or even obligation for the governor: he 'may not' be blind to the chaos brewing and 'moste' be alert. The words 'forthi' (*as a result*) and 'therto' make honour dependent upon service: it is only because he knows how to protect his crew that he wins his 'wage' and 'honour'. The topos of the king as a naval commander not only conveys his absolute authority but also his absolute commitment to the realm.

Yet these lines again mistranslate Vegetius' more practical account of the navy, when the poet transforms the *gubernator* or steersman into 'the gouernour'. This is a common metaphor for the good ruler. An army or a ship offers a perfect analogy for a political community: in these tightly knit units, even the loftiest man must contribute towards the common 'salus' or well-being—perhaps echoed here in the 'port saluz'; a selfish tyrant would flounder at sea. The metaphor of the steersman as ruler appears in the writings of Aristotle and Cicero and was popular with philosophers in the thirteenth and fourteenth centuries; it also appears in English poems and pamphlets of the fifteenth century.[76] In *Knyghthode and Bataile*, the metaphor lets the poet reflect upon the rule of Henry VI. Although several writers responded to the decay of Henry VI's rule by stressing obedience and the king's absolute power, others did defend the king's obligations in return. Even the loyal

[76] M. S. Kempshall, *The Common Good in Late Medieval Political Thought* (Oxford: Clarendon Press, 1999), 39, 45, 153–5. See Robbins (ed.), *Historical Poems*, 191–3; *Wars in France*, II.ii.605–6 (Normandy's complaint); BL, MS Arundel 249, ff.6v–7v (lyric on Henry VI sailing home to aid the commonweal); Fortescue, *De Laudibus*, 50, 168.

Sir John Fortescue remembered the old piety that the king was servant of the servants of God, ruling for the realm and not vice versa. The king's obligation was particularly strong in the task of military protection from enemies without and within. The usually absolutist George Ashby warned the king to have 'Inspeccion' of trouble brewing which could harm the commonweal, a phrase similar to that quoted from *Knyghthode and Bataile*.[77] Finally, the poet of *Knyghthode and Bataile* also voices a sense of the king's obligation. By 1 March 1460 Henry VI had still not brought the civil war to an end, and the poet says so, when he sights his home town of Calais but cannot dock there:

> Hail, porte saluz! with thi pleasaunt accesse,
> Alhail Caleis! ther wolde I faynest londe;
> That may not I [−] oo, whi so? for thei distresse
> Alle, or to deye or with her wrong to stonde. [...]
>
> O litil case, o pouere hous, my poort
> Saluz thou be, vntil that ayer amende,
> That is to sey, vntil an other soort
> Gouerne there, that by the kyng be sende.   (2980–90)

The poet, who says in the prologue that he is a parson of Calais (33), cannot return home until the stormy 'ayer' of sedition is dispelled by someone sent by the king. The Duke of Somerset had been indentured to recover the town on 9 October 1459 but had failed to do so.[78] The translator, then, has interpreted Vegetius' master mariner in the light of wider philosophical tradition, of ideas of kingship among the Lancastrians and of his personal predicament. He reads his source with freedom.

Yet his freedom is not whimsy or incompetence: he develops his reading consistently elsewhere in the poem. For example, just before he encourages us that ancient wonders may be revived, he stresses that military reforms will also bring civil renewal:

Quis autem dubitet artem bellicam rebus omnibus esse potiorem, per quam libertas retinetur et dignitas, propagantur provinciae, conservatur imperium? [...]

Dux ergo cui tantae potestatis insignia tribuuntur, cuius fidei atque virtuti possessorum fortunae, tutela urbium, salus militum, rei publicae creditur gloria, non tantum pro universo exercitu sed etiam pro singulis contubernalibus debet esse sollicitus. Si quid enim illis eveniat in bello, et ipsius culpa et publica videtur iniuria.   (III.x.2, 4–5)

---

[77] Watts, *Henry VI*, 39–41; Fortescue, *De Laudibus*, 88–90; Fortescue, *Governance of England*, 116, 127, with sources on 201–2; George Ashby, *The Active Policy of a Prince*, in his *Poems*, ed. Mary Bateson, EETS es 76 (London: Kegan Paul, Trench, Trübner, 1899), 12–41 (lines 772–8).

[78] Harriss, 'The Struggle for Calais', 48–9.

Certeyn it is, that knyghthode and bataile
So stronge is it, that therby libertee
Receyued is with encreste and availe;
Therby the Croune is hol in Maiestee
And vche persone in his dignitee,
Chastised is therby rebellioun,
Rewarded and defensed is renoun.

Forthi the duke, that hath the gouernaunce,
Therof may thinke he is a Potestate,
To whom betakyn is the prosperaunce
Of al a lond and euerych Estate.
The Chiualers, if I be fortunate,
The Citesens, and alle men shal be
If I gouerne wel, in libertee.

And if a faut is founden in my dede,
Not oonly me, but al the commyn wele
So hurteth it, that gretly is to drede
Dampnatioun, though noman with me dele; [...]   (1622–39)

In translating these lines, he shifts the emphasis from military to civic
life. He ignores the desire to increase one's external colonies or provinces
('propagantur provinciae') and ignores the praise of the military arts as being
better than statecraft ('rebus omnibus esse potiorem'). He instead lists the
three civil benefits of warfare. For both him and Vegetius, warfare can halt
rebellion. For Vegetius, it can preserve liberty ('libertas retinetur'), but for the
translator it can increase liberty further. For Vegetius, the leader of the army,
protects his men in war ('illis [...] in bello'), but for the translator he protects
the citizens and the whole commonweal. Moreover, the translator's choice of
words—*potestate, liberty, citizen, commonweal*, and *fault*—evoke the military
life less than they evoke the concepts of contemporary urban government. It
has been said that Thomas More's political thought may reflect the nature of
London government; similarly, this poem, presented after the king entered the
city of London, may echo local legal traditions.[79] Most strikingly, the insignia
of power ('potestatis insignia') are translated into 'Potestate', a term which
recurs later (1954, III.xviii.1). The 'Potestate' sounds more like the elected
podestà of an Italian city state. The term was familiar: an English translation
of Giles of Rome rendered the Italian republican *podestà* as 'a potestate oþer

---

[79] *OED, citizen*, 1(a), 2; *MED, citisein*, 1, 2; *OED, liberty, n.*^{1}, 1(a), 2(a), 7; *MED, liberte*, 2(b),
4; Sarah Rees Jones, 'Thomas More's "Utopia" and Medieval London', in *Pragmatic Utopias:
Ideals and Communities, 1200–1630*, ed. Rosemary Horrox and Sarah Rees Jones (Cambridge:
Cambridge University Press, 2001), 117–35 (119). *Citizens* may imply a citizen militia, an
important feature of Vegetius' army and of humanist theories of war.

a lord' who must help others 'as heere astat axeþ', just as *Knyghthode and Bataile*'s 'potestate' must help 'vche persone in his dignitee'.[80] The translator misreads the Roman text through a fifteenth-century civic lens.

Yet this misreading of Vegetius as a manual of contractual government is not so mistaken here. The lines about the military commander, like the lines about the master mariner, are overall fairly close to the Latin; they are certainly a closer translation than is the partisan story of the storm at sea, Tethys, and her tormentors. These lines reproduce, too, the tone of firm instruction found throughout Vegetius' book, which is composed as a set of rules issued with a firm command to powerful men. Overall, by borrowing the advice of an imperial administrator, Vegetius, to the empire's generals, the poet borrows a voice which imposes duty—but speaks in that voice to the king. The teacherly tone may be allowed, given that it is glorious to be seen to learn from the ancients; it is no diminution of prestige to be a humanist student. But, overall, the thorough reading and translation of a classical text has disrupted the usual plundering of the classics for flattery and ornament. As a form of reading, the humanist translation is not necessarily superficial or prince-pleasing. The fleeting allusions often serve to glorify the speaker or the listener, and some more extended classical comparisons can do the same. But even in *De Consulatu Stilichonis*, Stilicho is praised for serving the 'peas of commoun welthe', when no such phrase appears in the Latin (27; XXII.25). Some humanist readers or translators, if only at some times, find in their books support for good government and responsibility to the commonweal, and they find it simply by reading the classics closely.

---

[80] *Trevisa's Aegidius Romanus*, 326:2–12 (III.ii.2); *OED, potestate*, 3. *MED, potestate*, omits the Italian sense and glosses the word in *Knyghthode and Bataile* as a 'A ruler, Lord; an individual possessing power or authority, a superior'. *Knyghthode and Bataile*, 154, also uses the word for a rank of angel.

4

William Worcester and the commonweal
of readers

Although many classical allusions and translations offer specious praise and
fanciful rhetoric, the poet of *Knyghthode and Bataile* also began to read—or
rather to misread—Vegetius' *Epitoma* and to find in it a conception of royal
commitment to the commonweal, a conception which contrasted his work to
glorify the king. However, a self-professed translation is a little more restricted
in its freedom to misread than are looser responses to classical literature;
writers in other genres can go further. They do so, however, with a similar
set of conceptions about public service. A political treatise called *The Boke
of Noblesse* also quotes Vegetius' lesson in military responsibility as a lesson
in domestic rule: to the military leader is committed the care of the army,
whereas 'a prince is office' is 'the gouernaunce of comon publique' which
'is clepid vulgarilie the comon profite'. But, unlike a translation, *The Boke
of Noblesse* can draw upon more, and more diffuse, models of serving the
'comon profite' or commonweal. In fact, when *The Boke of Noblesse* seems
to quote Vegetius, it quotes instead Christine de Pizan's *Le livre des fais
darmes et de chevalerie*.[1] However, if in *The Boke of Noblesse* the model of
serving the commonweal does not only come from classical reading-matter,
nevertheless the activity of humanist reading constitutes the commonweal or
community.

It is possible to see *The Boke of Noblesse* within a community of read-
ers, because the reader who made it left more traces than others did.
The Boke of Noblesse was composed by the scholar William Worcester
(1415–*c*.1483), sometime secretary to the war veteran Sir John Fastolf of
Caister (*c*.1380–1459). Unlike the imagined readers of other translations,
Worcester is very much a real reader whose activities, books, and companions

---

[1] All parenthetical page numbers come from [Worcester], *Noblesse*, here citing 55; however,
the quotations use the spelling and punctuation of the original manuscript, BL, MS Royal 18. B.
xxii. Compare Vegetius, *Epitoma rei militaris*, ed. M. D. Reeve (Oxford: Clarendon Press, 2004),
III.x.2–5, and Christine de Pizan, *Lart de cheualerie selon Vegece* (Paris: Verard, 1488; classmark
BL IB.41088), sig. b7v (I.xv).

in learning we can track. Some six rough notebooks survive to record his reading, four of them in an unusual elongated format, often called a holster book. The notebooks contain manorial records, topographical facts and memoranda from his travels between 1478 and 1480, medicine, and military and political memoranda.[2] Besides his notebooks, still surviving are twenty-three manuscripts with marginalia or at least an *ex libris* in his distinctive handwriting. In his notebooks and marginalia, he shows his catholic tastes: chronicles, which are sources for parts of *The Boke of Noblesse*, astronomy, calendrical science, and other subjects.[3] However, both his notebooks and his marginalia reveal his extensive study of classical antiquity. The most important evidence for Worcester's humanist study is in two notebooks, British Library, MS Royal 13.C.i (cited here as 'Ro') and in the holster book, British Library, MS Cotton Julius F.vii (cited here as 'Ju'). The former is a bulky set of chronicles and notes on classical history; the latter book is Worcester's own set of notes on classical and historical subjects. In it, he plunders Guarino's *Floriferus ortus* for extracts of Terence and plunders the highlights from book I of Ovid's *De Arte amandi*; he also compiles lists of texts or *incipits* from Statius, Lucan, and Cicero.[4] Beyond them, he also owned or annotated manuscripts in humanist hands of Cassiodorus and Diodorus Siculus, and ancient Greek tragedies and verse.[5] He also read or owned Boccaccio's *De Casibus virorum illustrium*, a French translation of the pseudo-Senecan *Des Quatre vertus cardinaulx*, and Chaucer's translation *Boece* (the latter noted in Chapter 1 above).[6] Twentieth-century accounts often used Worcester as the 'medieval' ignoramus against whom the famous humanists such as Free and Tiptoft were defined, and his grammar and handwriting are ugly. However, even Roberto Weiss, who criticized Worcester's Latin, grudgingly conceded that

---

[2] BL, MS Additional 28208, discussed by G. Poulett Scrope, *History of the Manor and Ancient Barony of Castle Combe* (London: privately printed, 1852), 262–6; CCCC, MS 210, partly edited in Worcestre, *Itineraries*, and William Worcestre [*sic*], *The Topography of Medieval Bristol*, ed. Frances Neale, Bristol Record Society's Publications, 51 (Bristol: Bristol Record Society, 2000); BL, MS Sloane 4; London, College of Arms, MS Arundel 48.

[3] For example: BL, MS Cotton Julius E.iv (4), BL, MS Royal 13.C.i, ff.62r–130r, and London, College of Arms, MS M.9, ff.31r–66r (chronicles); BodL, MS Laud misc. 674 (astronomy); 'The Chronicle of John Somer, OFM', ed. Jeremy Catto and Linne Mooney, in *Camden Miscellany XXXIV: Chronology, Conquest and Conflict in Medieval England*, Camden Society 5th series, 10 (Cambridge: Cambridge University Press, 1997), 197–285 (213–14 on calendars). Daniel Wakelin, 'William Worcester Writes a History of his Reading', *NML*, 7 (2005), 53–71 (71), lists his books.

[4] Ju ff.105r–111v, ff.20r–21r, f.59r, ff.3r–5v, ff.22r–23v, ff.49r–54v. The excerpts he claims are Traversari's translation of Diogenes Laertius (Ju ff.93r–96v, ff.99r–101r) do not come from that work, for they mention authors who lived centuries after Diogenes Laertius.

[5] OMC, MS lat. 166, flyleaf f.iv^v; OBC, MS 124, f.242v; BodL, MS Auct. F.3.25., f.1v.

[6] OMC, MS lat. 198, flyleaf f.ii^v; CUL, MS Additional 7870, f.30v.

his notebooks reveal how many Italian humanist texts circulated in Yorkist England.[7] His marginalia and notebooks invite us to include his reading and writing within a history of humanism in England.

Finally, from Worcester's reading emerged two important surviving works: a translation of Cicero's *De Senectute*; and the prose political treatise *The Boke of Noblesse*. K. B. McFarlane's rigorous biography of Worcester convincingly argued for his authorship of *The Boke of Noblesse*, and some close correspondences (noted below) between this work and Worcester's marginalia confirm the attribution.[8] McFarlane also cautiously proposed that Worcester composed *The Boke of Noblesse* in stages: a reference to Charles VII of France (d. 1461) as living and some passages of heated lament suggest that he first composed it soon after the loss of the French territories in the 1450s. He then revised it for rededication to Edward IV when Edward IV decided to renew the wars in France in the mid-1470s. One final revision is more visible: the only manuscript, British Library, MS Royal 18.B.xxii, was originally a fair copy in a professional-looking late fifteenth-century secretary hand, but it now has many marginal rubrics and several marginal and interlinear additions in Worcester's own hand, and he dates these additions to 15 June 1475. A collection of documents about the English campaigns in Normandy in London, Lambeth Palace Library, MS 506, probably once accompanied *The Boke of Noblesse* as a factual supplement to it.

The revisions suggest that, in this case, *The Boke of Noblesse* itself is really a 'work in progress', a witness to Worcester's reading, writing, and revising. Therefore, this chapter places it among the processes of Worcester's reading, re-reading, and rewriting. How do his studies of antiquity feed his political concerns? Is his humanist reading exemplary or eulogistic, like that advocated in *De Consulatu Stilichonis*, say? In fact, Worcester rejects such a seemingly simple but actually problematic imitation of antiquity. Instead, his reading of the classics is political not only in the ideals he finds in the books, but also in the processes of reading those books, and of transmitting his knowledge to a new readership.

---

[7] R. J. Mitchell, *John Free: From Bristol to Rome in the Fifteenth Century* (London: Longmans, Green, 1955), 12–14; Weiss, *Humanism*, 177–8.

[8] K. B. McFarlane, 'William Worcester: A Preliminary Survey', in his *England in the Fifteenth Century: Collected Essays*, ed. G. L. Harriss (London: Hambledon, 1981), 199–224 (212–15). Anne F. Sutton and Livia Visser-Fuchs, 'Richard III's Books: XII. William Worcester's *Boke of Noblesse* and his Collection of Documents on the War in Normandy', *The Ricardian*, 9 (1991), 154–65 (155–7), and Christopher Allmand, 'France-Angleterre à la Fin de la Guerre de Cent Ans: Le 'Boke of Noblesse' de William Worcester', in *La 'France Anglaise' au Moyen Âge* (Paris: CTHS, 1988), 103–11 (104), support this account of the composition.

A COMMUNITY OF READERS

After studying in Oxford in the late 1430s, Worcester was employed by Sir John Fastolf until Fastolf's death in 1459; thereafter he fought to defend Fastolf's inheritance from unkind executors. During his life, Fastolf's household emerges as a cultivated place, home to Stephen Scrope, another translator, and to a collection of French books, including many fourteenth-century French translations of classical literature.[9] These elegant works no doubt seemed fit adornments to the household of a grand old soldier. But Worcester's scholarship also seems to emerge from Fastolf's financial business: Fastolf sent him and other servants around the country collecting information about his estates. The journeys might have provoked Worcester's well-known topographical interests, and they also allowed him to build a network of bookish friends: when most knowledge still travelled in rare and scattered manuscripts, whom one knew determined what one knew. For example, in May 1449 one John Crop was seeking genealogies and titles for Fastolf in the west of England; in a letter to Worcester about this, Crop writes that:

I spake with Mayster Hoby as for ij queyers, as that ⌐ letter ¬ made mencion, and he seid me hys bokis ⌐ were ¬ remevid of his chaumbre, for a lady that lay in his chaumbre, like as he told yow. But he seid me that it shuld be redy ⌐ lokid vp ¬ in that wike. Also, he graunte me the copye of Wallens *De vita et doctrina philosoforum*, also the queiere of Oved, *De vetula, De remedio moris, De Arte amande*, and of the verse vp-on Boicius.[10]

Master Ralph Hoby offers several books: John of Wales's *Breuiloquium de uirtutibus*, which is an account of ancient philosophy, Ovid's *De Arte amandi* and Boethius' *De Consolatione Philosophiae*, and the pseudo-Ovidian *De Vetula*. There is evidence that Worcester later went on to study all four of these works.[11] His scholarship was made possible by the 'knowledge transactions' in his service of a rich old man.[12]

[9] Richard Beadle, 'Sir John Fastolf's French Books', in *Medieval Texts in Manuscript Context*, ed. Graham Caie and D. Reveney (London: Longmans, 2007), 163–89, and K. B. McFarlane, 'The Investment of Sir John Fastolf's Profits of War', in his *England in the Fifteenth Century: Collected Essays*, ed. G. L. Harriss (London: Hambledon, 1981), 175–97.

[10] Richard Beadle and Colin Richmond (eds.), *Paston Letters and Papers of the Fifteenth Century: Part III*, EETS ss 22 (Oxford: Oxford University Press, 2005), no. 969:23–9; P. S. Lewis, 'Sir John Fastolf's Lawsuit over Titchwell 1448–55', *Historical Journal*, 1 (1958), 1–20 (12–16), and *BRUO*, II.939, discuss Crop and Hoby.

[11] As noted below. And he added a cross-reference to *De Vetula* into [Worcester] (trans.), *Tullius de senectute*, sig. f5r. [William Worcester (trans.)], *Caxton: Tulle of Olde Age*, ed. Heinz Susebach, Studien zur Englischen Philologie, 75 (Halle: Niemeyer, 1933), offers a misleadingly interventionist edition.

[12] The term comes from Lisa Jardine and William Sherman, 'Pragmatic Readers: Knowledge Transactions and Scholarly Services in Late Elizabethan England', in *Religion, Culture and Society*

Eventually, much of Fastolf's estate was diverted into funding William Waynflete's new foundation of Magdalen College and School in Oxford (an institution which reappears in Chapter 5 below). Worcester's exchange of books with Bishop Waynflete also becomes part of his financial dealings and, perhaps, the tawdry but important activities of advancement or patronage: for example, in 1461 Worcester received a copy of Boccaccio's *De Casibus virorum illustrium* from the powerful bishop Waynflete, and a decade later reciprocated with his version of *De Senectute* and a *Liber de sacramentis ecclesiae*; around then, in 1472, he was trying to prevent a legal judgement in Waynflete's favour and to his own detriment.[13] His exchanges of books are therefore, to some extent, an investment in ownership and 'networking'; however, simultaneously, they create a more whimsical image of his identity as a reader. The gifts of Cicero and Boccaccio identify Worcester not only as a claimant for favour but also as a fellow humanist. Indeed, the colouring is so striking that Worcester even describes his gift to Waynflete of the religious *Liber de sacramentis ecclesiae*, in pious memory of Sir John Fastolf, as a humanist gesture. He inscribes the flyleaf:

Suo domino Colendissimo magistro Willelmo Waynfleete Sedis Ecclesie Cathedralis sancti Swythun Wyntoniensis Episcopo que olim ante tempus consecracionis dicte Ecclesie Templum dagon vocabatur tempore paganorum gencium[14]

To his most worshipful master William Waynflete, bishop of the seat of the cathedral church of St Swithin of Winchester, which once before the time of the consecration was called the temple of Dagon in the era of the pagan people.

It is important to register just how odd is the imaginary humanist: for, oddly, given the context, there is no request for prayers but there is this antiquarian posing. The more selfish motivations behind such 'knowledge transactions' have been well studied. There is more to say, though, about the odd images chosen to conceal those motivations and about their scholarly colour, as in this wholly needless note about the temple of Dagon.

In many of his notebooks and inscriptions of ownership, Worcester casts himself as a humanist. Firstly, his notebooks record his dealings with other men known to be humanist readers sometimes: with John Hall of Garboldisham, with John Argentine of King's College, or with the pioneer of Greek studies,

---

in Early Modern Britain: Essays in Honour of Patrick Collinson, ed. Anthony Fletcher and Peter Roberts (Cambridge: Cambridge University Press, 1994), 102–24 (102–3).

[13] OMC, MS lat. 198, flyleaf f.ii[v]; Worcestre, *Itineraries*, 252–5; Colin Richmond, *The Paston Family in the Fifteenth Century: Fastolf's Will* (Cambridge: Cambridge University Press, 1996), 213–22, 255–6, describes their legal dealings.

[14] OMC, MS lat. 26, flyleaf f.ii[v].

William Sellyng.[15] Moreover, Worcester would surely register these men as humanist readers, for he registered the myth that new trends of study were recently introduced to England by Humfrey, Duke of Gloucester. In revising *The Boke of Noblesse*, Worcester added to his military praise of the duke some praise for the gift of books to nurture Oxford's scholars in the seven liberal arts and both laws (45); elsewhere one of his notebooks records the death of Humfrey, who is described as a 'lover of virtue and of the commonweal and in particular a unique promoter of scholars' ('amator virtutis et rei publice atque precipue clericorum promotor singularis').[16] Wherever we look, Worcester's notes on his friends and books trace a network of learned imitators of Duke Humfrey.

So, for example, Worcester recognized the humanist studies of John Free, too. When he donated a copy of Poggio Bracciolini's translation of Diodorus Siculus and of some notes from Pliny by Free to Free's former college, Balliol College in Oxford, he described the notes from Pliny on the front page as:

[...] compilata per magistrum Johannem ffreas de Brist<ow>natus et in Italia padue de eius propria manu scriptus [...] et idem magister fuit in Collegio vocato Balyollo et ex postea in Italiam studens Padue et Rome doctor professus in medicinis et lege ciuili ac greca lingua[17]

[...] compiled by master John Free born in Bristol and written in his own hand in Italy at Padua [...] and the same master was at Balliol College and afterwards a student in Italy and at Rome professed a doctor of medicine and of civil law and of the Greek language

The inscription here insists upon the humanist studies for which Free is now known, recording the trip to Italy and the knowledge of Greek. Worcester owned two further manuscripts that once belonged to Free, and cited a fourth,[18] and we can sense some excitement that this book is Free's autograph copy. Worcester, in this inscription, imagines humanism embodied in the fingerprints of Free's human presence, and in his own presence as transmitter of the knowledge. Later in the Diodorus Siculus, Worcester marks a cross-reference to a geographical work by the roving classicist Cristoforo Buondelmonti which, he notes superfluously, was compiled for Cardinal

---

[15] Respectively Ju f.47v, Worcestre, *Itineraries*, 364–7, *BRUC*, 281 and *n*. 80 in Chapter 6 below (Hall's *sententiae* from Palladius, Seneca, Poggio Bracciolini); Ju f.165r, and Oxford, New College, MS 162, on which see Dennis E. Rhodes, *John Argentine Provost of King's: His Life and his Library* (Amsterdam: Hertzberger, 1967), 12, 18–24, 27, and D. Riehl Leader, 'John Argentein and Learning in Medieval Cambridge', *HL*, 33 (1984), 71–85; and Ju f.118r, f.205r, *BRUC*, 15–16 and Weiss, *Humanism*, 157 (Sellyng).

[16] London, College of Arms, MS Arundel 48, f.126v. This note is not in Worcester's hand.

[17] OBC, MS 124, f.1r; R. A. B. Mynors, *Catalogue of the Manuscripts of Balliol College* (Oxford: Clarendon Press, 1963), 102; Weiss, *Humanism*, 110–11.

[18] Ju f.204v, ff.211r–231v; BodL, MS Auct F.3.25, f.1v; *Humfrey 1970*, 42, no. 85, no. 99.

Giordano Orsini and now 'remains with William Worcester once owner of this book' ('remanet cum willelmo Worcestre quondam possessore huius libri'). Sure enough, Worcester did elsewhere copy much of Buondelmonti's work from a book once owned by Fastolf; and Buondelmonti did dedicate the work to Orsini.[19] Yet why does Worcester tell us these facts in a lengthy note about Crete at the end of some jottings from Pliny? As in the note on the Temple of Dagon at Winchester, there is a surplus of information: a delight in building up a picture of his own and of others' scholarship. In Free's book Worcester writes of a community of readers fixated by the Italian fashion for antiquity. He notes the use of Greek, the visit to Padua twice or Orsini, because he expects people—to whom, after all, he donated the books—to recognize the import of these notes. Here in the front of his books, he proudly links himself with the renowned scholars of Italy and with their English followers. If modern historians or codicologists can recognize in such inscriptions the history of humanism, it is because Worcester expects those in the know to do so. He is forging bonds among people not only materially, by the exchange of books, but also imaginatively, by keeping records of the exchange. He imagines a readership *in* these records, and he imagines a readership *for* these records.

POLITICAL READING: CICERO, JOHN OF WALES, AND CHARTIER

However, do his bonds through shared books simply tie up some coterie, like that imagined by the poet of *On Husbondrie?* Do his 'knowledge trans-actions' merely exclude other people or promote himself? Kevin Sharpe, in his account of a voracious seventeenth-century note-taker, Sir William Drake, wondered in passing whether Drake's references to the friends with whom he swapped books revealed what one might call an 'interpretive community' or 'textual community' of readers with shared modes for interpreting those texts. As books circulated among Drake's friends, their stock of shared ideas and examples grew and allowed their opinions to coalesce; similarly, the opinions of his friends shaped his reading, rather like 'living commentaries' on it.[20] Some of Worcester's notes record him sharing scholarship that is

---

[19] OBC, MS 124, f.242v; CCCC, MS 210, pp. 279–94; Worcestre, *Itineraries*, 372–3.

[20] Kevin Sharpe, *Reading Revolutions: The Politics of Reading in Early Modern England* (New Haven, CT: Yale University Press, 2000), 178. These ideas develop from Stanley Fish, *Is There a Text in This Class? The Authority of Interpretive Communities* (Cambridge, MA: Harvard University Press, 1980), 147–73, and Brian Stock, *The Implications of Literacy* (Princeton, NJ: Princeton University Press, 1983), 88–90, 522.

innocuously antiquarian, rather than sharply political like Drake's.[21] However, the scholarly heroes sometimes become political ones: for example, in
Worcester's notebook, the aforementioned record of the mysterious death of
Duke Humfrey links his unique promotion of scholars to his love of virtue *and*
of the commonweal.[22] The useless loveliness of *On Husbondrie* composed for
Humfrey might throw doubt upon the connection between scholarship and
political virtue, but Worcester's marginalia and then *The Boke of Noblesse* do
bear witness to the productive political outcome of humanist reading.

Colin Richmond characterizes Worcester's bookishness as overwhelmingly
'active', always dedicated to some purpose, and a recent cluster of histories of
early-modern readers emphasize this model of the process; texts were 'studied
for action'.[23] Sure enough, Worcester's sheer bulk of notes does imply hours
of activity and throughout his margins the exhortation 'nota' is, note well, an
imperative verb; it imagines active and committed reading by those who read
his note in turn. Yet claims that Worcester's—or anyone else's—reading was
'active' might be inevitable, for the only reading in the past which we might
describe now is reading that was active enough to lead to the writing of notes.
Yet Worcester obviously thought that lots of his reading was worth noting.
One sign of his self-importance is his habit of dating his notes and marginalia
with knowing timeliness: his reading occurs in history. Dates by scribes are rare
in English manuscripts; such dates are recorded more commonly by Italian
humanist scribes for whom, Pamela Robinson has suggested, the addition of
new dates to old texts may express an awareness of the conjunction of past
and present. For example, the English humanist Richard Bole notes the recent
Battle of St Albans in his colophon to Sallust's account of a country torn
apart in *Jugurtha*, but he is rare in so doing.[24] However, William Worcester
notes the date of a full quarter of his two-hundred or so recorded moments of
reading.[25] Moreover, in several marginalia he directly links recent politics and
his humanist reading: in 1453 some description of the ancient traitors Calchas
and Curion reminds him of the recently murdered Duke of Suffolk and
Bishop of Salisbury; a chronicle of Richard II's reign reminds him of Cicero's
emphasis on princely justice.[26] So as well as remembering his bookish friends,
he also remembers the polity within which he studied; his two self-images as

[21] For example Ju f.169r and Worcestre, *Itineraries*, 262, 312.   [22] See *n.* 16 above.

[23] Richmond, *Fastolf's Will*, 76–80. On 'active reading' see Sharpe, *Reading Revolutions*, 189,
and Anthony Grafton and Lisa Jardine, '"Studied for Action": How Gabriel Harvey Read his
Livy', *Past and Present*, 129 (1990), 30–78 (30–1, 40).

[24] P. R. Robinson, *Dated and Datable Manuscripts c.737–1600 in Cambridge Libraries*, 2 vols.
(Cambridge: Brewer, 1988), II.5, II.12; Rundle, 'Republics and Tyrants', 268–9, noting OBC,
MS 258, f.148r.

[25] Wakelin, 'William Worcester', 65, discusses his dating further.

[26] Ro f.138v, Ro f.105r.

humanist reader and timely or overtly political reader often coincide. Yet (as Chapter 1 noted) humanist reading and a civic politics do not *necessarily* go together: so how did Worcester link them?

The clearest example is his study of Cicero, evidently his favourite writer. He makes fleeting references to Cicero throughout his notebooks and summarizes three of the philosophical works more fully in Latin, evidently while reading through the works themselves.[27] He eventually writes his own translation from Cicero's *De Senectute*, and he retranslates or paraphrases part of it in *The Boke of Noblesse* (58–71). The differences between his Latin summary and his two English translations reveal that Worcester returned to *De Senectute* at least three times—a persistent and diligent reading. He knew well that studying Cicero required an act of scholarly retrieval by his humanist 'textual community': a letter sent to him, now folded into his notebook, contains a list of 'The works of Cicero, as Leonardo Bruni relates when he wrote his biography' ('Opera tullij vt refert leonardus aretinus cum eius vitam scripsit').[28] The tense-change in that heading, though presumably unconscious, is nevertheless revealing: the correspondent moves from the eternal present tense in which one describes literary works ('vt refert') into a past tense ('scripsit'). That past tense implies some hazy sense that Cicero's oeuvre is not timeless but is known through the particular humanist work of retrieval by Bruni, which Bruni himself describes in his prologue.[29] Moreover, Worcester's knowledge of Cicero's career only comes from the now-anonymous friend who sent the letter, that is, from the humanist community once more.

However, those studies of Cicero not only link Worcester to his friends, in knowledge transactions or friendships; they further his political reflections. Where the letter to Worcester lists Cicero's lost work, *De Republica*, some hand has doodled a small cross to highlight it.[30] Elsewhere Worcester himself tried to recover this lost text. *De Republica* was largely unknown until it was uncovered in a palimpsest in 1819, yet Italian humanists often cited the few known fragments: some cited them to support their civic political arguments, particularly in Venice; some from a fetish for its 'lostness' or obscurity. There is mention of its loss in the French translation of Cicero's *De Amicitia* by Laurent de Premierfait, a work which Worcester most likely knew, as he knew de Premierfait's paired translation of *De Senectute*.[31] Worcester's

---

[27] For example Ju ff.71r–73r and Worcestre, *Itineraries*, 250–1.

[28] Ju ff.67v–68r; Leonardo Bruni, *Vita Ciceronis*, in his *Opere Letterarie e Politiche*, ed. Paolo Viti (Turin: Unione Tipografico-Editrice, 1996), 413–99 (470–4).

[29] Bruni, *Vita Ciceronis*, 416–18. Worcestre, *Itineraries*, 274–7, records the date of Bruni's death.

[30] Ju f.67v.

[31] 31 David Rundle, 'Carneades' Legacy: the Morality of Eloquence in the Humanist and Papalist Writings of Pietro del Monte', *EHR*, 117 (2002), 284–305 (291–2), and M. S. Kempshall,

own reconstruction of *De Republica* occurred when he read and annotated a manuscript of a classical dictionary, Nonius Marcellus' *De Conpendiosa doctrina*, itself a recondite work favoured by humanist collectors such as William Gray, John Tiptoft, and Humfrey, Duke of Gloucester.[32] On his first reading of the dictionary, Worcester marked with his customary 'Saturn' symbol nearly two-hundred quotations which illustrate diverse words and idioms from a good range of classical works: a general study of the Latin language. However, he then transcribed some seventy-seven of the quotations into a notebook, citing the folio numbers he had added to the manuscript, and he mostly transcribed the excerpts from Cicero's *De Republica*, ignoring his other marginalia. In fact, he transcribed two thirds of Nonius' excerpts from it.[33] We can trace his reading in stages: firstly, he pottered among an arcane and curious book; then he focused on the more serious scholarly job of reconstructing *De Republica*. However, did he aim simply to reconstruct a lost masterpiece? In fact, this philology also, as a process, led him to study many of Cicero's political ideas. The excerpts which Worcester copies into his notebook are not universally political in flavour, but several of them are: definitions of sedition and servitude, of helping and supporting the state, of concord, of brave senators, and so on. Did he realize the political focus of these excerpts? It seems so, for eventually this reading fed directly into his praise for the commonweal in *The Boke of Noblesse*. In his final editing of *The Boke of Noblesse*, he added to a list of other Ciceronian works on the commonweal one more reference to *De Republica*, 'that Nobius Marcellus makyth mencion of yn dyuers chapiters' (57). He engages in the humanist project of recovering the lost heritage of the ancients, but his philological reading—like that of others—fed his political concerns. One must not separate the textual and conceptual elements of his reading, the unpredictable outcome of even superficial philology.

'*De Re Publica* I.39 in Medieval and Renaissance Political Thought', in *Cicero's Republic*, ed. J. G. F. Powell and J. A. North, Bulletin of the Institute of Classical Studies: Supplement, 76 (London: Institute of Classical Studies, 2001), 99–135 (124–33); Carla Bozzolo, 'La lecture des classiques par un humaniste français Laurent de Premierfait', in *L'Aube de la Renaissance*, ed. D. Cecchetti, L. Sozzi, and L. Terreaux (Genève: Slatkine, 1991), 67–81 (75).

[32] OMC, MS lat. 206, ff.113r–243v. For the other copies in England, see Mynors, *Balliol*, 281 (MS 262 from Gray); Alfonso Sammut (ed.), *Unfredo duca di Gloucester e gli umanisti italiani*, Medioevo e Umanesimo, 40 (Padua: Antenore, 1980), 83 (inventory no. 264, now lost); and Nonius Marcellus, *De Conpendiosa doctrina I–III*, ed. J. H. Onions (Oxford: Clarendon Press, 1895), p. xxv.

[33] There are sixty-six annotations of quotations from *De Republica* in OMC, MS lat. 206, ff.113r–243v; fifty-six of them, and three more, are copied into Ju ff.124r–128r. There are 118 annotations of quotations from other works in OMC, MS lat. 206, but only three of them, and fifteen more, are copied into Ju. Worcester's 'Saturn' annotation is illustrated in Norman Davis (ed.), *Paston Letters and Papers of the Fifteenth Century*, 2 vols. (Oxford: Clarendon Press, 1971–6), plate XVI.

His political concerns are perhaps made most explicit in a second example of his reading, namely of the French versions of two works on the cardinal virtues, now bound together in Cambridge University Library, MS Additional 7870 (hereafter cited as Cu). Worcester dates to July 1450 his marginalia on the first work, John of Wales's *Breuiloquium de uirtutibus*, a copy of which John Crop had found for him the previous year. As it happens, his employer, Fastolf, owned a further deluxe copy of this rare work, also dated to 1450 by its scribe, Ricardus Franciscus.[34] What is the significance of July 1450? On 1 or 2 July that year, Fastolf's palace in Southwark became a target for the rebels with Jack Cade, who surprisingly identified Fastolf with the men responsible for the loss of France, when, in fact, the opposite was true.[35] But during this tumultuous month, Worcester coolly perused these two works. When he did so, he did not escape from the world in turmoil but, in fine Ciceronian style, reflected upon it. In his numerous marginalia on the works, Worcester frequently finds stern lessons for the government which had allowed Cade's mayhem to brew. For example, in a chapter on financial business, Worcester can only doodle a giant accusing finger on the page and urge 'note well for the realm of England proven at the time of our king now', presumably alluding to Henry VI's profligate largesse and avoidance of reform even as the crisis erupted ('nota bene pro Regno Anglie verificato tempore Regis nunc').[36] In the manuscript's second work, a French translation of *Des Quatre vertus cardinaulx* which was ascribed to Seneca, Worcester once more highlights the exhortation that if fortune treats you poorly, then you must reform your situation with good policy ('quando fortuna venit ex parte [sinistra] debet per bonam policiam reformare').[37] His reading offers specific consolation at a time when English troops in France faced successive defeats at the hands! of Charles VII.

---

[34] Cu f.30v; BodL, MS Laud misc. 570, f.93r; OMC Archives, MS Additional 99 (Lovell Papers), f.21r. Rosemund Tuve, 'Notes on the Virtues and Vices', *Journal of the Warburg and Courtauld Institutes*, 26 (1963), 264–303, 27 (1964), 42–72 (264), and Gianni Mombello, 'Notizia su due manoscritti contenenti "l'Epistre Othea" di Christine de Pizan ed altre opere non identificate', *Studi francesi*, 31 (1967), 1–23 (13–21), identify Fastolf's copy but do not mention Worcester's (Cu). Considerable textual differences suggest that neither manuscript is copied from the other, despite the circulation of both within Fastolf's household.

[35] I. M. W. Harvey, *Jack Cade's Rebellion of 1450* (Oxford: Clarendon Press, 1991), 87–91.

[36] Cu f.23v. This is also the only passage annotated in Fastolf's copy (BodL, MS Laud misc. 570, f.18r). Harvey, *Cade's Rebellion*, 71, traces the political context.

[37] Cu f.44r; Jean Courtecuisse (trans.), *Sénèque des IIII vertus: La* Formula Honestae Vitae *de Martin de Braga (pseudo-Sénèque)*, ed. Hans Haselbach (Berne: Lang, 1975), 375:69; the edition does not mention this manuscript. Worcester actually writes 'ex parte dextra' ('from the right hand') but presumably means 'sinistra' ('left'), as he has just used 'the right hand' to denote good fortune.

Moreover, although these are not genuine classical texts, Worcester often ties his political lessons to their copious classical stories and the wise saws in them ascribed to Aristotle and Cicero. For example, John of Wales, one of the so-called 'classicizing friars' of earlier centuries, praises the princes of 'long ago' ('jadis') described by Valerius Maximus who sought power principally in order 'to defend the commonweal and diligently to protect it'. In the margin, Worcester highlights the references to Valerius and Aristotle and recommends how ancient men served the commonweal ('pour la chose publique deffendre et diligentement garder').[38] Elsewhere, he notes that the method of the Roman generals for breaking the news of defeat should enlighten England's unlucky leaders.[39] Then we hear how Hanon the wise Carthaginian senator foretells that a humiliated enemy will recover to be a more furious victor: Worcester's jerky *nota bene* jumps all over the page; he optimistically if wrongly observes that the warning bodes well for the recovery of England's lost territories ('pro Recuperacione terrae perditi' [*sic*]; 'pour le courage dez anglez'). As with his study of Cicero's *De Republica*, his reading of these works feeds directly into *The Boke of Noblesse*, where he retells the tale of Hanon the senator, with verbal echoes of this translation, in order to recommend the renewal of old alliances in order to fight one's enemies; this is what Hanon prophesied the Romans would do.[40] Worcester's notes on his reading, then, frequently connect the deeds or wisdom of the ancients and the military and political dilemmas of the fifteenth century. One can be encouraged by ancient models, as *Knyghthode and Bataile* urged Henry VI to be; indeed, the words *courage, encouraged*, and their cognates appear some thirty-one times in *The Boke of Noblesse*, often linked to the stories cited there from the works of Cicero or pseudo-Seneca. Worcester's marginalia and treatise turn to antiquity for lessons which fit his particular political moment.

However, Worcester in this manuscript peruses works by authors who are not genuinely classical: John of Wales and Pseudo-Seneca. Did he need to turn to the ancients for his 'active' and political reading? Would not the compilations of the friars suffice? One final example confirms the importance to him of a specifically classical history. The example also reveals how his humanist reading alters, even as it handles, the classicism of his closest predecessors. Through the reading process cultural change occurs, but occurs not as a rupture but as

[38] Cu f.23r–v, translating John of Wales, *Breuiloquium de uirtutibus antiquorum principum et philosophorum*, in *Summa Johannis Ualensis de regimine vite humane seu Margarita doctorum ad omne propositum prout patet in tabula*, ed. Johannes Ualentis (Lyons, 1511), ff.cci[v]–ccxvii[r] (f.ccix[v]).

[39] Cu f.51r; Courtecuisse (trans.), *Sénèque*, 389:238–42.

[40] Cu ff.52v–53r; Courtecuisse (trans.), *Sénèque*, 393:275–92; Worcester, *Noblesse*, 49–50, borrowing the words 'muys', 'discomfiture', and 'demaunded'.

a gentle shift. The shift occurs when Worcester reads *Le Quadrilogue invectif* (1422) and *Le Livre de l'espérance* (1428–30) by the French poet and moralist Alain Chartier (*c*.1385–1433). These works are dream visions, inspired by Boethius, in each of which the three theological virtues or the three estates discuss France's waning fortunes in war and conclude that France will only revive through moral and spiritual reform. Despite his connections to the court of Charles VII, enemy of the English, the works proved popular in England too; for example, English translations circulated among the Norfolk gentry with connections to Fastolf.[41] One of Worcester's notebooks contains long excerpts from these works in French handwriting; those excerpts were then annotated by Worcester himself. Whoever copied the excerpts proceeded sequentially through both works, giving folio references to a copy in two columns, and he copied from Chartier's works almost every classical exemplum and, notably, almost exclusively the classical exempla—just as Worcester lifted little except Cicero from Nonius Marcellus.[42] Thus, Worcester's knowledge of antiquity is not new, for it comes from Chartier; but what is new is the exclusivity of his interest in such knowledge.

However, once more Worcester's interest in antiquity also accompanies a keen interest in the commonweal, for these classicizing excerpts directly feed *The Boke of Noblesse*. *The Boke of Noblesse* names or borrows from Chartier's works in eight passages, five of them classical narratives found in the notebook of excerpts. As has been proposed by others, Chartier's works offer a good precedent for the composition of a reforming treatise.[43] For example, *The Boke of Noblesse* borrows from Chartier's *Quadrilogue* a list of doomed empires. There is some evidence of complex and diligent scholarship: here as elsewhere *The Boke of Noblesse* omits and includes slightly different details from the excerpts found in the notebook; so Worcester consulted a manuscript of Chartier's *Quadrilogue* like that from which his excerpts come, but he must have read the whole work afresh.[44] Moreover, in *The Boke of*

[41] Margaret S. Blayney (ed.) *Fifteenth-Century English Translations of Alain Chartier's* Le Traité de l'Esperance *and* Le Quadrilogue Invectif, EETS os 270, 281, 2 vols. (Oxford: Oxford University Press, 1974–80), II.7–8, II.12.

[42] Ro ff.136r–141r. Compare for example Ro f.136r with Alain Chartier, *Le Quadrilogue invectif*, ed. E. Droz, 2nd edn. (1923; Paris: Champion, 1950), 3:9–4:3, 12:7–15, 15:3–12, 16:7–8, 16:12–14, 17:18–22, 23:26–31.

[43] Ro f.136r–v, f.139v; [Worcester], *Noblesse* 26, 51, 75, 83; Chartier, *Quadrilogue*, 3:8–21, 35:17–23, 31:4–14, 31:15–19; Chartier, *Espérance*, Pr.VIII.310–20. [Worcester], *Noblesse*, 25, 33, 58, cites Chartier further, on which see Christopher Allmand and Maurice Keen, 'History and the Literature of War: The *Boke of Noblesse* of William Worcester', in *War, Government and Power in Late Medieval France*, ed. Christopher Allmand (Liverpool: Liverpool University Press, 2000), 92–105 (102).

[44] Ro f.136r; Chartier, *Quadrilogue*, 3:8–31. For example, [Worcester], *Noblesse*, includes Nineveh, omitted in Ro f.136r, but both texts simplify Carthage's fate ('fut arse toute en cendre';

Noblesse his reading supports his hope for political action: Chartier's topos of the transfer of power 'frome one nacion to another straunge tong' comes to offer useful and sufficient lessons to 'who so wolle considre welle the histories of olde Croniclers' (51–2). Worcester implies that his reader should think about these examples for himself: everyone ('who so', *whosoever*) actually now should 'considre' such histories either 'welle' to some advantage or 'welle' with some care. The phrase might translate the usual wording of marginalia: *nota bene* or 'considre welle'. Then, to facilitate this good consideration, Worcester supplements Chartier's list of doomed empires with the further stories of Boethius, Lucius Valerius, and other 'worshipfulle senatours'. He insists and repeats that their stories offer lessons to contemporary worthies who might be guilty of 'hauyng no consideracion to the comen wele' or 'not hauyng consideracion to the generalle profit and vniuersalle wele of a comynalte' (51, 52). Bad rulers, it seems, do not 'considre welle' the histories of old chroniclers. Luckily, to amend this thoughtlessness, *The Boke of Noblesse* digests for the reader lots of histories to consider; it guides its reader to retrace Worcester's own active and hopeful reading through these second-hand ancient tales.

However, if Chartier provides some of Worcester's classical histories, what is so new about his humanist reading? What is new is that *The Boke of Noblesse* uses classical history with optimism quite unfound in its lugubrious source. For example, *The Boke of Noblesse* presents the list of doomed empires as a history which one can 'considre welle' in order to keep oneself off the grim list. However, Chartier's *Quadrilogue* presents the same list as the story of *translatio imperii*, the inexorable transfer of power. This story does not help us in this world but cruelly rebukes us: nobody can prevent this transfer of power, for human comprehension of it is limited ('descognoissance de la cause'). We ascribe to random fortune what is in fact God's just and ordained vengeance on sinful nations, which he destroys as a potter breaks his wares.[45] Chartier implies that there is little hope in considering the chronicle well, without religious renewal, whereas Worcester finds in it practical lessons in government, thus rather misreading Chartier's book. His optimism frequently diverges from Chartier in this way. For example, after that list of doomed empires, *The Boke of Noblesse* introduces the philosopher Boethius as someone who 'loued rightwisnesse to be kept and the pore comyns of Rome in that susteyned and maynteyned' (52–3). By contrast, in Chartier's *Le Livre de l'espérance*, a wicked character called Ugly Indignation mocks Boethius for ruing his futile public service and warns that there is no hope of reforming

---

'was rent to asshes'), compared to Droz's edition (*Quadrilogue*, 3:31), which sadly lacks a textual apparatus.

[45] Chartier, *Quadrilogue*, 2:27–32, 4:10–20, with echoes of Psalms 2: 9, Jeremiah 19: 11.

society: Seneca, Cicero, Demosthenes, and Boethius have all met their doom in trying.[46] Strikingly, the excerpt of this brief history in Worcester's notebook omits Ugly Indignation's snide verdict and leaves Boethius as the heroic citizen he becomes in *The Boke of Noblesse*.[47] Thus, Worcester's emphasis upon the usefulness of classical history is a departure from the ambivalence of his predecessor towards it.

Moreover, his worldly optimism reflects precisely the shift towards pagan antiquity which prompted Worcester's amanuensis to fillet the classics from Chartier's writing. In *Le Livre de l'espérance*, Faith relates how pagan philosophy and the brutal dominion of wicked emperors have been defeated by simple Christian folk; the 'tyrans' rest now 'en damnation pardurable' whilst the humble saints live in eternity.[48] Therefore, although Chartier's speakers sometimes cite classical examples to support their arguments, the first such allusions come from the devil's advocates, and later the godly character, Hope, rejects any 'exemple' which might incite the suicidal *accidia* of the Romans. Such narratives provide:

[...] plus exemples de fuir que de suir. Encore te dy je que cest argument qui procede par comparaison resemblable se peult souldre par similitude. Car foy crestienne t'a baillé provision de si haulte esperance que lez paiens et les ydolatres n'y peurent attaindre.[49]

[...] more examples to avoid rather than to follow. Again I say to you that this argument which proceeds by outward comparisons can dissolve itself similarly. For Christian faith has equipped you with so high a hope which pagans and idolaters could not attain.

The reader simply cannot learn so blithely from the period of human history before the revelation of Christ: one must distinguish how to deploy each classical *exemplum* and which should be shunned rather than followed. This interpretative skill is demanded by the historical rupture between Chartier's fatalist and fatally doomed pagans and the hope of Christian sufferers. The rupture prevents any useful lessons from the pagan past. Hope grants that these fictions could be a sop to worldly listeners who seek to compare their deeds with those of the ancients 'humainement', that is, with their limited human comprehension; but she warns that these listeners will soon find that 'providence divine' perplexes such insufficient mortal cognition.[50] We may

---

[46] Alain Chartier, *Le Livre de l'espérance*, ed. François Rouy, Bibliothèque du XVe siècle, 51 (Paris: Champion, 1989), Pr.II.138–54. Despair even advocates suicide as the only escape, citing Cato in Utica (Pr.IV.12–61).

[47] Compare Ro 138v; Chartier, *Espérance*, Pr.II.149–54.

[48] Chartier, *Espérance*, Pr.VI.67–76.   [49] Chartier, *Espérance*, Pr.XI.128–32.

[50] Chartier, *Espérance*, Pr.XIV.71–84.

not want to ascribe such statements by allegorical speakers to Chartier himself, who had personal ties to the early French humanists.[51] Nevertheless, in the works which Worcester and his amanuensis read, it is the godly figures who voice unease about classical culture; by contrast, Worcester's notebook and then his own work refine Chartier's writing into an anthology of classical tales, and trust them to guide us in this world.

THE LIMITS OF EXEMPLARY READING

However, *The Boke of Noblesse* itself reveals some limitations in this form of humanist reading. Firstly, although classical histories constitute much of *The Boke of Noblesse*, they are not its only ingredient. Worcester was also an antiquarian and biographer, and the first quarter of *The Boke of Noblesse* offers a 'recordacion' of the military deeds of English kings, princes, and knights (3). Moreover, if, as was probably intended, we read *The Boke of Noblesse* alongside the documents about the wars in France, now preserved in London, Lambeth Palace Library, MS 506, then the classical histories are dwarfed by records of recent history. His humanist reading did not obliterate other forms of study. Secondly, does the historical record, whether of recent times or of antiquity, offer useful lessons?

In the first quarter of *The Boke of Noblesse*, Worcester only once explicitly states that the recent history appears 'for an example' (9). However, although the language of exemplarity is hidden, the practice is not. Like *De Consulatu Stilichonis*, the treatise treats heroes from both antiquity and modernity as role models. Even when Worcester went collecting the documents which are still so useful for historians, he did so with an occasional frank nod to the political notions he sought to illustrate. For example, he annotated an account of Somerset's blunders in France with further praise for one Thomas Gower, who fought 'for the preservation of the commonweal' ('pour le conseruacion du bien publique').[52] His political notions do indeed shape the gathering of those historical collections into *The Boke of Noblesse*, even in the apparently rare data of the 'litille codicelle' of supportive documents. After Worcester's death, his son offered the codicil—and presumably *The Boke of Noblesse* too—to Richard III. He introduced these scrappy writings about the wars in

---

[51] As noted by François Rouy, *L'Esthétique du traité moral d'après les œuvres d'Alain Chartier* (Genève: Droz, 1980), 287–8, and Regula Meyenberg, *Alain Chartier Prosateur et l'Art de la Parole au XVe Siècle: Études Littéraires et Rhétoriques* (Bern: Francke, 1992), 32–7.

[52] London, College of Arms, MS Arundel 48, f.288r; f.284r–284v contain further documents about Gower.

France not only as a 'perpetuelle memorialle' to the Duke of Bedford and his peers, but also as a distinctive lesson for 'auauncing and preferring the common publique' of the realms of England and France. Throughout the collection, some headings provided by the original scribes and by Worcester note the value of the documents 'for the benefit of the commonweal' and so on ('pro comodo reipublice Regni' [*sic*]).[53] So as he reads various documents, and then anthologizes them to accompany his own treatise, Worcester does sometimes suggest the political lessons in more recent history, just as in Chartier's or Cicero's classical tales. Moreover, even without the brief commentary, any collection of historical documents has an editorial logic as much as any historical narrative does; this is true even of modern textbooks or sourcebooks in fashionable areas of research. Worcester's decision to offer records of recent wars to the king is underpinned by habits of 'active' reading and a faith in the use of precedent.

But does such exemplary reading work? How, exactly, do the dry military records in the codicil instil such an abstract thing as fervour for the commonweal? After all, the dull documents in the codicil make warfare look more like a matter of economic nous than Ciceronian zeal: there are lists of wages, account books, and inventories of essential equipment. Of course, Worcester's intended reader, Edward IV, sought from 1472 to 1475 to persuade parliament to grant him funds for an invasion of France, and these financial documents could provide the crucial justification or calculation.[54] But even in Worcester's brief headings to them, it is unclear precisely what the reader should learn. For example, an inventory of articles found in Rouen Castle upon the death of Bedford looks not like a theory of the commonweal, but like a shopping-list. Worcester notes that:

hic ponitur pro exemplo aliorum principum sed in prima emptione constabant dicta artelleria multo plus in precio quam hic notantur[55]

It is placed here to be an example for other princes; but at their first purchase the said armaments cost much more than is noted here.

So he concedes that historical evidence is patchy and limited, and that historical flux renders it impossible to apply the lessons of the past to the present in any detailed way. Captains, like homeowners, face price inflation and property devaluation which change the demands upon their resources.

---

[53] I quote from LPL, MS 506, hereafter cited as La, but give page references for the sections printed in *Wars in France*, II.ii.519–607; here citing La f.2r, ff.3v–4r (*Wars in France*, II.ii.521, II.ii.524–5), La f.13v (*Wars in France*, II.ii.534). Sutton and Visser-Fuchs, 'Richard III's Books: XII', 156–7, clarify the link between the treatise and the codicil.

[54] Charles Ross, *Edward IV*, 2nd edn. (London: Methuen, 1974), 214–18.

[55] La f.32r (*Wars in France*, II.ii.566).

Worcester sounds, like Christine de Pizan on Vegetius, uncertain about the value of history or sounds as though he prefers recent, practical experience.[56] In these doubts he demonstrates that the fifteenth century does not witness an uncontested shift *towards* deference to the past and its exemplarity.

Nevertheless, elsewhere *The Boke of Noblesse* does defer to the ancient histories which Worcester found in his reading. The classical allusions increase in frequency as *The Boke of Noblesse* progresses, especially in its second half, after the list of doomed empires from Chartier's *Le Quadrilogue*. Eventually, one continuous fifth of the work paraphrases or translates some exemplary tales of serving the commonweal from Cicero's *De Senectute*. This is not usually recognized. Yet even in this section, Worcester's classical imitation is second-hand: both his full translation of *De Senectute* and the excerpts in *The Boke of Noblesse* come not from the original Latin but from the French version by Laurent de Premierfait, whose version of Boccaccio Lydgate used.[57] In fact, in the section of *De Senectute* translated in *The Boke of Noblesse*, Cicero writes only a cursory list of the names of heroes, a typical stylistic trick; however, de Premierfait in French expands the list hugely into a set of exemplary lives, and it is this which Worcester translates, still more expansively.[58] His obsessive interest in the exemplary lives of Roman senators is betrayed by his prose, in which he strings them together by accrual rather than argument. He begins the lives paratactically one after another: 'Also to haue in remembraunce', 'Also it is remembrid' (for example 66, 67). The verb is essential though: these seem to be histories fit to be remembered or noted—as in a *memorandum*—and presumably imitated by the active reader.

In some ways this work develops the stylistic trend for fleeting comparisons and allusions in other contemporary speeches, polemics, and tracts, which glorify the present with antique precedent and glamour (as Chapter 3 showed). This style had been tried in Fastolf's household before. Stephen Scrope had translated two French works which borrowed the prestige of classical philosophy and history, to support moralizing and Christian allegory.[59] More

---

[56] De Pizan, *Lart de cheualerie*, sig. f6r–v, discussed in *n.* 60 in Chapter 3 above.

[57] [Worcester (trans.)], *Tulle of Olde Age*, ed. Susebach, pp. xiii–xiv, identifies BL, MS Additional 17433 as Worcester's manuscript of de Premierfait; in fact, it is minutely different from the source of Worcester's translations; nevertheless I cite its text, which is very close.

[58] [Worcester], *Noblesse*, 58–71, especially 64; Marcus Tullius Cicero, *Cato Maior de senectute*, ed. J. G. F. Powell, Cambridge Classical Texts and Commentaries, 28 (Cambridge: Cambridge University Press, 1987), XX.75; BL, MS Additional 17433, ff.44v–46v (French); [Worcester] (trans.) *Tullius de senectute*, sigs. g8r–h3v.

[59] See in general Jonathan Hughes, 'Stephen Scrope and the Circle of Sir John Fastolf: Moral and Intellectual Outlooks', in *Medieval Knighthood IV*, ed. Christopher Harper-Bill and Ruth Harvey (Woodbridge: Boydell, 1992), 109–46.

comparably, in August 1449 Fastolf, perhaps with Worcester's secretarial help, offered to the king some unsolicited advice about a military campaign; and, amid the technicalities, he recommended finding leaders prudent enough to lead the troops with foresight and flexibility, 'for in the Trojan War the prudence of one Antenor is said to have been of greater assistance than the strength or fortitude of ten Hectors' ('nam plus profuisse dicitur in bello Trojano providentia unius Antenoris quam strenuitas aut fortitudo decem Hectorum').[60] As it happens, *The Boke of Noblesse* takes a similar distinction between Ajax's doughtiness and the aged Nestor's sagacity from the French *De Senectute* (63–4).[61] Worcester's treatise, then, in both its specificities and in its general favour for classical history, echoes the wider trend for giving authority to one's work with classical dressings, the trend found in other fifteenth-century writings.

However, two things distinguish Worcester's allusions from those of his peers. One distinction is the bulk of them. For example, in *The Governance of England*, another reforming tract from the 1470s, Sir John Fortescue makes classical allusions half a dozen times and claims after one such allusion that 'Off such ensamples mony of the bokes off cronycles be full; and in especiall þe cronycles off þe Lacidemonies, and off þe Authenences'. But he does not offer many more of these examples.[62] Moreover, the other writers of the time—with the exception perhaps of Fortescue here, who is, as ever, more subtle—use their fleeting and flimsy allusions to impress and persuade rather than to educate. Of course, Worcester probably hoped that his humanism gave his book an air of authority. But as he expands his allusions in bulk, into translations of whole stories, so he expands their significance too. His is not an epideictic rhetoric designed to impress or to flatter the reader; his is a deliberative rhetoric which is designed to help the reader to think. This is why he uses the idea of exemplarity to introduce his classical tales: 'In example I rede in the Romayns stories […]' (53). And this is why, when he borrows from Chartier, he assumes that he has an 'active' reader who will 'considre welle' how Boethius and others served the commonweal, and why he exhorts, us, with each story, that we should remember it.

However, although he imagines an active, considering reader, he cannot predict or secure the response he desires—as no writer can. His own interest in the commonweal emerges as much from misreading the works of Alain

---

[60] *Wars in France*, II.ii.725.

[61] BL, MS Additional 17433, f.19v; [Worcester] (trans.) *Tullius de senectute*, sig. d2r–v. However, Worcester's reference to six Nestors is a variant in some Latin manuscripts listed in the *apparatus criticus* to Cicero, *De Senectute*, ed. Powell, X.31.

[62] Sir John Fortescue, *The Governance of England*, ed. Charles Plummer (London: Oxford University Press, 1885), 150.

Chartier or Nonius Marcellus as from reading them. So how does *The Boke of Noblesse* ensure that we do not misread its examples in turn? The risk of misreading emerges during a catalogue of heroes who gave their lives to defend the Roman republic, the list which Worcester plucks from the French expansion of *De Senectute*. Among the brave and noble men, he describes how the consul Publius Decius, while leading troops into battle, made a rash and ultimately fatal charge upon the enemy in order to inspire his men to similar ferocity, and how Marcus Actilius submitted to gruesome torture rather than assist Rome's enemies (64–6).[63] Worcester presents them as heroes who exemplify service of the commonweal: Marcus Actilius' 'voluntarie dethe […] for the welfare prosperite and comon profit of Rome causithe hym to be an example to alle othir' (66). These seem to be noble sacrifices worthy of Tennyson's Light Brigade. Or are they? Publius Decius may have been noble, but in personal terms, he failed—and glorious failure is evidently not yet considered an English virtue. For in the margin next to Publius Decius' demise Worcester adds a formal and rubricated note which warns the reader that this rash behaviour 'is not recommended', and similar warnings sit beside some other examples of sweet and glorious patriotism ('non est recomendandus' [*sic*]).[64] Moreover, despite the length of the anecdotes, in his final revisions of *The Boke of Noblesse* Worcester added in the margin a further detailed distinction made by 'myne autor Fastolfe' between the 'manlye man' and the 'hardye man'. According to Sir John Fastolf, the hardy man rushes forward into battle, heedless of all bar the personal glory he hopes to win, and leaves his comrades to care for themselves, but the manly man—a term used by Lydgate too, which might echo the Ciceronian *uir uirtutis*—[65] discreetly obtains the upper hand over his adversary and so saves himself and his company. This passage attractively suggests that the aged Fastolf dispensed chivalric lore to 'yong knyghtys and nobles at hys solasse'. This passage perhaps slyly defends Fastolf's behaviour at the Battle of Patay, given his reputation, sealed by Shakespeare, for believing that discretion is the better part of valour. Yet on a closer look Fastolf's comment is more challenging: Worcester, reporting it, seems to share the qualms of Alain Chartier about classical reading. He concludes that the manly man is 'more to be commended' whereas Publius Decius' escapade 'ys not aftyr cristen lawes comended by hys willefulle deth' (64–5). Why is Worcester uncertain whether or not the humanist allusion to Publius Decius is useful for his readers?

[63] Cicero, *De Senectute*, XX.75; BL, MS Additional 17433, ff.44v–45v; [Worcester] (trans.) *Tullius de senectute*, sigs. g7v–h1v.
[64] [Worcester], *Noblesse*, 64, 70–1, with marginalia in BL, MS Royal 18.B.xxii, f.32v, f.35r.
[65] Quentin Skinner, *The Foundations of Modern Political Thought*, 2 vols. (Cambridge: Cambridge University Press, 1978), I.87–91, describes the *uir uirtutis*.

His doubts could stem from academic discussions of how to serve the commonweal. The Aristotelian commentaries of the preceding two centuries argued that suicide deprived the community of one's potential service to others. Nicole Oresme's French translation of Aristotle's *Ethics*—which Fastolf owned—also distinguished between rashness and rational fortitude.[66] These interpretations could be in Worcester's mind when he worries that these heroes' stoical fearlessness might be wilful suicide. However, in his mind too might be the more general difficulties of teaching through *exempla*. What is an *exemplum*? Examples are, as examples, chosen for their very freakishness: Publius Decius and Marcus Actilius are memorable primarily thanks to their elaborate deaths and personal failures; their public service is so noticeable because it is so gory. What, then, should one imitate? The reader should not re-enact these narratives blithely, but should select the key lesson which pervades them: one should, in the next examples given, 'folow the steppis' of the doomed Scipios, not in failing to serve, but in trying (66). To follow their example to the letter would kill us, but the spirit gives life to a hazy ideal towards which we should aspire. In a subtle account of sixteenth-century rhetorical theory, Victoria Kahn interprets humanist concepts of political prudence and of literary decorum as concepts impossible to teach, unamenable to theorization, and embodied only in practice, that is, in instances or examples. For writers from Castiglione to Puttenham, the skill of learning from past events what to do in the present or future does not allow for generalization; all one can learn is the ability to consider situations well.[67] In a similar manner, Worcester's examples provide not specific prudent policies or actions to imitate, but rather samples of virtue to inspire the reader to act 'as the case shall require', as Worcester's son put it when *he* read the book.[68] Hence it is not always clear what the exemplary lives in *The Boke of Noblesse* teach, apart from offering food for thought. The classical examples need interpretation before they can be of any use; otherwise in the space between past model and future practice there is room for misreading their lessons, and in warfare mistakes can be fatal. Worcester's worries about Publius Decius are to a large extent worries about

[66] Cicero, *De Senectute*, XX.75; Aristotle, *Nicomachean Ethics*, trans. H. Rackham (Cambridge, MA: Harvard University Press, 1934), V.xi.1–3; M. S. Kempshall, *The Common Good in Late Medieval Political Thought* (Oxford: Clarendon Press, 1999), 120, 122; Alexander Murray, *Suicide in the Middle Ages*, 2 vols. (Oxford: Clarendon Press, 1998–2000), II.138–9, II.228–31; Beadle, 'Fastolf's French Books', 179. Michael Jones, 'The Battle of Verneuil (17 August 1424): Towards a History of Courage', *War in History*, 9 (2002), 375–411 (388, 398), notes that fifteenth-century strategists often praise egregious risk-taking.

[67] Victoria Kahn, 'Humanism and the Resistance to Theory', in *Literary Theory/Renaissance Texts*, ed. Patricia Parker and David Quint (Baltimore, MD: Johns Hopkins University Press, 1986), 373–96 (377–8, 380).

[68] In his preface to the codicil: La f.2r (*Wars in France*, II.ii.521).

the freedom of readers to misread the hopeful lessons about the commonweal in the classical history he has read and translated.

Therefore, Worcester allows us to hear Fastolf's interpretation of Publius Decius' hardiness; he gives us not only an exemplary tale, but also an exemplary reading. Although he undertakes some humanist reading and anthologizing for us, when he gathers and arranges these materials, he also critiques that reading. Moreover, because of the state of the manuscript in which *The Boke of Noblesse* uniquely now survives, with Worcester's final revisions in his hand, we can see him re-reading his treatise and responding to it. Of course, the tiny revisions clutter the manuscript's leaves, and so if Edward IV or Richard III ever received a copy they likely received a tidier one which incorporated the revisions. In a similar manner, Worcester made revisions to Scrope's *The Dicts and Sayings of the Philosophers*, still visible in his hand in one copy, but in later copies silently integrated. However, his revisions to Scrope's work are smaller interlinear additions, bar two short phrases which did not fit between the lines.[69] By contrast, his eleven marginal responses to *The Boke of Noblesse* offer more formal additions, most fairly lengthy and three even rubricated. As it survives in this manuscript, then, Fastolf's commentary on courage bears witness to the exegesis which classical texts require. These responses, and especially the other briefer, tidier, and red Latin marginalia, structure the reading of the work as much as do the fiddly page designs of *On Husbondrie* and such poems. *The Boke of Noblesse* resembles one of Worcester's own heavily handled manuscripts, replete with adversaria which criticize the treatise's own study and imitation of antiquity.

However, Worcester's revision may also sidestep the politics which an exemplary reading inculcates. The exemplary story is individualistic: it exhorts one man to follow another lone hero. Earlier translations demonstrated this focus: in *De Consulatu Stilichonis*, say, the reader was told to mark the autocratic consul, Stilicho, and the purpose was to teach one aristocratic reader, York—or rather to bring him personal glory. One critic of humanist political rhetoric has criticized its focus upon personal virtue at the expense of 'class consciousness'.[70] Whether or not he shares quite those objections, Worcester does express qualms about personal glory because of his commitment to communal action. This commitment may reflect his interest in the great

[69] Compare Worcester's annotations in Cambridge, Emmanuel College, MS I.2.10, for example f.58v, f.73r, then silently included in CUL, MS Gg.I.34 (ii) and TCC, MS O.5.6, and edited in Stephen Scrope (trans.) *The Dicts and Sayings of the Philosophers*, ed. Curt F. Bühler, EETS os 211 (London: Oxford University Press, 1941), 224:12, 180:5–7.

[70] John Najemy, 'Civic Humanism and Florentine Politics', in *Renaissance Civic Humanism: Reappraisals and Reflections*, ed. James Hankins (Cambridge: Cambridge University Press, 2000), 75–104 (92–3).

republican Cicero—whereas *De Consulatu Stilichonis* and *Knyghthode and Bataile* translate works from imperial Rome. His model is the communal body of senators and not 'singular' or selfish individuals. Thus the politics of the exceptional example is ill-suited, as he at one point explains, to the welfare of the community:

For it was neuer sene that any Countre. Cite or Towne did encrece welle wherouer many nedeles officers and Gouernours that onlie wolde haue a renomme and vndre that colour be a extorcioner piller or briboure was reignyng and ruling ouer theym (72–3)

Like many who have dealt with officious bureaucrats, Worcester feels that seeking 'renomme' in positions of public service is selfish rather than helpful, and liable to conceal malpractice and greed. He contrasts 'singular' or selfish behaviour with communal spirit, and he more frequently discusses the Latin *res publica*. He mentions it or some translation of it, such as *commonweal*, *common profit*, and so on, fifty times throughout the book.[71] Where did he develop this interest in the commonweal? Is it the product—as the dangerous heroic examples seem to be—of his humanist reading, or of some other influence?

SOURCES OF THE COMMONWEAL IN *THE BOKE OF NOBLESSE*

Worcester uses the phrases *res publica*, *commonweal*, and *common profit* apparently interchangeably and never really defines them explicitly; yet he does declare the primary importance of the commonweal to his book above 'alle other thingis':

And it is forto remembre among alle other thingis that is made mencion in this Epistille that euery man after his power and degre shulde principallie put hym in deuoire and laboure for the auaunsment of the comon profit of a Region Contre. Cite. Towne. or householde ¶ For as alle the famous Clerkis writen and inespecialle that wise Cenatoure of Rome Tullius in his booke de Officijs ⌐ de republica. that Nobius Marcellus makyth mencion of yn dyuers chapiters ¬ And in other bookis of his de Amicicia paradoxis and Tusculanis questionibus that Res publica welle attendid and obserued. It is the grounde of welfare and prosperite of alle maner peple (56–7)

---

[71] The word *singular* appears eleven times, in a sense which neither *MED, singuler,* 1(a) nor *OED, singular,* II.8.a and II.8.b, distinguishes. For Worcester's other political terms, see *n.* 33 in Chapter 6 below.

The poem *Knyghthode and Bataile* betrayed that the idea of the *res publica* cannot always be drawn from classical literature without misreading; in that poem the references to the common good sounded strikingly English and urban. But Worcester declares that his fervour for the commonweal comes from Cicero's Roman republican prose. Worcester had actually read many of these works with care (as was noted above) and he gives gravitas to his fervour by alluding to the diligence with which he had to reconstruct one of the works, Cicero's *De Republica*, from 'dyuers chapiters' in Nonius Marcellus' dictionary. To bolster his account further, in subsequent lines he gives definitions from St Augustine and Cicero, with further quotations from John of Wales, Cicero's 'Rethorik', and finally his *De Officiis*. The passage quoted above continues:

> And first to wete the verray declaracion of these. ij. termys Res publica ¶ As seint Austyn seiethe in the. v. booke and. xxviij. Chapitre of the Cite of God ¶ And the saide Tullius the famous Rethoricien accordithe withe the same saieng in latyn termes ¶ Res publica est res populi […] (57)

It is evidently impressive to link one's political ideas to one's humanist reading; the link between the two seems clear. But is it? As we saw, some of Worcester's humanist reading was second-hand and in these lines too, as it happens, the Latin quotations in fact all come from the opening chapters of John of Wales's thirteenth-century *Communiloquium*. Even the first quotation which Worcester says is Cicero's is ascribed by John of Wales to St Augustine; Worcester has confused it with an adjacent reference to St Augustine's paraphrase of part of Cicero's *De Republica*.[72] Yet Worcester seems to offer us Cicero and, as when he read Nonius Marcellus, he evidently thinks that he has selected only Cicero from John of Wales's work, creating a humanist source by deceit.

Such well-meaning fakery recurs elsewhere in *The Boke of Noblesse*, where Worcester compares the lord's care for his farm or household to one's commitment to the commonweal. The comparison allegedly follows Cicero's *De Senectute*. In that work, one character says that nothing better befits noble men than to study land management, for this subject is closest to philosophy and will bring prosperity to the realm, and he then describes King Cyrus' labours in his garden. Again, though, Worcester follows de Premierfait's expansion of Cicero's text: the original Latin only briefly

---

[72] Compare [Worcester], *Noblesse*, 57, with John of Wales, *Communiloquium*, in *Summa Johannis Ualensis de regimine vite humane seu Margarita doctorum ad omne propositum prout patet in tabula*, ed. Johannes Ualentis (Lyons, 1511), ff.i^r–cxxxix^v: f.iiii^r (I.i), f.v^r, conflating two passages (I.iii); compare [Worcester], *Noblesse*, 58, with John of Wales, *Communiloquium*, f.vii^r (I.vii). See Marcus Tullius Cicero, *De Republica*, ed. K. Ziegler (Leipzig: Teubner, 1969), I.25.39, and St Augustine, *The City of God Against the Pagans*, ed. and trans. George E. McCracken and others, 7 vols. (Cambridge, MA: Harvard University Press, 1957–72), II.xxi.

mentions Cyrus the green-fingered monarch in the hope that people 'would understand that nothing so befits the ruler as study of the cultivation of fields' ('ut intellegatis nihil ei tam regale videri quam studium agri colendi'); but the French and English versions imagine in detail what Xenophon's praise for agriculture might be and describe farming at length.[73] In *The Boke of Noblesse* agriculture is 'one of the principalle dedis of a Prince' (69). The expansions suit the spirit of the original *De Senectute*, which does, in other sections, beautifully digress on this theme. The expansion is also typical of humanist writing, which often used this Ciceronian topos to idealize the government of one's estate as a symbol for other forms of mastery.[74] But it is not genuine classical scholarship; once more, Worcester makes his ideas about the commonweal look like humanist ones, even though his sources are faulty. He writes in harmony with classical sources, even if he is not quite reading them.

However, given their tenuous connections to classical literature, it is fair to ask how important humanist reading was in forming these ideas about the commonweal. What is the real source of them, and how necessary are the classical tales in communicating them? The connection between the commonweal and land economy is particularly curious in this regard. The earlier agricultural translation, *On Husbondrie*, neglected to highlight the political connotations of its matter: its hints at Duke Humfrey's good governance were only implicit; more prominent were hints at the duke's glory as a textual critic. So classical agricultural writing does not *necessarily* yield lessons about the commonweal. Nor, conversely, is the political symbolism in agriculture necessarily read in classical authorities. Other books could inspire the theme: for example, Worcester also inserted some praise of agriculture as service of the 'comon profite' when he revised Scrope's *The Dicts and Sayings of the Philosophers*.[75] Then, back in *The Boke of Noblesse*, he explicitly aligns political governance with household governance according to fifteenth-century practical experience:

the terme of Res publica whiche is in englisshe tong clepid a comyn profit it ought aswelle be referred to the prouision and wise gouuernaunce of a mesuage or a householde as to the conduit and wise gouernaunce of a village Towne. Citee. Countree. or Region (68)

---

[73] Cicero, *De Senectute*, XVI.56, XVII.59–XVII.60; BL, MS Additional 17433, f.34r, ff.35r–36v; [Worcester] (trans.) *Tullius de senectute*, sigs. f3v–f4v, f5r–f7r.

[74] Cicero, *De Senectute*, VII.24–5; on which, see Lorna Hutson, *The Usurer's Daughter: Male Friendship and Fictions of Women in Sixteenth-Century England* (London: Routledge, 1994), 28–9, 36–7.

[75] Cambridge, Emmanuel College, MS I.2.10, f.3v; Scrope (trans.) *Dicts and Sayings*, 28:19–30:2, and 328–9, *n.* 28.18–29, noting that 'bien commun' is not in the French source here.

At this point in his argument, Worcester interrupts Cicero's account of agriculture with another page of text squeezed at the last minute into the margins. As when he criticizes Publius Decius, the process of revising and reading again turns away from Cicero to Sir John Fastolf, Worcester's employer. The revision discusses Fastolf's successful garrisoning of the Bastille, then an English fortress in Paris, in 1421; he had ensured that it had food and armaments sufficient to endure sieges and attacks (68–9). So can contemporary heroes, Fastolf rather than Cyrus, exemplify service of the *res publica* in their skilful domestic economy?

Apparently so. Historians of the twelfth to fifteenth centuries have keenly demonstrated that notions of the commonweal were available to thinkers long before the influence of humanist studies, in the academic theories of Parisian theologians, in the practice of burghal life or even in the more flexible feudalism of England. Walter Ullmann even suggested that civic humanism had little influence in England because the aristocracy and nobility there had long been accustomed to negotiate with their vassals. Some of these vernacular notions seemed to influence the politics of the humanist translation *Knyghthode and Bataile* (in Chapter 3 above).[76] In his more useful writings, account books and letters and so on, Worcester often finds service of the commonweal unfolding in the domestic business of English life. For example, he once comments in a notebook that Fastolf's skills in governing his estates were 'the main causes of the increase of the commonweal' at Castlecombe, a manor he acquired through his wife ('cause principales augmentacionis rei publice'); as it happens, economic studies have confirmed Fastolf's wise governance of his tenants there. Elsewhere Worcester expresses his concern to aid the 'comyn weelle' with bequests from Fastolf's will, or praises William Canynges, the mayor of Bristol, for serving the *res publica* of that town.[77] Unsurprisingly, then, *The Boke of Noblesse* can turn from a classical example of good governance, Cyrus in his garden, to the concern for the commonweal in the responsibilities of the English landowner or burgess. Yet the example concerns Fastolf's military household, his garrisoning of the Bastille. How is *military* governance relevant? Does not warfare harm rather than destroy?

[76] Kempshall, *The Common Good, passim*; James M. Blythe, '"Civic Humanism" and Medieval Political Thought', in *Renaissance Civic Humanism: Reappraisals and Reflections*, ed. James Hankins (Cambridge: Cambridge University Press, 2000), 30–74 (36–43); Walter Ullmann, *Medieval Foundations of Renaissance Humanism* (London: Elek, 1977), 185–8; and *n*.79 in Chapter 3 above.

[77] BL, MS Additional 28208, f.2v; Davis (ed.) *Paston Letters*, nos. 912, 461, 727, 878, 888; Worcestre, *Itineraries*, 52–3. On Fastolf's business, see E. M. Carus-Wilson, 'Evidences of Industrial Growth on Some Fifteenth-Century Manors', *Economic History Review*, 2nd series, 12 (1959–60), 190–205 (198–9), and Anthony Robert Smith, 'Aspects of the Career of Sir John Fastolf (1380–1459)' (unpublished D.Phil. thesis, University of Oxford, 1982), 43, 50–1.

In fact, some political writers of the 1450s to 1470s grounded the popular idiom of the commonweal in nostalgia for the achievements of the military governance of Henry V and Bedford, under whom Fastolf served.⁷⁸ Sure enough, one important inspiration for *The Boke of Noblesse* is the conduct of the English wars in France. Financial reforms in the military will benefit all: if the king ensures that the officers feed and pay the soldiers well, he will preserve their morale and discipline and prevent them from plundering—and so alienating—loyal French civilians (71–4). This can be learnt from Fastolf's records of the army in France or from the statutes issued by Henry V and Bedford. Worcester reminds the king, his imagined reader, that he delivered a copy of the statutes 'to your hyghenes enseled' on 29 May 1475 (31). One early sixteenth-century reader of *The Boke of Noblesse* noted that he must enquire after a copy of them too, and others in Worcester's milieu collected them.⁷⁹ Readers could apparently learn to serve the commonweal from their near contemporaries, whether in husbandry or in warfare. So was the humanist reading pointless?

It seems so. In the first half of *The Boke of Noblesse* classical history is dwarfed by practical counsel. Nevertheless, it remains important. Firstly, Worcester still adorns his most practical lessons with classical allusions, as other fifteenth-century writers did. To stay with Bedford's men, we hear that they never stole from their foes 'in semblable wise' to the ancient Gauls, and that Bedford too rejected pillage 'aftyr the Romayns condicion' (31–2), a comparison that adorns but does not explain. Secondly, there are limits to the extent to which fifteenth-century military governance might be a model for good civil governance. We must not ignore the vernacular sources of Worcester's republican ideology, but nor must we idealize them. Do seductive myths of 'horizontal' political responsibility accurately represent the hierarchical fifteenth century? Some have argued that they do not and that even letters about the commonweal by Fastolf and company might employ such phrases merely to bolster their private interests.⁸⁰ Moreover, moral questions hover

---

⁷⁸ David Morgan, 'The Household Retinue of Henry V and the Ethos of English Public Life', in *Concepts and Patterns of Service in the Later Middle Ages*, ed. Anne Curry and Elizabeth Matthew (Woodbridge: Boydell, 2000), 64–79 (73–4, 78).

⁷⁹ BL, MS Royal 18.B.xxii, f.15r. For Bedford's statutes, see B. J. H. Rowe, 'Discipline in the Norman Garrisons under Bedford, 1422–35', *EHR*, 46 (1931), 194–208 (201–6); and for others owned by Worcester's associates, see G. A. Lester, *Sir John Paston's 'Grete Boke'* (Cambridge: Brewer, 1984), 167–72; Richard Beadle and Lotte Hellinga, 'William Paston II and Pynson's *Statutes of War* (1492)', *The Library*, 7th series, 2 (2001), 107–19 (109).

⁸⁰ Christine Carpenter, *The Wars of the Roses: Politics and the Constitution in England, c.1437–1509* (Cambridge: Cambridge University Press, 1997), 46, 57–9; Helen Castor, *The King, the Crown and the Duchy of Lancaster: Public Authority and Private Power, 1399–1461* (Oxford: Oxford University Press, 2000), 163–4.

over whether warfare could ever serve the commonweal well: a sceptical search easily undermines any idealization of warfare. For example, although *The Boke of Noblesse* discovers that Bedford's well-paid and well-ordered troops never harmed the French civilians, it then betrays that they did also win worship and riches, after their initial selflessness (31–2). More horrifically, Fastolf issued a military despatch in 1435, copied into *The Boke of Noblesse*'s codicil of documents, in which he recommended the defeat of France through the burning of crops and 'alle bestaile' to starve the French into submission. The despatch ponders how to deflect 'any noote of tirannye' from such an act, and reassures its readers that the civilian subjects of one's foes deserve famine.[81] In the light of this accompanying document, *The Boke of Noblesse* looks more like a textbook for 'tirannye'—it does advocate invading France—and the classical allusions seem, again, vague and specious distractions from the real argument.

However, *The Boke of Noblesse* does not advocate war for war's sake, but as a means to justice and peace. Like several parliamentary documents of the 1470s, it argues that the kingdom should occupy its more troublesome subjects in foreign conflict where their energies might win prosperity for themselves and the realm (44–5). As such, it might support the efforts in the parliament of 1472–5 to win an experimental tax so that the king would have enough funds for his phoney war in France.[82] Yet *The Boke of Noblesse* pursues its campaign for peace on many less martial fronts. It requests not only the opening of a war-chest to allow the king's campaigns to thrive but also charity to nurture the whole community. The treatise exhorts the king, addressed in person, to 'let youre riche tresours be spradde and put abrode' in order not only to finance his impending conquest but to bring 'the relief of youre indigent and nedie peple', already overtaxed (80). This request for relief from taxation might recall the doctrines of Sir John Fortescue, Worcester's acquaintance and contemporary. Yet Fortescue attacks taxation as a redistribution of the gentleman's hard-defended wealth; his only concern for the poor is their political flammability and the dishonour to the king's magnificence of having mean subjects.[83] By contrast, Worcester's prayer to the king to 'let youre riche tresours be spradde and put abrode' is not a plea for small government but a plea for sharing the burden of supporting the whole realm:

---

[81] La ff.40v–41r (*Wars in France*, II.ii.580–1), on which see M. G. A. Vale, 'Sir John Fastolf's "Report" of 1435: A New Interpretation Reconsidered', *Nottingham Mediaeval Studies*, 17 (1973), 78–84 (80–3).

[82] J. Brigstocke Sheppard (ed.), *Literæ Cantuarienses: The Letter Books of the Monastery of Christ Church, Canterbury*, RS 85, 3 vols. (London: HMSO, 1887–9), III.275–8; Kekewich and others (eds.) *Vale's Book*, 145–7; on which see Ross, *Edward IV*, 217.

[83] Fortescue, *Governance*, 114–17, 138–40.

[…] for it is saide that ⌐ An empyre or ¬ Roiaume is bettir without tresoure of golde than without worship ¶ And also bettir it is to lyue a pore life in a riche Roiaume in tranquillite and pease than to be riche in a pore Roiaume where debate and strife reignithe (81)

Such a policy, apparently, will make life better for everyone in a Rawlsian sense: the general level of well-being will be greater, even if some individuals are not as wealthy as they once were. The immediate intention of financing the 1475 invasion lies only in the background of this bigger idea.

Moreover, at this most bold stage in the argument, these ideas about the commonweal are less a reflection of contemporary feudal platitudes than of Worcester's study of antiquity. In fact, we can trace the models for this most bold of the propositions in *The Boke of Noblesse* directly back to Worcester's reading. When he reminds the king that 'bettir it is to lyue a pore life in a riche Roiaume in tranquillite and pease than to be riche in a pore Roiaume where debate and strife reignithe' (81), he is translating the French version of John of Wales's *Breuiloquium*, where this axiom sums up some inspiring tales from Aristotle and Valerius Maximus: 'Car vng chascun amoit mieulx viure et conuerser comme poure homme en vng Rice Roiaume que estre riche et viure en vng poure roiaume'. In his manuscript of John of Wales, Worcester marked this sentence as an 'Exemplum notabile' and the note-making has allowed him to transfer it to his own treatise.[84] Now, he may here import John of Wales's characteristic Franciscan contempt for worldly goods, a financial selflessness with a different distinguished heritage.[85] However, he bolsters his interest in selfless service and generosity not with further pious sources, but with further stories of ancient Rome from Chartier's *Le Quadrilogue invectif*: the Romans replaced their slaughtered equestrians of 'Auncien gentille bloode' with 'bounde men' promoted to knighthood in order to save the state; the Roman ladies gave 'liberallie of theire juellis' to pay soldiers' wages and secure victory (83). The terms such as *gentility* and *liberality* sound quaint and chivalric but Worcester's own notes on Chartier mark these stories as lessons 'pro re publica'.[86] Finally, Worcester demonstrates the selfless disbursement of private goods for a common cause with a long and close paraphrase from Livy's history *Ab Urbe condita*, a copy of which he probably acquired from William Sellyng.[87] As we join the story, a colony of Rome has been tempted to align itself with the enemy; when a levy is called to support Rome's defence of the colony, the Roman citizens refuse. Suddenly, Valerius Laevinius, who is

[84] Cu f.23r–v; John of Wales, *Breuiloquium*, f.ccix[v].
[85] Jenny Swanson, *John of Wales: A Study of the Works and Ideas of a Thirteenth-Century Friar* (Cambridge: Cambridge University Press, 1989), 59; Kempshall, *Common Good*, 15–16.
[86] Ro f.136v; Chartier, *Quadrilogue*, 31:4–19.
[87] According to a letter copied into Ju f.205r.

called 'Lenius' in *The Boke of Noblesse*, persuades the senators themselves to give freely as befits their estate, thereby 'yeuyng the Comons Example'. The populace take 'gret courage' and also give 'largelie of here golde and tresour for the comon wele'; noble magnanimity and service inspire widespread action (83–5).[88] There are clear parallels with English affairs as seen by the pro-war party, who called upon their countrymen to defend the unloved and unwilling English territories in France. Yet, essentially, in this most daring of political exhortations—to the idea of national charity—Worcester exceeds the inspiration of Bedford and Fastolf and turns instead to antiquity.

Moreover, here *The Boke of Noblesse* seems to overcome the difficulties inherent in imitation, for imitation is the triumphant element in this final Roman exemplum. The noble senators give an 'example' to every member of the body politic that he should consider every other member; they almost demonstrate how Worcester's classical stories and allusions might urge every fifteenth-century reader, royal or otherwise, to follow the magnanimous senators in doing good. The imitation, furthermore, is not one that is followed blindly, as we might follow a kamikaze general into battle. Royal or noble generosity must provide an 'example' to inspire each man 'after his degree' to contribute to the commonweal (81). Public service is here not lazy imitation, but a careful interpretation of the exemplum, in order to gauge the most prudent contribution according to one's abilities and 'degree'. *The Boke of Noblesse* develops neither the lordly generosity ascribed to Fastolf nor the grievances of the ignored Commons from fierier manifestos; it is not that the rich give and the poor receive—nor vice versa. It offers a bold but simple idea, that all should *think carefully* about their place in the commonweal and act fittingly—with the humanist quality of decorum.

THE COMMONWEAL OF READERS AND COMMON KNOWLEDGE

As Worcester says (quoted above), the main purpose of the book is to inspire service of the commonweal:

And it is forto remembre among alle other thingis that is made mencion in this Epistille that euery man after his power and degre shulde principallie put hym in deuoire and laboure for the auaunsment of the comon profit [...] Res publica welle attendid and obserued. It is the grounde of welfare and prosperite of alle maner peple (56–7)

[88] Livy, *Ab Urbe condita*, ed. and trans B. O. Foster and others, 14 vols. (Cambridge, MA: Harvard University Press, 1919–59), XXVI.xxxv.1–XXVI.xxxvi.12.

The 'grounde' of prosperity—and 'of alle maner peple' too—is not just that there *is* a communal unit called the *res publica*; there might be such thing as society, and one might ignore it. The 'grounde' of prosperity is that one should *attend to* that communal unit, give it one's active attention: it must be 'welle attendid and observed'. *Res publica* does not denote an institution like the state or an economic goal; it is an ethical imperative to act, namely, to do some intellectual activity—remembering, attending, and observing—as well as 'deuoire and laboure' in the wider world. Elsewhere reading and thinking are exhorted as the first points of public service: one must 'considre welle the histories of olde croniclers'. The style of *The Boke of Noblesse*, veering from example to exhortation to example, and the interpolated or marginal notes, all demand an active, alert reader. Moreover, if the process of attending to the commonweal is the 'grounde' of prosperity, then merely by attending to the examples and exhortations one serves the commonweal—or begins to, at least. The classical examples and histories are not mere trimmings here, then, but are an essential action of this book, of the active experience of reading it. The reader imitates the 'deuoire and laboure' of Worcester's own scholarship.

Moreover, just as Worcester's records of his reading in his notebooks or marginalia conjure up a coterie of humanist scholars, so in this longer work he conjures up a coterie by his style of writing. The constant stream of histories draws the reader into a virtual library, as it were, of other ever-present books from which the argument is bolstered. Worcester frequently directs the reader to other works, whether the military statutes composed by Bedford, which he had given to the king, or the works of Josephus, Orosius, and Livy (51); as it happens, these three were available in Sir John Fastolf's household in French translation.[89] His reminders in red marginalia of the sources of his quotations, or of passages for which the text itself does not give a source, further direct the reader to the wider culture from which the book gets its authority. Even the stories of one-off heroes, about whom Worcester was so nervous, are supposed to homogenize the readers rather than to individualize them. Marcus Actilius' fatal zeal 'causithe hym to be an example to alle othir'; tales from Cicero, Livy, Chartier, and de Pizan must guide 'euery wise gouernoure is hert' (66, 58). The words 'alle' and 'euery' are important in this book. Then for 'alle' men and 'every' governor to play a part, everybody must read and share the same models. The sense that the models are shared emerges in one other important word in the references to 'that vaillaunt citezin' Publius Decius and

---

[89] See the inventory in OMC Archives, MS Fastolf Papers 43, f.10r, and Worcester's notes from French translations of Orosius, Lucan, and Suetonius, also owned by Fastolf, in Ro f.135r–v, ff.142r–146r. For Livy, Vegetius, Josephus, and Bartholomaeus Anglicus, all owned by Fastolf, see [Worcester], *Noblesse* 2, 21, 26, 29, 51, 53, 55, 83. Date computations from Josephus also appear in Worcester's notebook, London, College of Arms, MS Arundel 48, f.94v.

'that verray trew louer of the comon wele' Marcus Actilius (64, 65). When he uses the word 'that', Worcester writes as though the reader already knows the stories he's referring to, and thus insinuates that the readers are already bound together to some degree. It is like the reference to 'those' ('hec') humanities with which *we* are all familiar in Pietro del Monte's writings, or the names of Humfrey's friends in *On Husbondrie*. Worcester draws the reader into an imaginary readership of people familiar with certain literary and historical materials, by making these histories and Latin tags to some extent common knowledge or 'classical' in the typicality and familiarity of 'the classic'. That sense of binding a readership together seems the other important feature of Worcester's use of his humanist reading in *The Boke of Noblesse*.

One of Worcester's own favourite works suggests the imagined effect of these shared heroes and 'touchstones'. The suggestion lies in two important passages of Cicero's *De Amicitia* (cited here in Tiptoft's translation, which Caxton printed alongside Worcester's translation of *De Senectute*). Cicero suggests that mutual goodwill among citizens is crucial to the preservation of the commonweal: without friendship and 'acorde', 'neyther hows ne cytee · ne tylthe of londe shal remayne'. Friendship aids governance, and what doomed tyrants essentially lack is the friendship of fellow men. And how will one generate friendship? Obviously, like attracts like: 'one cyteseyn drawe rather to an other · than one straunger to another'. One could well interpret these ideas as exclusionary; however, Cicero emphasizes that the elite which wins friendship is an elite based upon virtue, and that the virtue which prompts friendship can be found throughout 'the multitude of peple'. Moreover, such virtue prompts selflessness rather than selfishness, helping 'alle maner of paple' [*sic*]. The English translation calls the attitude to be cultivated 'loue of the comunyte', a phrase much warmer and more communitarian than Cicero's snooty 'charity for the crowd' ('caritate vulgi').[90] So one's care for the commonweal is like one's virtuous friendships. Moreover 'the multitude of peple' can all model their virtuous friendships on 'such as we remembre · that ben here in this comyn lyf emonge vs': that is, we can imitate those noble friends whose names are preserved in memory and who are familiar to all in common from history and literature, such as Publius Emilius and Lucinius, or Marcus Curius and Titus Cornucacius.[91] Cicero's *De Amicitia* suggests that a political community will share certain forms of literary and historical culture, certain rhetorical forms.

---

[90] John Tiptoft (trans.), *De Amicitia*, printed in [Worcester] (trans.), *Tullius de senectute*, but separately foliated; here citing sigs. a6v–a8r, b7r–v; Marcus Tullius Cicero, *Laelius de Amicitia* in his *Cato Maior. Laelius*, ed. K. Simbeck (Stuttgart: Teubner, 1971), 5.19–7.23, 14.50–15.52.

[91] Tiptoft (trans.), *De Amicitia*, sig. b4r; Cicero, *De Amicitia*, 11.38.

There is no evidence that Worcester's book is informed by precisely this reading of *De Amicitia*. However, this theory does illuminate Worcester's practice as Ciceronian by analogy. Moreover, Aristotle makes a similar point.[92] And as it happens, Worcester studied Cicero's *De Amicitia* and the book of Aristotle's *Ethics* on friendship at considerable length. More fittingly still, he shared those works with his friends![93] The sharing of books was typical of Worcester's reading habits. That emerges in the fifty-two donors or recipients of his books named in his notebooks and marginalia, and the other men implied by vaguer notes or by the name of their institution. It emerges in his correspondence, too, swapping books or proverbs: in one of Worcester's notebooks is a letter from William Sellyng, asking 'vmfrido Gentyll lucano'—perhaps one of the Luccan merchants in London—to show to the bearer a copy of Livy, 'for your friendship to me and your outstanding *humanitas* towards all men' ('pro tua erga me beniuolentia et pro tua in omnes homines singulari humanitate').[94] It was *humanitas* which (as Chapter 1 noted) drove one young scholar to hunt out plays in the vulgar tongue for his friend. This sort of sharing of learning is a communal act and expresses *humanitas*, now in the sense of *kindness*, between men. So in his reading Worcester shared in the goodwill on which the manuscript literary community depended, and with *The Boke of Noblesse* he fixes that reading and that community into writing. Simply by dint of sharing these stories, he binds the reader into a community of the like-minded.

But did his imagined reader, Edward IV, listen? Did anybody else? Unfortunately, *The Boke of Noblesse* only survives in one manuscript and so, for all we know, Worcester's commonweal of readers was most likely imaginary.

[92] Aristotle, *Ethics*, VIII.ix.1–6; Kempshall, *Common Good*, 49–50; Miriam Griffin, 'From Aristotle to Atticus: Cicero and Matius on Friendship', in *Philosophia Togata II: Plato and Aristotle at Rome*, ed. Jonathan Barnes and Miriam Griffin (Oxford: Clarendon Press, 1997), 86–109 (86).

[93] Ju f.71r–v, ff.74r–78r (copious notes from *De Amicitia* and *Ethics*, VIII and IX); Davis (ed.), *Paston Letters*, no. 316 (borrowing *De Amicitia* from John Paston II); Worcestre, *Itineraries*, 262 (lending Aristotle's *Ethics*).

[94] Ju 205r; and exchanges of books or proverbs in Davis (ed.), *Paston Letters*, nos. 537, 604, 780; Worcestre, *Itineraries*, 312 (again mentioning John Crop); and *n*. 10 above.

5

Print and the reproduction of humanist readers

William Worcester's use of classical literature does not fit those recent histories which have described humanism as a pedantic philological activity married to absolutism and discipline. For Worcester, the process of reading the classics was itself suffused with civic commitment. However, there is little evidence of the wider circulation of Worcester's treatise, *The Boke of Noblesse* (as the last chapter noted). To explore the feasibility of a commonweal of readers, we need to explore what happened when a wider vernacular readership turned to classical literature. Just over a year after Worcester completed *The Boke of Noblesse*, William Caxton began printing books in England for the first time, and was swiftly followed by Theodoric Rood in Oxford and an anonymous printer in St Albans. In 1481, around the very end of Worcester's life, Caxton printed Worcester's other surviving English work, a translation of Cicero's *De Senectute*. When these printers began engaging in vernacular humanism, did they cultivate a wider, politically engaged readership, or simply foster a humanist pedagogy of grammar and flagellation?

What cannot be doubted is that writers and readers in late fifteenth-century England often employed printed books in their humanist studies. One might miss the quantity of classical and neo-Latin books read in England, because most of them were not produced there; recent statistics have hinted at the scale of the imported 'Latin trade', much of which was classical literature. One study even suggests that English readers owned as many classical texts from Venice as books printed in London,[1] although Venetian classical editions, many of them large and sturdy, all of them prestigious, are more likely to survive safely in academic libraries. This world of imported books is not

---

[1] The calculation combines two figures given by Margaret Lane Ford, 'Importation of Printed Books into England and Scotland', in *CHBB: III*, 179–201 (183–5, 188–90). For similar figures, see Lotte Hellinga, 'Importation of Books Printed on the Continent into England and Scotland before c.1520', in *Printing and the Written Word: The Social History of Books, circa 1450–1520*, ed. Sandra Hindman (Ithaca, NY: Cornell University Press, 1991), 205–24 (221–4).

separate from the world of England's own first printer, Caxton. He was a busy importer of books, and his biography does link him with several humanist scholars. His early career as a merchant and diplomat in the Low Countries introduced him frequently to collectors of the Latin classics in print, such as the clerics and ambassadors of humanist taste John Gunthorpe, John Russell, and John Morton.[2] He printed several works created by Italian humanists, as did the other presses in fifteenth-century England; he printed works by Cicero in English, not to mention Cato, Aesop, and Chaucer's *Boece*. Moreover, within his books he refers to classical authors such as Virgil, Homer, Ovid, Lucan, and Statius—almost in that familiar order—and to the Italian scholars Boccaccio and Poggio Bracciolini. He may note the origin of the *studia humanitatis* in Italy: Virgil is a popular subject for schools, he says, 'specyally in Ytalye and other places'.[3]

Nevertheless, hitherto only Luigi Balsamo has recognized Caxton's early move into the market for humanist textbooks, while Seth Lerer has shown that Caxton describes his recovery of Chaucer's poems as a textual scholarship analogous to humanist research.[4] Other critics have belittled the humanist influences upon Caxton's career, and have cast him as representative of the ignorance or 'medievalness' of his age.[5] Even David Carlson's invaluable discussion of Tudor printing considers only fifteen English incunables to have any humanist interest: but by including the vernacular some thirty-eight editions can be judged to further the study or imitation of classical antiquity. Carlson argues that the biggest concern of fifteenth-century printers was marketing their newly voluminous quantities of books and, as they 'seem not to have perceived much of a market' for humanist books, 'they contributed little indeed to creating one'. In his account, the sheer multiplication of books by the press creates the problem of finding a market, and humanism does not until the 1520s offer a solution.[6] In fact, though, it seems that by the 1470s a humanist readership was no longer a desideratum, something still to be

[2] Martin Lowry, 'The Arrival and Use of Continental Printed Books in Yorkist England', in *Le Livre dans l'Europe de la Renaissance*, ed. Pierre Aquilon and Henri-Jean Martin (Paris: Promodis, 1988), 449–59 (449–50); Martin Lowry, 'Diplomacy and the Spread of Printing', in *Bibliography and the Study of 15th-Century Civilisation*, ed. Lotte Hellinga and John Goldfinch, British Library Occasional Papers, 5 (London: British Library, 1987), 124–46 (132–3).

[3] *Caxton's Own Prose*, 96:45–55 and 36a:21; see also 44:1–3, 71b:1–6, 72a:58–61.

[4] Luigi Balsamo, 'The Origins of Printing in Italy and England', in *Journal of the Printing Historical Society*, 11 (1976: special issue *Eight Papers Presented to the Caxton International Congress*), 48–63 (58–60); Seth Lerer, *Chaucer and his Readers: Imagining the Author in Late-Medieval England* (Princeton, NJ: Princeton University Press, 1993), 150–1, 166–8.

[5] N. F. Blake, *William Caxton and English Literary Culture* (London: Hambledon, 1991), 7–8; N. F. Blake, *Caxton and his World* (London: Deutsch, 1969), 196–200; and J. B. Trapp, 'The Humanist Book', in *CHBB: III*, 285–315 (288–9); Weiss, *Humanism*, 175–6.

[6] Carlson, *English Humanist Books*, 130–5.

invented, as it was for *On Husbondrie*; humanism had already shaped some forms of English literature, book production and reading habits long before printing came to England.

So what happens to humanist writing when technology makes a wider readership yet more convenient? Within the classroom or lecture hall, the ability to reproduce more quickly and more cheaply guides to Ciceronian rhetoric or phrase books from Terence allowed the 'institutionalization' of humanism. Several printers in England cultivated the lucrative market in textbooks and several teachers exploited the opportunity to reproduce their books mechanically. Some of these works (in the first half of this chapter) seem to revert to the narrow philology and discipline of minds and bodies criticized by recent historians of humanism. However, when we turn from classical Latin and neo-Latin works to the English books produced by William Caxton, we find (this chapter finally argues) that he echoes the forms and ideas of the specifically vernacular humanism found in *Knyghthode and Bataile*, say, or similar works. His prologues and epilogues imagine the possibilities of textual reproduction and dissemination which humanist pedagogy imagines; not in order to discipline or limit his readers, but to ennoble them. These hopes emerge in his epilogue to *Boece* (as shown in Chapter 1) and in his prefaces to various other works, including William Worcester's version of Cicero's *De Senectute*. This translation originally emerged from a close-knit network of patrons and friends, like so many earlier works in manuscript, but it now survives in more copies than they do, because it was printed. Worcester did not dream in vain of a larger commonweal of readers; Caxton actually sent this work out to them. Yet it is not that technology alone determined the spread of humanism. It is the ideas of humanist writers, printers, and patrons, and the choices of their readers, which made reproduction and dissemination possibilities worth pursuing—once in turning to the vernacular, now in turning to print.

REPRODUCING HUMANISM IN PRINT

Although it was long standard to grant the new technology a completely revolutionary influence, as in Elizabeth L. Eisenstein's influential *The Printing Press as an Agent of Change*, recent historians of printing have warned against this assumption. They have quibbled with the belief that printing transformed European culture by the sudden possibilities for standardization, textual fixity, and the increased dissemination of ideas. They have observed that printed books only acquired their reputation for stability and trustworthiness because of conscious efforts by authors, printers, booksellers, and readers to treat them thus, rather than because of any inherent quality in print. Early editions did not in fact contain fixed and stable texts, and there was not a radical shift from manuscript to print; readers continued to consult both media as complementary forms of one thing (the book) rather than as opposed entities, and they continued to alter, annotate, and read aloud from both media.[7]

These insights are borne out by the uses of printed books by humanists in fifteenth-century England. Giovanni Gigli (1434–98), a papal official in England from 1476 to 1490, wrote by hand at the front of Cicero's *Tusculanae disputationes* some verses which instructed the 'lector' to read the book for its moral wisdom. One will learn how to endure mortality and embrace virtue, lessons picked out by most of the marginal notes which the book contains.[8] Similarly, when Pietro Carmeliano (*c.*1451–1527), an Italian at the English court, gave Edward IV a printed edition of Cicero's *De Oratore* he prefixed some Latin verses, and added marginal notes throughout. Scholars thus impeded the perfect duplication of printed books by hand-finishing some copies for presentation with that personal touch.[9] With such additions, the printed book becomes as solicitous and as intimate a lesson or a request for patronage as a manuscript can be. The printed books personalized in this way recall the manuscripts circulated by English writers with, say, prologues addressed to Duke Humfrey or Worcester's windy inscriptions. Some humanist books were not finished until finished by hand, whether the text itself was copied or printed.

However, by appearing in a printed book, such verses balance that deluxe intimacy with participation in shared scholarly endeavour. Firstly, it is not always certain whether the 'lector' addressed on flyleaves denotes only one particular reader or instead stands in for a wider possible readership—as in some books dedicated to English princes. Certain other books decisively offer their intimacy to the wider community, for their liminary verses are themselves printed. Caxton's edition of Chaucer's *Boece* concludes with a verse epitaph of Chaucer, made by the 'poete laureat' Stefano Surigone, which Caxton claims could be found on Chaucer's tomb; thus readers can mentally

---

[7] Adrian Johns, *The Nature of the Book: Print and Knowledge in the Making* (Chicago: University of Chicago Press, 1998), 1–6, 10, 18–20; David McKitterick, *Print, Manuscript and the Search for Order* (Cambridge: Cambridge University Press, 2003), 20, 36–7, 99–100, 117–18.

[8] Cicero, *Tusculanarum quaestionum libri* (Venice: Jenson, 1472; CUL, classmark Inc.3.B.3.2 [1353]), flyleaf f.iii[v] and notes *passim*. On Gigli, see David R. Carlson, 'Three Tudor Epigrams', *HL*, 45 (1996), 189–200 (193–6), and *n.* 13 in Chapter 3 above.

[9] This book, described by Thomas Tanner, is now lost: see David Carlson, 'The Occasional Poetry of Pietro Carmeliano', *Aevum*, 61 (1987), 495–502 (496–7). For another annotated copy of this edition with an English provenance, see Cicero, *De Oratore* (Venice: Catharensis, 20/8/1478; CUL, classmark Inc.3.B.3.27 [1478]).

travel to Westminster and listen to an Italian poet.[10] There are other examples: Caxton also printed six elegant neo-Latin letters 'diligently revised by Pietro Carmeliano, poet laureate, in Westminster' ('diligenter emendate per Petrum Carmelianum Poetam Laureatum / in Westmonasterio'); the colophon was followed by verses which urged the purchaser to buy these letters if he saw himself as cultivated:

> Eloquij cultor sex has mercare tabellas
> Que possunt Marco cum Cicerone loqui
> Ingenijs debent cultis ea scripta placere
> In quibus ingenij copia magna viget[11]

O cultivator of eloquence, buy these six letters which are fit to speak even with Cicero. These writings, in which a great breadth of wit thrives, ought to please cultivated wits.

Carmeliano also supplied verses to accompany the first humanist grammar composed in England, John Anwykyll's *Compendium totius grammatice*, and an edition of Griffolini's translation of the *Epistole* ascribed to Phalaris, both printed in Oxford: 'O studious reader, I beg and I beg,' he asks, 'that you read this book' ('Hunc precor. atque precor lector studiose libellum | Perlege'). Similar poems appear in many grammatical textbooks, usually on the first printed page or, when a blank front leaf or title page appears, on the back of it, facing the start of the text.[12] The name-dropping and the prominent placing of these verses suggest that the printers imagined that to brandish a book's humanist connections could help to sell it. The verses draw the buyer, in personal tones, into a community of elite scholars like that offered to readers of *On Husbondrie*.

Nevertheless, in early printed books the addressee of humanist writing does change. If the name-dropping and invitations to intimacy in these verses have any purpose, then the implication must be that the reader is not yet part of the community—at least not until he has bought the volume. These verses are *invitations to join* the humanist endeavour, and the invitations would be meaningless without the possibility that the readers were as yet uninitiated. From the confidence of a poet that Duke Humfrey will receive his manuscript, we move to the uncertainty of addressing an unknown 'lector'. Carmeliano

---

[10] *Caxton's Own Prose*, no. 7:49, noted in Chapter 1 above.

[11] [Pietro Carmeliano. (ed.)], *Sex quamelegantissimæ epistolæ printed by William Caxton in 1483*, facsimile ed. James Hyatt, trans. George Bullen (London: Lawrence and Bullen, 1892), sig. c8r.

[12] Francesco Griffolini (trans.), *Epistole Phalaridis* (Oxford: Rood and Hunt, 1485; *STC* 19827; Oxford, Wadham College Library, classmark A.4.31), sig. a1v; Carlson, 'Occasional Poetry', 497–9; Anna Modigliani, 'Un nuovo manoscritto di Pietro Carmeliano: Le "epistolae" dello Pseudo-Falaride nella Trinity College Library in Dublin', *HL*, 33 (1984), 86–102 (89–90, 101).

must 'beg' his reader to examine Phalaris's *Epistole* ('precor') and can describe the reader as somebody still 'searching' for a learned master ('Munificum queris. doctum iustumque piumque. | Inuenies vnum. phalaris ille fuit').[13] His verses on the six elegant letters make no secret of the need to buy the book ('mercare'), rather than receive a personal presentation copy. Although these slim volumes share the verbal tricks of the manuscripts for princes, there is one important difference: they are relatively 'mass-produced' and can address more readers.

However, it is not only the advent of mechanical reproduction that makes the address to a wider readership necessary or even possible. Adrian Johns has argued that the stability and credibility of print was a tacit illusion shared by their readers and fostered by their makers, quite contrary to the facts.[14] Could it be that, in a similar manner, the reproduction of English humanist books also appears a process which is demanded from, rather than caused by, the new technology? There were already precedents for the reproduction and wider dissemination of humanist literature in England: the scribes of *On Husbondrie* and *Knyghthode and Bataile* had already reproduced works with imitative care by hand, even down to the layout and minute textual corrections (as Chapter 2 showed); in the 1480s Carmeliano gave bijou manuscripts of one Latin poem to different patrons with different prefatory verses, but in formats and designs otherwise closely duplicated for multiple readers.[15] It was as if these men already required from their books the fixity and reproductive capacity which people would later ascribe to print. Why might they have done so? Well, they sometimes sought multiple patrons. Yet the core humanist activities of retrieving and imitating classical literature with fidelity, of evangelizing its eloquence, and of fusing humanist communities by such reading, are all sustained by a belief in textual reproduction, whether mechanical or scribal. For example, Lydgate's *The Fall of Princes* was aimed not at one prince but at the many important men who had something to learn about political life; it survives only in thirty-nine manuscripts, alongside the run of 600 copies—most of them now lost—which Richard Pynson printed in 1494.[16] In the case of vernacular humanism, it is not that printing created a new conception of the widely disseminated text; rather, it is almost as if such a conception needed printing to reach its fullest potential.

Yet, even avoiding technological determinism, one cannot deny that print was distinguished for its greater speed and facility of reproduction, even by

---

[13] Griffolini (trans.), *Epistole Phalaridis*, sig. a1v.

[14] Johns, *The Nature of the Book*, 18–19, 30–1.

[15] Carlson, *English Humanist Books*, 43–7.

[16] Alexandra Gillespie, *Print Culture and the Medieval Author: Chaucer, Lydgate, and their Books 1473–1557* (Oxford: Oxford University Press, 2006), 101–3.

the earliest commentators.[17] This is a very practical benefit and the humanists working in England imagine a very practical use for it. When, in their liminary verses or insinuating prologues, they imagine reproducing their 'textual community', they often imagine one very real community: the classroom of pupils. Many editions suggest how they exploited the increased circulation of print for education. They were among the earliest sponsors of bespoke editions—though not necessarily humanist ones—from Caxton's press and the press in Oxford. As well as the aforementioned elegant neo-Latin letters, Caxton printed two rhetorical guidebooks by Lorenzo Traversagni, a friar and humanist who taught at Cambridge in 1478–80.[18] He most likely printed them at Traversagni's personal request, but one was apparently worth reprinting by the anonymous printer of St Albans known to his followers as a schoolmaster. And, in fact, besides these bespoke humanist books, the English printers issued other schoolbooks for what must have seemed a lucrative market, as if to challenge the more copious imports. The printer of St Albans also issued Agostino Dati's best-selling guide to Ciceronian idiom. In Oxford, the printer Theodoric Rood, who often worked in partnership with Thomas Hunt, the university stationer, issued Aristotle's *Ethics* and Cicero's *Pro Milone* in the cheaper, handier quarto formats typical of schoolbooks.[19] These works all suggest that scholars employed the press to duplicate classical and humanist works for the classroom and that the risk-averse printers shared in their efforts.

The verses of Carmeliano fit into this pedagogic project. His lines in a *Compendium totius grammatice* urge a community of young scholars, in the plural ('iuuenes'), to celebrate the book's author:

> Vos teneri iuuenes vestrum celebrate ioannem
> Qui bene vos docuit verba latine loqui
> Barbara que fuerat prius. est nunc facta latina.
> Lingua. breui spacio quam didicisse licet

[17] McKitterick, *Print, Manuscript and the Search for Order*, 31–6; Alexandra Walsham and Julia Crick, 'Introduction: Script, Print and History', in their *The Uses of Script and Print, 1300–1700* (Cambridge: Cambridge University Press, 2004), 1–26 (20).

[18] David R. Carlson, 'A Theory of the Early English Printing Firm: Jobbing, Book Publishing, and the Problem of Productive Capacity in Caxton's Work', in William Kuskin (ed.), *Caxton's Trace: Studies in the History of English Printing* (Notre Dame, IN: University of Notre Dame Press, 2006), 35–68 (46–7, 55–6); for another example, see A. C. de la Mare and Lotte Hellinga, 'The First Book Printed in Oxford: The *Expositio Symboli* of Rufinus', *TCBS*, 7 (1978), 184–244 (184–5, 193–5).

[19] [Marcus Tullius Cicero, *Oratio pro T. Milone*] ([Oxford: Rood, 1483]; *STC* 5312; Oxford, Merton College Library, classmarks P.3.2 and P.3.3a), with sigs. c1r-c2v, c5r-c6v, d1r-d2v, and d5r-d6v; [Leonardo Bruni (trans.)], *Aristotelis ethicorum libri* (Oxford: [Rood], 1479; *STC* 752; BodL, classmark S. Selden e.2), annotated for lecturing, as noted by Kristian Jensen, 'Text-books in the Universities: The Evidence from the Books', in *CHBB: III*, 354–79 (355).

> Nam que valla dabat. vel que precepta perottus
> Longa nimis. paruus continet iste liber

O you tender boys, praise your John who has taught you to speak the Latin tongue well. The tongue which once was barbarous has now become Latin, which it was able to learn to do in only a short time, for the rather lengthy lessons of Valla or Perotti are encompassed in this short book.

He then praises Bishop William Waynflete:

> Te gulielme pater. multum celeberrime qui nunc
> Ecclesie presul vintoniensis ades
> Fama canet. tantos et te celebrabit ad annos
> Dum fuerit stabili firmus in axe Polus
> Hoc opus auctor enim te persuadente ioannes.
> Edidit. vnde tibi fama perennis erit[20]

Fame will sing of you, O father William—you who are now famous as the bishop of Winchester—and will celebrate you as long as the pole star remains on its firm axis; for John, the author, issued this book at your persuasion, for which eternal fame will be yours.

These brief poems allow us to identify the author of the *Compendium totius grammatice* as John Anwykyll (d. 1487), then grammar master at Magdalen College School, newly founded by Waynflete. They also reveal a pedagogic intention to proselytize: the bishop deliberately persuaded the schoolmaster to compose his grammar ('te persuadente'). Like many early founders of humanist schools, Waynflete apparently did see his school as a way of disseminating and enforcing a particular standard of Latin.[21] This dream of reproducing the textbook and, thereby, reproducing a better style also underpins the notion that Waynflete will earn eternal fame, which of course requires the verses to reach many people over a long time. Yet in these verses it is a now unfashionable 'top-down' metaphor of pedagogy and cultural transmission which is implicit. The textbook's reform of barbarous Latin ('Barbara que fuerat prius') is a sort of Roman conquest of the boys. England too is infantilized by the veneration of the Italian scholarly heroes, Valla and Perotti, on whom Anwykyll's grammar

---

[20] John [Anwykyll], *Compendium totius grammatice* (Deventer: Pafraet, 4/5/1489; *STC* 696.1; BL, classmark IA.47600), sig. a1v; earlier editions were printed in Oxford but are now fragmentary. Carmeliano's verses might echo some prefatory verses from 1482 by Domenico Mancini, who came to England 1482–3 and apparently knew Carmeliano: see Dominic Mancini, *The Usurpation of Richard the Third*, ed. C. A. J. Armstrong (Oxford: Oxford University Press, 1969), 2–3 (especially *n.* 1), 19 (*n.* 1).
[21] Nicholas Orme, *Education in Early Tudor England: Magdalen College Oxford and its School 1480–1540*, Magdalen College Occasional Papers, 4 (Oxford: Magdalen College, 1998), 5, 8, 16; Virginia Davis, *William Waynflete, Bishop and Educationalist* (Woodbridge: Boydell, 1993) 84–8; Nicholas Orme, 'Schools and School-books', in *CHBB: III*, 449–69 (458–9).

is based. Elsewhere Carmeliano describes the importation of a printing press to England as a transfer of Venetian brilliance—notably not German—to these shores.[22] The model of cultural transmission rests upon imbalanced authority: the dissemination of learning from above or abroad, with the press as enforcer, and reproduction of it below in many copies and in many minds. Critics of such pedagogy, from Roger Ascham to recent historians and sociologists, have argued that humanist teaching was a form of discipline or indoctrination. For Ascham and others, this fierce discipline of the tongue and mind is exemplified in the learning of 'latins' or *vulgaria*: they were bilingual collections of phrases to parrot in one's own familiar speech—under threat of the violent beatings portrayed in woodcuts at the front of grammars. Such pedagogy forces a 'reproduction' of hierarchical divisions within the classroom and a 'reproduction' of elite language in the pupil's own mouth.[23]

REPRODUCIBLE ENGLISH IN ANWYKYLL'S *VULGARIA*

However, although these criticisms surely hold true of many teachers, how do writers meet the challenge of reproducing antiquity in their 'latins' or *vulgaria*? And what did writers achieve who were writing for reproduction? These questions can be answered by considering the 'latins' earliest printed in England. They were produced by the John Anwykyll whose grammar was praised by Carmeliano. He was a pioneering vernacular humanist, who used classical literature both in school and in print. In 1487 his superiors at Magdalen College School praised the 'new and very useful form of teaching conceived and prescribed by him for the school' ('novam et perutilem formam docendi pro eadem Schola conceptam et præscriptam per eundem'). His novelty was clearly the cultivation of the *studia humanitatis* or, as the college put it, 'grammaticumque [...] ac poemata, elegantias, et alias humanitates' or what one pupil at the school called 'humanite'.[24] Anwykyll's *Compendium*

[22] Griffolini (trans.), *Epistole Phalaridis*, sig. m6r.

[23] Alan Stewart, *Close Readers: Humanism and Sodomy in Early Modern England* (Princeton, NJ: Princeton University Press, 1997), 108–9, 145–50; Richard Halpern, *The Poetics of Primitive Accumulation: English Renaissance Culture and the Genealogy of Capital* (Ithaca, NY: Cornell University Press, 1991), 25–6, 31–4; and more generally Pierre Bourdieu and Jean-Claude Passeron, *Reproduction in Education, Society and Culture*, trans. Richard Nice, 2nd edn. (1970; London: Sage, 1990), for example, 36.

[24] Orme, *Education in Early Tudor England: Magdalen College*, 15–17; John Rouse Bloxam (ed.), *A Register [...] of Saint Mary Magdalen College in the University of Oxford*, 8 vols. (Oxford: Graham, 1853–85), III.8; William Nelson (ed.), *A Fifteenth Century School Book* (Oxford: Clarendon Press, 1956), no. 280.

totius grammatice allegedly taught Italian standards of grammar (as seen above) while his *Vulgaria quedam abs Terencio* offered boys the chance to imitate the Latin of a genuine ancient author, Terence, by comparing various phrases from his plays with an accompanying translation. These works were printed as a set at Oxford in 1483, perhaps for Anwykyll's students. Magdalen College in Oxford, to which his school was attached, was wholly familiar with the possibilities of print: the fellows had many financial and legal dealings with the printers in the town and on one recorded occasion they purchased multiple copies of a commentary on Aristotle from the Oxford press.[25] Given such contacts and precedents, Anwykyll or some colleague might have arranged for Theodoric Rood to reproduce this textbook for the school. Of course, it can seldom be proven whether textbooks were actually used; their cost may have prohibited all but a few pupils from owning them, and teachers may not have followed their directions so slavishly.[26] It should be said that only one of the extant copies of Anwykyll's *Vulgaria* (as far as I have examined) contains many annotations which suggest linguistic study.[27] However, in this book the provision of printed translations perhaps removed the need for further glossing. After all, several copies of Anwykyll's *Vulgaria* did find early owners in education: one was paid for by the friends of John Grene, a friar studying in Oxford; another was bound with guides to Ciceronian Latin, model letters, and so on.[28] Yet rather than consider the readers, it is worth asking how Anwykyll himself presents classical literature for reproduction in the classroom. What does he take and offer from it?

His *Vulgaria* firstly show the place of the vernacular in classical education. Contrary to our nostalgic belief that the schoolboys of the past

[25] Constance Blackwell, 'Niccolò Perotti in England, 1: John Anwykyll, Bernard André, John Colet and Luis Vives', *Studi umanistici Piceni*, 2 (1982), 13–28 (14–15); Joseph A. Dane, 'A Note on American Fragments of Grammatical Texts from the Oxford Press of Theodoric Rood (STC 315 and 695)', *The Library*, 6th series, 20 (1998), 59–61 (60); Christine Ferdinand, 'Magdalen College and the Book Trade: The Provision of Books in Oxford, 1450–1550', in *The Book Trade and its Customers 1450–1900: Historical Essays for Robin Myers*, ed. Arnold Hunt, Giles Mandelbrote, and Alison Shell (Winchester: St Paul's Bibliographies, 1997), 175–87 (177–9).

[26] Fred Schurink, 'An Elizabethan Grammar School Exercise Book', *BLR*, 18 (2003), 174–96 (192), begins to develop this major point.

[27] *Uulgaria Therentij in anglicanam linguam traducta* (London: Faques, [*c.* 1505]; *STC* 23907.3; bound into CCCC, MS 386): someone writes in the margin the word exemplified by each phrase.

[28] [John Anwykyll], *Vulgaria quedam abs Terencio in Anglicam linguam traducta* ([Oxford: Rood and Hunt, *c.*1483]; *STC* 23904; BodL, classmark Arch G. e.5), on which see *Humfrey 1988*, no. 120; *Vulgaria Therentij in anglicanam linguam traducta* (Antwerp: Leeu, 1486; *STC* 23907; CUL, classmark Inc.5.F.6.2 [3353]), on which see J. C. T. Oates, *A Catalogue of the Fifteenth-Century Printed Books in the University Library, Cambridge* (Cambridge: Cambridge University Press, 1954), no. 3889, and nos. 3486, 3479, 749, 2910, 3442, 2978, 3542, 2798, 645, and 4209.

conversed readily in Latin, it is clear that in the 1480s English was commonly used by teachers of Latin at Magdalen and elsewhere. Readers added
English glosses to copies of Anwykyll's *Compendium totius grammatice*,[29]
while the marginalia of John Stanbridge, Anwykyll's most famous successor
at Magdalen, show that even this distinguished teacher glossed his imported
classical editions in English.[30] Looking further afield, other English incunables show that Terence's works were also enjoyed by readers who preferred
to gloss them. Richard Pynson printed Terence's complete works in 1497,
printing some plays with 'heavy leading' which left generous white space
between the lines for notes, and printing one play with a glossary of difficult archaisms. Both extant copies of this edition contain a few handwritten
English glosses.[31] By writing his bilingual *Vulgaria*, Anwykyll simply enshrines
this use of the vernacular in the Magdalen schoolroom and in the study of
Terence.

Yet as he secures English a place in the institutional study of classics,
so he relinquishes the inventiveness of earlier translations. Palladius and
Vegetius forced the poets of *On Husbondrie* and *Knyghthode and Bataile*
to mine English's stylistic resources, until they exceeded their sources in
brilliance. By contrast, most of Anwykyll's textbook offers banal conversation
in a plain style. For example, he converts the Latin 'adolescenciam' into the
wholly ordinary 'ʒouthe', whereas *On Husbondrie* called its young chickens
'adolescentis', a striking and anthropomorphic coinage.[32] Anwykyll also pares
down the pseudo-classical imagery which earlier translators expanded: for

---

[29] John [Anwykyll], *Compendium totius grammatice* ([Oxford: Rood and Hunt, 1483]; STC
696; BodL, classmark Inc.e.E2.1483.1), sigs. g7r-v, h5v, k3r-v, with glosses largely on verses
which list vocabulary; John [Anwykyll], *Compendium totius grammatice* ([London: Wynkyn de
Worde, *c*.1517]; STC 696.7; OMC, classmark Arch. C.I.1.20), sigs. A6r-A8v, E4r.
[30] Plutarch, *Virorum illustrium uitae* (Venice: Jensen, 2/1/1478; OMC, classmark Arch.
B.III.4.4–5), sigs. l10r-v, m1v, m3r-v, m4v, m6r, m7v, m9r-v, n1r-n2r; and Cicero, *Epistolae ad
familiares* (Venice: de Tortis, 24/5/1485; OMC, classmark Arch. B.III.1.13), sigs. a3v, a4r, a5r-v,
a6v-a7r, d4r-d5r (and glosses in another hand on sigs. g1v, g2r, g3v, g4v, g5v-g6r, g7v, h1v, h3v,
n3r, A1v). His signature appears at the front of each book.
[31] Terence, *Comoediae* (London: Pynson, 1497; STC 23885; BL, classmark C.4.g.13), with
the glossary on *Andria*, sig. d5v, wider spacing on *Heauton Timorumenos*, *Adelphoe*, and
Phormio, and MS glosses throughout *Andria* and *Heauton Timerumenon* especially (for example
Andria, sigs. a4r, c3r, d4v), almost invisible due to washing of the leaves. The leaves from this
edition's *Phormio*, now bound into BodL, MS Fairfax 18, have English glosses on sigs. b1v, b2v.
Bibliographers date the edition to 1495–7, but the colophons to both *Andria* and *Hecyra* specify
1497; the 'ii' on the 'lxxxxvii' in *Hecyra* is almost invisible due to smudging.
[32] Quotations and parenthetical folio references come from [John Anwykyll], *Vulgaria
quedam abs Terencio in Anglicam linguam traducta* ([Oxford: Rood and Hunt, 1483]; STC 23904;
CUL, classmark Inc.5.J.2.2 [3585]), with Latin line numbers from Terence, *Comedies*, ed. and
trans. John Barsby (Cambridge, MA: Harvard University Press, 2001). Compare here sig. p4r
(*Adel.* 152) with Mark Liddell (ed.), *The Middle-English Translation of Palladius De Re Rustica*
(Berlin: Ebering, 1896), 4.869, discussed in *n.* 79 in Chapter 2 above.

example, when Terence refers allusively to Ceres, as goddess of hops, and to Venus, Anwykyll mentions alcohol and lust:

This is a trew saynge that men say comenly whyth oute mete and drynke bodily lust coleth or abateth.

Verum hercle hoc verbum est quod vulgo aiunt Sine cerere et libero friget venus (o2v, *Eun.* 732)

This is to some extent very sensible of Anwykyll, whose purpose was not poetry but the most rudimentary education. It might be that the ubiquitous Venus really was unfamiliar to the schoolboys: in one copy of Anwykyll's grammar a handwritten gloss is needed to explain that this *Venus, -ris, -i* is in English a goddess ('anglice a goddis').[33] Rather than stretching the boys with pseudo-classical pomposity, Anwykyll uses English simply as a means to access Latin itself. In the editions of Anwykyll's from 1483 to *c.*1505, the Latin text appears in a larger fount than the alternating English, albeit usually in the same style of typeface. In one edition from the 1480s a paraph introduces each snippet from Terence, while in a copy of another edition someone has added a red paraph to highlight each Latin phrase only.[34] Thus printers and readers present Anwykyll's *Vulgaria* with an emphasis upon the Latin text, and treat English merely as a propaedeutic. Anwykyll retreats from the experimental poetry and politics of previous works to a more limited writing for the curriculum.

However, if they seem usefully plain in style, Anwykyll's *Vulgaria* have one distinction which made his teaching 'new', as his employers claimed. Although the genre of *vulgaria* was not in itself new, for other collections circulated at Magdalen in the late fifteenth and early sixteenth centuries, Anwykyll's set was the first to take the Latin phrases predominantly from an identified classical author.[35] As in his *Compendium totius grammatice*, the idioms are actually classical. Yet, once more, when Anwykyll offers the classics in a form digestible in the curriculum, he must dilute the humanist return *ad fontes*. So he cannot fully or accurately reproduce Terence's plays, if the phrases are to make sense outside of the plots from which they spring. One study of his book has traced only 399 of the 530 phrases to Terence; those excerpts appear in loose groupings

---

[33] John [Anwykyll], *Compendium totius grammatice* ([Oxford: Rood and Hunt, 1483]; *STC* 696; BodL, classmark Inc.e.E2.1483.1), sig. m5v.

[34] *Vulgaria quedam abs Terencio in anglicam linguam traducta* ([London: de Machlinia, 1483?]; CUL, classmark Inc.5.J.3.5 [3609]), with printed paraphs; and *Vulgaria quedam abs Terencio* (Oxford: Rood and Hunt, 1483; *STC* 23904; BodL, classmark Arch G. e.5), with rubrication. However, when Wynkyn de Worde later reprinted Anwykyll's *Vulgaria*, he let the English text dwarf the Latin (*STC* 23907.7 and *STC* 23908).

[35] Compare Nelson (ed.), *A Fifteenth Century School Book* (with the provenance on pp. xvi–xix), and Nicholas Orme (ed.), 'An Early-Tudor Oxford Schoolbook', *Renaissance Quarterly*, 34 (1981), 11–39, the latter with only thirteen references to classical authors in eighty-eight phrases.

play-by-play, but with numerous exceptions and with lines sometimes out of dramatic sequence.[36] The first few pages of the book are arranged in imitation of conversation, with words of greeting and introduction. Some sections are reorganized in order to illustrate syntactical points, such as the workings of the verb *videor*, an illustration followed by the book's only explanatory note (n3v). Even though the textbook's second half follows the plays more closely in its order of speeches, it still frequently interrupts the original phrases to demonstrate how to re-use Terence's vocabulary or idiom in a new, invented sentence:

There is no thynge more esy than to say a worde
Nichil est facilius dictu
Itt is esyere to say than to do
Facilius multo est dictu quam factu   (q3r, with only the first line from *Pho.* 301)

Anwykyll's phrases must diverge from Terence, in order to make grammatical sense out of context, as in the following example where Terence's *cui* lacks an antecedent now that the line stands alone:

It is harde to disceyue hym
Difficile est ei verba dare Teren. Cui verba dare difficile est   (n5r, *And.* 211)

Here, Terence's original phrase is also dutifully noted and such conscientiousness perhaps alerts the schoolboy to the Terentian pedigree of the idiom. However, Anwykyll only admits such divergences on three occasions (all on n4v-n5r). Usually, the phrases further conceal their source by omitting the characters' names which appeared in the original plays; the one exception is a reference to the old man Crito in the book's opening phrase.[37] Here too Anwykyll is wise: the schoolboys' classical imitation would be bizarre were they to reproduce Terence's dialogue precisely, addressing their friends as Crito, and so on; they need to turn away from the classical text to some extent. But here too Anwykyll impoverishes his book as a work of humanist imitation in its own right—unlike *On Husbondrie*'s faithful reproduction of Palladius, say. The book's primary function is to direct the new act of reproduction by the pupil, rather than to reproduce the text of Terence. It is useful as an education in Latin, but limited as a reading of the classical text.

Moreover, nor does the book offer much more than education in Latin. Modern observers often assert that the book is full of moral sentence; this is not true. Although fifteenth- and sixteenth-century scholars universally

---

[36] Alexander H. Brodie, 'Anwykyll's *Vulgaria*: A Pre-Erasmian Textbook', *Neuphilologische Mitteilungen*, 75 (1974), 416–27 (422–3).

[37] [Anwykyll], *Vulgaria*, sig. n1r (*And.* 802); for other cuts, see sigs. n4r (*And.* 254), o3v (*Eun.* 864–5), q2v (*Phor.* 151).

advocated Terence's fine diction, they were less unanimous about his moral worth: some found the plays morally improving; others found them scurrilous and in need of bowdlerizing.[38] Sure enough, Anwykyll finds in Roman drama about as much morality as Stephen Sondheim and Zero Mostel found there: for what else can Terence provide phrases, if not for wooing beautiful girls, hiring courtesans and gulling the old? Take one sample lesson:

I giff no fors so that I may haue hyr
mea nichil refert dum pociar modo.　(n8v, *Eun.* 320)

This phrase is authentically classical: the translator rightly interprets the verb *potiar* to allude to a girl ('hyr'), even though she is not mentioned in the Latin line actually quoted; he shows some knowledge of Terence's *Eunuchus* as a whole.[39] However, in *Eunuchus* itself Chaerea's urgent quest to 'haue' his beloved was to be pursued through chauvinistic 'force or stealth' no matter what. Such dubious morality is not untypical of the phrases borrowed by Anwykyll's *Vulgaria*: in other passages the boys learn how to express *Schadenfreude* and selfishness, how to discuss the sexual foibles and charms of women, or how to deceive fathers (o4v, *Eun.* 1041; o5r, *Eun.* 1070; o3r-o3v, *Eun.* 812–13; n8v, *Eun.* 361). Some censoring occurs but mostly, it seems, by accident when the specific contexts of the plays are obscured in order to make phrases more generally reproducible: for example, a pimp becomes simply 'hym' or 'illo' (q2v-3r, *Pho.* 171). By contrast, when Anwykyll invents some phrases, which demonstrate how to reproduce Terence's idioms for oneself, he simply continues the playwright's misbehaviour: for example, the idiom *pereo funditus* is dragged from an innocuous phrase in *Andria* into a new but strangely Terentian scenario—invented by Anwykyll:

If he espy that I go aboute to disceyfe hym I am loste vttirly.
Si senserit quicquam me fallacie conari pereo funditus. [40]

In no sense does he edit Terence to produce a handbook of moral wisdom. Of course, such a large selection did yield one or two maxims for the instruction of the young, like the advice to 'subdue the desyres of the flesh' or to beware of fortune (n7r-n7v, q2v). However, such outcrops of sententiousness are rare among the workaday conversation and the immorality. One would guess that the boys loved this book, which is jollier than Cato's *Disticha* or the worthy textbooks of modern languages today. But it must be registered that

[38] As reported by Howard B. Norland, *Drama in Early Tudor Britain 1485–1558* (Lincoln, NE: University of Nebraska Press, 1995), 67, 84, 88, 79–81, 95–110.

[39] Terence's *mea* is a feminine singular ablative possessive agreeing with the ablative of *res* implied in *refert*: 'as far as it concerns *my* business'; *potiar* has no subject and means 'so that I might take possession'.

[40] [Anwykyll], *Vulgaria*, sig. n4r. Compare *And.* 244, using 'pereo funditus'.

Anwykyll reproduces—in this book for some elementary class no doubt—a very elementary form of humanist study, not very classical, not very moral, and not even very exciting English.

This is surely the effect of dilution in the classroom. One historian has portrayed the learning of good Latin in the schools and universities from the 1480s through to Colet's day as the first successful establishment of humanism in England.[41] In fact, the opportunities for reproduction in printing and schooling lead Anwykyll away from the experiment of earlier fifteenth-century writers in English. He exceeds even the narrow stylistic concerns of *On Husbondrie*, for at least that work preserved its source's integrity, whereas he breaks his source into fragments. Some have found that sixteenth-century humanist teachers treat the classics as a discontinuous sequence of linguistic lessons. Others have suggested that a more searching reading could have occurred in universities, rather than elementary schools.[42] We do not know for certain how people truly read Anwykyll's book, for the surviving copies are few. Yet the humanists in England seem to be reproducing an impoverished humanism through the press. Did anybody imagine a more complex reading of the classics in printed books?

CICERO BETWEEN GRAMMAR AND PHILOSOPHY

This intellectual economy—where the better study of Latin means a less thoughtful reading than that practised by vernacular writers—was discussed by men at the time. One instructive discussion appears in Lorenzo Traversagni's *Nova rhetorica*. Traversagni (*c*.1425–1503), an Italian friar, taught in Cambridge in the 1470s before resuming his career on the continent; he wrote his *Nova rhetorica* while in England and had it printed by Caxton around 1479 from an autograph manuscript; it was then reprinted in St Albans in 1480.[43]

[41] Denys Hay, 'England and the Humanities in the Fifteenth Century', in his *Renaissance Essays* (London: Hambledon, 1988), 169–231 (192, 206–12).

[42] For different views, see Grafton and Jardine, *Humanism*, pp. xii–xiii, 9–23, 136–45; Halpern, *Poetics of Primitive Accumulation*, 46–7; Rebecca W. Bushnell, *A Culture of Teaching: Early Modern Humanism in Theory and Practice* (Ithaca, NY: Cornell University Press, 1996), 118, 124–34, 143; Eugene R. Kintgen, *Reading in Tudor England* (Pittsburgh, PA: University of Pittsburgh Press, 1996), 18–57; Robert Black, *Humanism and Education in Medieval and Renaissance Italy: Tradition and Innovation in Latin Schools from the Twelfth to the Fifteenth Century* (Cambridge: Cambridge University Press, 2001), 22–30.

[43] Blake, *William Caxton and English Literary Culture*, 7–8; José Ruysschaert, 'Les manuscrits autographes de deux œuvres de Lorenzo Guglielmo Traversagni imprimées chez Caxton', *BJRL*, 36 (1953) 191–7 (194–5); Nicolas Barker, 'St Albans Press: The First Punch-cutter in England and the First Native Typefounder?', *TCBS*, 7 (1979), 257–78 (258, 268); Weiss, *Humanism*, 175.

Traversagni's title recalls the traditional title of the rhetoric *Ad Herennium* ascribed to Cicero, a work he plundered fully. In the prologue to book III, Traversagni worries about his favour for Cicero: should he have learnt a lesson from St Jerome's famous dream of being whipped by an angel for being a Ciceronian ('cautionem sumere a divo Hieronimo doctore probatissimo atque clarissimo : qui se Ciceronista foret')? No, he answers, and in his wording he belittles the danger of his Ciceronianism. Whereas in St Jerome's dream the 'Christianus' was contrasted with the 'Ciceronianus', Traversagni changes the word. In his prologue the sinful 'Ciceronista' sounds, in the suffix —*ista*, less like the devotee of a pagan religion and more like a professional teacher within some quattrocento university, by analogy with the *humanista*. His tone is very sarcastic, aside from one short prayer, and he sophistically asks: if eloquence is so wicked, why was Jerome only whipped the once, before he went on to defend and flaunt his pagan style further?[44] This prologue defends the classical curriculum not as a pagan world-view but as a course in Ciceronian stylistics, harmful to no one. It confirms, as Anwykyll's book did, humanism as a simple curriculum in grammar and style, now in order to defend it.

Of course, despite the cheekiness of this fascinating prologue, Traversagni's limitation of his interest in Cicero to the language may in fact reflect his notion that pagan eloquence was necessary simply in order to preach the Christian faith. Traversagni was a keen reforming friar later in his career, and in his other prefaces and lectures he dreams of marrying eloquence with Christian wisdom in the service of faith. For example, elsewhere he writes praise of Magdalen College and School not only, as Carmeliano did, because they civilize the barbaric tongues of the boys, but because they cultivate the human arts alongside theological ones.[45] He opens the *Nova rhetorica* too by exhorting all Christian soldiers to turn their pagan rhetorical weapons against the impious; to serve this purpose, his manual focuses exclusively upon demonstrative oratory 'which most and particularly pertains to the salvatory conversion of souls' and to 'the public good, as much ecclesiastical as civil' ('quod maxime et proprie spectat ad animorum salubrem conuersionem', 'ad bonum publicum : tam ecclesiasticum quam ciuile'). His purpose seems strikingly pietistic. If teaching young men to replicate pagan eloquence is only

---

[44] Quotations from Lorenzo Traversagni, *Nova rhetorica* (Westminster: Caxton, [1479]; *STC* 24189; CCCC, classmark EP.H.6), sigs. k5r-k6r (with corresponding page and line numbers from Lorenzo Guglielmo Traversagni, *Margarita eloquentiae castigatae*, ed. Giovanni Farris (Savona: Sabatelli, 1978), here 168:5–169:29). Compare Saint Jérôme, *Lettres*, ed. and trans. Jérôme Labourt, 8 vols. (Paris: Budé, 1949–63), I.145 (no. XXII.30).
[45] LPL, MS 450, f.3r (praise for Waynflete's school), on which see P. R. Robinson, *Catalogue of Dated and Datable Manuscripts c.888–1600 in London Libraries* (London: British Library, 2003), no. 83; Giovanni Farris, *Umanesimo e religione in Lorenzo Guglielmo Traversagni (1425–1505)* (Milan: Mazorati, 1972), 44–7, 68–9.

the beginning of a wider campaign of Christian preaching, then his survey of pagan literature can indeed be limited.[46] Indeed, it could be reduced and purified—castigated or *castigata*, as his alternative title for the work had it (*Margarita castigata eloquentie*). The emphasis is again not on the original works being reproduced, for Cicero's teaching is moulded into a new form, but on the use of them for evangelism: a different form of reproduction.

Yet should we believe his excuse that eloquence will serve preaching and theology? Later on, when he advises orators on how to win goodwill, he confesses that to promise that one will address matters essential to the commonweal or to faith is merely one of the many devices that a speaker can use to make an audience willing to listen.[47] One might well, then, suspect that Traversagni's apology for rhetoric simply seemed necessary to justify the humanist studies to the scholars of Cambridge. For, indeed, once Traversagni has justified himself with these fanciful preliminaries, he can wallow for the rest of his book in verbal detail and technique. Like *Ad Herennium* itself, this textbook concerns not the common good or faith, but rhetorical figures and structures; it teaches us *how* to write well, but not *why* to do so.[48] Of course, it is possible that Traversagni did preach with zeal in the lectures which this book prompted, and which have been largely lost to us. But the textbook which remains contains only two brief dalliances in philosophy: a brief excursus upon the useful and the good in *De Officiis*, where he scandalously calls Cicero 'almost a theologian' ('quasi theologus'), and one upon the cardinal virtues, where he leaves the theological virtues for theologians to handle.[49] Although Traversagni justifies his curriculum with classical beliefs about the nobility and wisdom of the orator, he usually treats ideas, Ciceronian or Christian, with brevity; most of his book plunders Cicero for style, rhetoric, and language.

There may be historical reasons for this avoidance of philosophy and theology: in England the legitimacy of doctrinal teaching was not entirely clear in the century after Arundel's Constitutions; schoolmasters were not supposed to instruct their students in the faith.[50] Yet Traversagni's brisk reprocessing of classical literature into a style sheet largely reflects the demands of a curriculum: having lectured on *Ad Herennium* itself in Cambridge in 1476,

---

[46] Traversagni, *Nova rhetorica*, sigs. a2v-a3v, a4v-a5r, a6r (*Margarita*, ed. Farris, 29:36–31:30, 33:15–29, 35:17–30). According to Farris, Traversagni's autograph urged care of 'souls' ('animarum') rather than Caxton's erroneous 'minds' ('animorum').

[47] Traversagni, *Nova rhetorica*, sig. b2r-v (*Margarita*, ed. Farris, 38:42–39:4, 39:19–27).

[48] Contrary to James J. Murphy, 'Caxton's Two Choices: "Modern" and "Medieval" Rhetoric in Traversagni's *Nova rhetorica* and the Anonymous *Court of Sapience*', *Medievalia et Humanistica*, 3 (1972), 241–55 (243–4).

[49] Traversagni, *Nova rhetorica*, sigs. g6r-g7v (*Margarita*, ed. Farris, 117:24–119:35).

[50] Rita Copeland, *Pedagogy, Intellectuals and Dissent in the Later Middle Ages: Lollardy and Ideas of Learning* (Cambridge: Cambridge University Press, 2001), 11.

two years later Traversagni advertised to an audience there his forthcoming *Nova rhetorica*, which reduced Cicero's *Ad Herennium* into a more pithy and pertinent form; then, his opening lecture in Paris on this textbook promised to survey the topic in brief time ('brevi tempore').[51] Other readers were invited to abbreviate Traversagni's treatise in turn by an elaborate sequence of rubricated notes which seem to be reproduced by a stationer in the first edition or perhaps by readers in others; the notes usually just fillet out rhetorical figures and summarize the gist, to obviate fuller reading.[52] Finally, the constraints of time, one assumes, are what encouraged Traversagni himself to compress his treatise into a shorter *Epitoma*.[53] All these devices are utilitarian, serving the future reproduction of Cicero's or Traversagni's style, without any concern for their own intentions or ideas; Traversagni's fascinating prologue, for example, is never annotated or excerpted. His printed works and lecture courses encourage the whole hall of students to imitate him imitating Cicero, but, in so doing, the humanist knowledge of antiquity is spread thinly.

Cicero never faded into Traversagni's shadow, of course: readers had the chaste neo-Latin manual copied out or bound alongside the original *Ad Herennium* or Cicero's speeches.[54] However, even in that choice of companions we see a continuation of Traversagni's narrow vision of Cicero as a readily imitable wordsmith, able to be plundered for the production of new Latin rather than for new ideas. Such a focus recurs in other humanist textbooks printed in England. For example, Agostino Dati's *Libellus super Tulianis elegantiis*, a European best-seller reprinted at St Albans in about 1479, teaches the tyro how to imitate Cicero's distinctive word order, idiom, and style. In Dati's classroom, Cicero is the final arbiter of proper usage: true definitions and unusual forms are authorized with phrases like 'Cicero mostly follows that formation in his *Epistles*' or 'Cicero accepts it' ('id plurimum Cicero in epistolis consueuit', 'M. Cicero accepit'). Elsewhere, as we saw, Carmeliano sells his collection of elegant neo-Latin epistles by asserting that they are so good they 'are fit to speak even with Cicero' ('possunt Marco cum Cicerone loqui').[55] The only genuine Ciceronian work printed in Latin in fifteenth-century England,

[51] Farris, *Umanesimo e religione*, 71, 77, 85.
[52] See marginalia in Lorenzo Traversagni, *Nova rhetorica* (Westminster: Caxton, [1479]; STC 24189; CCCC, classmark EP.H.6), throughout; and in Lorenzo Traversagni, *Nova rhetorica* (St Albans: [anon.], 1480; STC 24190), in BL, classmark C.11.a.29, sigs. t4r-t6r, and in BodL, classmark Auct.N.5.8, throughout.
[53] Lorenzo Traversagni, 'The *Epitoma Margarite Castigate Eloquentie* of Laurentius Gulielmus Traversagni de Saona', ed. and trans. Ronald H. Martin, *Proceedings of the Leeds Philosophical and Literary Society*, 20 (1986), 131–269.
[54] Respectively BodL, MS Laud. lat. 61, ff.74r-160v; Traversagni, *Nova rhetorica* (STC 24190; BodL, classmark Auct.N.5.8) discussed in *n.* 65 below.
[55] Agostino Dati, *Libellus super Tulianis elegantiis* (St Albans: [anon.], [1479]; STC 6289; CUL Inc.5.J.4.1 [3632]), sigs. b5v, c2v; [Carmeliano. (ed.)], *Sex quamelegantissimæ epistolæ*, sig. c8r.

the speech *Pro Milone,* is perhaps Cicero's most conventional and exemplary oration, again an ideal model for schoolboys.[56] Educational historians note that among the few real innovations of quattrocento curricula was the use of Cicero in the secondary levels of grammatical and rhetorical schooling,[57] and he certainly appears important in fifteenth-century English educational publishing. However, those schoolbooks suggest the intellectual poverty of English printing in this line.

Of course, these English editions were outnumbered, incalculably, by the imported editions of Cicero's works. Yet if we take a sample of incunables of his works which contain the names of early English owners, then the same intellectual poverty is glimpsed in several readers' responses.[58] These books confirm that people read Cicero for an education, as Traversagni and others suggest, in grammar and style. Englishmen owned a wide range of texts in various designs and formats, yet there were some trends: they most commonly owned *De Officiis* and *Epistolae ad familiares.* This first tendency may suggest that Cicero was read in the classroom: people most often annotated with any thoroughness only book I of each work—unless they read on and just stopped writing about it—and that patchiness of attention could betray not a lack of stamina but a set text.[59] Educational readers select only as much as they can comfortably cover. Secondly, the use of Cicero for basic linguistic study is suggested by the addition of at least a few handwritten glosses in English in a third of the incunables owned by Englishmen; moreover, the only works thus glossed are again, with one exception, *De Officiis* or *Epistolae ad familiares.*[60]

---

[56] See *n.* 19 above and, on *Pro Milone,* see M. L. Clarke, *Rhetoric at Rome: A Historical Survey,* 3rd edn., rev. D. H. Berry (1953; London: Routledge, 1996), 67–8.

[57] Black, *Humanism and Education,* 262, 353–5.

[58] I examined the thirty incunables of Cicero with an English provenance in the libraries SJC, TCC, CUL, and OMC, and incidentally one copy each in BodL and LPL. The provenance of *Orationes* ([Venice]: Valdarfer, 1471; SJC, classmark Ii.1.6), rested on a solitary English gloss (f.105v, 'Asiatici Iewes'). It was impossible to date most marginalia precisely. On Italian incunables of Cicero, see Howard Jones, *Master Tully: Cicero in Tudor England,* Bibliotheca Humanistica et Reformatoria, 58 (Nieuwkoop: De Graaf, 1998), 117–25.

[59] Cicero, *De Officiis* (Louvain: de Paderborn, 2nd edn. after 1483; CUL, classmark Inc.3.F.2.2 [4088]), with frequent notes in five hands on book I (sigs. a4v-q1r), and thereafter only two handwritten titles (sigs. t7r, D2r); Cicero, *Opera Omnia,* 2 vols. (Milan: le Signerre, 1498–9; CUL, classmark Inc.1.B.7.26 [1927]), owned by Thomas Linacre, with fifty-one notes on book I of *De Officiis* (sigs. a3r-b2r) but only one on book II (sig. b3v).

[60] Cicero, *De Officiis, etc.* (Mainz: Fust and Schöffer, 4/2/1466–7; classified as LPL, MS 765); Cicero, *De Officiis, etc.* (Mainz: Fust and Schöffer, 4/2/1466–7; TCC, classmark VI.14.24); Cicero, *Epistolae ad familiares* ([Louvain: de Veldener, *c.*1470s]; CUL, classmark Inc.3.F.2.1 [3166]); Cicero, *Epistolae ad familiares* ([Venice: printer of the 1480 Martial, *c.*1480]; CUL, classmark Inc.3.B.3.152 [1857]); Cicero, *De Officiis* (Louvain: de Paderborn, 2nd edn. after 1483; CUL, classmark Inc.3.F.2.2 [4088]); Cicero, *De Officiis, etc.* (Lyons: Guillaume Le Roy, *c.*1485; OMC, classmark Arch. B.III.2.7); Cicero, *Epistolae ad familiares* (Venice: Locatellus, 22/9/1494; CUL, classmark Inc.2.B.3.85 [1659]); Cicero, *De Officiis, etc.,* with a few glosses on *De Senectute* and *De*

Of course, readers more commonly add Latin glosses and, if they use both languages, Latin dwarfs English by ten glosses to one. But one copy of the letters contains some 800 English glosses, predominantly on book I, and often on the simplest vocabulary: 'necesse est' becomes 'yt ys need', for example.[61] This is the sort of rudimentary reading found in copies of Chaucer's *Boece* or other English translations. Thirdly, even when the annotations suggest more advanced study, it is of the part of the *studia humanitatis* concerned with grammar and style: as that most prolific English glosser remarks, in a Latin gloss this time, 'humanitas' is 'eloquencia'.[62] Eloquence is what most of the readers pursue. In Cicero's *Epistolae*, the readers often highlight the bland letters asking for references, and so on, or typical epistolary phrases, as if reading them is the preliminary to writing workaday letters of their own.[63] Even in works notable for their moral sentence, some readers identify the rhetorical devices such as simile, vituperation, or the device, which so many fifteenth-century readers like to point out, of irony.[64] Typically, then, the reading of Cicero feeds the creation of a whole classroom of new Ciceronians: a focus on reproducing new Latin among the pupils and other readers.

It is, though, possible to nuance this critique. Firstly, we cannot deny the veneration for the classics which prompted this linguistic analysis. Although the marks in these early editions seldom grant to Cicero the careful attention that, for example, Worcester gave to Cicero's *De Republica*, reading in the classroom sometimes differs only in quality and not in kind from the textual castigation and analysis of other humanists. English schoolboys no longer allegorize the text, but some of them do try to understand it diligently and lovingly: like the scribes of *Knyghthode and Bataile*, they correct misprints, dot minims to distinguish the letters, or add helpful brackets or *lunulae*.[65] Secondly, although their comments are often philological, in the broadest

---

Amicitia too (Venice: Pincius, 3/3/1496; CUL, classmark Inc.3.B.3.104 [1736]); Cicero, *Epistolae ad familiares* (Lyons: de Vingle, 12/3/1496; CUL, classmark Inc.2.D.2.25 [2713]); Cicero, *Opera Omnia* (Milan: le Signerre, 1498–9; SJC, classmark Ii.2.10), with glosses only on *Epistolae ad familiares*; and Stanbridge's copy in *n.* 30 above.

[61] Cicero, *Epistolae ad familiares* ([Venice: printer of the 1480 Martial, *c.*1480]; CUL, classmark Inc.3.B.3.152 [1857]), sig. b2v, with most other glosses on book I (sigs. b1r–d4v).

[62] Cicero, *Epistolae ad familiares* ([Venice: printer of the 1480 Martial, *c.*1480]; CUL, classmark Inc.3.B.3.152 [1857]), sig. b3r.

[63] Cicero, *Epistolae ad familiares* (Venice: Locatellus, 22/9/1494; CUL, classmark Inc.2.B.3.85 [1659]), for example sigs. a5v, d3r, e2r, e5r; Cicero, *Epistolae ad familiares* (Milan: de Lavigne, 1478; CUL, classmark Inc.2.B.7.2 [4336]), sigs. E4v, P7r, R6r.

[64] For example, Cicero, *Opera Omnia*, 2 vols. (Milan: le Signerre, 1498–9; CUL, classmark Inc.1.B.7.26 [1927]), sigs. a6v, a8r, b1v ('prouerbium', 'Ironia', and 'Figura').

[65] Cicero, *Pro Lege Manilia, etc.* ([Paris: Martineau, *c.*1482]; CUL, classmark Inc.5.D.1.10 [2429]), for example sigs. a2v, a3r, b12v, c3v–c4r, c8v (on which see Oates, *Catalogue*, no. 2910); and another copy now bound in BodL, classmark Auct.N.5.8, with Traversagni's *Nova rhetorica* discussed in *n.* 54 above.

sense, encompassing language, literature, and history, they are not *always* framed at a basic level; philology is an art sometimes. Some readers spot the connections to other works by Cicero or to other classical authors; when editions contain the latest neo-Latin commentaries, some readers highlight interesting synonyms or the more arcane allusions.[66] Moreover, not all the scholars were schoolboys: for example, Thomas Linacre studied Cicero's rhetorical devices in an *Opera Omnia* printed in 1498–9, when Linacre was nearly forty years old; similarly, John Gunthorpe annotated Dati's *Libellus super Tulianis elegantiis* long after he had produced humanist orations of his own.[67] When Gunthorpe reads *De Officiis* most of his marginalia concern language and allusions, but by one passage he writes 'the other text has the passage thus' and quotes an alternative reading ('alter textus habet sic'). He seems to be collating Cicero's text.[68] Printed editions of Cicero are read in ways similar to manuscripts in the service of an enthusiastic and accomplished philology.

Furthermore, that close philological reading does sometimes reveal political lessons to Gunthorpe. Can one make a close reading of a political work without being caught out suddenly by its opinions? Defining terms is an essential preliminary to political discussion, and so it is important to distinguish, say, the terms *plebs* and *populus* as Gunthorpe does in one note on Cicero's work ('plebs et populus differunt'). He also notes some passages about revolution, that scourge of fifteenth-century England.[69] Bishop John Russell (*c*.1430–94) also reveals the different sorts of reading to which Cicero was amenable. Russell bought two copies of the first printed edition of *De Officiis* in 1467 in Bruges on a diplomatic mission with Caxton and others. In the first twenty pages of one copy there are tiny interlinear annotations which are mostly linguistic; indeed, in places they are so thorough that they provide a crabbed translation of the work. Yet in the other copy, someone notes the philosophical themes instead,

[66] Cicero, *Orator, etc.* (Venice: Locatellus, 17/8/1492; TCC, classmark VI.15.21¹), sigs. A4r, A5v, m4v; *De Officiis, etc.* (Mainz: Fust and Schöffer, 4/2/1466–7; TCC, classmark VI.14.24), f.12v (Seneca), with marginalia almost invisible due to washing of the leaves; Cicero, *Epistolae ad familiares* (Venice: Locatellus, 22/9/1494; CUL, classmark Inc.2.B.3.85 [1659]).
[67] Cicero, *Opera Omnia*, 2 vols. (Milan: le Signerre, 1498–9; CUL, classmark Inc.1.B.7.26 [1927]), sigs. a6v, a8r, and b1v, on which see *BRUO*, II.1147–9; Agostino Dati, *Elegantiole* ([Louvain: de Westfalia, *c*.1485]; BodL, classmark Auct.N.5.3), on which see *Humfrey 1970*, no. 94.
[68] Cicero, *De Officiis* (Louvain: de Westfalia, [*c*.1483]; CUL, classmark Inc.3.F.2.2 [3184]), sigs. s1v-s2r (Greek), s4r (collation). Gunthorpe's name is stamped into the binding and the marginalia resemble the hand in *Humfrey 1970*, plate XV. Compare his marginalia in *n*. 18 in Chapter 1 above.
[69] Cicero, *De Officiis* (Louvain: de Westfalia, [*c*.1483]; CUL, classmark Inc.3.F.2.2 [3184]), sig. m5r; *De Amicitia, De Senectute* (Louvain: de Westfalia, 17/5/1483; CUL, classmark Inc.3.F.2.2 [3180]), sig. b1r-v.

themes to which Russell would later allude in his parliamentary speeches in 1483.[70] And other readers too who note the rhetorical devices in Cicero's works do also note, sometimes more frequently, the content of the work.[71] We must not be too dismissive about the evidence of rudimentary linguistic understanding written in the margins and between the lines of these books. What else does a narrow margin allow the annotator to show? Many scholars who have researched the history of reading have spoken with dejection of the simplistic marks left in so many books.[72] But all reading begins with basic comprehension, and 'reading' in the metaphorical senses of *interpreting* and *responding* requires further consideration and further space. It requires, in fact, room for writing.

REPRODUCING THE COMMONWEAL OF READERS IN CAXTON'S PROLOGUES

A more expansive account of humanist reading is offered in the writings of one English printer of Cicero, and Traversagni's collaborator, William Caxton. In his famous prologues and epilogues, Caxton also expresses zeal to reproduce his works and to accumulate readers, no doubt partly through a keen mercantile spirit. Printing itself was still an expensive process; what made the early printers their money was their ability to pass on books 'wholesale' to stationers. The early printers made money not through the process of printing, but through their skill in marketing.[73] So how did Caxton encourage his reader to buy his humanist books in English, beyond the more clearly saleable schoolbooks in Latin? He wrote prologues and epilogues advertising his books. And in some of them he offers the readers a chance to participate in a political humanism unlike the stylistic and grammatical studies of Carmeliano and Traversagni. He does offer brief stylistic commentary in the epilogue to *Boece* (as in Chapter 1) and famously in his prologue to his *Eneydos*, from a

---

[70] Cicero, *De Officiis, etc.* (Mainz: Fust and Schöffer, 4/2/1466–7), in LPL, MS 765, with glosses, and in CUL Inc.3.A.1.3a [12], with ideas summarized (sigs. b1r-v, b6r). See *BRUO*, III.1609–11, and *nn.* 2–3 in Chapter 6 below for Russell.

[71] For example, on *De Officiis, De Senectute* and *De Amicitia* in Cicero, *Opera Omnia*, 2 vols. (Milan: le Signerre, 1498–9; SJC, classmark, Ii.2.10), there are twenty-five notes on rhetorical devices but 502 on the content.

[72] William H. Sherman, 'What Did Renaissance Readers Write in their Books?', in *Books and Readers in Early Modern England: Material Studies*, ed. Jennifer Andersen and Elizabeth Sauer (Philadelphia, PA: University of Pennsylvania Press, 2002), 119–37 (130–3).

[73] Peter W. M. Blayney, *The Stationers' Company before the Charter, 1403–1557* (London: Worshipful Company of Stationers and Newspaper Makers, 2003), 21, 35–6.

French retelling of Virgil's *Aeneid*. Yet it is in his *Eneydos* that he sounds most uneasy about the classical style: he has been uncertain how to translate its recherché diction, for some people dislike over-curious terms:

> I doubted that it sholde not please some gentylmen whiche late blamed me sayeng that in my translacyons I had over-curyous termes whiche coude not be understande of comyn peple and desired me to use olde and homely termes in my translacyons.

Yet, on the other hand, the fashion for aureate language is growing:

> For in these days every man that is in ony reputacyon in his countre wyll utter his commynycacyon and maters in suche maners and termes that fewe men shall understonde theym. And som honest and grete clerkes have ben wyth me and desired me to wryte the moste curyous termes that I coude fynde.

He then decides to use a middling style, but worries that he still may sound rather abstruse:

> And yf ony man wyll entermete in redyng of hit and fyndeth suche termes that he cannot understande, late hym goo rede and lerne Vyrgyll or the *Pystles* of Ovyde, and ther he shall see and understonde lyghtly all yf he have a good redar and enformer. For this booke is not for every rude and unconnynge man to see, but to clerkys and very gentylmen that understande gentylnes and scyence. [74]

What are the curious terms? These 'termes' sound like a humanist style recommended by what sound like ecclesiastical humanists such as Russell, Traversagni, or Waynflete ('grete clerkes'). To understand the terms, one must seek their models in Virgil and Ovid, and one will need a lecturer or teacher to help ('redar and enformer'). Only John Skelton, an Oxford graduate who has just translated 'the *Epystles* of Tulle', that staple textbook, is fit to judge Caxton's translation, he says (36a:90–6). Now, it has been argued that Caxton's tropes of humanist scholarship in his *Eneydos* and elsewhere sever the new Tudor dynasty from its 'medieval' past in favour of an ancient and imperialist heritage.[75] Yet we must be cautious in finding teleology in the supposed transition from 'medieval' to 'Renaissance': could Caxton know, in 1491, that Henry VII's dynasty was secure and advancing towards absolutism? Furthermore, even within this prologue, Caxton sounds disenfranchised from the humanist inheritance: it requires a teacher to explain it and produces a style that only a poet laureate is fit to judge. Then he criticizes this style as a tool of political mystification: many a nobleman speaks in this humanist style

---

[74] All quotations, usually with parenthetical references, come from the numbered excerpts in *Caxton's Own Prose*: here citing 36a:27–31, 60–5, 75–82.

[75] Lerer, *Chaucer and his Readers*, 172–4; Seth Lerer, 'William Caxton', in *The Cambridge History of Medieval English Literature*, ed. David Wallace (Cambridge: Cambridge University Press, 1999), 720–38 (736–8).

in order to awe his affinity in his 'countre'; they use it so that 'fewe men shall understonde theym'. In fact, Caxton usually ignores an academic agenda, and sometimes even a lordly agenda, and addresses instead the 'comyn peple'.

His customary manifesto for the study and imitation of antiquity by a wide range of readers recalls that of other writers in English, yet his reasoning is still rooted in classical sources. To provide a proem to John Trevisa's *Polychronicon* (1482) Caxton translates the preface to Diodorus Siculus' *Bibliotheca Historica*, originally composed in Greek. It has been assumed that Caxton used some lost French intermediary for this proem,[76] but Caxton's language here is uncharacteristically Latinate and fairly close to the vocabulary and syntax of Poggio Bracciolini's fifteenth-century Latin version. The source need not surprise us: Poggio's translation of the *Bibliotheca Historica* was available in England to readers such as William Worcester or to the papal protonotary Giovanni Gigli; as Caxton himself records, John Skelton had made an English translation of it by 1491. Gigli's and Worcester's notes on it are, in fact, predominantly observations on unusual names and places in the customary philological vein, but Caxton borrows Diodorus Siculus' defence of reading histories.[77] In sum, histories make their common readers into rulers:

Historyes ought not only to be juged moost proffytable to yonge men whiche by the lecture, redyng and understandyng make them semblable and equale to men of greter age and to old men, to whome longe lyf hath mynystred experymentes of dyverse thynges, but also th'ystoryes able and make ryght pryvate men digne and worthy to have the governaunce of empyres and noble royammes. Historyes moeve and withdrawe emperours and kynges fro vycious tyrannye, fro vecordyous sleuthe unto tryumphe and vyctorye in puyssaunt bataylles. Historyes also have moeved ryght noble knyghtes to deserve eternal laude, whiche foloweth them for their vyctoryous merytes, and cause them more valyantly to entre in jeopardyes of batayles for the defence and tuicion of their countrey and publyke wele.   (86a:40–53)

Firstly, Caxton's translation portrays educational reading by the young not as mere grammar, but as the acquisition of wider experience or 'experymentes'; whatever the evidence of marginalia, the latent political opportunities within reading are at least imagined here. Yet then Caxton moves from children to the reading of historical literature by politically enfranchised adults. The later ubiquity of ideals about a liberal education leaves this passage sounding

[76] Blake, *Caxton and English Literary Culture*, 138–43; Samuel K. Workman, 'Versions by Skelton, Caxton, and Berners of a Prologue by Diodorus Siculus', *Modern Language Notes*, 56 (1941), 252–8 (254).

[77] Compare Thomas E. Marston, 'A Book Owned by Giovanni Gigli', *Yale University Library Gazette*, 34 (1959), 49; OBC, MS 124, ff.153r-242v (where Worcester ascribes Poggio's translation to John Free), especially as annotated ff.154v-160r; *Caxton's Own Prose*, 36a:92–3.

commonplace and perhaps vacuous. However, to compare the near-contemporary translation by Skelton reveals that Caxton's political emphases still sounded a distinctive note in the 1480s. Skelton says that reading history has led men 'of baas and lowe progenye' to disreputable social climbing; this is the snobbery which feeds his later bile against Wolsey the butcher's son. By contrast, Caxton's translation says that such 'private' ordinary citizens are wholly 'worthy' to take on public offices in government. Then, when they do serve, Skelton's heroes demonstrate a more chivalric 'valyaunt prowesse and marcyal fayttis' in defence of 'theyr countreye', whereas Caxton's heroes sound more like civic leaders who avoid 'tyrannye' in order to defend both 'their countrey and publyke wele', adding an idea of the commonweal to Poggio's more neutral word 'patria'.[78] Caxton next further contrasts good governance of the commonweal with tyranny by adding to his source a reference to the failings of Nero (86a:57–8). John Skelton's reading misses the possible political tenor of the *Bibliotheca Historica*, and his ensuing translation seems most concerned with developing a Latinate style. By contrast, William Caxton insistently employs humanist political slogans, and brings those slogans to life with a fleeting allusion. This is a fresh and idealistic statement.

Furthermore, besides its political character, Caxton's imagined humanist reading is also striking because it shapes not one princely reader, but a wider community of readers. To some extent it becomes clear in other prologues and epilogues by Caxton that the interest in service of the 'publyke weal' by 'pryvate men' is determined not only by classical sources but also by the very function of prologues to solicit business. Caxton and his one-time business partner Colard Mansion are rare among fifteenth-century printers for the rambling introductions they add to their books.[79] These prologues invite Caxton's contemporaries to purchase, of course, but also to read his editions as if they were members of the bookish community mentioned therein; as such, then, Caxton's prologues work analogously to those prefatory Latin verses in humanist schoolbooks. Some echoes of educational metaphors linger: Caxton's translation of Diodorus Siculus (quoted above) initially defines reading as a process that will refashion the younger reader to make him 'semblable' to, or an imitation of, certain older, wiser men. As when we or the Duke of York are told to 'Marke' Stilicho, the usefulness of studying history would itself work by the imitation and reproduction of the past. These prologues suggest that each work's ideas will be reproduced within each reader's mind as the book is distributed.

[78] John Skelton (trans.), *The Bibliotheca Historica of Diodorus Siculus*, ed. F. M. Salter and H. L. R. Edwards, EETS os 233, 239, 2 vols. (London: Oxford University Press, 1956–7), 6:27–35; Poggio Bracciolini (trans.), *Diodorus Siculus* (Paris: Petit, 1508), sig. a3r.
[79] Painter, *Caxton*, 72–7.

Critics have long recognized Caxton's preference for the fanciful exemplary histories of Troy and Jason alongside the Nine Worthies.[80] What is less often recognized is that Caxton's interest in imitating the classical world does also, in some books, echo humanist idioms. For example, the focus upon reading as a service to the wider commonweal in *Polychronicon* originates in a response to Diodorus Siculus, and elsewhere there are apparently Ciceronian sources. One of them comes in Caxton's exhortation to us to purchase the work *Caton* (1484). The presence of humanist ideas in the prologue to *Caton* is curious. The work is not—though critics often say it is—yet one more edition of Cato's *Disticha* in Burgh's bilingual form, which Caxton had printed, presumably for schools, in earlier years. In *Caton* the Latin *Disticha* come overwhelmed by a version of Philippe de Pergamme's enormous Christianizing commentary known as the *Speculum regiminis* (*c*.1385).[81] This is not a humanist schoolbook, but a pious homily: Caxton refers to it as 'the myrour of the regyme and gouernement of the body and of the sowle'. The commentary cites St Augustine and the Church Fathers far more than Caxton's 'noble Romaynes'. And even when Cato in his *Disticha* recommends reading classical authors for technical advice, the commentator in *Caton* dismisses them. Virgil's advice on husbandry is worthless, because:

the auncyentes dyte put theyr cure and studye for to laboure and cultyue the erthe / but thys oppynyon is false / for the soueryn good of thys worlde is to serue and loue god

Macer, Lucan, and Ovid are similarly rejected. The commentator interprets his few other classical exempla as 'moral allegories' about Christ's relationship with the soul ('To speke now morally').[82] Caxton's oeuvre as printer encompasses diverse genres, and many of his supposedly classical texts are not genuinely so. This commentary is totally unlike the secular interest of the humanists in agriculture and statecraft; it is the sort of grim misreading of the classics found, for example, in Walton's commentary on Boethius.

Therefore it is even more striking how far Caxton, in turn, misreads his own *Caton* in its prologue, for in the prologue he presents this pious philistinism—as he presents other spurious classical texts such as his *Eneydos*—with humanist packaging. He knew his market: his readers did have the work bound with the almost-classical *Boece*, and one even spotted an

---

[80] On which, see William Kuskin, 'Caxton's Worthies Series: The Production of Literary Culture', *English Literary History*, 66 (1999), 511–51 (511).

[81] Joseph Nève, *Catonis Disticha: Facsimilés, Notes, Liste des éditions du XVe siècle* (Liège: Vaillant-Carmanne, 1926), 13, describes *Speculum regiminis*. William Caxton (trans.), *Caton* (Westminster: Caxton, 1484; *STC* 4853; CUL, classmark Inc.3.J.1.1 [3505]), sig. i9r.

[82] Caxton (trans.), *Caton*, sig. e3r-v, and also sigs. c2r-v, d2v-d3r. *Caton* cites Christians forty-five times and pagans thirty-five times (eighteen of which cite the moralistic pseudo-Seneca).

echo of *Boece* in *Caton*.[83] In the prologue, Caxton justifies his printing of *Caton* by invoking the approval of Poggio Bracciolini 'of Florence', he says, who 'helde *Cathon Glosed* for the best book of his lyberarye'.[84] An Italian again authorizes this choice of edition, as in the name-dropping prefaces to grammars. Furthermore, Caxton imagines a classical pedigree for the work he is about to translate, in a passage where he ponders why London's prosperity is declining:

And the cause is that ther is almost none that entendeth to the comyn wele, but only every man for his singuler prouffyte.

O whan I remember the noble Romayns that for the comyn wele of the cyte of Rome they spente not only theyr moevable goodes, but they put theyr bodyes and lyves in jeopardy and to the deth, as by many a noble ensample we may see in th'actes of Romayns, as of the two noble Scipions, Affrican and Asyan, Actilius and many other, and amonge al other the noble Catho, auctor and maker of this book whiche he hath lefte for to remayne ever to all the peple for to lerne in hit and to knowe how every man ought to rewle and governe hym in this lyf. And as in my jugement it is the beste book for to be taught to yonge children in scole; and also to peple of every age it is ful convenient, yf it be wel understanden.   (15a:22–36)

Whether by confusion or by sleight-of-hand, Caxton has made two mistakes here. His first error is sly: despite having already printed and so known Cato's *Disticha*, he here conflates Philippe de Pergamme's religious commentary with the poems themselves. The second error is more comprehensible: the third-century poems known as Cato's *Disticha* had been ascribed to the second-century BC republican Cato at least since the time of Aulus Gellius,[85] and sure enough, this prologue continues that ascription to 'the noble Catho'. Caxton thereby exhorts his customers to read what *seems to be* a work of the classical republican era. In fact, he even emphasizes the connection of this work with the famous Cato by alluding to Cato's role as a character in Cicero's *De Senectute*. It is in *De Senectute* that Cato tells people to offer their 'moevable goodes' and 'bodyes' to serve the 'comyn wele' instead of their 'singuler prouffyte'; it is there too that the two Scipios and Marcus Actilius appear as examples of such sacrificial service. Or, rather, they appear not in Cicero's original *De Senectute*, beyond one passing reference, but in William Worcester's expansion of their

---

[83] William Caxton (trans.), *Caton* (Westminster: Caxton, 1484; *STC* 4853), in BodL, classmark Arch G. d.13, and in Oxford, Exeter College, classmark 9.M.4815(3), especially sig. h1v (reference to *Boece*), a book recently discussed by Lucy Lewis, 'A Newly Discovered Lyric from Exeter College, Oxford on the Theme of 'know thyself'', *Medium Ævum*, 75 (2006), 123–7, and in *n.* 38 in Chapter 1 above.

[84] *Caxton's Own Prose*, 15a:61–8. Italian humanists did still teach from Cato: Black, *Humanism and Education*, 225–35.

[85] Nève, *Catonis Disticha*, 5.

stories in his translation (as Chapter 4 noted). Caxton had printed Worcester's translation only two-and-half years previously and here he alludes to it.[86] Once more, an English writer offers us a classical work of somewhat spurious pedigree, misreading *Caton* as worthy of humanist study.

He also misreads *Caton* in hoping that it will inspire service of the commonweal. The commentary *Caton* does not tell us to serve the commonweal, except in one brief section where it promises that charity begins at home, so if we help the commonweal we will end up benefiting our 'synguler prouffytes'; Worcester would be dismayed with such selfish calculations.[87] But Caxton sells the book for its political lessons. There may be timeliness in this prologue: it might criticize London's citizens for supporting the usurper Richard III.[88] However, in fact, the prologue does not criticize readers but invites them in: Cato created 'this book', this very work you are holding, to 'remayne' like a monument beyond his death for 'all the peple'; every reader is invited to commune with Cato. Moreover, this book will teach 'every man' who reads it to 'governe' himself. Once again, an educational model appears: it is fit for 'yonge children in scole' as the bilingual editions of Cato's *Disticha* would have been; but adults 'of every age' are to be formed and informed too, as children are. There are the inclusive words found in *The Boke of Noblesse*: *ever, all the people, every man, every age*. In this prologue, Caxton imagines the number of readers reproducing to transform the whole polity. He boastfully implies that his reproduction of this book in multiple copies is an act of communal service.

Seth Lerer has suggested that Caxton's imagined readership of Chaucer's poetry is an 'elegiac' readership, radically separated from the poems they study by humanist dreams of the recovery of those texts;[89] such a separation would obviously apply to classical texts even more powerfully. However, alongside the feeling of diachronic distance comes a feeling of synchronic community: as in *Knyghthode and Bataile*, the two seem to go hand in hand; for reforming oneself, one must have a model to follow. The pairing of attitudes appears most clearly in Caxton's edition of two genuinely classical works, Cicero's *De Senectute* and *De Amicitia* (1481), issued along with Buonaccorso da Montemagno's *Controversia de nobilitate*, a recent neo-Latin dialogue. *De Senectute* is (as noted in Chapter 4 above) surely translated by William Worcester and the other two works are ascribed to John Tiptoft, Earl of

---

[86] Compare [Worcester], trans., *Tullius de senectute*, sigs. g8v-h2r; the French translation in BL, MS Additional 17433, ff.45r-46r; Marcus Tullius Cicero, *Cato Maior de senectute*, ed. J. G. F. Powell, Cambridge classical texts and commentaries, 28 (Cambridge: Cambridge University Press, 1987), XX.75.

[87] Caxton (trans.), *Caton*, sig. a8v; the phrase 'comon wele' is used fleetingly in two passages on other topics (sigs. d4r, g5v).

[88] Painter, *Caxton*, 138.   [89] Lerer, *Chaucer and his Readers*, 150–2, 162.

Worcester, a man famous for his support of humanist scholarship (as noted in Chapter 6 below). Caxton's prologues to these three printed works emphasize the book's classical origins. Despite the presence of Buonaccorso's work, he introduces the book as essentially Cicero's, by summarizing each Ciceronian work and relating Cicero's original order of composition in order to justify putting *De Senectute* first (79a:88–98, 79c:10–12). Moreover, Caxton's Cicero is the master of Greek learning and of eloquence:

> th'ystoryes of this book [...] were drawen and compyled out of the bookes of th'auncyent phylosophers of Grece, as in th'orygynal text of *Tullii: De Senectute* in Latyn is specyfyed compendyously, whiche is in maner harde the texte. But this book reduced in Englyssh tongue is more ample expowned and more swetter to the reder, kepyng the juste sentence of the Latyn.   (79a:44–50)

Despite an admission elsewhere that *De Senectute* has been translated from a French intermediary, Caxton boasts that the English text still follows 'the juste sentence of the Latyn' and is itself a work of skilful grammar and rhetoric. Indeed, the translation surpasses the Latin in its 'more swetter' and 'more ample expowned' style, but paradoxically does so by its rigid fidelity to the 'the juste sentence of the Latyn'. Caxton's 1481 edition of Cicero, then, echoes the interest in Cicero as a model of style discernible in Latin textbooks and imported editions.

However, here the Latin text sounds like something of an encumbrance; the translation is better, ampler, and sweeter. Indeed, rather than pursue literary aims in printing this book, Caxton lauds the political importance of it: repeatedly he calls it 'requisite' and emphasizes its 'polytyque' wisdom (79a:3, 10, 29, 100; 79c:13; 79d:16, 27). As in *Caton*, but now more fittingly, he explains that Cicero will cite authorities who discuss how the old Roman heroes 'toke grete thought and charge for the governaunce of the comyn prouffyght [...] named in Latyn *Res publica*, kepyng the Romaynes prosperous and defendyng them fro theyr adversaryes and rebelles'; his words echo William Worcester's translation again.[90] The slogans of the commonweal and the deference to ancient examples all recur in many of Caxton's prologues, especially in the early 1480s, such as those for Malory's *Le Morte Darthur*, *The Game of Chess*, or Ramon Lull's *Order of Chyualry*. These works are usually taken as typical of Caxton's 'medieval' taste but, in fact, there are close similarities between his prologues to the chivalric and to the supposedly classical works. They all affirm the efficacy of history, whether tales of the Nine Worthies or 'th'old hystoryes of the Romayns', to teach us to reform our ways: they all

---

[90] Compare *Caxton's Own Prose*, 79a:17–21, and [Worcester] (trans.), *Tullius de senectute*, sig. b1r; Cicero, *De Senectute*, I.1.

share a zeal for the 'comyn' rather than the 'synguler wele'.[91] It is not provable which way the influence flows, or even whether chivalry and humanism are distinct categories in the 1480s. The political slogans found in the prologues to Cicero, Cato, and Boethius, and that adapted from Diodorus Siculus, are not anomalies but align much of Caxton's work with other humanist writing in the vernacular.

However, although his idioms come from the vernacular tradition, his teacherly stance and manner of address to the reader recalls the prefatory verses to Latin grammars (explored earlier in this chapter). He invites the reader to use these books as lessons or as instruction so that he might reproduce the *mores* of the ancients. Many of the books, he says, are translated or printed at the instance of older, wiser, or nobler men and women; some, such as William Pratt or Henry VII, openly aim to teach something or other.[92] This pedagogic zeal appears in the preface to *De Senectute* again as a form of 'top-down' dissemination:

[...] and the mater and commynycacion of this said book bytwene that wyse and noble man Cato on that one parte and Scipio and Lelius, two yonge knyghtes, on that other parte is moche behoefful to be knowen to every man vertuous and wel-disposed, of whatsomeever eage resonable that he be; thenne bycause I have not seen ony of the same heretofore I have endevoured me to gete it with grete difficulte, and so goten have put it in enprynte, and dilygently aftir my lytil understandyng corrected it to th'entente that noble, vertuous and wel-disposed men myght have it to loke on and to understonde it. And this book is not requysyte ne eke convenyent for every rude and symple man whiche understandeth not of science ne connyng and for suche as have not herde of the noble polycye and prudence of the Romaynes, but for noble, wyse and grete lordes, gentilmen and marchauntes that have seen and dayly ben occupyed in maters towchyng the publyque weal [...]   (79a:57–73)

A pedagogic authority underpins the original *De Senectute*, in which the wiser, nobler Cato teaches the younger senators; through the sombre form of a Ciceronian dialogue, he aims to mould the men in his own image, to reproduce his values. A similarly patrician attitude prompted the work's reproduction in English, Caxton alleges: it was translated at 'the ordenaunce and desyre of the noble auncyent knyght, Syr Johan Fastolf'.[93] Worcester's translation was originally a coterie work of small readership: he seems to have shared the interests of his neighbours, the Pastons, with whom he swapped copies of Cicero's treatises, and he presented his translation to Bishop William

---

[91] Quoting *Caxton's Own Prose*, 80:6–24 and 45c:1–13; see also 16a:7–13, 45a:15–22, 50e:34–44, 72a:11–34, 72a:104–17, 96:1–16, 96:44–56, as well prologues discussed above.
[92] *Caxton's Own Prose*, 9:6–18 and 38:4–16; see also 11:37–60, 16a:14–30, 29:9–35, 47a:75–86, 50b:47–58, 72a:4–9, 35–40, 75a:33–45.
[93] *Caxton's Own Prose*, 79a:5–6; 22–4.

Waynflete in 1472.[94] Caxton apparently knew of this translation and acquired it through some coterie, by rumour and connections, one assumes, for he 'endevoured […] with grete difficulte' to obtain it. Yet when he did so, he transformed it, for he duplicated it in print so that other men 'myght have it to loke on'. The process of downward dissemination from the private few to the public many is completed by Caxton through the reproductive capacities of print. And he assumes the right to judge what is 'behoefful' for his readers, like the literary arbiters, the Latin schoolmasters, able to discriminate between barbarous boys and the worthiness of Tully. He is the agent of reproduction just as Anwykyll and others were.

However, although he aims to reproduce something little known for many more readers, he says something odd here: it sounds as if the ideal reader would already know what the commonweal is and how to serve it. Firstly, Caxton suggests what *Knyghthode and Bataile* and *The Boke of Noblesse* adumbrated: the scholar who turns his attention to reading of classical antiquity, in the process of so doing, serves the commonweal. Secondly, Caxton conflates two groups: he conflates the *cognoscenti* who, dialectically defined, are already familiar with the 'Romaynes', with the aristocrats or oligarchs who govern our 'publyque weal'. Alongside that conflation appears a further, strange manoeuvre: the phrasing implies that knowledge of the classics has *already* spread: Caxton alludes to 'the' Romans as if his readers 'have' already 'herde' of them; the reader who turns to this book for advice on governance has previously heard about the exemplary heroes of antiquity. He may simply flatter the purchaser of this book; the purchaser cannot be 'rude and symple' but 'wel-disposed', he twice proposes, and elsewhere 'disposed to rede' (79a:43–4). Yet, beyond a circular flattery, this manoeuvre alters the pedagogic stance from a 'top-down' dissemination of learning to an assumption or insinuation of common culture horizontally shared. This sense of shared knowledge does fleetingly emerge within the prologues: for example, in *Caton* in 1484 he recalls the two Scipios and Marcus Actilius briefly and allusively, as if we too might recall their exploits—perhaps from the 1481 *De Senectute*; in *Polychronicon* in 1482 he adds a passing reference to Nero as if we know what that name stands for. Caxton implies a wider humanist readership by speaking to his readers *as if* they were already one.

In one historical sense, by the 1480s there were already humanist readers for him to speak to: the printer will not create but, instead, meet a market for this book. After all, the scribes who duplicated *On Husbondrie* from the 1440s on were already imagining a commonweal of learned readers. And (as

[94] Norman Davis (ed.), *Paston Letters and Papers of the Fifteenth Century*, 2 vols. (Oxford: Clarendon Press, 1971–6), no. 316; Worcestre, *Itineraries*, 252–5.

Chapter 4 traced) the shared allusions and exemplars in *The Boke of Noblesse* not only inculcate an idea of the commonweal, but also, simply by dint of being shared, unite the members of the commonweal. However, with only one manuscript intended for the king, in *The Boke of Noblesse* the commonweal of readers seemed a mere dream; by contrast, when Caxton prints Worcester's *De Senectute* the dream is feasible. The printing press speeds the transformation of the historically classical ideas and exempla into 'classic', or shared and ubiquitous, knowledge which can bind citizens together. Yet we must not—as we might be tempted to—trust technology alone to create this community. It is the idea which drives how Caxton imagines uses for the technology.[95]

CAXTON'S CICERO AND ITS MISREADERS

Yet this readership is so far still imaginary, existing only in these written prologues. It remains to ask: did readers use Caxton's book as he invited them to do? In some of his romances Caxton describes an ideal aristocratic readership even though the real readers were far less than aristocratic; the description is aspirational rather than factual.[96] Is something similar true of the 1481 edition of Cicero offered to humanist readers?[97] A few inventories of people's books and a few names which recur in more than one book suggest that the 1481 edition of Cicero was read by people who read other works of vernacular humanism or who owned other notably educational books. Much of the evidence is sixteenth century rather than evidence about the first owners, but it is nevertheless informative. An inventory in one copy shows that by the late sixteenth century it was worth eight pence and was bought by

[95] This point develops hints from Elizabeth L. Eisenstein, *The Printing Press as an Agent of Change: Communications and Cultural Transformations in Early Modern Europe*, 2 vols. (Cambridge: Cambridge University Press, 1979), I.126–7, and Benedict Anderson, *Imagined Communities: Reflections on the Origins and Spread of Nationalism*, rev. edn. (1983; London: Verso, 1991), 33–4, 44, with useful modifications by William Kuskin, ' "Onely imagined": Vernacular Community and the English Press', in William Kuskin (ed.), *Caxton's Trace: Studies in the History of English Printing* (Notre Dame, IN: University of Notre Dame Press, 2006), 199–240 (222).

[96] Yu-Chiao Wang, 'Caxton's Romances and their Early Tudor Readers', *Huntington Library Quarterly*, 67 (2004), 173–88 (179).

[97] I have examined thirteen copies of [William Worcester] (trans.), *Tullius de senectute* (Westminster: Caxton, 1481; STC 5293), from those listed by Seymour de Ricci, *A Census of Caxtons*, Bibliographical Society Illustrated Monographs, 15 (Oxford: Oxford University Press, 1909), 39–42, 119–21. In what follows, I cite each copy of the edition only by the library and classmark. For bibliographical detail, see E. Gordon Duff, *Caxton's Tully of Old Age and Friendship 1481 now for the first time collated* ([n. p.]: Pearson, 1912), and N. F. Blake, *William Caxton: A Bibliographical Guide* (New York, NY: Garland, 1985), 41.

someone in a set of books which included many educational and Reformist tracts.[98] A much earlier inventory of the books of James Morice, clerk of works to Lady Margaret Beaufort, lists the English *De Senectute* with some other early Tudor editions, including a set of quartos bound together. This reader also owned a 'prologue of Caton', which might be Caxton's *Caton* or even—though it seems unlikely—just the humanist prologue, rather than the rest of the text; the prologue to *Caton* was printed in a separate quire with separate leaf signatures.[99] Another copy of the 1481 Cicero was signed by a 'Fra: Laxton' who also owned a copy of *Caton*. Some twenty-three of the thirty-three marginalia in the *Caton* pick out the quotations from other authors, rather than marking the pious argument.[100] In the sixteenth century a John and a Thomas Culpeper signed a copy of the 1481 Cicero; these names seem common, but in the same period one John Culpeper wrote in a manuscript of *The Fall of Princes* an inventory of his books, which were largely classical texts and humanist educational texts, but which included some 'Vulgaria ex Terentio'. These men might be from the family of lawyers known as the Culpepers.[101] Other copies of the 1481 Cicero were owned by lawyers, such as Sir Edmund Molyneux.[102] Some of the people who owned the 1481 Cicero were, then, of a scholarly bent or also read other English books influenced by humanism.

What did they think of the 1481 Cicero? With the freedom of all readers they write rather varied marginalia in the many extant copies; the commonest themes noted are the dangers of 'flesshely lustys' and the immortality of the soul, not the most important themes in Cicero's work.[103] Many annotators

---

[98] BL, classmark C.10.b.6, sig. f8v.

[99] CUL, classmark Inc.3.J.1.1. [3497]; Michael K. Jones and Malcolm Underwood, *The King's Mother: Lady Margaret Beaufort, Countess of Richmond and Derby* (Cambridge: Cambridge University Press, 1992), 154, 201, 224, 234, 279.

[100] De Ricci, *Census of Caxtons*, 31.23; and see William Caxton (trans.), *Caton* (Westminster: Caxton, 1484; GUL, classmark Hunter Bv.2.16), flyleaf f.ii^r, with annotations on sigs. a5v, a7r, b6v-b7r, b8v-c1r, c2v, c3v, c5r, c7r, d3v, d4r, d6r, d8r-v, e2r, f1r, f4r, f6v, h2v, h8r, i2r, i6v. The owner may be the Laxton who was M.A. by 1458–9 or Richard Laxton, rector of Felbrigg, Norfolk, 1448–82 (*BRUC*, 357).

[101] HEHL, classmark 82872, sigs. i2r, $_2$b7r, $_2$f8v; BL, MS Additional 21410, f.168v. One Thomas Culpeper, who moved in a legal milieu, gave a copy of *Brut* to one Richard Culpeper in 1568 (JRL, MS Eng. 102, f.37v, f.39v) and one William Culpeper signed another manuscript of *The Fall of Princes* in a hand of similar date (BodL, MS Hatton 2, f.169v).

[102] SJC, classmark Ii.1.49, sigs. $_2$e1r, $_2$f1r. As the book also contains the name of 'James wynge Churchmaysters of harton next newarke', the Molyneux is possibly the lawyer (d.1552) from Haughton, Nottinghamshire (*DNB*, <http://www.oxforddnb.com/view/article/18920>, accessed 28 August 2005).

[103] CUL, classmark Inc.3.J.1.1 [3495], sigs. a1v, a5r-v; CUL, classmark Inc.3.J.1.1 [3496], sigs. e1r-v, g3r, g4v; CUL, classmark Inc.3.J.1.1 [3497], sigs. a1v-a2r; Oxford, Queen's College Library, classmark Sel.a.111, sigs. a1v-a2r; SJC, classmark A.1.4, sigs. a4r-a5v. However, Caxton does mention the lessons in the book about bearing one's old age (79a:76–81).

do, however, engage in some grammatical studies, adding Latin texts to the margins, as in manuscripts of *Boece*, or spotting and glossing classical names.[104] Moreover, these studies begin to build up that network of 'classic' references which Caxton exploits: one prolific annotator picks out Fabius, who fought for 'the welfare of the comon profyte of his countrey', and the political martyrs Lucretia, Publius Decius, and Marcus Actilius—without Worcester's qualms about their suicides.[105] As these readers highlight the classical heroes, they suggest a shared interest in those 'classic' allusions which bind a culture together. Indeed, to mark up those allusions with a pen, rather than simply to skate over them with one's eyes, may suggest the continuing attempt to secure them as reference points. If Caxton's readers had not already 'herde' of the old Roman heroes, they made an effort to learn. Moreover, they often record explicitly the importance of the commonweal and of one's service to it in *De Senectute*. This is not the only or the most important theme: in one copy, only a single passage concerning the 'comyn prouffyt' is flagged, compared to two on lust and four on the afterlife.[106] Nevertheless, readers do attend to it.[107] One anonymous reader writes marginalia with a predilection for abstract humanist concepts such as virtue, liberty, and servitude: 'virtue and fame are most greatly to be sought' ('virtus et bona ffama sunt maximis appetenda'). He mistakes some of Cato's words in the work for the author's own: 'Tully comendythe owld age in hys owne person The tyme off hys olde age beyth prophetabyll ffor the comon weelle'.[108] The mistake reveals a lazy classicist but an earnest one. In these books, the readers of Cicero are not the parroting schoolboys, often mocked in descriptions of humanist reading, from Skelton's time to our own: they seek not only to reproduce Cicero's style, but to imitate his ideas. Yet they do not reproduce slavishly the lessons which Caxton would have them learn; they are inconsistent, independent, and unpredictable in this response. Sometimes, though, in these marginalia, the readers imagine their humanist community for themselves.

---

[104] BL, classmark C.10.b.6, sigs. b2v-g3v; Oxford, Queen's College Library, classmark Sel.a.111, sigs. b3r, c2r-v, d2v and flyleaf f.iii^r; CUL, classmark Inc.3.J.1.1 [3495], sig. h5r; CUL classmark Inc.3.J.1.1 [3496], sig. d8v.

[105] Oxford, Queen's College, Sel.a.111, sigs. c2v, d2v and flyleaf f.iii^r; CUL classmark Inc.3.J.1.1 [3495], sigs. g7v, h5r; CUL, classmark Inc.3.J.1.1 [3496], sigs. b6r, g7v, g8v.

[106] CUL, classmark Inc.3.J.1.1 [3495], sigs. i4r-a5v.

[107] Oxford, Queen's College Library, classmark Sel.a.111, sigs. 2b4r, 2b5r, 2c5v.

[108] CUL, classmark Inc.3.J.1.1 [3496], sigs. b6r, g7v, g8v, e3r, c2v.

6

Eloquence, reason, and debate

Caxton's commonweal bound together in reading is a writer's fantasy. The unpredictable readers do not always read his 1481 edition of Cicero, say, as he expects them to. But his fantasy is underpinned by its similarity to some notions of long and good pedigree not about reading but about speaking. The theory was that speaking—eloquence, reasoning, and debate—could bind together the commonweal. It was familiar to Caxton's contemporaries from the works of Cicero. In *De Inventione* and *De Oratore*, Cicero tells us that speech forms society, as people talk each other into peace, and it can do so because what distinguish human beings from animals are the abilities to reason and to speak.[1] One fulsome expression of this notion comes in the speeches of Bishop John Russell, the humanist, cleric and public servant. One of his speeches was given on embassy to the Duke of Burgundy in the 1470s and then printed by Caxton. In it, Russell cites Cicero's view of man as the 'animal sociale' who seeks concord in order to survive; delightfully, his examples are Arthur's Round Table and the Order of the Garter.[2] The other speech was prepared in 1483 for the first parliament of Edward V. In this one, Russell compares parliamentary debate to the public debates in the Roman senate and alludes to several other Roman heroes who took or gave counsel. This is a way of flattering his listeners, of course, like the less-purposeful allusions in other political writing of the time. But behind these allusions lies some deeper theory of the nature of humanity:

Man that ys callyd *Animal ciuile*, namely for that he ys endued whythe speche, whyche no best hathe but onely man, and whereby thynges ellys unknowen may be broughte to knowleche from one to a nother, takithe hys lernynge by herynge.

---

[1] Marcus Tullius Cicero, *De Inventione*, in his *De Inventione; De optimo genere oratorum; Topica*, ed. and trans. H. M. Hubbell (Harvard, MA: Harvard University Press, 1949), I.2; Marcus Tullius Cicero, *De Oratore*, ed. and trans. E. W. Sutton and H. Rackham, 2 vols. (Harvard, MA: Harvard University Press, 1942), I.viii.32.

[2] *Propositio Johannis Russell printed by William Caxton circa A.D. 1476*, ed. Henry Guppy (Manchester: Manchester University Press, 1909), sig. a2r–v, reprinted in Pierre Chaplais (ed.), *English Medieval Diplomatic Practice*, 2 vols. (London: HMSO, 1982), I.253–5.

For human beings to flourish, they must use their reason and eloquence; the prosperity of the commonweal, Russell urges, requires 'eche amyabilly to harken apon other'.[3] What he urges the members of parliament to do is to listen to each other, in debate rather than monologue, and in a friendly or amiable style. Yet we might be sceptical about Russell's concern for eloquent debate. He wrote this oration for the parliament of Edward V, but then revamped it for the parliament of the man who usurped the throne, and perhaps killed the king, Richard III. Neither the parliament nor England in general was fully open to debate; this was no true democracy. So is the Ciceronian humbug a smokescreen? Is the commonweal of eloquent discussion, like the commonweal of readers, only a fantasy? Is there any real value in debating with each other?

The question is pressing because a good number of humanist works of the fifteenth and sixteenth centuries use the form of the debate or dialogue. For centuries people had composed debates and dialogues in courtly and religious traditions. In English there were wonderful poems which debated faith or love, such as *The Owl and the Nightingale, The Thrush and the Nightingale,* or Chaucer's *The Parliament of Fowls.* Then in the fifteenth century the humanists composed more debates, in a different set of forms with classical precedents.[4] They composed dialogues in imitation of Plato and Cicero—like those exemplified in Caxton's 1481 edition—and they composed declamations, in which two or more people deliver opposing orations in classical style. The humanists in Italy were prolific in these forms and the humanists writing in England or in English followed suit, often closely following classical or neo-Latin models. For example, Lydgate translated a declamation by Salutati in *The Fall of Princes,* with the debate between Lucretia and her husband about shame and suicide. Some unknown writer adapted from Lucian a declamation between the three classical heroes about who was greatest, and in this adaptation Henry V joins in the discussion and wins. (These examples were noted in Chapters 2 and 3 above.) Somebody from Winchester School translated Petrarch's *Secretum,* his spiritual dialogue, into English rhyming couplets.[5] The imitation of classical dialogues, then, fed into the literature of

---

[3] 'Bishop Russell's Parliamentary Sermons in 1483', printed in S. B. Chrimes, *English Constitutional Ideas in the Fifteenth Century* (Cambridge: Cambridge University Press, 1936), 167–91 (171–2, 174, 177–8), on which see John Watts, '*The Policie in Christen Remes*: Bishop Russell's Parliamentary Sermons of 1483–84', in *Authority and Consent in Tudor England: Essays Presented to C. S. L. Davies,* ed. G. W. Bernard and S. J. Gunn (Aldershot: Ashgate, 2002), 33–59 (47–8); and *n.* 11 in Chapter 3 and *n.* 70 in Chapter 5 above.

[4] David Marsh, *The Quattrocento Dialogue: Classical Tradition and Humanist Tradition* (Cambridge, MA: Harvard University Press, 1980), surveys some.

[5] Available only in facsimile in Wilson and Fenlon (eds.), *Winchester.*

England during the fifteenth century. (Some such debates are the subject of the first part of this chapter.)

The most pronouncedly humanist exercise is perhaps the debate printed in the 1481 edition of Cicero, as a third work bound with Cicero's dialogues. Caxton calls this third work *The Declamacion of Noblesse* and says that it was translated by Sir John Tiptoft, who he says translated Cicero's *De Amicitia* too. It is a translation of the *Declamatio de vera nobilitate* by Buonaccorso da Montemagno (1391/3–1428). Buonaccorso was a humanist scholar and a lawyer in Florence. In his *Declamatio* he establishes, very briefly, that one Lucretia, the daughter of a senator in republican Rome, must choose her husband from two suitors, Cornelius and Gaius. Cornelius comes from the aristocracy but his virtue is less than that of Gaius, the self-made man. Each man delivers an oration defending his claim to true nobility and therefore to Lucretia's hand.[6] But no outcome is given; it is merely a *declamatio*, the rhetorical exercise of arguing 'for and against'. The English version printed by Caxton preserves the open-endedness. Is this, then, the exercise of pure debate, without the political or spiritual lessons of the ones adapted from Lucian or Petrarch, say? (This debate is the subject of the middle part of this chapter.)

The open-endedness seems a gift to readers, who might here have practice in the polite debate which will bind the commonweal. However, it seems that few readers bothered to record in marginalia or notes their opinions of *The Declamacion of Noblesse*. Although many of them annotated the genteel dialogues of Cicero in the 1481 edition, only one person (in the thirteen copies which I have seen) annotates *The Declamacion of Noblesse* too.[7] Yet this work did excite one reader, Henry Medwall (1462–after 1501), to write an English interlude which tells its story, the interlude of *Fulgens and Lucres*.[8] (Medwall's plays are the subject of the last part of this chapter.) The main plot of the interlude is an expansion of the action which lies behind Buonaccorso's story; it leads to the two opposing speeches which are then rehearsed, with some verbal echoes of Tiptoft's translation. Here, then, is a fuller response than any marginal note could offer, extending the argument over two hours before a present audience of people listening amiably—as Russell might wish. But Medwall responds to the open-ended debate by ending it: his Lucres judges

[6] *Prose e rime de due Buonaccorsi da Montemagno*, ed. G. B. Casotti (Florence: Manni, 1718), 6–40, prints the whole; Buonaccorso da Montemagno, *De Nobilitate*, in *Prosatori Latini Del Quattrocento*, ed. Eugenio Garin (Milan: Ricciardi, 1952), 141–65, prints only the second half.
[7] The sixteenth-century annotator Nicholas Leigh in Oxford, Queen's College Library, classmark Sel.a.111; he gives up on sig. 2c4v.
[8] Quotations, with parenthetical act and line references, come from *The Plays of Henry Medwall*, ed. Alan Nelson (Cambridge: Brewer, 1980).

whom she will wed. Why was Medwall unwilling to let his audience, unlike Caxton's readers, listen and judge for themselves? Was the purpose of the humanist writers to provoke debate, or to preach?

ELOQUENT DEBATE IN THE FIFTEENTH CENTURY

The interest of English writers in humanist forms of debate can be traced by comparing two very different debates, Thomas Chaundler's *Libellus de laudibus duarum civitatum* and the anonymous *Somnium Vigilantis*. Chaundler's *Libellus* shows how English writers of the fifteenth century could endorse the Ciceronian theories energetically. Chaundler (*c.*1417–90) had a distinguished career at the University of Oxford and at Wells Cathedral as an educator and ecclesiastic.[9] He earned his living with the good use of words. In the course of his career he edited some dialogues called the *Collocutiones*, allegedly by one of his students, wrote his own *Allocutiones* and might have given an oration in response to Cornelio Vitelli, who taught Greek at Oxford.[10] He gave his written debate, the *Libellus de laudibus duarum civitatum*, to his patron, Bishop Thomas Bekynton of Bath and Wells, before 1464. In it, Andreas of Wells and Peter of Bath deliver letters and then speeches to the bishop; because the see is split between the two cities, each man solicits for his city the bishop's love. Yet what we learn of Bath and Wells is negligible, because Chaundler lifts large parts of the orations word-for-word from a pair of works by Leonardo Bruni in praise of Florence and Piercandido Decembrio in praise of Milan. As when classical allusions are borrowed to adorn political life, the borrowed passages here offer little room for comment on the English scene. Indeed, Chaundler somehow manages to plunder Bruni's work to praise both English cities; he plunders Decembrio's work for a few more points on Bath.[11] The content—the qualities of Bath and Wells—does not concern Chaundler.

[9] *DNB*, Chaundler, Thomas (<http://www.oxforddnb.com/view/article/5200>, accessed 28 August 2005); M. R. James, *The Chaundler MSS.* (London: Nichols, 1916), 29–31, 33–4; Thomas Chaundler, *Liber apologeticus de omni statu humanae naturae*, ed. Doris Enright-Clark Shoukri, Publications of the MHRA, 5 (London: MHRA, 1974), 9, citing earlier unpublished work.

[10] Guy Fitch Lytle, ' "Wykehamist Culture" in Pre-Reformation England', in *Winchester College: Sixth-Centenary Essays*, ed. Roger Custance (Oxford: Oxford University Press, 1982), 129–66 (138–9); Cecil H. Clough, 'Thomas Linacre, Cornelio Vitelli, and Humanistic Studies at Oxford', in *Essays on the Life and Work of Thomas Linacre c.1460–1524*, ed. Francis Maddison, Margaret Pelling, and Charles Webster (Oxford: Clarendon Press, 1977), 1–23 (17–21).

[11] Thomas Chaundler, *Libellus de laudibus duarum civitatum*, ed. George Williams, *Proceedings of the Somersetshire Archaeological and Natural History Society*, 19 (1873), 99–121. Compare Andreas's speech (106–10) with Leonardo Bruni, *Laudatio Florentine urbis*, ed. Stefano U. Baldassarri (Florence: SISMEL-Edizione del Galluzzo, 2000), 1.1–3, 1.6–7, 1.9–12, 2.6–9, 3.1–4.9, 5.4–5, 5.7–21, 6.4, 6.6–7.2, 7.4–11, 7.14–8.6, 8.10–11, 23.1–11, 26.10–12, 29.1–3,

It is the form—the eloquent debate—which is his true concern. The debate could be intended for exercises in argument and style, some work for teaching rhetoric to young men. Yet, beyond teaching rhetoric, the work also contains self-conscious reflection upon it. Firstly, in the preface Chaundler discourses on the nature of eloquence, over some length, often following Decembrio's work here.[12] Then each orator begins his speech by speaking about how to speak, once more over some length: Andreas wonders how to find words fit for his task; Peter attacks Andreas's words and Andreas attacks Peter's.[13] In the verdict, the judge commends both men for having eloquence like that of the ancients and commends eloquence in general:

[...] quæ primum efficit ut ea quæ ignoramus discere, ac ea quæ scimus alios docere possimus. Cum eadem coartamur, persuademus afflictos, consolamur perterritos, a timore deducimus, gestientes comprimimus, cupiditates iracundiasque restinguimus; ac per eam juris, legum, urbium societate conjungimur, cum nos ab inani et ferâ vitâ segregârit.[14]

[...] which first made it possible for us to learn things we don't know and teach things we do. With it we are drawn together, we rally the afflicted, console the terrified, and lead them from fear, we restrain the warlike, we quench lust and anger; and through it we are joined together in a society of right, law, and cities, when it removes us from a poor and beastly life.

He professes to follow Cicero in this theory of eloquence, and in fact he lifts these lines word-for-word from book II of Cicero's *De Natura deorum*. The work continues to endorse broadly Ciceronian theories that it is eloquence which civilizes humankind and binds society.[15] The work also exemplifies how eloquence will restore peace. Chaundler talks up the false controversy of Bath and Wells by reiterating words such as *controversia*—when, like most things billed as a controversy, it is not very controversial at all—and then is able to celebrate the return of peace by reiterating words such as *otium*, *quies*, *concordia*, and *pax*. These words seem especially common in the sections

29.5–9, 88.3–5, 88.7–8, 90.1–10, 93.3–5, 93.7–9. Compare Peter's speech (111–14) with Bruni, *Laudatio*, 15.6–12, 6.1–2, 12.12–14, as well as Pier Candido Decembrio, *De Laudibus Mediolanensis urbis panegyricus*, in *Pier Candidi Decembri Opuscula Historica*, ed. A. Buti, F. Forsati, and G. Petraglione, Rerum italicarum scriptores, 2nd series, 20 (Bologna: Zanichelli, 1958), 1013–25 (1015.12–13, 1016.19–27, 1016.37–8).

[12] Chaundler, *Libellus*, 99–100; Decembrio, *Panegyricus*, 1015.3–4, 1014.45–7, 1014.38–43.
[13] Chaundler, *Libellus*, 106–7, 111, 114–15.
[14] *Ibid.*, 117.
[15] Marcus Tullius Cicero, *De Natura deorum*, in his *De Natura deorum; Academica*, ed. and trans. H. Rackham (Harvard, MA: Harvard University Press, 1933), II.148. The passage also evokes Cicero, *De Inventione*, I.2, where he contrasts something feral with human life ('et sibi victu fero vitam propagabant').

which Chaundler wrote without 'sources'.[16] Thus the pointless debate offers the opportunity both to discuss and to prove nebulous theories of eloquence as the unifier of society.

However, as we might of Russell's speech to parliament, so we might be sceptical about Chaundler's eloquence. The work really seems a form of flattery for Bekynton, as the orators fawn for his favour and praise him as a fit judge of the contest, just as Duke Humfrey was flattered for his judgement of metre in *On Husbondrie*. Does eloquent debate truly unite the commonweal, or is it—like much humanist oratory and writing—an indirect form of praise for the powerful? This question seems especially pertinent to the second example, the work known as *Somnium Vigilantis*. The unknown writer of this debate had some genuine controversies and dissensions to settle. In the autumn of 1459 the Yorkists had at last marched openly against the king but, when their support had dwindled, had fled overseas. At parliament that November the Lancastrian loyalists took revenge with a harsh attainder on the Yorkists. *Somnium Vigilantis* was probably composed at that time for it seems to be a veiled defence of the attainder. As such, it was probably composed by someone deeply loyal to Henry VI or Queen Margaret of Anjou. Her household included several authors among its clerics and lawyers, such as Ashby and Fortescue; John Morton, later the patron of Medwall, helped to draft the attainder. This is the moment and milieu of *Knyghthode and Bataile*, too, and it shares that poem's loyalism.[17] Yet, despite the loyalism, in *Somnium Vigilantis* a speaker is given the opportunity to defend the rebels in a formal oration. Moreover, whoever wrote this work was concerned with an ideal of polite speech quite different from the usual rabid polemics and prosy 'articles' of this time. The loyal orator begins by telling the rebels' spokesman how to speak with measure and politeness:

It is ayenste the curtayse of rethorique namely before eny prynce or high astat, to whom alle honoure and dredfulnesse be du with lauly subjeccioun, to entremedle eny wordis that ben sounynge to menasses offeringe, and ye nevertheles amonge your presumptuous blastes toke none erubescennce or shame to uther such langage that longeth more for a soverain unto his subget than unto you that ar but an unknowen

[16] Chaundler, *Libellus*, 101, 103, 104, 121 (*concordia*), 101, 103 × 3, 104, 105, 117 (*pax*), 102, 115 (*quies*), 102 × 2, 115 (*otium*), and 108 (*tranquilitas*), besides 100, 105 × 2, 106, 120 (*controversia*), and 105 × 2, 120 (*lis*).

[17] For its origins, see Margaret Kekewich, 'The Attainder of the Yorkists in 1459: Two Contemporary Accounts', *Bulletin of the Institute of Historical Research*, 55 (1982), 25–34 (26, 30); Anthony Gross, *The Dissolution of the Lancastrian Kingship: Sir John Fortescue and the Crisis of Monarchy in Fifteenth-Century England* (Stamford: Watkins, 1996), 58–60, 108–9 (n. 62); Christopher Harper-Bill (ed.), *The Register of John Morton, Archbishop of Canterbury 1486–1500*, Canterbury and York Society, 75, 78–9, 3 vols. (Leeds: Duffield, 1987; Woodbridge: Boydell, 1991–2000), pp. vii–viii.

gest. But that ye may openly undyrstonde the grete curyalite of this moste noble auditte, youre rudnes and undyscrete demeanynge shalle put none obstacle but that ye shalle have audience, safe oon thinge ye most observe in this partie, that ye be as succynt and compendious as ye may, reducinge into your mynde before whome ye make your peroracion; and yf ye be not fully avysed ye shalle of the exuberant cortesye of this noble place have respitte in tyme of bettere delyberacyon.[18]

Once more there is not only eloquent debate, but some self-consciousness about it, its decorum and its effects; the form is itself discussed. Here, although the rebel is short of polish and judgement ('rudnes and undyscrete demeanynge'), the loyalist promises to listen and evokes an ideal of polite discourse. How should he speak before a prince or lofty jury ('auditte')? He should attempt the 'curtayse of rethorique', yet not sound too haughty. And how is this high style achieved? In this speech it is achieved with fancy inkhorn words, the common humanist markers of high style, which then continue throughout the debate ('perniciosite', 'sogregat', 'caryllous', 'inveterat', 'consuetude', 'reyterat'). Some are ponderous new borrowings or nonce-words, and some are words long since borrowed from French but here respelled in a more Latinate form.[19] There are classical allusions too, as well as quotations from St Augustine and St Gregory—and nor do they seem taken (so far as I could trace) second-hand from *florilegia* used by others at this time.[20] Thus, the writer uses the Latinate style and allusions found in other translations and polemics in order to compose the 'curtayse of rethorique'. The style is self-consciously eloquent, so much so as to be mannered.

Yet the style is surely meant to sound imposing; it is telling that the losing rebel spokesman does not get to use this bomphiologia. Although the work is structured as a debate between a loyalist and a rebel, the eloquence is the preserve of one side more than the other. Moreover, the Lancastrian who wrote this work does not in fact engender genuine discussion. After the rebel speaks,

---

[18] J. P. Gilson (ed.), 'A Defence of the Proscription of the Yorkists in 1459', *EHR*, 26 (1911), 512–25 (514).

[19] *OED* dates *erubescence, n.*, and *erubescent, a.*, from 1736; *curiality* from 1626; *audit, n.*, sense 1 ('A hearing, an audience') from 1598, but in the fifteenth century with a financial sense; *succinct, pa. pple., ppl. a.*, and *a.*, sense B.1.a ('Of a narrative') from 1585, but with reference to belts from the fifteenth century; *peroration* only from 1440; *exuberant, a.*, from 1513; *perniciosity, n.*, from 1568; *inveterate, a.*, from 1528; *reiterate, pa. pple.* and *ppl. a.*, from 1471. *OED* and *MED* omit *sogregate* and *caryllous*.

[20] Compare Latin quotations in Gilson (ed.), 'Defence', 524, with Gaius Sallustius Crispus, *Catilina, Iugurtha, Fragmenta Ampliora*, ed. Alphonsus Kurfess (Leipzig: Teubner, 1968), *Catilina*, 52.18, 52.29; 517 with Lucan, *De Bello civili*, ed. D. R. Shackleton Bailey (Stuttgart: Teubner, 1988), VI.527–8; 517, later translated as 'inveterat consuetude' (521), with St Augustine, *The City of God Against the Pagans*, ed. and trans. George E. McCracken and others, 7 vols. (Cambridge, MA: Harvard University Press, 1957–72), VI.12; 522 with St Augustine, *City of God*, XVI.19; 525 with St Augustine, *City of God*, VIII.19; 522 with Jeremiah 13:23; and see also *n.* 22 below.

the loyalist rebuts his points one-by-one and finally a third speaker gives a judgement in French in favour of punishing the rebels severely. *Somnium Vigilantis* offers some debate but ends by justifying the tough attainders. Given its origins, *Somnium Vigilantis* seems written to convince 'persons of moderate persuasion to support the attainders';[21] the 'curtayse of rethorique', in eloquent style and formal debate, lets the persuasion seem moderate when it is not.

This sense of debate offered and then quashed is developed through misreading a classical source. It is not usually recognized that *Somnium Vigilantis* is modelled on the debate at the end of Sallust's history *Catilina*, a work cited explicitly in a couple of places. In *Catilina* a debate unfolds before the senate between Caesar and Cato, to decide whether to execute the rebels who have disturbed the state; Caesar advocates leniency but it is the severe Cato who wins. So too *Somnium Vigilantis* allows a spokesman to defend the rebels before the argument for rigour wins. There is an interest in classical forums for debate in selecting this model. But the response to Sallust's orations is selective. The stern judge gets to quote Cato's speech in favour of punishment: the poor rebel does not get to quote Caesar's speech in support of leniency. Nor does *Somnium Vigilantis* incorporate all of Cato's speech: the loyalist alludes to an example from Cato's speech, one which glorifies severity; but in the full history Cato goes on to admit that it is the weakness and moral softness of the republic which has brought insurrection, and so necessitated this hawkish vengeance. The English writer ignores those rebukes in Cato's finely balanced argument.[22] Even though the traitor is heard and told how to speak politely, and even though Sallust has inspired a *form* of oratory and debate, still Sallust has not inspired any *intellectual* argument. This is no surprise given the occasion. In order to defend the Lancastrian throne, many writers advocated a form of absolutism, and repudiated the right to counsel and advise that was usually so integral to the English monarchy. *Somnium Vigilantis* is perhaps the best example of that absolutist tradition.[23] The winning speaker, in fact, condemns the rebels' claim to serve the commonweal with the story of Manlius Torquatus, a story told by Cato in *Catilina*, about the importance of political obedience before political service.[24] So how could one use Ciceronian eloquence or debate in a country as undemocratic and as divided as fifteenth-century England? Chaundler's debate and *Somnium Vigilantis* both defer to

---

[21] Helen Maurer, *Margaret of Anjou: Queenship and Power in Late Medieval England* (Woodbridge: Boydell, 2003), 169–70.

[22] Gilson (ed.), 'Defence', 524; Sallustius, *Catilina*, 52–3 especially 52.19–23. Gilson (ed.), 'Defence', 524, also quotes out of context Claudius Claudianus, *Carmina*, ed. John Barrie Hall (Leipzig: Teubner, 1985), XVII.239–40: Claudian praises mercy for achieving what violence cannot, the contrary message to that of *Somnium Vigilantis*.

[23] Watts, *Henry VI*, 40–50.

[24] Gilson (ed.), 'Defence', 519–20; Sallustius, *Catilina*, 52.30.

the ideal of eloquent debate, and self-consciously stress it. The stress, though, betrays the fragility of the ideal. Humanist debate seems just an otiose show of rhetoric or, worse, a screen for flattery or political control.

DEBATING BUONACCORSO'S *DECLAMATIO*

So can we find any credit in debate? We might expect more of the debate raised in Buonaccorso da Montemagno's *Declamatio de vera nobilitate* and rehearsed in England by Sir John Tiptoft and Henry Medwall. The topic is bolder, and one which had provoked people for centuries. For its originator, Buonaccorso, the question mattered: he lived in the Florentine republic during the upheavals earlier in the century and he was an ardent republican. He composed his *Declamatio de vera nobilitate* in the 1420s as the republic seemed threatened by the Milanese monarchy. His prize, Lucretia, shares her name with the raped Lucretia, who had been a symbol of republican righteousness for Livy and for Salutati in his *Declamatio Lucretiae*. One of his speakers, Cornelius, is a cocky lout who gives the old nobility a bad name; the other, Gaius, is a virtuous defendant of the republic and modelled on Marius from Sallust's *Jugurtha*.[25] The caricatures invite a bold conclusion, but Buonaccorso leaves the conclusion unwritten, as if for further discussion.

Unwritten words can be read even more variously than written ones, and this debate was never short of readers; nor did they all judge immediately in favour of Gaius. For example, various Italian humanists composed further declamations and dialogues responding to the question of true nobility.[26] The competing responses can be heard in a letter by Lauro Quirini of Venice (*c*.1420–75/9). Quirini, tries, to discredit Poggio Bracciolini who had written his own well-known dialogue *De Nobilitate*. Quirini notes that Poggio was not the first to write of true nobility; Buonaccorso had that honour. Then Quirini tells of a debate on the Rialto in Venice, the site of conversation

---

[25] Hans Baron, *The Crisis of the Early Italian Renaissance: Civic Humanism and Republican Liberty in an Age of Classicism and Tyranny*, 2 vols. (Princeton, NJ: Princeton University Press, 1955), I.365–6, II.623–8.

[26] For responses, see Albert Rabil, Jr., (ed.), *Knowledge, Goodness, Power: The Debate over Nobility among Quattrocento Italian Humanists*, Medieval and Renaissance Texts and Studies, 88 (Binghampton, NY: Center for Medieval and Early Renaissance Studies, 1991); Arjo Vanderjagt, 'Il pubblico dei testi umanistici nell'Italia settentrionale ed in Borgogna: Buonaccorso da Montemagno e Giovanni Aurispa', *Aevum*, 70 (1996), 477–86 (482–4); A. J. Vanderjagt, 'Three Solutions to Buonaccorso's *Disputatio de nobilitate*', in *Non Nova, Sed Nove: Mélanges de civilisation médiévale dédiés à Willem Noomen*, ed. Martin Gorman and Jaap van Os (Groningen: Bouma, 1984), 247–59 (252–6).

and commerce, among some friends who have come there from many lands. Some of the friends contrast the elegance of Buonaccorso's words with the viciousness of Poggio's, perhaps influenced by Poggio's reputation for scurrility. Yet the professed reason for attacking him and for preferring Buonaccorso is Buonaccorso's eloquence: 'he found better arguments, arranged them more fittingly and declaimed more eloquently'; he broached the controversy 'modestly without offending anyone' whereas Poggio broached it in a way which caused offence ('acutius invenit, aptius disposuit et eloquentius declamavit'; 'modeste sine ullius iniuria').[27] And, indeed, Buonaccorso's declamation has prompted this further civilized debate, here on the Rialto, in which men are united in talking of the question still. Yet despite all this modesty and eloquence, the nature of true nobility remains undecided: Quirini, too, says that his reader must 'judge who should be the husband for Lucretia' ('per te Lucretie sponsus fuerit adiudicatus').[28] The continuing flow of eloquent debate seems like an avoidance of judgement.

The debate provoked further responses in northern Europe, especially in Burgundy in a popular French version.[29] The Latin work was printed in Cologne in 1473 by a printer with whom Caxton seems to have worked, and the French version was printed in Bruges around 1475 by Colard Mansion, somebody else associated with Caxton.[30] There is no surprise then in the decision of Caxton to print so popular a book in English. He says that the translator into English was Sir John Tiptoft, Earl of Worcester (1427–70), and he states that Tiptoft also translated Cicero's *De Amicitia* in the same 1481 edition. This statement of the authorship by an earl might seem unlikely, as some people suggest. For example, Caxton could easily have confused the Earl of Worcester with William Worcester, who wrote the translation of Cicero's *De Senectute* in the same book.[31] William Worcester certainly knew

---

[27] 'Laurus Quirinius, Franciscus Conatrenus, Nicolaus Barbus et socii Petro Thomasio prestantissimo phisico suo S.P.D.', in Vittorio Branca (ed.), *Lauro Quirini Umanistà*, Civiltà Veneziana Saggi, 23 (Florence: Olschki, 1977), 67–73 (69–70, paras 11–12, 15–16).

[28] 'Laurus Quirinius [...] Petro Thomasio', 73, para. 35.

[29] This story is fully told by Arjo Vanderjagt, *Qui sa vertu anoblist: The Concepts of* noblesse *and* chose publique *in Burgundian Political Thought* (Groningen: Miélot, [1981]), especially 72–3, 83, 86, 104–5, 124, 154–6.

[30] E. Ph. Goldschmidt, *Medieval Texts and their First Appearance in Print* (1943; repr. New York: Biblo and Tannen, 1969), 5–6. If the 'printer of the Flores S. Augustini' was John Veldener and he printed Buonaccorso's *Declamatio* in 1473, then it was not during Caxton's short collaboration with him. On Caxton's stay in Cologne, see Severin Corsten, 'Caxton in Cologne', *Journal of the Printing Historical Society*, 11 (1976–7: special issue *Eight Papers Presented to the Caxton International Congress*), 1–18 (2, 8, 16).

[31] John Tiptoft (trans.), *The Declamacion of Noblesse* is reprinted in R. J. Mitchell, *John Tiptoft (1427–1470)* (London: Methuen, 1938), 215–41. David Rundle, 'Humanism before the Tudors: On Nobility and the Reception of the *studia humanitatis* in Fifteenth-Century England', in

Buonaccorso's declamation, although it is not clear how well.[32] However, the manner of translation and the habits of phrasing in Worcester's *De Senectute* differ from those in *De Amicitia* and *The Declamacion of Noblesse*, so there is likely some difference in their authors.[33] Whereas Worcester worked from French, the works ascribed to Tiptoft seem to follow the Latin and quite closely. *The Declamacion* is accurate with only five little mistranslations and very few omissions beyond a couple of words. It does alter the opening lines which set the scene, but the other additions are tiny and just clarify the syntax or vocabulary. It has some fine doublets, parallelisms, and rhetorical questions which give pattern and drama to the writing—quite unlike Worcester's wandering, bureaucratic prose.[34] Until there is more proof, we must say that *The Declamacion* is not like Worcester's writing and—more importantly for this study—it was published and so read *as if* it were Tiptoft's.

Yet to be published as Tiptoft's lumbers the work with Tiptoft's complex reputation. He was recognized in his lifetime for cultivating Italian humanist studies, and he had a fine library of classical, neo-Latin, and other books. He might conceivably have encountered Buonaccorso's work on his travels in Italy in 1459–61.[35] His reputation would link *The Declamacion* to somebody

---

Reassessing Tudor Humanism, ed. Jonathan Woolfson (Basingstoke: Palgrave Macmillan, 2002), 22–42 (34–5), and Anne F. Sutton and Livia Visser-Fuchs, 'Richard III's Books: XII. William Worcester's *Boke of Noblesse* and his Collection of Documents on the War in Normandy', *The Ricardian*, 9 (1991), 154–65 (160–1), reasonably question the authorship.

[32] [Worcester], *Noblesse*, 1, quotes Cornelius' argument that the word *nobiles* should refer to men of high birth (*Prose e rime de due Buonaccorsi*, 22). He might have misunderstood that Cornelius was supposed to sound silly or he might use the quotation strategically, to spur the king to emulate his ancestors. The translation ascribed to Tiptoft uncharacteristically omits a sentence here (Tiptoft (trans.), *Declamacion*, 220 line 28—221 line 1) which Worcester's quotation does include ('Dein ii, qui litterarum eruditi sunt, nonne nobiles dicunt generosos, quasi in genere nobilitas sit.'); this divergence might suggest that Worcester and Tiptoft/the translator had different exemplars.

[33] Most telling are the translators' different preferred versions of *res publica*: [Worcester], *Noblesse*, uses *common profit* nineteen times, *commonweal* fifteen times and Latin *res publica* thirteen times; [Worcester] (trans.), *Tullius de senectute*, uses *common profit* twenty times and Latin *res publica* twice. By contrast the translations of *De Amicitia* and *The Declamacion of Noblesse* ascribed to Tiptoft never use *common profit* or Latin *res publica* and only use *commonweal* twice in total. Instead the two works ascribed to Tiptoft use *weal public* three and nine times respectively and *estate public* thirteen and eight times respectively. Worcester never uses those terms.

[34] Critics are undecided over whether it follows the Latin or the French: H. B. Lathrop, 'The Translations of John Tiptoft', *Modern Language Notes*, 41 (1926), 496–501 (499–501); Mitchell, *John Tiptoft*, 177. The five errors appear in Tiptoft (trans.), *Declamacion*, 222 line 17, 223 line 18, 232 line 33, 234 line 18, 235 line 31. For parallelism, see for example Tiptoft (trans.), *Declamacion*, 216 lines 16–17 (*Prose e rime dei due Buonaccorsi*, 10); for rhetorical questions, see Tiptoft (trans.), *Declamacion*, 221 lines 29–30 (*Prose e rime dei due Buonaccorsi*, 26).

[35] R. J. Mitchell, 'Italian «nobiltà» and the English Idea of the Gentleman in the XV Century', *English Miscellany*, 9 (1958), 23–37 (31); *Humfrey 1988*, nos. 53a–65; *Humfrey 1970*, nos. 70–51; Mitchell, *Tiptoft*, 150–71.

erudite and elite. But he was also a busy nobleman. He served Edward IV as constable of England and as constable he was well known for being severe in justice and brutal in punishment. For example, there is one terrible report of the verdict he delivered over Ralph Grey, just before he had him killed. This sort of duty, and these reports of it, would link *The Declamacion* with somebody who delivered speeches in judgement on others. The speech over Ralph Grey is not obviously influenced by the ancients; it is legalistic in expression and chivalric in thought.[36] Yet would Tiptoft's reputation as a cruel judge in such cases affect people's reading of *The Declamacion*, with its own invitation to judge? Does this tough justice not expose the mildness and open-endedness of *The Declamacion* as a charade? It might do. Yet David Rundle warns that we must not believe clichés about the Renaissance villain cultivated in fine letters and finer violence.[37]

Rather than see Tiptoft's literary studies as a perverse mirror of his judicial career, it is better to see them as simply irrelevant to it, for it is hard to gauge the purpose, if there was one, of Tiptoft's studies. Rundle has noted some moral and political works among Tiptoft's books, but has stressed the predominance of belle-lettres and curious literary exercises among them.[38] Tiptoft's clients worried about the irrelevance of his studies: in a letter preface to Tiptoft—and sent to Bekynton, the patron of Chaundler—Tiptoft's secretary John Free defends Tiptoft's studies in Italy while there's a war in England. He notes that Tiptoft's learning will, in fact, help the state to regain its former strength ('tua sapientia antiquam gentis tuae gloriam reperares').[39] Tiptoft himself says little about his interests, but his few hints do suggest some stylistic and rhetorical interests. In his earliest surviving letter he rues his own prolixity and praises the 'Ciceronian style' of his correspondent ('stilo tulliano').[40] But in fifteenth-century courts and the curia, to study rhetoric was something useful. Tiptoft announces so much in a letter made public by being sent to the University of Oxford in 1459–60. He offers to donate some books to the

---

[36] '*Warkworth's*' *Chronicle*, in Lister M. Matheson (ed.), *Death and Dissent: Two Fifteenth-Century Chronicles* (Woodbridge: Boydell, 1999), 61–124 (97:4–10, 101:22–102:6, 106:18–107: 1). See also the speech quoted by the editor of [John Warkworth], *A Chronicle of the First Thirteen Years of the Reign of King Edward the Fourth*, ed. James Orchard Halliwell, Camden Society, o.s. 10 (London: Camden Society, 1839), 38–9, and in general Mitchell, *Tiptoft*, 87, 89, 97–9, 131–5.

[37] David Rundle, 'Was There a Renaissance Style of Politics in Fifteenth-Century England?', in *Authority and Consent in Tudor England: Essays Presented to C. S. L. Davies*, ed. G. W. Bernard and S. J. Gunn (Aldershot: Ashgate, 2002), 15–32 (19–21).

[38] Rundle, 'Humanism before the Tudors', 33–5.

[39] 'A Letter Preface of John Free to John Tiptoft Earl of Worcester', ed. R. Weiss, *Bodleian Quarterly Record*, 8 (1935–8), 101–3 (102–3).

[40] W. A. Pantin (ed.), *Canterbury College, Oxford*, Oxford Historical Society, new series, 6–8, 3 vols. (Oxford: Clarendon Press, 1946–50), III.103 (no. 122).

university, imitating Duke Humfrey surely, with hopes that from these books the students will recover the ancient dignity of Latin. He wants them to be well equipped if ever employed as 'oratores' for the king on an embassy to the Italians, the princes of all eloquence. This is an extremely specific aim, which probably reflects the fact that Tiptoft had been so employed to represent his country before the pope. The scholars of Oxford write back, noting his comment on the Italians and vowing to devote themselves to 'eloquence, which both they and we call divine' ('quam et ipsi et nos divinam vocamus, eloquencia').[41] So Tiptoft suggests that the humanist studies will school young men in eloquence of a most useful kind.

Could such schooling in eloquence be what *The Declamacion* is for? The debate without a judgement was a tried and tested training in the arts of persuasion: the argument *in utramque partem* where the outcome mattered less than the skills acquired.[42] This is how the English work begins, by establishing that the two suitors who speak were being tested on their speech: each man is invited to bid for a bride 'in as goodly langage as he coude'; then before the senate each man had 'suche langage for his parte by waye of Oracion as ensieweth.' The first reference to language is not found in the source.[43] Moreover, in the edition of 1481 Caxton ends the work by linking it with Tiptoft, dodging the judgement and hinting instead at the 'playsyre' of its eloquence:

As touchyng the sentence dyffynytyf gyven by the Senate aftir thise two noble knyghtes had purposed and shewed theyr oracions, I fynde none as yet pronounced ne gyven of whiche myn auctour maketh ony mencion of in his book. Thenne I wolde demaunde of theym that shal rede or here this book whiche of thies tweyne, that is to saye Cornelius Scipio and Gayus Flammyneus, was moost noble and in whiche of theym bothe aftir the contente of theyr oracions that noblesse resteth. And to hym juge ye this noble and vertuous lady Lucresse to be maryed.

And here I make an ende of this mater for this tyme, prayeng and requyryng all theym that in this sayd werke shal have ony playsyre that ye wil remembre hym that translated it into our maternal and Englyssh tongue, and not only this said werke but the book of *Tullius: De Amicicia* heretofore enprynted which treateth so well of frendship and amyte: I mene the right vertuous and noble erle, th'Erle of Wurcestre, whiche late pytously lost his lyf, whos soule I recommende unto youre special prayers; and also in his tyme made many other vertuous werkys whiche I have herd of.

---

[41] James Tait (ed.), 'Letters of John Tiptoft, Earl of Worcester, and Archbishop Neville to the University of Oxford', *EHR*, 35 (1920), 570–4 (572); Anstey (ed.), *Epistolae*, II.355.

[42] M. L. Clarke, *Rhetoric at Rome: A Historical Survey* (1953; London: Routledge, 1996), 89–92, 136–7; Quentin Skinner, *Reason and Rhetoric in the Philosophy of Hobbes* (Cambridge: Cambridge University Press, 1996), 27–30.

[43] Tiptoft (trans.), *Declamacion*, 216 lines 27–8 (not in *Prose e rime de due Buonaccorsi*, 10), 217 lines 18–20.

O good, blessyd Lord God, what grete loss was it of that noble, vertuous and wel-disposed lord! Whan I remembre and advertyse his lyf, his science and his vertue, me thynketh (God not displesyd) overgrete a losse of suche a man, consyderyng his estate and conning; and also th'excercise of the same with the grete laboures in gooyng on pylgremage unto Jherusalem, visytyng there the holy places that oure blessyd Lord Jhesu Criste halowed with his blessyd presence and shedyng there his precious blood for oure redempcion and from thens ascended unto his fader in heven. And what worship had he at Rome in the presence of oure Holy Fader the Pope; and so in alle other places unto his deth.[44]

In this epilogue Caxton claims the authorship of Tiptoft as a way of character-izing the debate. Much of his epilogue prays for the writer's soul, a necessary piety. But he also alludes to the famous occasion on which Tiptoft performed an oration before the pope and won 'worship' for it. The oration was reported in England in the letter preface of his secretary Free, who said that Pius II wept for joy when he heard Tiptoft orating ('lacrymans prae gaudio').[45] (Those tears are open to interpretation.) Caxton hints at this public acclaim for his eloquence. Yet as well as esteeming Tiptoft and the characters for their eloquence, Caxton esteems the readers for their ability to respond to such eloquence. He notes that there is no 'sentence dyffynytyf' for the debate and so he invites the readers to 'juge'. The invitation could be evasiveness: he was a toadying man and he might here be taking care not to offend any aristocratic customers by judging for Gayus. Yet this quest to win readers once more (as in Chapter 5) leads him to a lofty view of them, their intelligence, and their judgement. The readers must judge the men 'aftir the contente of theyr oracions'; that is, by their words, rather than by prejudices. These orations become not ephemeral tools to impress, as Tiptoft's words impressed the pope; they become an exercise for us in intelligent and independent reading.

REASONS FOR RHETORIC IN MEDWALL'S *FULGENS AND LUCRES*

One reader, Henry Medwall, took up Caxton's invitation to 'juge' *The Declamacion of Noblesse* in his play *Fulgens and Lucres*. In his play Medwall lets the lady Lucres judge her suitors, and she chooses the humble Gayus. With this move to judgement, the play might seem a predictable lesson. Yet in some ways the play still seems an exercise in oratory, and in this it seems to reflect

---

[44] *Caxton's Own Prose*, 79f:2–33.   [45] 'A Letter Preface of John Free', 102.

the household where the writer and the first actors and auditors probably lived.

In the later fifteenth and early sixteenth centuries, English drama often unfolds within the household. There is a telling mistranslation in the version of Cicero's *De Amicitia* by Tiptoft. Cicero refers to applause 'throughout the auditorium for a new fable by my host and friend' ('tota cauea nuper in hospitis et amici mei M. Pacuvi nova fabula'); Tiptoft refers to a 'tragedye playd in the hous of myn hoost and my frende', naming the genre and setting the show within a household on some amiable occasion.[46] Medwall's play also seems to emerge from a household on some amiable occasion, to judge by references in the play. In the 1490s Medwall worked in the household of John Morton, by then the Archbishop of Canterbury, until 1501 when Medwall seems to have died.[47] Morton did business with many learned men, including some of humanist taste such as Gigli, Argentine, Gunthorpe, Kendal, Sellyng, Caxton, and William Hatteclyff. Like most senior ecclesiastics, he kept a household of men skilled in writing and arguing for him, including the humanist Robert Sherborne, and he kept boys as pages, who were being educated in those skills; a household this grand would also have had choirboys. He employed as tutor to the boys the grammarian John Holt, who praised Morton's nurturing his 'nephews' ('nepotes'). And among the many scholars who worked in his household was once the young Thomas More.[48] A letter from More to Holt copied around 1500 (noted in Chapter 1 above) shows that some of these men were interested in drama. In general, then, the household was an educated one and also, to some degree, one where young men and boys were educated.

Is this household education the prompt for the debate in *Fulgens and Lucres*? It is recorded that in other large fifteenth-century households the pages and

[46] John Tiptoft (trans.), *De Amicitia*, printed in [Worcester], trans., *Tullius de senectute*, but separately foliated; here citing sig. 2a8r; Marcus Tullius Cicero, *Laelius de Amicitia*, in his *Cato Maior. Laelius*, ed. K. Simbeck (Stuttgart: Teubner, 1971), 7.24.

[47] Alan H. Nelson, 'Life Records of Henry Medwall, M.A., Notary Public and Playwright; and John Medwall, Legal Administrator', *Leeds Studies in English*, 11 (1980), 111–55; Sally-Beth MacLean and Alan H. Nelson, 'New Light on Henry Medwall', *Leeds Studies in English*, 28 (1997), 77–98 (83).

[48] *DNB*, Morton, John (<http://www.oxforddnb.com/view/article/19363>, accessed 30 August 2005); Christopher Harper-Bill, 'The *Familia*, Administrators and Patronage of Archbishop John Morton', *Studies in Religious History*, 10 (1979), 236–52; BL, MS Arundel 366, f.1r (dedication by Giovanni Gigli); Harper-Bill (ed.), *Register of Morton*, no. 408 (Argentine), nos. 7, 65, 445a, 446b, 447c (Sellyng); R. N. Swanson, 'Caxton's Indulgence for Rhodes, 1480–81', *The Library*, 7th series, 5 (2004), 195–201 (Kendal); Daniel Wakelin, 'The Occasion, Author and Readers of *Knyghthode and Bataile*', *Medium Ævum*, 73 (2004), 260–72 (267, 272 *n*. 38: Caxton, Hatteclyff); *Humfrey 1970*, nos. 23, 96, *Humfrey 1988*, no. 86, and *BRUO*, III.1685–7 (Sherborne); Nicholas Orme, 'John Holt (d.1504), Tudor Schoolmaster and Grammarian', *The Library*, 6th series, 18 (1996), 283–305 (287–8, 291–3); John Holt, *Lac puerorum* (London: de Worde, *c*.1508; *STC* 13604), sig. a1v.

choirboys sometimes acted in plays. No such records survive for Morton's household; however, given the precedents, it is possible that Medwall's plays were also performed by the choristers and pages of Morton's household.[49] The text of *Fulgens and Lucres* would certainly offer an educational exercise in oratory, to the actors as pupils and to the audience of men professionally literate—an educational use like that which Tiptoft claimed for his studies. The mock-debate, the *controversia* or *declamatio*, would allow one to practise and display one's skill in oratory, and so these forms were used in schools in antiquity and again by the humanists, often as exercises in the use of good grammar and rhetoric.[50] In sixteenth-century English schools, Roman drama was often used to train the boys. The printing of bits of Terence in 1483 and in full in the 1490s reveal that he was already saleable to schools before 1500. Morton's grammar-master, John Holt, included a few excerpts from Roman drama in the grammar which he wrote a few years later.[51] The libraries of Oxford and Cambridge often had copies of Roman plays and, despite statutes forbidding it, there were plays performed in the universities in the 1480s and 1490s; in fact, Medwall's visits to his old college often coincided with the performance of plays.[52] It is a record from a household, though, which hints what drama might teach. In the royal household in the 1470s ordinances specified that the chaplains and clerks of the chapel should study grammar and so on and should be:

endowed with vertuouse, morall and speculatiff, as of theyre musike, shewing in descant clene voysed, well relysed and pronouncyng, eloquent in reding, sufficiaunt in organez playyng, and modestiall in other maner of behauing.[53]

Drama offered the chance to practise so many of these aptitudes: the rhetorical arts of *memoria* in conning lines and of *pronuntiatio* in uttering them and gesturing fitly; even reading here seems to be reading aloud in a way that is 'eloquent'. And being 'modestiall' too meant not reticence but fitness or

[49] Suzanne R. Westfall, *Patrons and Performance: Early Tudor Household Revels* (Oxford: Clarendon Press, 1990), 14–18, 56–9, 115–21.

[50] K. J. Wilson, *Incomplete Fictions: The Formation of English Renaissance Dialogue* (Washington, DC: Catholic University of American Press, 1985), 50–4, 57–60.

[51] John Holt, *Lac puerorum*, sigs. e8v, g2r (Terence), a4v, g2v (Plautus). Chapter 5 above discusses printed editions of Terence.

[52] Joel B. Altman, *The Tudor Play of Mind: Rhetorical Inquiry and the Development of Elizabethan Drama* (Berkeley, CA: University of California Press, 1978), 3–7, 28–34; Bruce R. Smith, *Ancient Scripts and Modern Experience on the English Stage 1500–1700* (Princeton, NJ: Princeton University Press, 1988), 15–16; Glynne Wickham, *Early English Stages 1300–1600: Volume III. Plays and their Makers to 1576* (London: Routledge and Kegan Paul, 1981), III.44; Ian Lancashire, *Dramatic Texts and Records of Britain: A Chronological Topography to 1558* (Toronto: University of Toronto Press, 1984), 241–4.

[53] Myers (ed.), *Household of Edward IV*, 135.

decorum.[54] The skills of choristers and clerks shade so easily into rhetorical skills in which drama might offer training.

The interlude of *Fulgens and Lucres* offers an especially rich training in these skills of speech and decorum, as critics have noted.[55] The virtuous and successful orator, Gayus, offers a notably good role model. How does he go about his task? Firstly, his servant reminds him how to speak. Before he addresses an 'honorable audyence' he should 'study' and seek 'Such argumentis as ye can best fynde' (I.1318–22); that is, he should undertake *inventio*, the first element of rhetoric, whereby one tries to 'fynde' the best things to say before opening one's mouth. Then he begins his oration itself in textbook style:

> With ryght gode will I shall go to,
> So that ye will here me with as grete pacience
> As I have harde you—reason wolde soo.
> And what so ever I shall speke in this audience,
> Eyther of myn owne meritis or of hys insolence,
> Yet fyrst unto you all, syrs, I make this request:
> That it wolde lyke you to construe it to the best.
>
> For lothe wolde I be as ony creature
> To bost of myne owne dedis—it was never my gyse.   (II.585–93)

He pledges to answer Cornelius's charges:

> To make a grete rehersall of that ye have saide
> The tyme will not suffre, but never the lesse
> Two thingis for your self in substaunce ye have layd [...]   (II.599–601)

When he begins speaking he solicits the goodwill of his hearers, the move known as the *captatio benevolentiae*, by flattering them and by establishing his own good character, his *ethos*. Then he addresses his opponent's points methodically ('Two thingis'). So despite fighting for his love, he strikes a mild and orderly tone, shy of reproofs and boasting—like the 'modestiall' household clerks. The unwillingness to boast comes from the source, Buonaccorso's *Declamatio*, but the other moves can be traced in classical manuals of rhetoric, such as Cicero's *De Oratore*.[56] Cicero in particular insists that a moderate tone will recommend the speaker to the audience; this moderation is essential to

---

[54] *OED* and *MED* ignore *modestiall*. *MED*, *modestite* (n.), records an isolated earlier form; otherwise, *OED*, *modesty*, *n.*, is first recorded in Elyot, *The Boke named the Gouernour* (1531), meaning both temperateness (sense 1) and 'Decorum, propriety; scrupulous sobriety of thought, speech, conduct' (sense 2).

[55] Eugene M. Waith, 'Controversia in the English Drama: Medwall and Massinger', *PMLA*, 68 (1953), 286–303 (294); Altman, *Tudor Play of Mind*, 3–7, 19–25.

[56] Tiptoft (trans.), *Declamacion*, 225 line 34–226 line 6; *Prose e rime de due Buonaccorsi*, 38. Compare for example Cicero, *De Oratore*, I.xxxiii.149, II.xxiv.102–3 (*inventio*); II.xlii. 178–xliii.184 (*captatio benivolentiae*); II.vii.30 (*ethos*); II.liii.215–16 (methodical refutation).

his ideal in *De Oratore*. A mild manner will placate the audience to milder passions, and thus make them sensible and receptive, rather than prejudiced.[57]

So Medwall's Gayus could train the men of Morton's household in the practical arts of oratory, just as Tiptoft hoped to train the students of Oxford. It is this banausic training which has won humanist education, and *Fulgens and Lucres* too, a bad name, for teaching the self-interested arts of rhetoric which allowed the young boys and bureaucrats of Tudor England to advance themselves as 'new men', all the while kowtowing to the established hierarchy.[58] However, this interlude is not only an exemplification of rhetoric; like Chaundler's *Libellus*, it is also a reflection upon rhetoric: these people keep talking about how to talk. And what they talk about are mostly not the practical skills of rhetoric, but the wider ethics of these skills. The ethics of speech seem informed by the loosely Ciceronian notions about how speech forms society (sketched at the start of this chapter). Later moralists often note that a mild manner is an essential part of the mutual forbearance or 'manners' which make it possible to live in civil society.[59] If we believe such notions, the mild speech which will render others receptive to our words will also prevent us from asserting ourselves over others too aggressively. So the characters say in *Fulgens and Lucres*. For example, Cornelius, the grander orator, needs to be reminded to avoid flattering 'wordis' (I.306), verbal fireworks, or incitement:

> Of all suche wordis as may gyve occasion
> Of brallynge or other ungodely condycion.   (II.371–4)

Later, in his oration, he speaks too harshly and Lucres warns him:

> No more therof, I pray you! Suche wordis I hate,
> And I dyde forbid you them at the begynnyng
> To eschue thoccasyon of stryfe and debate.   (II.536–8)

The interruption does not appear in the source. Elsewhere Gayus takes some twenty lines to promise to speak in 'short and playne' words (I.519–39). And so on through the play. What matters is not just what one says, but how one says it.

This self-consciousness seems to arise from the particular theme of true nobility. The topic was known to be inflammatory. For example, in his *Epitoma* of rhetoric, printed in England after he lectured in Cambridge, Lorenzo Traversagni warns that when one is praising good deeds before

---

[57] Cicero, *De Oratore*, I.xxvi.119, I.xxxviii.136–7, II.xliii.182–II.xliii.184, II.xlv.189–II.lii.211. Skinner, *Reason and Rhetoric*, 127–33, gives the wider tradition.

[58] Simpson, *Reform*, 548–51; Olga Horner, '*Fulgens and Lucres*: An Historical Perspective', *Medieval English Theatre*, 15 (1993), 49–86 (52–61).

[59] Skinner, *Reason and Rhetoric*, 77–81.

breeding one must not be too zealous, for fear of seeming spiteful.[60] Similarly, in a comic prologue in *Fulgens and Lucres* the two servants, called just 'A' and 'B', worry how to broach the theme:

> *A* [...] What? Wyll they afferme that a chorles son
> Sholde be more noble than a gentilman born?
> Nay, beware, for men wyll have therof grete scorn—
>
> It may not be spoken in no maner of case.
> *B* Yes, suche consyderacions may be layde
> That every resonable man in this place
> Wyll holde hym therin right well apayde—
> The matter may be so well convayde.
>
> [...] Wherfor I can not think or suppose
> That they wyll ony worde therin disclose
> But suche as shall stond with treuth and reason
> In godely maner according to the season.
>
> *A* Ye, but trouth may not be sayde alway,
> For somtyme it causith gruge and despite.
> *B* Ye, goth the worlde so now a day
> That a man must say the crow is white?
> *A* Ye, that he must, be God allmyght.
> He must both lye and flater now and than
> That castith hym to dwell amonge worldly men.
>
> In some courtis such men shall most wyn!
> *B* Ye, but as for the parish where I abide,
> Suche flaterye is abhorride as dedly syn.   (I.130–7, 157–70)

Despite the concerns of 'A' and 'B', the most important point about this passage is that the theme is not controversial at all. It had been common for centuries, in works by Dante, Chaucer, and others, to consider whether the meek but moral might be better than the rich and rotten. In a Christian culture, this question will always be worth considering.[61] So, indeed, 'A' does not say that to choose the humble husband is unthinkable; he says it's unsayable. One must not 'afferme' it; it 'may not be spoken' even though it is 'trouth'. It is in response to the concern with speaking of the theme that 'B' reassures him that what will make the audience listen will be the style, how things will be 'convayde' with decorum, 'In godely maner according to the season'.

---

[60] Lorenzo Traversagni, 'The *Epitoma Margarite Castigate Eloquentie* of Laurentius Gulielmus Traversagni de Saona', ed. and trans. Ronald H. Martin, *Proceedings of the Leeds Philosophical and Literary Society*, 20/2 (1986), 131–269 (116–19).

[61] A. J. Minnis, 'From Medieval to Renaissance? Chaucer's Position on Past Gentility', *Proceedings of the British Academy*, 72 (1986), 205–46, traces the tradition.

The terms he uses are a rhetorician's: the 'season' might nod to the feast at which the play is being performed, or to the virtue of *temperantia* or temperance, one element of which involves being seasonable or fitting for the time and place. In *De Officiis* Cicero explains that decorum is one element of temperance. As he describes it, fervent or persuasive oratory must be reserved for the senate, whereas a tempered manner must be used in informal gatherings—like an interlude in a household, perhaps.[62] Yet in Cicero's *De Officiis*, decorum sounds like deceit.[63] What is the difference between temperance and complaisance? After all, there is flattery in the temperance of the prologue. 'B' flatters the audience for being immune to flattery: in 'some courtis' one must lie and flatter to get on, but in 'the parish where I abide' people hate that. He might be contrasting the secular royal court and the archbishop's household in his reference to the religious 'parish'. Certainly he is praising the audience, for he says that 'every resonable man *in this place*'—that is, here in the archbishop's hall—will gladly hear the debate. In a valuable analysis of temperance, Jennifer Richards concedes that temperance and decorum can become acquiescence, with social convention and political power, as many critics of humanism and sixteenth-century culture allege. Yet Richards argues, by contrast, that for sixteenth-century writers temperance not only leads to political quiescence, but to social harmony too.[64] This might be a workable defence of *Fulgens and Lucres*. Being 'godely' had aesthetic implications but also moral ones, both met by acting or speaking fitly and in due season.[65]

One word used by servant 'B' suggests the ethical implications of treating the audience with temperance. 'B' appeals to 'every *resonable* man in this place'. He reminds them that the theme is one susceptible to rational analysis: words of 'treuth and *reason*', a cool and bookish word. How one writes or speaks implies certain things about one's addressee: for example, to create a Latinate translation larded with glosses implies that one's reader is a classicist like Duke Humfrey. Here the mild manner implies the audience to be reasonable: able to follow reasoned debate and to judge well.[66] Moreover, in the speeches where

---

[62] Cicero, *De Officiis*, ed. and trans. Walter Miller (Cambridge, MA: Harvard University Press, 1913), I.xxviii.132.

[63] Cicero, *De Officiis*, I.xxxvii.134; I.xxxv.126–31.

[64] Jennifer Richards, *Rhetoric and Courtliness in Early Modern Literature* (Cambridge: Cambridge University Press, 2003), 26–7, 50–1, 56–8, 60–1. My argument in this chapter is indebted to Richards's account.

[65] *OED*, goodly, *adv.*; *MED*, godli (adj.); *OED*, ungoodly, *adv.*; *MED*, ungodli (adj.). Later Lucres will answer Gayus' suit 'Evyn as sone as I godely may' (I.552); Gayus says that nobility is 'vertue and godely maner' (II.668).

[66] *OED*, reasonable, *a.*, A.3a, and *MED*, resonable (adj.)[2], 1, have an unfamiliar sense: 'Able to discourse or discuss matters; ready of tongue or speech'.

they dwell on their manner of address, the characters seek this reasonableness from each other. For example (as we saw), Gayus begins his oration with a hope that people 'will here me with as grete pacience | As I have harde you—reason wolde soo' (II.585–7). He proceeds methodically and calmly as if the others were patient and he does so because he wants 'reason' to determine the way they hear him. When Lucres and her father arrange the debate—in a scene which Medwall added to the story—she wishes for a moderate debate so that she can follow its reasoning and judge well:

> *Lucres* Than syth I have so greate lyberte
> And so gode choyce, I were unfortunable
> And also to unwyse yf I wolde not see
> That I had hym whiche is moste honorable.
> Wherfore may it lyke you to be agreable
> That I may have respyte to make inquisycyon
> Whiche of this two men is better of condicyon.
>
> *Fulgens* I holde me content, that shall be well done.
> It may be respyted for a day or twayne,
> But in the meane tyme use this provysyon:
> Se that ye indyfferently them both entertayne
> Tyll that youre mynde be sett at a certayne
> Where ye shall rest now. Can ye do so?
> *Lucres* At the leste, my gode wyll shall I put thereto.   (I.452–65)

Here we have her motive for seeking decorum and a moderate argument: to allow her to choose 'indyfferently'. Gayus, too, seeks from Lucres 'indifference' to his rank (II.645). The word *indifferent* and its cognates in fifteenth- and sixteenth-century English only seldom mean 'not caring'. Being indifferent usually means a more positive impartiality, being fair or disinterested, as we now say. It is quite often applied to the art of listening to what might not seem appealing: in *The Bouge of Court* Skelton hopes that we will hear his satire 'indifferently', and writers from Lydgate to Heywood hope for the monarch to be 'indifferent' to his suitors, which means, unprejudiced to their rank.[67] This indifference is important in forming the plot of *Fulgens and Lucres*, of course, a debate with an outcome still undecided. But it is also important to argue mildly and judge indifferently because to do so implies an anthropology, a theory of

---

[67] John Skelton, *The Bouge of Court*, in his *Complete English Poems*, ed. John Scattergood (New Haven, CT: Yale University Press, 1983), 46–61 (line 535); John Lydgate, 'A Mumming at Hertford', in Lydgate, *Minor Poems*, II.675–82 (lines 220–1); John Heywood, *The Play of the Wether*, in *The Plays of John Heywood*, ed. Richard Axton and Peter Happé (Cambridge: Brewer, 1991), 183–215 (lines 161, 281, 376, 885, 956); *OED*, *indifferent*, a.[1], I; *indifferently*, *adv.*, especially 2; *indifference*, *n.*[1], 1. *OED* records the sense 'not caring' first in an interlude in 1519.

human life: it implies that the human mind enjoys a certain rationality and liberty to choose. The interlude implies that its audience is not only one of students of rhetoric, but one of masters of reason.

THE IDEA OF REASON IN MEDWALL'S *NATURE*

At one point Medwall sets out his theory of the human ability to reason. Early in the play, Fulgens firstly considers the nature of all human beings and how God 'of his grace is ever indifferent' (I.207). Then he considers his daughter and her gifts from God:

> She is so discrete and sad in all demeanyng,
> And therto full of honest and verteous counsell
> Of here owne mynd, that wonder is to tell
> The giftes of nature and of especiall grace.   (I.267–70)

She has the power of discretion ('discrete'), a form of judgement, and of determining 'here owne mynd'. These powers are, after all, the essential premise of the play, for Fulgens refuses to tell his daughter which suitor to choose:

> How be it, certeynly I am not the man
> That wyll take from her the liberte
> Of her owne choice—that may not be!   (I.336–8)

She and others insist upon her 'so greate lyberte | And so gode choyce' (I.428, I.542–3, I.670). This liberty depends upon a certain manner of speaking which will allow her to judge indifferently. Yet it also depends upon the mind which human beings are given by 'nature' and 'especiall grace'. What is Medwall's view of that mind?

It is set out more fully in his other interlude, *Nature*, which throws useful light on *Fulgens and Lucres*. *Nature* is a psychomachia, an allegory of the battle within the human soul: in it, 'Man' is seduced from virtue by various vices, but finally returns to righteousness, the first time by becoming shamefast, and the second by recalling the virtues in his old age. Even the shortest summary suggests that *Nature* is very different from *Fulgens and Lucres* and more like the other fifteenth-century morality plays. Yet in performance, without speech headings, the sins or the virtues in *Nature* might seem less allegorical; they might seem more like the braggards, bawdy lads, and self-righteous bores of *Fulgens and Lucres*. For example, 'Sensualyte' spurns 'Reason' by treating him as an arriviste; 'Pryde' sounds especially like Cornelius in his obsession with high birth.[68] We would need to know more about costume, though, to clarify the effects in performance. What links Medwall's two plays more firmly is that the speeches in *Nature* theorize the practice of reason and judgement in *Fulgens and Lucres*.

It is in the scope for reason and judgement that Medwall's play differs from the other morality plays, despite its generic conventions. Like the other morality plays, *Nature* ends with Man returning from vice to virtue, an ending so predictable that it would seem to deny free choice. In the other morality plays this moment is a dramatic lapse as a 'deus ex machina', or a priest from the local church, steps in to save the human character, no matter how feisty he has been beforehand. For example, in *Mankind*, Mercy asks Mankind to save himself, but very quickly instead prays to the Virgin to save him and then takes on the job himself. He greets Mankind as 'predylecte' and 'my precyose redempt son' long before Mankind asks for love and redemption, and the words borrowed from Latin passive participles betray that he is already passively redeemed by somebody else with power over him.[69] In Medwall's play, by contrast, it is Man who saves himself. Reason hides 'In secrete' to watch his progress and see whether he has 'Some token of grace in hym' to save himself—divine grace, but 'in' himself (I.1312–18). What occurs is that Man interrupts his own misbehaviour, with a sudden query about what Reason would do, and when he is saved he stresses that he is saved 'Of myne owne mocyon' (I.1335–6, I.1403–4). After he has fallen again in the second act, he summons the virtues to help him—rather than having them foisted on him—and as he does so, he keeps saying words such as *self* and *will*, as if to stress his self-determination, and people call the help he seeks *counsel*, suggesting advice rather than commands. By contrast, it was when he relinquished the 'dyscrecyon' to choose what to do and considered himself 'predestynate' that he fell.[70] Medwall's interlude does not differ in its essential plot from the other morality plays, but it does differ in the theory it sets out behind the plot.

[68] Quotations from *Nature*, with parenthetical act and line numbers, also come from *Plays of Henry Medwall*, ed. Nelson; for references to rank see especially I.264–5, I.731–8, I.1006–7, I.834+, II.497. John Alford, ' "My Name is Worship": Masquerading Vice in Medwall's *Nature*', in *From Page to Performance: Essays in Early English Drama*, ed. John A. Alford (East Lansing, MI: Michigan State University, 1995), 151–77 (157), makes this point about speech prefixes.

[69] Mark Eccles (ed.), *Mankind*, in his *The Macro Plays*, EETS os 262 (London: Oxford University Press, 1969), 153–84 (lines 72, 756–9, 765; 771, 811, and the debate at 811–70).

[70] Medwall, *Nature*, II.1008, II.1046, II.1056, II.1136, II.1200 ('selfe'); II.1040–2, II.1227 ('good wyll'); II.1083–5 ('own brest', 'voluntary'); II.1223 ('intent'); II.1400 ('my best power'); II.1003, II.1137, II.1149, II.1164, II.1199, II.1207, II.1372, II.1408 (counsel). See also his earlier free will (I.140, I.168, I.301, I.331) and abandonment of it (I.705, I.866–9).

As he saves himself by trying to recover his reason, Man actually pauses to explain this theory:

> Man wythout Reson ys but blynde,
> And yf I shuld speke after my mynde,
> I can well a dyfference fynde
> Bytwyxt man and a beste
> Whan he hath Reason in presence [...]   (I.1343–7)

Like John Russell describing man as a talking animal, here Man theorizes how he differs from the beasts. Yet it is the opening of the interlude where Medwall sets out his theory of humanity most fully. The morality plays often begin with a sermon or colloquy in which some figure of authority expounds the theory behind the play: that mercy is required, that only good deeds outlast death, and so on. *Nature* has such a colloquy: Nature and Reason teach Man, who parrots their lesson back to them. What Nature teaches Man is how he will excel the other beasts, rather than how miserable he is, if he will follow Reason. As if the exposition were not enough, Man then repeats the lesson, giving thanks to God:

> And over all thys thou hast gyven me vertue
> Surmountyng all other in hygh perfeccyon,
> That ys, understandyng, wherby I may avew
> And well dyscerne what ys to be done.
> Yet for all that have I fre eleccyon
> [To] do what I wyll, be yt evyll or well,
> And am put in the hande of myne owne counsell.   (I.134–40)

Nature responds with one more warning:

> Let Reason the governe in every condycyon, [...]
> Thou hast now lyberte and nedest no maynmyssyon,
> And yf thou abond the to passyons sensuall,
> Farewele thy lybertye—thou shalt wax thrall.   (I.159, I.166–8)

What is emphasized is the power to 'dyscerne' right from wrong through 'fre eleccyon' or 'lybertye', a point stressed later (I.298–302). Here the power to reason and choose demonstrated in the story of *Fulgens and Lucres* is in *Nature* expounded in full and set within a fuller theory of the human intellect, from its first principle, the free will of the soul. Yet by expounding the theory so explicitly, the interlude loses something. The form is the dialogue, but it is not dialogic in spirit. The wording is abstract with hollow echoes of theology ('perfeccyon', 'fre eleccyon', 'maynmyssyon') and, though it is clear, the argument is knotted ('That ys', 'wherby', 'Yet', 'be yt', 'And yf'). Moreover, the scene is repetitious, as Man reiterates everything he is told, so that he sounds weirdly robotic. In this dialogue, as in the catechism, the answer to every question is already known. There is a paradox here: Medwall limits our freedom to reason for ourselves in order to assert a theory of human rationality and freedom. Despite the form, there is no debate in this interlude about the ideas which underlie it.

THE RECEIVED IDEAS IN MORTON'S HOUSEHOLD

This is no surprise, though: through the long tradition of dialogue one seldom hears Socrates or Cato learning something from his young friends. Nor is this a surprise when we consider Medwall's interlude not just within the tradition of debate, but within its immediate and wider intellectual milieu. The theories sketched or expounded in Medwall's interludes were so ubiquitous that there seems to have been little room for debating them. With theories as ubiquitous as they seem to be, open debate is unlikely. Some sense of the ubiquity and predictability of these notions comes from considering some of the possible sources for them in books which Medwall might have read or some of the other books read by members of the household where he worked. These men, after all, were likely, or were like, the first men who saw the interlude. Then Medwall's interludes can be understood not as open dialogues, but as works which express the reading, beliefs, and interests of the community of readers within which he moved. Thus the theory of humanity in Nature's opening sermon seems preachy, but preaching to the converted.

In fact, so ubiquitous were the received ideas in Medwall's interludes that it is difficult to identify exact sources for *Nature*. For example, in the opening sermon of this work, Nature describes the whole cosmos and then sets Man in the middle; she describes how Man is superior to the other animals for his rationality and free will, and how the sign of his immortal inclinations is his upright posture:

> Pluck up thyn harte and hold thyn hed upryght,
> And ever more have heven in thy syght.
>
> Ovyde, in hys boke cleped The Transformacyon,
> Among all other hys fables and poesyes
> Maketh specyall mensyon of thy creacyon,
> Shewyng how God wonderously gan devyse
> Whan he the made and gave to the thempryse
> Of all thys world, and feoffed the wyth all

As chyef possessyoner of thyngys mortuall.

In token wherof he gave the upryght vysage
And gave the in commaundement to lyft thyn eye
Up towarde heven, [...]   (I.76–87)

Where did Medwall find this sign of the superiority of Man in his posture? One direct source has been proposed in the delightful poem *Reson and Sensuallyte*. There Nature is described in her decorated coat, on which is portrayed all the cosmos and humankind in the middle, with 'Towarde heven erecte hys face' for 'He passeth bestys of reson'. Moreover, in the only fifteenth-century manuscript of the poem some marginalia quote from Ovid's *Metamorphoses*:

¶ Vnde Ouidius de transformatis prona q[ue] cum spectent etc
¶ Os homini sublime dedit. celumque videre // Iussit et erectos ad celum tendere vultus[71]

Whence Ovid, *Metamorphoses*: while they look around from below, and so on. He gave to man an upright face, and commanded him to look to the heavens and to direct his upright face there.

Medwall might be following the text given in the marginalia, which mention the heavens ('celum') rather than the stars ('sidera') of the established text of Ovid. However, there are no other close parallels between the interlude and the poem or its marginalia, and the poem and its marginalia exist now in only one fifteenth-century copy, so it is unclear whether Medwall could ever have known it. Could he have known Ovid's poem itself? To read Ovid would not require special erudition; after all, like other fifteenth-century allusions to Ovid (sketched in Chapter 3 above), this one only comes from book I. Yet whether he used *Reson and Sensuallyte* or *Metamorphoses* is beyond settling, and there are two more important things to note. Firstly, no matter which he really used, Medwall tells us that the theory of human reason comes from Ovid's 'boke'; he presents the theory as the outcome of humanist reading. Secondly, no matter which he really used or which he cites, the possibility of his reading either the Latin or the English poem tells us just how commonplace this theory was.

Even when we turn to the books which were more likely read in Medwall's world, we uncover not obvious sources, but analogues, echoes between his works and others. The books, classical, humanist or otherwise, owned by the

---

[71] W. Roy Mackenzie, 'A Source for Medwall's *Nature*', *PMLA*, 29 (1914), 189–99; John Lydgate, *Reson and Sensuallyte*, ed. Ernst Sieper, EETS es 84, 89, 2 vols. (London: Kegan Paul, Trench, Trübner, 1901–3), lines 393–401; Ovid, *Metamorphoses*, I.84–6; John Norton-Smith (ed.), *Bodleian Library MS Fairfax 16* (London: Scolar Press, 1979), f.207r–v, briefly mentioned in *n*. 18 in Chapter 3 above. Mackenzie ignores the marginalia. His other parallels for *Nature*, I.1–7, I.22–8, I.12–14, I.92–8, I.123–6, I.134–7, and I.141–3, are not close; those for I.57–63, I.99–103, I.157–68, are nonsense.

men in the household of Cardinal Morton often offer theories of human reason like those in Medwall's interlude. We do not know whether Medwall read these books, but they did put the theories found in his interlude within the experience of his likely friends and audience. For example, the theories appear in a commentary on Plato's dialogue *Phaedo*, composed between 1473 and 1486 by John Doget, a scholar at King's College, Cambridge, and an ecclesiastic; Medwall was also a student at King's College, during the early 1480s. Doget gave the sole surviving copy of his commentary to the archbishop of Canterbury before Morton. It was later owned by Robert Sherborne, the secretary to Morton during his first eight years as archbishop; perhaps Sherborne acquired the book from the estate of the late archbishop when Morton took over.[72] It is not clear whether or not he owned it while both he and Medwall worked for Morton. It is clear, though, that Doget's commentary offers some striking parallels to Medwall's *Nature*. Doget's commentary begins with praise of the world of nature: the movements of the heavenly bodies; the plants and the trees; the animals, birds, reptiles, silkworm, and honeybee. Then he notes that although humanity shares its vegetative and sensitive motions with the plants and beasts, it excels them in that it alone is rational and able to comprehend the workings of nature and of God. Doget's description of the tripartite soul—which is not in Plato's *Phaedo*, on which he is commenting—is close in thinking and detail to the sermon of Nature.[73] Both works also drift slowly from a tripartite view of the soul to a more dualist one, in Medwall's case in order to build the punchy conflict or psychomachia needed for the plot.[74] There is no point which Medwall's interlude definitely borrows from Doget's commentary, but the interlude and the commentary offer similar ideas. Moreover, despite the different genres—an interpretation of a classical dialogue, a new dialogue of sorts—both works begin not with debate, but with exposition in Doget's prologue and in Medwall's opening speeches. But the works preach the importance of reason.

The unanimity becomes more striking if we consider further books read or owned by the men who passed through the same household as Medwall. They seem to be interested in the notions which interested him. For example, many

[72] *DNB*, Doget [Doket], John (<http://www.oxforddnb.com/view/article/7766>, accessed 30 August 2005); Weiss, *Humanism*, 164–7; Harper-Bill, 'Familia, Administration and Patronage', 239–40; *BRUO*, III.1685–7; *Humfrey 1970*, no. 6.

[73] BL, MS Additional 10344, ff.2r–3v, ff.74r–75r. James Hankins, *Plato in the Italian Renaissance*, Columbia Studies in the Classical Tradition, 17, 2 vols. (Leiden: Brill, 1990), II.497–9, prints the prologue.

[74] For Doget's slowly shifting theory, see BL, MS Additional 10344, f.43r–v, f.60r–v. Christopher Tilmouth, *Passion's Triumph over Reason: A History of the Moral Imagination from Spenser to Rochester* (Oxford: Oxford University Press, 2007), 16–18, 44–5, explains tripartition and psychomachia.

works, classical, humanist, or otherwise,[75] allegorize the upright posture of humankind as Medwall does, and these works were often of interest to the men of Morton's household. For example, the upright posture of humanity is noted in Peter Lombard's *Liber sententiarum* as a symbol of rationality. This work was owned by one of the chaplains to the household, Clement Browne.[76] The image is sketched in Lactantius' *Divinae institutae* too, and in one chapter with support from the quotation from Ovid. Medwall differs from Lactantius a little when he names Ovid's 'boke' outright—a humanist gesture—for Lactantius quotes his source without naming it; well he might, for he is supposed to be criticizing the pagans. Lactantius' work was owned by another of the chaplains to the household, Roger Bower. One of two surviving copies is Bower's; it is now unsure which. In neither is the quotation from Ovid noted, but in both somebody notes the following chapter where Lactantius refers to the upright posture to remind us why we must not stoop to beastly idolatry.[77] We cannot say whether Medwall knew this image from the Roman poem, from the works of theology or somewhere entirely different. But we can say that it was already available to the readers in his world, and that some readers were interested enough to annotate it.

Finally, even the wider ideas of human rationality which underpin Medwall's work were found in books owned by members of the household. In fact, Archbishop Morton, the head of the household, owned one such work. He owned a copy of the letters of Seneca, made in Italy in 1409, in which somebody annotates certain lines by putting bracketing down the margin and writing 'nota' there, sometimes with a maniculum. What is intriguing is that the majority of marks cluster in a group of letters on the nature of humanity as expounded in Medwall's interludes (letters 72–5, 91–5, 104–5). For example, in letter ninety-two the reader noted the observation that although humankind is not equal to the gods, through our reason we become like them, and that our upright posture—once again—is the sign of the likeness. Elsewhere the reader marked the lines which teach that we share the senses with the animals, but that each animal has distinct qualities and that ours is reason: 'Quid in

---

[75] C. A. Patrides, 'Renaissance Ideas on Man's Upright Form', *Journal of the History of Ideas*, 19 (1958), 256–8, lists them.

[76] BL, MS Royal 9.B.vi, f.115r–v (II.xvi.4.2), owned by Browne, on whom see *BRUO*, II.283–4, and Harper-Bill, '*Familia*, Administration and Patronage', 247–8.

[77] Peter D. Clarke, with R. Lovatt (eds.), *The University and College Libraries of Cambridge*, Corpus of British Medieval Library Catalogues, 10 (London: British Academy, 2002), 402 (UC45.20), 439 (UC49.187–200), 668–9: Bower donated to Pembroke College, Cambridge, Lactantius, *Divinae institutiones* (Venice: John of Cologne and John Mathem de Chernetsem, 1478). But two copies survive at Pembroke (classmark C.28 and classmark C.29); notes kept in the library specify that Bower donated C.28, but, given the late date of the notes, the correct copy might be C.29. For unannotated Ovid see II.i (sigs. d7r–d8r); for annotated Persius see II.ii (sig. d9r).

homine proprium / ratio'.[78] This is again the tripartite view of the soul, sharing natural motions with the plants, sensuality with the beasts, but unique in its rationality. Thus the anthropology in Medwall's *Nature* was common property in the books owned by the community of readers among whom he worked. He was expounding a theory of humanity with which his first listeners might already agree.

However, this muddle of notes of ownership or reading brings only possibilities or likelihoods; there is no conclusive evidence that Medwall read any of the works in question. Nor is there conclusive evidence of who left the notes in these books; or whether they did so before, during, or after Morton or his men owned the books; or whether those owners or readers knew this interlude. The history of reading often encounters problems in identifying whose pointing finger is doodled in the margin or specifying when he doodled it. Yet this problem is, in this case, yet one more sign of the ubiquity of the theories expounded in Medwall's interlude. Many different readers in this community found these theories in many different books on many different occasions. Indeed, the books begin to merge in themselves and in the readers' responses. For example, Doget's description of the place of man in the universe parallels book II, chapters xiv–xvi, of Peter Lombard's *Liber sententiarum*, both of which truly follow the description in Genesis. Doget's awed admiration of the sky parallels some lines in Lactantius' second chapter, marked in one copy perhaps owned by the chaplain Bower. In that copy of Lactantius, some humanist hand also notes a reference to Seneca. In Morton's copy of Seneca, somebody in a late fifteenth-century secretary hand transcribed the sayings of some other spurious philosophers.[79]

Moreover, these theories were of interest well beyond Morton's household at this time. For example, the philosophical sayings found in Morton's copy of Seneca were also copied twice by William Worcester, and in one copy he

---

[78] BodL, MS Laud lat. 70, f.96v (Seneca, *Ad Lucilium epistulae morales*, ed. and trans. Richard M. Gummere, 3 vols. (Cambridge, MA: Harvard University Press, 1917–25), XCII.27, XCII.30), f.61r (Seneca, *Ad Lucilium*, LXXIV.16), f.64r (Seneca, *Ad Lucilium*, LXXVI.8–10). The annotator also marked meditations on death: for example f.73v (Seneca, *Ad Lucilium*, LXXVI.2–3), f.94r (Seneca, *Ad Lucilium*, XCI.12–18). A second set of marks, consisting only of tiny black dots, cover the first few pages (ff.1r–29v). The scribe often misnumbers the letters. For Morton's ownership, see his rebus and arms (f.1r) which reappear in BL, MS Arundel 366, f.1r, Gigli's work dedicated to Morton, and on f.1r of his legal manuscripts BL, MS Arundel 435, BL, MS Arundel 454, and BL, MS Arundel 461. BL, MS Harley 5015, a legal manuscript, has just a note alleging his ownership.

[79] BL, MS Additional 10344, f.9r (Doget borrowing from Genesis 2: 2); Peter Lombard, *Sententiae in IV libris distinctae*, Spicilegium Bonaventurianum, IV–V (Rome: Collegium S. Bonaventurae ad Claras Aquas, 1971–81), II.xiv.4, II.xiv.9, II.xv.1–2; Lactantius, *Divinae institutiones* (Cambridge, Pembroke College, shelfmark C.28), sigs. b2v (I.ii.5), d9r (I.ii); BodL, MS Laud lat. 70, f.144v (Seneca with sayings of the philosophers).

appended some further sayings from Seneca's letters and his *De Beneficiis*; one reader of *Knyghthode and Bataile* owned a copy of Lactantius too, in which somebody wrote 'Nota de homine' by the theory about our upright posture; another reader even found comments on the gifts of nature in the dry rhetorical textbook by Traversagni.[80] The theories of human reasoning get well expressed by writers throughout the fifteenth century, including John Lydgate and Thomas Chaundler.[81] The blending of these theories not with rhetorical practice of reasoning but with religious thinking on free will is another important trend around 1500, i.e. in the works of Colet and other neo-Platonists.[82] The most complex expression beyond Medwall's comes in one other work of dialogue, in the translation of book I of Petrarch's *Secretum*, which survives in a manuscript, copied after 1477 or perhaps after 1487, connected to Winchester School.[83] In Petrarch's *Secretum* St Augustine argued that what distinguishes humankind is 'wytt resonable | Dystincte in dyfference / fro brutes vnresonable'.[84] In these books there emerges an 'interpretive community' who spotted shared theories, images, and expectations in one text after another. Yet it is no wonder that, in some recent theories of reading, the 'interpretive community' seems like a closed circle.[85] In these books reading comes to seem less like a free and unpredictable practice (as Chapter 1 suggested it was), and more like a confirmation of certain received ideas.

Within the community of readers linked to Medwall or within the received ideas of the late fifteenth century, what room can there be for debate? It is no surprise, then, that Medwall decides to judge the debate in *Fulgens and Lucres*. Despite using the vigorous language of argument, Medwall never engages intellectually in debate. He reads Tiptoft's open-ended *The Declamacion of*

---

[80] Respectively, BodL, MS Laud lat. 70, f.144v (with eyeskip from the middle of the fourth saying to the middle of the fifth), BL, MS Cotton Julius F.vii, f.47r–v, and Worcestre [*sic*], *Itineraries*, 364–6 (Worcester's second copy); GUL, MS Hunter 274 (U.5.14), f.7r, signed by Edward Hatteclyff on f.A[v] and f.72r, on whom, see Chapter 2, *n*. 118 above; Lorenzo Traversagni, *Nova rhetorica* (St Albans: [anon.], 1480; *STC* 24190; JRL, classmark 9114), sig. c5r.

[81] Lydgate, *Fall*, VI.3375–409; Chaundler, *Liber apologeticus*, ed. Enright-Clark Shoukri, 57–9, 67–9.

[82] J. B. Trapp, *Erasmus, Colet and More: The Early Tudor Humanists and their Books* (London: British Library, 1991), especially 134–5, offers the best comparisons. For possible neo-Platonism in Morton and Medwall's milieu, see Clarke, with Lovatt (eds.), *University and College Libraries of Cambridge*, 405 (UC45.38), 437 (UC.47.174), 676, on which see Harper-Bill, 'Familia, Administration and Patronage', 247, and *BRUC*, 247, and M. E. Moeslein (ed.), *The Plays of Henry Medwall: A Critical Edition* (New York: Garland, 1981), 252–3, 272.

[83] Wilson and Fenlon (eds.), *Winchester*, 9–16, sketches the humanist connection, on which see also Lytle, ' "Wykehamist Culture" ', 135, 141–4, 147–50.

[84] Wilson and Fenlon (ed.), *Winchester*, f.17v.

[85] I am modifying some ideas from Stanley Fish, *Is There a Text in This Class? The Authority of Interpretive Communities* (Cambridge, MA: Harvard University Press, 1980), 329–32.

Noblesse and ends it, refusing to write, as Buonaccorso, Tiptoft, and Caxton did, a mere exercise in rhetoric. At the end, Lucres chooses her husband and she chooses, of course, Gayus. The choice is predictable, given the biased presentation of the two suitors. Moreover, Lucres insists, before she makes it, that her choice will be predictable by others:

> I shall go enquyre as faste as I may
>
> What the commune fame wyll theryn reporte [...]   (II.725–6)

Gayus too has just said that he will let 'the commune voyce of all the contrey' report his nobility (II.721). What steers her judgement is not personal whimsy but the esteem for the qualities exemplified in Gayus, according to the received ideas of the whole community. Gayus is a selfless servant of the community. Moreover, his life as a self-made man also proves the theory of self-determination so essential to Medwall and his contemporaries in the archbishop's household. As such, he must conclude his interlude in favour of Gayus. In fact, the debate is not so much concluded as never even begun, for the interlude opens with a statement of the outcome (as quoted above). The few real debates of these years, Chaundler's *Libellus de laudibus duarum civitatum* or Tiptoft's *The Declamacion of Noblesse*, seem to be mere exercises in rhetoric. But behind Medwall's interludes—or other works one could consider, such as the English version of Petrarch's *Secretum*—lie notions of human reason, and of the self-determination it brings, which were too ubiquitous to escape, perhaps, and certainly too important to debate.

7

Some Tudor readers and their freedom

The first years of the sixteenth century might seem like the beginning of humanism in England or in English literature. This is because the writers of those years often boast that their method of studying and imitating antiquity is new or often spend time prescribing it as if it were new. Of course, to read the classics was never wholly new; there were earlier readers in earlier 'renaissances', and Lydgate, Worcester, Caxton, and others often relied on the work of earlier compilers, translators and so on. But what was new with the humanists was this self-conscious sense of being new, so that they boasted that their programme of reading was a novelty or prescribed it as if it were. When Duke Humfrey's clients gave him books, they were stunned by his life of relentless newness, with which they hurried to keep pace: 'Oon nouelte vnnethe is hym to profre'. When the Duke of York was given a book about the consulate of Stilicho, the poet evoked a cultural revival in which the muses were 'newly ageyn in mynde', just as York hoped that his own fortunes would be renewed. Similarly, as David Carlson has uncovered, in the best study of humanism in the early Tudor period, the sixteenth-century humanists also announced their methods of studying antiquity to be new and improved in order to bolster their own careers or as a sort of correlative to the new Tudor monarchs whom they were sensibly keen to please.[1] From the fifteenth century to the sixteenth there were continuities in the self-consciousness with which the humanists describe their work.

There were the strongest continuities in two methods of reading the classics: in the use of English in educational reading and in the use of the classics for political and moral reading. The continuity in schoolbooks is easy to see: Anwykyll's *Vulgaria Terentii* was reprinted from 1483 to 1529—evidently a hit despite the flaws in it. It was followed by another more complex phrase book from Terence, by Nicholas Udall, equally popular over the next half century from 1534 on.[2] There were continuities too in the fuller classical

---

[1] Carlson, *English Humanist Books*, for example 55–6, 62–3.
[2] For Anwykyll, see *STC* 23904, 23905, 23906, 23907, 23907.3, 23907.7, 23908 and Chapter 5 above; for Udall, see *STC* 23899, 23900, 23900.5, 23901, 23901.3, 23901.7, 23902, 23903.

translations of moral and political works: for example, Walton's version of Boethius' *De Consolatione Philosophiae* and the version of Cicero's *De Amicitia* supposedly by Tiptoft were printed in 1525 and 1530 respectively.[3] More broadly, the influence of Cicero strengthened in the 1530s as ever more of his works were printed in English. English printers in fact suddenly printed hugely more classical translations after about 1530, and seem to have stopped printing the classics in Latin alone; they stopped competing with foreign printers, then, and pursued the vernacular tradition.[4] If there is a good point to interrupt this survey of English humanism, it is around 1530 when these vernacular forms of humanism, moulded on lines established in the fifteenth century, were secure.

Some of the continuities emerge in the sweet series of books printed by Thomas Berthelet in the 1530s and 1540s. He printed several works of advice translated from classical sources: Cebes, Cicero, Frontinus, Isocrates, Livy, Plutarch, and Xenophon on morality, education, friendship, military strategy, agriculture, etc. The direct use of Greek sources is newly pronounced in this series; Berthelet even printed the first English translation direct from the Greek.[5] Otherwise, though, somebody from the fifteenth century would not be surprised by the topics for which the ancients were consulted in this series nor by the terms used to justify consulting them. These were books of advice for the 'Actife lyfe' of winning 'effecte or profite' or serving the 'commune weale'. Berthelet sometimes prints these books with short prefaces or a table or side-notes—like some fifteenth-century translations in manuscript—highlighting their usefulness for 'the welthe of this realme' which renders them 'very profitable to be redde'. Thirteen of them, out of seventeen, were printed in an octavo or sextodecimo format, small enough to carry around on business: 'Lette hym in hand take this historie', the printer orders the reader of one book, and he might mean it literally. Somebody from the fifteenth century would not be surprised by the gothic typeface, or at the most foreign a 'rotunda', while the erudite might recognize the colophons in roman type, which announce that Berthelet's shop was 'nere to the Cundite at the sygne of Lucrece'. These colophons were a gently humanist sign, like the Greek signatures or snippets

---

[3] *STC* 3200, 5275.

[4] Traced in Daniel Wakelin, 'Possibilities for Reading: Classical Translations in Parallel Texts *c.*1520–1558', forthcoming in *Studies in Philology*, 105 (2008).

[5] Chapter 5 above notes that Caxton translated the prologue to Diodorus Siculus' Greek history from Poggio Bracciolini's Latin version, and that Skelton translated the whole thing thus, although Skelton's translation was seemingly not printed. Thomas Wyatt (trans.), *The quyete of mynde* (London: Pynson, 1528; *STC* 20058.5), is also translated not from Greek but from a Latin version. Works by Aristotle, Lucian, and Plutarch had been printed in Latin and continued to be so (*STC* 752, 16891, 16892, 16896, 20060).

of Latin in a humanist hand sometimes found in earlier English translations.[6] Here, then, were continuities in the humanist models of how to read from the fifteenth century to the sixteenth: one should read the classics for their useful advice on living in the commonweal.

The model of useful reading seems best expressed in two new works printed by Berthelet at this time in frequent small octavo editions. It seems best expressed in *An Exhortation to yonge men* by Thomas Lupset (*c.*1495–1530) and in book I of *The boke named the Gouernour* by Sir Thomas Elyot (*c.*1490–1546). Lupset wrote in 1529, and his work was printed posthumously; Elyot wrote just before his book was first printed in 1531.[7] (These two works are the subject of the latter part of this chapter.) These two works set out schemes of humanist reading imbued with the keen sense of the usefulness of it. In this respect Lupset and Elyot resemble earlier writers such as the poet of *Knyghthode and Bataile* or Caxton, and usefully set out the notions which the earlier writers only imply or sketch briefly. They directly propose how to educate young men and propose reading-lists of writers suitable for grammar, civil politics, or, for Lupset, steering one's soul. Yet what is there in such books of the unpredictability or freedom of humanist reading (a tendency noted in Chapter 1)? In offering such prescriptions, these books could limit the humanist reader. In the early sixteenth century, several writers do set out to fix humanist reading. The writers of statutes and textbooks in the early 1500s seek to fix humanist reading into the rules and routines of schools and universities. (These writers in the institutional tradition are the subject of the first part of this chapter.) But Lupset and Elyot codify humanist education and reading not within the schoolroom but within the wider commonweal. And they do not in fact codify it completely; for them, the process of deciding and codifying what to read is itself a vital exercise of the reader's reasoning—like reasoning imagined in Medwall's plays—and thus of his intellectual freedom.

---

[6] For the quotations, see Thomas Elyot (trans.), *The Education or bringinge vp of children* (London: Berthelet, 1532; *STC* 20057), sig. d2r; Gentian Hervet (trans.), *Xenophons treatise of householde* (London: Berthelet, 1532; STC 26069), sig. A1v; Anthony Cope (trans.), *Annibal and Scipio* (London: Thomas Berthelet, 1544; *STC* 5718), sig. a1v; Elyot (trans.), *Education*, sig. f4v. For Berthelet's others, see *STC* 4890.5, 4891, 5276, 5719, 11402, 14278, 14279, 16612a.7, 16894, 20052, 20056.7, 26071, 26072, 26073.

[7] Quotations come, with page:line references, from the diplomatic edition in *The Life and Works of Thomas Lupset*, ed. John Archer Gee (New Haven, CT: Yale University Press, 1928), 235–62, and with parenthetical chapter numbers and leaf signatures, from Sir Thomas Elyot, *The boke named the Gouernour* (London: Berthelet, 1531; *STC* 7635). No modern edition of Elyot's work is textually ideal or widely available, but I also give for convenience page:line references to *A Critical Edition of Sir Thomas Elyot's* The Boke named the Governour, ed. Donald W. Rude (New York: Garland, 1992).

PRESCRIBING HUMANISM IN THE 1510s

People propose, codify, and prescribe humanist reading in England in schools and universities because there, in the 1510s and 1520s, the methods of humanist reading were becoming institutionally endorsed and remunerated. (Chapter 5 traced an earlier phase of this institutionalization.) Some humanists insist at this time that their project is still new and is therefore vulnerable to perilous foes, yet their defences of it seem to be less defensive than offensive moves. Throughout the universities of northern Europe at this time, people rehearsed the debate between scholastics and humanists and they rehearsed it more urgently than in the past because there were now curricula, jobs, money, and influence for the humanists to seize.[8] Ironically, the noise from humanists defending their corner might be why their voices sound, to us, more prominent in the sixteenth century than the fifteenth. Humanism is not still insecure but is securing further power.

This seems the undertone of the most famous defence of humanism written in England: it is the open letter written in 1518 from Thomas More to the University to Oxford in defence of humanist studies there. In this letter, More worries that people in Oxford have begun to oppose the 'Greeks'—the advocates of Greek and other humanist studies—and to call themselves Trojans by contrast, one of them even preaching against the humanities in the university church.[9] Humanism sounds under threat. The threat might have been true: Oxford had been slow in revising its statutes to prescribe the humanities. Yet beyond the official prescriptions, there were signs of humanist reading and teaching occurring, and in the 1510s there were some institutional shifts too: Bishop Richard Fox founded Corpus Christi College, which held some distinctive lectureships in *humanitas* and Greek, and Cardinal Thomas Wolsey founded daily lectures in 'good literature' ('bonarum litterarum').[10] It is this endorsement of humanism by powerful men which is the context for the attacks on it, if they really occurred, and for More's defence.[11] More's letter is itself pressure from a man who had been newly appointed to the King's

[8] Erika Rummel, *The Humanist-Scholastic Debate in the Renaissance & Reformation*, Harvard Historical Studies, 120 (Cambridge, MA: Harvard University Press, 1995), 2–4, 83–95.

[9] Thomas More, *In Defense of Humanism*, ed. Daniel Kinney, Complete Works of St. Thomas More, 15 (New Haven, CT: Yale University Press, 1986), 132–3.

[10] J. M. Fletcher, 'The Faculty of Arts', in *The History of the University of Oxford, III: The Collegiate University*, ed. James McConica (Oxford: Clarendon Press, 1986), 157–99 (159, 172–5, 179–80); G. D. Duncan, 'Public Lectures and Professorial Chairs', in *ibid.*, 35–61 (336–8)

[11] In fact the chancellor of the university warned the scholars not to relinquish too much authority to Wolsey in letting him revise their statutes: W. T. Mitchell (ed.), *Epistolae Academicae 1508–1596*, Oxford Historical Society, 26 (Oxford: Clarendon Press, 1980), 77.

Council. His letter is signed from the nearby town of Abingdon where, early in 1518, the king was staying with More in tow; members of the university had attended the king there. Thus More's letter carries the prestige not only of his learning, but also of his power beside the throne. At the end of the letter, More reminds the university that many men have contributed money to support 'all kinds of literary study' ('omnigenam literaturam'); these other donations, presumably those of Wolsey and Fox, will inspire others to do the same by example ('exempla').[12] This is how people claimed that Duke Humfrey would inspire or guide others. The poor members of the university might have wished to resist the pressure from government on their curriculum but—as universities often are—they were urged to trim to fit the fads of politicians. Humanism is not under threat, but in triumph.

With hindsight, even if we might dislike this interference in education, is not More's goal of broadening the curriculum a good thing? He stresses that it is the opponents of humanism who wish to keep the curriculum narrow, by excluding the new subjects. We might support his defence then, whether we prefer the classical humanities or would prefer to broaden the curriculum in different ways today. However, More in fact speaks really of limiting the curriculum. Although he seeks to add Greek and secular Latin literature to the curriculum, he in effect seeks to add only some of the writing in these languages. Indeed he is most interested in Greek:

[…] etenim cui non perspicuum est, cum in caeteris artibus omnibus, tum in ipsa quoque theologia, qui vel optima quaeque inuenere, vel inuenta tradiderunt accuratissime fuisse Graecos? Nam in philosophia, exceptis duntaxat his, quae Cicero reliquit et Seneca, nihil habent latinorum scholae, nisi vel graecum, uel quod e graeca lingua traductum est.

For can anyone fail to perceive that not only in all other arts, but in theology as well, the most original thinkers and the most diligent interpreters of their thoughts were Greek? For in philosophy, apart from the works left by Cicero and Seneca, the schools of the Latins have nothing to offer that is not either Greek or translated from Greek.

After all, he adds, even the New Testament and the earliest patristic books are in Greek, and so Jerome, Augustine, and Bede all learned it:

Nec didicere solum, sed posteris consuluerunt etiam, his in primis qui vellent esse theologi, idem ipsi ut facerent.

[…] nor did they merely learn it, they also advised later scholars, especially those who were going to become theologians, to do the same thing.[13]

---

[12] More, *In Defense of Humanism*, pp. xxviii–xxxi, 144–5. The editor warns that the controversy was reported by Erasmus in April 1519, and so might possibly date from March 1519, a year later.

[13] More, *In Defense of Humanism*, 142–3; published translation.

These limited preferences are shared by Hythloday in More's *Utopia*: he finds nothing valuable in Latin beyond the work of Cicero and Seneca. Yet Hythloday is an extreme figure, difficult to take seriously; he seems a parody of extreme idealism in scholarship.[14] His attempt to introduce Greek in the new world is undermined by the fewness of books he can take there and by a marmoset which eats some pages from one of them.[15] More's letter to Oxford, though, seems more sincerely meant, given the genre of the letter, with its fiction of personality, given the insistent tone (in words such as *all* or *the very same* or *nothing*), or given the imposing examples. More seems alert to the narrowness of the humanist studies in *Utopia*, but in the letter to Oxford he is himself persuasively narrow. He seeks not to defend humanism but to define it and limit it.

It is this effort to limit and define which is more typical of English writing about humanism and education in the early sixteenth century. James Simpson suggests that the humanists, like people in other 'pedagogical movements' and 'revolutionary periods', rejected some books as 'cultural waste' in order to make their studies manageable and to sidestep some nerves about the fruitfulness of their own studies.[16] The rejection of some books in favour of others is especially frequent and vehement in textbooks, statutes for schools, or advice to teachers. In these works one must define with precision which studies are worthwhile, and which are not, because the definitions will determine how time and money will be spent. This occurs in the statutes of John Colet for his new school at St Paul's in London in the 1510s. From his school, Colet expelled:

all barbary all corrupcion all laten adulterate which ignorant blynde folis brought into this worlde and with the same hath distayned and poysenyd the olde laten spech and the varay Romayne tong which in the tyme of Tully and Salust and Virgill and Terence was vsid, whiche also seint Jerome and seint ambrose and seint Austen and many hooly doctors lernyd in theyr tymes. I say that ffylthynesse and all such abusyon which the later blynde worlde brought in which more ratheyr may be callid blotterature thenne litterature I vtterly abbanysh and Exclude oute of this scole […][17]

Colet's energetic prose distils the zeal with which some humanists prescribe reading and study in early Tudor England; it distils as well three assumptions

[14] Alistair Fox and John Guy, *Reassessing the Henrician Age: Humanism, Politics and Reform 1500–1550* (Oxford: Blackwell, 1986), 38–9, interprets Hythloday thus.
[15] Thomas More, *Utopia*, ed. Edward J. Surtz, S. J., and J. H. Hexter, Complete Works of St. Thomas More, 4 (New Haven, CT: Yale University Press, 1965), 50–1, 302, 180–1.
[16] James Simpson, 'Bonjour Paresse: Literary Waste and Recycling in Book 4 of Gower's *Confessio Amantis*', forthcoming in *Proceedings of the British Academy*.
[17] John Colet, 'Appendix A: Statutes of St. Paul's School', printed in J. H. Lupton, *A Life of John Colet, D.D.* (1887; repr. London: Bell and Sons, 1909), 271–84 (279–80).

found in such writing. Firstly, Colet tells the humanist story of 'olde' eloquence destroyed by 'later' idiocy but being newly recovered: more stress on novelty. This story of how 'humanist studies once nearly perished' and now revive recurs in humanist textbooks for the English market ('studijs humanitatis/quæ olim ferme perierant') as it did in prefaces from del Monte onwords.[18]

Besides this well-worn chronology, Colet secondly distils the essential humanist stress on style. Colet here and throughout the statutes, even in passing, insists on the study of 'good litterature' or 'clene and chast laten', and the words echo the humanist clichés of *bonae litterae* and *castigata* eloquence.[19] His criteria for good literature seem pinchingly stylistic, for with his word *blotterature* he redefines *literature* not in the old sense of *all learning* but in something like the current sense of *good writing*; he uses too the word *barbary* which was then developing a stylistic sense.[20] Colet does recommend the church fathers for study, for he prefers them;[21] under the influence of Erasmus the humanist curriculum widens a little to include them. Yet here Colet writes of limiting his boys in their reading on stylistic grounds, as do other humanist educators of the early sixteenth century. For example, Colet himself composed a textbook for his boys and in verses in it the first master of his school, William Lily, urges the boys to 'flee barbarian words' ('barbara verba fuge') or to shun clumsy grammarians or 'grammaticastros'—a bomphiologous coinage which parodies the style of the men whom it mocks.[22] Lily wrote similar clichés in verses in the *Vulgaria* or phrase book of William Horman, the master of Eton: the boys had expelled barbarity and now had to revive 'golden speech' ('Pulsa barbarie'; 'aurea dicta'). At the back of this book there is a list of words to be shunned, and it tidily divides good Latin from the terms of scholastic philosophy: on the list to shun are *determinatio* which is used 'for scholastic debate' ('pro scholastico agone') and the terms for the scholars known as the *canonista, Scotista,* and *Thomista.* Notably, the word *humanista* is not proscribed even though it was much newer.[23] From Duke Humfrey's

[18] For this example, see William Horman, *Vulgaria* (London: Pynson, 1519; *STC* 13811), sig. +2r–v, and also sig. +1v. Compare *nn.* 86–7 in Chapter 2 above.

[19] Colet, 'Appendix A: Statutes', 271, 272, 279.

[20] Sylvia Adamson, 'Literary Language', in *The Cambridge History of the English Language: Volume III. 1476–1776*, ed. Roger Lass (Cambridge: Cambridge University Press, 1999), 539–653 (543); *OED, literature, n.*, 1, 3a; *OED, Barbary, n.*, I.3, is first recorded to mean *linguistic style* by Hawes in 1509; *blotterature* may echo *blot, v.*, 2, 'To cover (paper) with worthless writing', used by Fabyan in 1494.

[21] See Fox and Guy, *Reassessing the Henrician Age*, 21–2, 25–6, on this difference.

[22] William Lily, 'Carmen […] ad discipulos de moribus', frequently reprinted, cited here from [John Colet and others], *Rudimenta grammatices et docendi methodus* (Southwark: Treveris, 1529; *STC* 5542.3), sig. I2v, discussed by Carlson, *English Humanist Books*, 126, 232, *n.* 5.

[23] Horman, *Vulgaria*, sigs. +1v, dd2v, dd4r–ee1r, ee2v–ee3r. On *humanista*, see *n.* 14 in Chapter 1 above.

'hih lettrure' to Colet's 'good' literature, the humanists define their interests by style: the superficiality which sees them now condemned.

Yet this process of defining good books forces them to dismiss other books in a negative sweeping movement. When Colet refers to 'good litterature' or 'chast laten', he uses adjectives which imply that other things are not good. Indeed, he dismisses other studies with vicious words evoking filth, detritus, or poison to be expelled. Humanist civilization is reliant upon the definition of barbarism. This is the third element which the lines from Colet's statutes distil. It underpins Horman's list of words not to use, and the mockery of theologians which that expresses. It is evident too in the statutes of one other foundation of the 1510s, Corpus Christi College, Oxford. Here the founder, Bishop Richard Fox, tells the lecturer in the 'artium humanitatis' which books to lecture on—all from antiquity and most of them in Fox's own donations to the library, helpfully. But he also tells him to 'root out and expel [...] barbarism, whenever it sprouts up', using terms as stylistic and as vicious as Colet's ('barbariem [...] si quando pullulet extirpet et ejiciat').[24] One vivid scene of rooting-out unfolds in a letter about one of Colet's former pupils and a future lecturer at Fox's college, one Thomas Lupset (c.1495–1530), when he was a student:

Lupsetus estimat se nostra renatum opera planeque ab inferis emersisse. Magistri moliuntur omnia quo retrahant adolescentem in suum pistrinum. Nam statim eodem die sophisticis libris distractis Graecos emerat.[25]

Lupset esteems himself born anew by our work and almost arisen from the underworld. The masters contrive everything so that they can draw the youngster back to their treadmill. For steadfastly the very first day he sold off his books of sophistry and bought Greek ones.

This is a letter to Thomas More from Erasmus. This year, 1513, Erasmus was editing the New Testament and St Jerome in Cambridge, with the help of students whom he tutored in recompense. Young Lupset found the official course in Cambridge old-fashioned and uncongenial, and found himself more inspired by Erasmus's tuition in Greek; therefore he sold off his books of the sophists or scholastic logic-choppers in order to buy the Greek classics. The scene is comic, as the tutor smiles on the enthusiasm of the pupil, but really it visualizes the opinions of Erasmus and his friends. They often dismiss scholastic books as nearly worthless: while they were 'reborn' ('renatum') in

[24] *Statutes of the Colleges of Oxford*, 3 vols. (Oxford: Parker, 1853): the statutes for Corpus Christi College are separately paginated in vol. II: see 48. On the foundation and books, see James McConica, 'The Rise of the Undergraduate College', in *The History of the University of Oxford: Volume III. The Collegiate University*, ed. James McConica (Oxford: Clarendon Press, 1986), 1–68 (18–22), and J. R. Liddell, 'The Library of Corpus Christi College, Oxford, in the Sixteenth Century', *The Library*, 4th series, 18 (1937–8), 385–416 (388–9).
[25] Cited and translated differently in Gee (ed.), *Life and Works of Thomas Lupset*, 45–6.

the study of Greek, they would let scholastic knowledge die. Lupset throws out scholasticism with fevered violence: the books being 'distractis' evokes both selling them off willy-nilly and ripping them to shreds. The humanist is rejecting the past and starting his reading list anew.

However, the prescriptions for educating people in statutes or textbooks will be, by genre, prescriptive: their job is to limit and define—a necessity for the busy tutor or schoolmaster—and their length and structure allow little else. Moreover, we seldom know whether either statutes or textbooks were followed to the letter; the evidence suggests often not. Even Colet's statutes were perhaps not written to prescribe the books which were read in his school, but merely to evoke the pious atmosphere of it.[26] There were other writers in the early sixteenth century who took time to define humanist reading more fully. There were several continental works, including some by Erasmus composed for St Paul's School, as well as *De Fructu* by the English scholar Richard Pace. And two men codified how to read at length in English: Thomas Lupset, once ardent in selling off his old books, and Sir Thomas Elyot, in *An Exhortation to yonge men* and *The boke named the Gouernour* respectively.

LUPSET AND ELYOT ON READING AND JUDGEMENT

Of the two, Elyot does sometimes sound like the superficial judge of style, when he recommends or rejects certain books. For example, he rejects the current Latin versions of Aristotle's *Ethics* as 'a rude and grosse shadowe of the eloquence and wisedome' of the Greek, and slights the 'barbarouse' style of legal or medical books. However, neither Elyot nor Lupset is concerned foremost with judging books by their style. Even in these few words, Elyot mentions the barbarism of legal books but promises that, nevertheless, the best students do not slight the 'lernynges' in them. He praises the study of the classics not for their style but for their usefulness to other activities (I.xi, F1r, 53:29–31; I.xiv, G7v–G8v, 68:8–69:2). This is true even when Elyot sounds most exclusive in his fetish for antiquity:

no noble autour specially of them that wrate in greke or latine before. xii.C. yeres passed / is nat for any cause to be omitted. For therin I am of Quintilianes opinion / that

---

[26] J. B. Trapp, *Erasmus, Colet and More: The Early Tudor Humanists and their Books* (London: British Library, 1991), 116–18. In fact, St Paul's School probably followed, and indeed influenced, the largely classical curriculum common to most Tudor grammar schools: T. W. Baldwin, *William Shakspere's Small Latine & Lesse Greeke*, 2 vols. (Urbana, IL: University of Illinois Press, 1944), I.126–30.

there is fewe or none auncient warke / that yeldethe nat some frute or commoditie to the diligent reders.[27]

The interest in classical literature does not require other books to be omitted, as Colet or Fox omit them; classical literature is 'specially' important but, the word implies, not exclusively so. Most importantly, Elyot's first concern is not style but utility. This concern with utility reflects (as was noted above) the longer tradition of humanism in English. It also reflects the particular occasions of Lupset's, and Elyot's books. Lupset wrote to advise an alderman's son, whose tutor he had been, how best to pursue his studies and why. He struggles to sell reading as an investment, both on earth and in heaven, to the worldly Londoners.[28] Elyot dedicated his book to the king, but he set out in it how to educate the men who would counsel and govern for the king, and he had it printed for this wider public.[29] Fittingly, then, both writers imagine the reading of men destined to live the active life as merchants, citizens, courtly counsellors, and kings, like their predecessors in *Knyghthode and Bataile* or Caxton's edition of Cicero. So, like Worcester in *The Boke of Noblesse*, Elyot weaves into *The boke named the Gouernour* a sort of anthology of classical stories, for:

the recreation of all the reders / that be of any noble or gentill courage / gyuynge them occasion to eschewe idelnes / beynge occupied in redynge this warke / infarced throughly with suche histories and sentences / wherby they shal take / they them selfes confessing no lytell commodite / if they will more than ones or twyse rede it. The first reding being to them newe / the seconde delicious / and euery tyme after / more and more frutefull and excellent profitable.   (I.iii, B7v)[30]

The metaphors used betray the practical focus: Elyot stresses that his book is useful with the terms of merchandise and farming (*commodity, infarced, fruit, fruitful, profit, profitable*) and these terms recur throughout his book and throughout Lupset's, too; metaphors from farming and gardening were, in fact, ubiquitous in educational writing at this time.[31] It is this dull profit which characterizes the reading of the classics from Lydgate and Caxton to Berthelet and Elyot.[32]

---

[27] Elyot, *Gouernour*, I.xiii, G4v, 65:18–21; John M. Major, *Sir Thomas Elyot and Renaissance Humanism* (Lincoln, NE: University of Nebraska Press, 1964), 163, discusses the source.
[28] Gee (ed.), *Life and Works of Lupset*, 124–6, 134–6.
[29] Major, *Elyot*, 21, and Greg Walker, *Writing Under Tyranny: English Literature and the Henrician Reformation* (Oxford: Oxford University Press, 2005), 142–3, 167–8, 179.
[30] Elyot cut this passage from later editions and so Rude's edition gives it in an appendix (271–2).
[31] Lupset, *Exhortation*, 236:12, 237:19, 237:20, 237:23, 237:27, 237:32, 238:4, 239:12, 256:30, 262:1; Elyot, *Gouernour*, I.x, D6v, 43:19; I.x, E3r, 47:28; I.xiii, G2v, 63:1; I.xiii, G5r, 65:30; and so on; and in general Rebecca W. Bushnell, *A Culture of Teaching: Early Modern Humanism in Theory and Practice* (Ithaca, NY: Cornell University Press, 1996), 119–20, 135–6.
[32] Fox and Guy, *Reassessing the Henrician Age*, 43–4.

The economic model of profit steers the humanists to a brisk efficiency in their studies. Brevity and selectivity were common to much humanist reading throughout the fifteenth and sixteenth centuries. Works from *The Fall of Princes* to Elyot's works offer selected, digested, and abbreviated ancient history; schools from Anwykyll's to Udall's used only a few or excerpted texts; even the choice of works translated from the 1430s to the 1530s is profitable for farming, warfare, public service, or at least grammar. Elyot and Lupset confess this economizing in their own lists of what to read. Elyot recommends slow and 'frequent' reading of his listed books, but he concedes that to read them 'throughly' in seven years would be impossible; the pupil should read only excerpts from them, chosen to suit him: only 'so muche instruction' in each as is needed to find 'some profite' (I.x, D8v–E3r, 45:2–47:31). Lupset often recommends works which are short or offer what he calls *picked* or selected merits. For him, profit comes not by reading widely and shallowly, but narrowly and deeply:

I wold you medled not greatly with any other bokes, then with these, that I shal name vnto you: It is not the reding of many bokes, that getteth increace of knowledge and iudgement: for the most parte of them, that redeth al indifferently, confound their wittes and memorie without any notable fruit of their redyng. It muste be a diligent reder, that shal take the profyte of his labour and diligence. No man (specially of them that haue other occupations) can vse redinge but in verye fewe workes, the whiche I wolde shuld be piked out of the best sorte, that the fruit of the reders diligence may be the greater. I se many lose theyr tyme, when they thinke to bestowe theyr time beste, because they lacke iudgemente or knowelege to pyke oute the bokes, the whiche be worthye to be studied.[33]

The passage sets out the equation for the economics of using little time and deep concentration for high profit. There is nothing original about this belief that reading should be 'intensive' rather than 'extensive'; this belief persisted from the slow monastic reader to the short shelf of classics in the puritan household, even in the face of the more readily available books in the first years of printing.[34] It is a practical belief about how much it will or will not be possible for a pupil to read and about what will be profitable in adulthood. Rejecting some books as waste ('I wold you medled not greatly with any other bokes') is pragmatic.

However, selectiveness not only helps to make reading profitable in terms of time; selectiveness helps to make it safe, because the reading recommended

[33] Lupset, *An Exhortation*, 237:14–28; see also 237:22, 237:22, 237:26, 245:10–31, 245:19–22, 245:26, 250:22, 262:19, 262:21, and 237:4, 242:31, 257:31–3.

[34] Robert Darnton, 'History of Reading', in *New Perspectives on Historical Writing*, ed. Peter Burke (Cambridge: Polity, 1991), 140–67 (148), and Heidi Brayman Hackel, *Reading Material in Early Modern England: Print, Gender, Literacy* (Cambridge: Cambridge University Press, 2005), 76, trace 'extensive' and 'intensive' reading.

is often of pagan literature. The concern with pagan literature emerged in the little cuts and emendations in many fifteenth-century translations, or in the defensive comments in Bokenham's *De Consulatu Stilichonis* or Traversagni's *Nova rhetorica*. The concern is common to other humanist works on education, such as Erasmus's, upon which Lupset and Elyot drew. Erasmus voices considerable nervousness about pagan literature and the student's skill in interpreting it safely; he takes time to suggest not only what to read but how to interpret it; for example, he allegorizes Virgil's homosexual second eclogue.[35] Lupset and Elyot too consider how to avoid the seductions of antiquity. For example, Elyot thinks that one should preferably read only some 'elect' parts of Lucian (I.x, D7r–v, 43:33–44:6). He then picks and translates over three pages of excerpts from Roman poetry and drama stiff with virtue (I.xiii, G2r–G3v, 62:7–64:11). But for Lupset and Elyot the solution is not normally to offer interpretations in advance but to nurture the exercise of judgement in reading. This interest in judgement might have an Erasmian source: in *De Ratione studii* Erasmus does stress the process of picking the most fruitful elements from the classics and says that in reading 'judgement' is essential.[36] However, in proportion to his volumes of advice, he discusses judgement quite fleetingly; Lupset and Elyot discuss it more keenly, not only as a defensive mode of censorship but as a positive process. From his excerpts of moral verse, Elyot concludes that 'good and wise mater may be picked out of these poetes'. It is the process of picking which is essential, and he describes it with one extended metaphor of the garden. This garden is not now the wholesome orchard of fruit to be harvested; it is like Eden. The wise man enters the garden but does not succumb to the 'redolent sauours of swete herbes and floures'; instead he 'treadeth the nettiles vnder his feete whiles he gadreth good herbes' (I.xiii, G3v–G4r, 64:15–29). Once one's mind is mature, 'none auncient poete wolde be excluded', for then one can select the good and reject the ill. While Erasmus glosses the classical text for his pupil, Elyot hopes that the reader or pupil himself will pick the herbs and trample the nettles.[37]

---

[35] Erasmus, *De Ratione studii ac legendi interpretandique auctores*, trans. Brian McGregor, in *Literary and Educational Writings 2*, ed. Craig R. Thompson, Collected Works of Erasmus, 24 (Toronto: University of Toronto Press, 1978), 661–91 (682:23–683:21, 683:25–687:7); Erasmus, *De Pueris statim ac liberaliter instituendis declamatio*, trans. Beert C. Verstraete, in *Literary and Educational Writings 4*, ed. J. K. Sowards, Collected Works of Erasmus, 26 (Toronto: University of Toronto Press, 1985), 291–346 (337–8). Major, *Elyot*, 82, traces Elyot's differences from Erasmus.

[36] Erasmus, *De Ratione studii*, 687:25–8, 669:16–20, 670:11–671:22.

[37] Elyot, *Gouernour*, I.xiii, G4r–v, 65:2–23, which may develop an implication from Erasmus, *Antibarbariorum liber*, trans. Margaret Mann Phillips, in *Literary and Educational Writings 1*, ed. Craig R. Thompson, Collected Works of Erasmus, 23 (University of Toronto Press, 1978), 1–122 (16:8–9).

Lupset spells out more fully how the skills of selecting or judging are not incidental, not just a way of avoiding danger, but are among the profits got from reading. You will need 'iudgemente or knowelege to pyke oute the bokes' which will be profitable, but through this picking you will in turn acquire 'knowledge and iudgement' or will 'ryse in iudgemente':

in redynge of these olde substanciall workes, the whiche I haue named vnto you, shal beside the perfection of knowledge, gender a certayne iudgement in you, that you shal neuer take delite nor pleasure in the trifles and vayne inventions that men nowe a daies write, to the inquietinge of all good order: by reason that the most part of men that rede these new flittering workes, lacke perfect iudgement to dyscryue a weyghtye sentence frome a lyghte clause, the whiche iudgement can not be gotten but by a longe exercysynge of our wittes with the best sort of writers.[38]

This process is not economical, but slow, but it shares with brisk selective-ness the development of critical judgement. Lupset stresses the exercise of judgement in wording which is ascetic and pietistic: we must judge what is weighty over what is 'vayne', a word which evokes some contempt of the world. Throughout *An Exhortation*, Lupset aims to instil some unworldly piety in his boy, and judging the mundane world 'vayne' is part of this: 'Let not any similitude deceyue your iudgement', he says (247:32). His judgement involves not only reading well but doing so as part of living well spiritually. Here then his ideal of judgement seems to reflect not Erasmus's textbooks for St Paul's School, but his ideals of self-directed spirituality, grounded in one's reading. These ideals come from his spiritual writings, his *Enchiridion* or *Paraclesis*, or even his new edition of the New Testament, the cover of which urged, 'Therefore whoever loves true theology, read, examine, and then judge' ('Quisquis igitur amas ueram Theologiam, lego, cognosco, ac deinde iudica'). This book was known to Lupset, who had publicly defended it.[39] Moreover, by reflecting the Erasmian ideal of piety, the ideal of reading instilled by Lupset and Elyot reflects too—by some loose or even subconscious analogy; nothing more precise—the doctrine of free will, which Erasmus was defending against Luther in the 1520s. In Erasmus's thinking, human beings can influence their salvation to some degree, although God in his grace does still influence them and does have foreknowledge of their free will. Elyot seems to have shared this view: he briefly mentions 'libertie of wille' and the importance of knowing oneself in *The boke named the Gouernour*; some years later in *A Preservative*

---

[38] Lupset, *Exhortation*, 262:4–16; see also 237:14–28, 245:12–13. Lupset's use of *judgement* to mean 'the faculty of judging' is an early use in this sense. *OED, judgement, n.*, 8.a, cites *judgement* first in this sense from 1535, although, *MED, jugement* (n.), 5.b, has some fifteenth-century quotations in this sense.

[39] Reproduced in Trapp, *Erasmus, Colet and More*, 70–1, fig. 24; on Lupset's involvement, see Gee (ed.), *Life and Works of Lupset*, 74–84.

Agaynste deth he defends more fully the ability of humanity to save himself by 'his owne counsaile, whiche is his free will'.[40] It is this sense of spiritual self-determination which is felt in Lupset's *Exhortation*, too. For example, when he discusses the virtues, he says less about what they are than about how to judge what they are; he says, 'No man shal counsel you better, then you shall doo your owne selfe, if in reding you wil examin secretly your conscience' (256:4–7). Godly reading and the wise judgement of this reading are essential for the exercise of free will and lay piety sketched in Erasmus's *Enchiridion*.

However, although we should judge our books with our free will, we must not judge with entire independence. Even when Elyot, in *A Preservative Agaynste deth*, tells us to shore up our sense of free will by reading scripture, he would have us guided not by prejudice or presumption, but by old teachers and 'the bokes of the moste aunciente and catholike doctours' of the Church.[41] And Lupset too recommends judgement not in a vacuum, but 'with the best sort of writers' in order to comprehend what is good for our souls (as quoted above). He tells his pupil to read the New Testament with the 'expositions' of the learned doctors and to 'conforme' his interpretation to the true doctrine. He should read Aristotle 'eyther vnder some expert philosopher, orels with comment of Futtiratus', and Epictetus 'To confirme you the faster in these ryghte opinions' with the help of 'a coment or a good mayster' such as a commentary which Lupset hopes to translate soon (244:16–17, 244:35–245:4, 261:34–262:6). The process of reading is not here informing oneself or *forming oneself from within* by one's own judgement, but conforming or confirming, etymologically *forming with someone else's help*.[42] In this respect, Lupset and Elyot seem more restrictive than Erasmus on free will: he suggested that the doctrines of free will and grace were so knotty that it was better not to interpret scripture with firmness, but to concede 'free choice over free choice'.[43] Lupset and Elyot more honestly express the wish to steer the freedom of the reader. This is because the reader whom they imagine is reading within the household, or in the city or the court. When education needs to be profitable or relevant in the world, there is little time for freedom of judgement.

[40] Elyot, *Gouernour*, III.iii, Y5v, 182:30–1; Sir Thomas Elyot, *A Preservative Agaynste deth* (London: Thomas Berthelet, 1545; *STC* 7674), sig. D3r; Major, *Elyot*, 86, 218–19; Pearl Hogrefe, *The Life and Times of Sir Thomas Elyot Englishman* (Ames: Iowa State University Press, 1967), 329–36. Brian Cummings, *The Literary Culture of the Reformation: Grammar and Grace* (Oxford: Oxford University Press, 2002), 156–9, 167–9, traces the Erasmian ideas, and warns that we must not conflate Christian free will with freedom in general (167).

[41] Elyot, *Preservative*, sigs. D3r–D4v.

[42] *OED*, *conform*, v., and *confirm*, v., gives etymologies for these words, then sometimes interchangeable.

[43] Cummings, *Grammar and Grace*, 150, 154. Cummings traces Erasmus's inconsistency in these claims, which he was making in part as an argumentative strategy.

There is some inconsistency, then, in how Lupset and Elyot treat the freedom of the reader. They insist upon it but they police it, too. On a philosophical level, there is inconsistency in their opinions on the influence of nature and nurture in education. The classical writers, whom Elyot follows, have mixed opinions of nature and nurture. Erasmus too suggests that children tend by nature to virtue but are also 'vulnerable to cultural decay', as one critic puts it.[44] Elyot continues this inconsistency throughout his child psychology. For example, he recommends that the wet-nurse be of good character, not because the child will follow her unthinkingly, but because even in infancy he will 'decerne good from iuell' just as he will 'decerne milke from butter / and breadde from pappe', gesturing his judgements with his hands.[45] There is some inconsistency here, then, in Elyot's philosophy of human judgement.

ELYOT'S UNPREDICTABLE READERS

Besides these philosophical inconsistencies, two more inconsistencies muddle the methods by which Lupset and Elyot argue. Like Worcester, Caxton, or even the poet praising Duke Humfrey's judgement, Lupset and Elyot esteem the independence of the humanist reader, and they seek therefore to theorize and encourage it. The first inconsistency in method is that if one encourages independence, one immediately impinges upon it and crushes it; one cannot insist upon a person's freedom to resist insistence. (This muddle persists in Medwall's plays in Chapter 6 above.) Lupset and Elyot seem alert to the need not to preach too much, for in order to encourage judgement, they avoid spelling out the lessons or judgements which might be reached. However, the refusal to spell out the lessons they'd like learned renders their books somehow useless. (Worcester realized this problem, and had to spell out the lessons of his histories in *The Boke of Noblesse*, as noted in Chapter 4 above.) Humanist educational theorists offered too little concrete advice on the utility and practical effects of the studies which they prescribed, and so the theories were never successfully put into practice.[46] Elyot does suggest the beliefs which a humanist might hold in books II and III, but neither he nor Lupset ever really

---

[44] Bushnell, *Culture of Teaching*, 101–2; Major, *Elyot*, 252–3; for example Elyot (trans.), *Education*, sig. a4v.

[45] Elyot, *Gouernour*, I.iiii, B8v–C1v, 30:10–31:2. In this conception of infant moral choice, he is more complex than his sources; compare for example Elyot (trans.), *Education*, sigs. b2v–b3r. For Elyot's interweaving of nature and nurture, see Elyot, *Gouernour*, I.v, C3v–C4r, 33:8–11; I.ix, D5v, 42:16–18.

[46] This is an essential criticism in Grafton and Jardine, *Humanism*, 27–8, 136–45.

describes how his reading scheme will lead one there; he does not impinge upon the freedom of the reader.

Moreover, the freedom of the reader bedevils the process of setting out a scheme of reading. The problem for Lupset and Elyot is that their theories of the free judgement of the reader must be expressed in words which will themselves be read—freely. Therefore they insist upon their theories in a style which is far from insistent. Elyot, especially, uses prose modest in tone and perspicuous in method, guiding our reason, seldom pressing our hearts; it is a fine, responsible style, still not duly esteemed by us. Moreover, and more oddly, each writer uses words which concede the freedom of his own readers to judge his book, and thus softens his instructions on how to read and judge others. Their words imply some nervousness that people might misread or misjudge *The boke named the Gouernour* or *An Exhortation to yonge men* themselves. Both men offer the humble words common to Tudor literature, when they worry whether the book is too tedious or could be briefer.[47] Yet both men more subtly concede the possibility of a hostile response, Elyot even to the level of sounding neurotic. In throwaway comments, he often imagines a hostile response from us, presses us to agree, or questions what our response will be. 'Perchance some wyll scorne me', he thinks; 'no man wyll denie', he hints; 'who shall dought?', he wonders. There are many short lines like these in which he acknowledges the freedom of his own readers to judge him adversely, and there are some longer sections in which he mollifies his readers; he cut some of them from the second edition.[48] Moreover, when these writers describe the reading which they would like to stipulate, they speak of mere hypotheses, possibilities or futures. So many of the descriptions of how one should read begin with *if* or sometimes with *when*. So many of the verbs of reading, responding, and thinking begin with the modal auxiliaries *may*, *might* or at the most, *must* or *shall*. Lupset often describes how to read with the genteel suggestion *I would that*, so there is nothing here but suggestion, never insistence.[49] They cannot control how people will read their own books, let alone whether or how they will read the other books they tell people to read.

[47] Elyot, *Gouernour*, I.i, A1r, 15.2–7; I.xii, F5v, 275 *n.* 57:36, cut from the second edition; Lupset, *An Exhortation*, 237:4, 242:8, 242:31. Lupset also, more personally, admits that his previous lessons have caused 'frayes' between him and his pupil (236:22–7).
[48] Elyot, *Gouernour*, I.iiii, B8v–C1v, 30:10–31:2. See also I.xiiii, G7v, 68:8–12; I.xviii, K1r, 84:29–36. Rude (ed.), *Critical Edition of Sir Thomas Elyot's* The Boke, 269–99, lists lines cut in the second and other editions; those cut lines which apologize to or imagine readers were in I.iii, B7r–v, 29.4; I.viii, D3v, 40:21; I.xii, F5v, 275 n.57:36; I.xiii, G5r–v, 70:25; II.xii, V6r, 168:11; III.xi, c1v, 204:24; III.xxi (rightly III.xxii), f6v, 236:9.
[49] The quotations above all exemplify these habits. See also the following uses, taken only from discussions of reading and responding in Lupset, *An Exhortation*: *if* nine times (237:5, 238:1, 239:12, 239:14, 245:13, 256:1, 256:7, 256:8, 256:10); *when* or *as* three times (237:12, 246:25, 251:20); *may* some three times (237:13, 238:8, 238:30); *shall* twenty-six times (238:1, 238:3, 238:3

Of the two, Sir Thomas Elyot is especially fretful about the unpredictability of the reader and the scope for misinterpretation by his own readers. His fretting extends from *The boke named the Gouernour* through all of his many later books, and is especially fevered in the prefaces and dedications to them. There he imagines the possible readings, keen or hostile, which his books will get. These trembling words were conventional in Tudor literature, of course, but the conventions do imply the same ideal reader as the theories in *The boke named the Gouernour* do. So in the prefaces he repeatedly hopes that the reader will be diligent (five times) and just in judging (three).[50] Moreover, he discusses his readers in the same hypothetical grammar with which he and Lupset set out their educations: Elyot introduces the reading he hopes for with the uncertain *if* some fourteen times and the modals *may, might* some twenty times.[51] Does he imagine this independent mind in order to circumscribe it? Is this a humanist attempt to limit intellectual independence? On the contrary. Independence is what he seeks to unleash, in order to control something else. This emerges in *Of the Knowledge whiche maketh a wise man* in 1533:

I toke my penne and assayde / Howe in expressyng my conceyte I mought profyte to them, whiche without disdayne or envye wolde often tymes reade it. [...] Finally if the reders of my warkis, by the noble example of our moost dere soveraygne lorde do justly and lovyngely interprete my labours, I durynge the residue of my lyfe wyll nowe and than sette forthe suche frutes of my study profitable (as I trust) unto this my countray.[52]

Elyot wishes for re-reading ('often tymes') and equitable judgement ('justly') to bring forth fruit and profit. However, in his prefaces his wish is not only to render reading profitable for the reader, as in *The boke named the Gouernour*; he wishes that the reader's diligence and judgement will in turn help the writer, by leading to recognition of his intentions. Moreover, this recognition will have real consequences in buying his books—though Elyot, being a gent, does not say so—and certainly in honouring him, as his 'soveraygne lorde' did. It is his own public reputation which Elyot here seeks to control, not our intellectual response. It is well documented that in the marketplace for

again, 238:10, 244:30, 245:6, 245:9, 245:12, 245:16, 245:17, 245:28, 246:25, 246:27, 246:27 again, 246:31, 250:22, 251:4, 251:19, 254:12, 254:14, 256:2, 256:6, 256:6 again, 256:11, 262:4, 262:8); *must* five times (241:21, 241:23, 241:25, 241:26, 241:27); *I would* eleven times (237:10, 237:12, 237:14, 244:11, 244:35, 245:2, 245:27, 246:25, 251:21, 257:33, 261:34).

[50] The prefaces are helpfully edited in 'The Letters of Sir Thomas Elyot', ed. K. J. Wilson, a special issue of *Studies in Philology*, 73 (1976), separately paginated: see 45, 47, 54, 75 (×2) (diligence); 43, 49, 75 (judgement). Elyot refers to diligence in other contexts on thirteen more occasions in the prefaces.

[51] 'Letters of Elyot', with *if* on 43, 44 (x 2), 45, 48, 49 (×2), 52, 54, 59, 69, 75 (x 2), 78; and *may* or *might* on 41, 43, 46, 47, 49, 50, 55, 64 (x 4), 66, 67, 68, 69, 70, 71, 72, 75, 76.

[52] 'Letters of Elyot', 49.

printed books, writers expressed anxiety about their anonymous readers and misreaders, and sought to foreclose their responses in order to defend the author.[53] Thus, meeting his unpredictable readers of print, Elyot begs their diligence and judgement and fears their 'disdayne or envye' or 'malice' which might make them 'conjecte' his meaning wrongly.[54] But he does not stress his importance as the author as arbiter of meaning; he hopes that the intellectual independence of the reader, judging equitably the profit of his books, will bring him profit.

The reference to the 'soveraygne lorde' as one reader suggests a second cause of Elyot's nerves. After *The boke named the Gouernour* in 1531, Elyot's other works were composed and published during some difficult times for English writers. Through the 1530s, Henry VIII and his chief minister Cromwell thickened their control over the writing, speaking, and finally thinking of their subjects, and punished people for crimes of the tongue with cruelty. There were also complex shifts in official doctrine as parliament, Cromwell, and the king pulled the English church in various directions. Such policies made writing, and being read, difficult. Even the idealistic Elyot eventually seems to have recognized, in some of his works, the ironies in trying to use humanistic learning in public life.[55] These difficulties have been well traced by critics and have been seen as the cause of some crucial changes in English literature: indeed, as the cause of changes which shift 'medieval' literature into 'early modern'. For example, James Simpson and others wonder whether Protestant writers and humanist writers were complicit with the difficult and cruel world in which they lived: for example, did they legislate on what could or could not be said, in preferring classical styles, for example and rejecting all else as 'waste'? Greg Walker, by contrast, sees the writers of the 1530s finding exciting new forms with which to resist Henry VIII's tyranny, but he suggests that humanist forms, especially the mirror for princes, proved insufficient in the 1530s. He thinks that some new forms arose in English literature in the 1530s under pressure from the tyranny of these years, and not from any '"liberating" possibilities' in humanism.[56] Yet in Elyot's prefaces we can see how the ideal of the humanist reader, diligent in effort, rational in judgement, profitable in effect, did offer possibilities for coping with these dreadful pressures. Indeed, it is the sense of possibility and unpredictability in reading which lets Elyot cope with them.

The pose of being a humanist reader is used most keenly when Elyot seeks to defend himself from the controls of the Reformation regime. In December

[53] Brayman Hackel, *Reading Material*, 73–4, 82–3, 88.
[54] 'Letters of Elyot', 42 (×3), 46, 47, 49, 66 (malice), 54, 57, 70 (disdain).
[55] Fox and Guy, *Reassessing the Henrician Age*, 68, 72–3.
[56] Simpson, *Reform*, 561 and throughout; Walker, *Writing Under Tyranny*, 416–17.

1534 or 1535 the king wrote to Elyot condemning some seditious books and demanding that they be given up; two months later Elyot wrote to Cromwell and begged for time to comply with this order to stop reading.[57] In his letter, he uses three defences, each developed from humanist ideas about reading. Firstly he tries to elicit Cromwell's goodwill by reminding him of their old 'amitie'—and they do seem to be former friends—which rests on 'the moste perfeict fundacion' of 'the similitude of our studies'.[58] This idea is the one seemingly stolen from Cicero by Worcester or Caxton (in Chapters 4 and 5 above): that the studies enjoyed by scholars will bind together the commonweal. Amid the factions and betrayals of the 1530s, the dream of reading bringing friendship is the first defence. Two other defences follow:

I have ben ever desyrouse to reade many bookes, specially concerning humanitie and morall Philosophy, and therefor of suche studies I have a competent numbre. But concerning holy scripture I have very fewe, for in questionistes I never delyted: unsavery gloses and comentes I ever abhorred: the bostars and advauntars of the pompouse authoritie of the Busshop of Rome I never esteemyd. But after, that by moche and seriouse reading, I had apprehendid a jugement or estimacion of thinges: I didd anon smell oute theire corrupt affections [...][59]

Elyot's second defence is the distinctness of the *studia humanitatis* or 'humanitie' from divinity or any religious concerns, and certainly from the theology of the scholastic universities. The self-consciousness and self-identification of this course of study saves him. This is why he is willing to reject whole libraries of scholastic knowledge ('questionistes'), as Colet, Horman, Lily, Lupset, and More seemed to do in the 1510s. With the suspicions of heresy or treason in the 1530s, and the horrid punishments they brought, we could forgive him for this discrimination. Elyot's third and final defence is to profess his intellectual freedom as a reader. He can discriminate between scholasticism and humanism, not from mere prejudice, but from 'jugement' formed in 'moche and seriouse reading'. He records his freedom to read books and judge them adversely ('I ever abhorred'). Elsewhere in the letter he records his freedom to read for style alone—that humanist vice: he does own one of Bishop John Fisher's sermons and enjoys it not for the religious content, but for the style of the humanist Latin translation. And he records his freedom not to read some of his books at all, as he says that he never read the popish works bound into one volume which he owns.[60] It is the freedom of the humanist reader which he thinks will save him—and which, as he defends his life and books, he hopes to save.

---

[57] Stanford E. Lehmberg, *Sir Thomas Elyot: Tudor Humanist* (Austin: University of Texas Press, 1960), 149–50; Walker, *Writing Under Tyranny*, 129–32.
[58] 'Letters of Elyot', 26.   [59] *Ibid.*, 26.   [60] *Ibid.*, 27; for similar defences see 67.

However, in his letter Elyot *is* writing strategically, in order to defend himself. Does he, or do other humanists, truly cherish the freedom of the reader? Is it really essential to humanism, or merely incidental? It is not really essential, for throughout the fifteenth and sixteenth centuries, the humanist writers in England sought to control the reader. These writers did themselves exercise the creative writer's prerogative to misread or mistranslate, when they interpreted Claudian, Vegetius, or Cicero freely. Yet how free were they? When the poet of *Knyghthode and Bataile* read Vegetius, or Medwall read *The Declamacion of Noblesse*, each seems to have had ideas which, having accepted himself, he found in the books which he read. Furthermore, and most importantly, each of these readers then fixed his thinking in a written translation, treatise, interlude, or even a marginal note, and in so doing he sought to persuade other readers to follow his thinking closely. In fact, many of the humanist works between 1430 and 1530 have as their essential job influencing how people read. There are translations in page layouts designed to ensure that we recognize their styles, such as *On Husbondrie*. There are translations tilted to ensure that we see the contemporary parallels, such as *De Consulatu Stilichonis*. There are documents which tell us what or what not to read, such as the letters about Duke Humfrey or the statutes of Tudor schools. There are interludes which end our debate with firm lessons, such as Medwall's *Fulgens and Lucres*. There are treatises which tell us what to 'considre welle' in the works of Boethius or Livy, such as Worcester's *The Boke of Noblesse*. There are prologues such as del Monte's or Caxton's, which advertise what we must enjoy in the works which follow. And there are marginalia and notebooks which tell us where to *nota bene*. In their instructions, Lupset and Elyot merely do explicitly what the other humanist writings of the previous hundred years did slyly. They sought to tell their readers—though they did not always succeed—how to study and imitate antiquity in a manner that was very directed, not very free at all.

This directedness might seem a fault; one might prefer, as John Russell did in the 1480s, to see social interaction as a dialogue. But there are some beliefs so urgent that dialogue must be replaced by insistence.[61] These writers preach at their readers because they believe in something urgently, so that reading their work becomes an act of great importance. Some of them insist upon the superiority of the classics: this sometimes is a fetish or a shibboleth of taste, but it can give authority to their ideas about the commonweal or true nobility. Some insist upon certain methods of studying and imitating: this sometimes promotes crabbed translation or showy allusion, but it can

---

[61] Raymond Gaita, *A Common Humanity: Thinking about Love and Truth and Justice* (1998; London: Routledge, 2002), 207–11, reflects on this dilemma in contemporary culture.

promote responsible methods of argument, citation, or enquiry. And some insist upon the fine political or ethical ideas which they found knotted in the books which they read. Of course, the humanist insistence on how to read sometimes seems silly: Horman snobbily mocked the books he disliked and Lupset sold them off; even the instructions in Caxton's or Berthelet's editions might seem reductive. But Elyot insists that the matter and methods of the humanists will dignify the reader with the freedom to think for himself. By contrast, the pious fanatics and the political opportunists of the time feared the people who wrote, read, or thought for themselves and sometimes—as Elyot dreads in this letter—murdered them.

Works Cited

Manuscripts

CCCC, MS 210
CCCC, MS 285
CCCC, MS 423
Cambridge, Emmanuel College Library, MS I.2.10
Cambridge, Pembroke College, MS 215
Cambridge, Pembroke College, MS 243
Cambridge, Peterhouse, MS 215
SJC, MS C.10
SJC, MS B.3
SJC, MS G.29
TCC, MS O.5.6
TCC, MS O.9.8
CUL, MS Additional 7870
CUL, MS Additional 8706
CUL, MS Ee.I.13
CUL, MS Gg.I.34 (i)
CUL, MS Gg.I.34 (ii)
CUL, MS Gg.IV.18
CUL, MS Ii.I.38
CUL, MS Ii.III.21
CUL, MS Ll.I.18
CUL, MS Mm. IV.42
Chicago, University Library, MS 565
GUL, MS Hunter 5 (S.1.5)
GUL, MS Hunter 104 (T.5.6)
GUL, MS Hunter 185 (T.8.7)
GUL, MS Hunter 274 (U.5.14)
BL, MS Additional 4713
BL, MS Additional 10304
BL, MS Additional 10340
BL, MS Additional 10344
BL, MS Additional 11814
BL, MS Additional 12028
BL, MS Additional 16165
BL, MS Additional 17433
BL, MS Additional 21410
BL, MS Additional 28208
BL, MS Additional 39659

BL, MS Additional 44922
BL, MS Arundel 249
BL, MS Arundel 366
BL, MS Arundel 435
BL, MS Arundel 454
BL, MS Arundel 461
BL, MS Cotton Cleopatra, E.iii
BL, MS Cotton Julius E.iv (4)
BL, MS Cotton Julius F.vii
BL, MS Cotton Titus A.xxiii
BL, MS Cotton Vitellius E.x
BL, MS Harley 43
BL, MS Harley 44
BL, MS Harley 116
BL, MS Harley 1245
BL, MS Harley 1705
BL, MS Harley 1766
BL, MS Harley 4197
BL, MS Harley 4203
BL, MS Harley 4835
BL, MS Harley 5015
BL, MS Royal 5.F.ii
BL, MS Royal 8.E.xii
BL, MS Royal 9.B.vi
BL, MS Royal 13.C.i
BL, MS Royal 18.B.xxii
BL, MS Royal 18.B.xxxi
BL, MS Royal 18.D.iv
BL, MS Royal 20.B.xv
BL, MS Sloane 4
BL, MS Sloane 372
BL, MS Sloane 686
BL, MS Sloane 2945
London, College of Arms, MS Arundel 12
London, College of Arms, MS Arundel 48
London, College of Arms, MS M.9
LPL, MS 425
LPL, MS 450
LPL, MS 506
NA, MS PROB 11/11
NA, MS PROB 11/43
NA, MS C 54/288
NA, MS C 54/295
NA, MS C 54/296
Manchester, Chetham's Library, MS Mun. A.3.131 (27929)

JRL, MS Eng. 2
JRL, MS Eng. 102
OBC, MS 121
OBC, MS 123
OBC, MS 124
OBC, MS 316 A
OBC, MS 316 B
OBC, MS 258
BodL, MS Additional A.369
BodL, MS Ashmole 45 (ii)
BodL, MS Auct. F.3.25
BodL, MS Auct. F.3.5
BodL, MS Auct. F.5.22
BodL, MS Auct. F.5.26
BodL, MS Bodley 587
BodL, MS Bodley 797
BodL, MS Bodley 915
BodL, MS Duke Humfrey d.2
BodL, MS Hatton 2
BodL, MS Laud lat. 61
BodL, MS Laud lat. 70
BodL, MS Laud misc. 570
BodL, MS Laud misc. 674
BodL, MS Rawlinson C.448
Oxford, Corpus Christi College, MS 242
OMC, MS lat. 26
OMC, MS lat. 30
OMC, MS lat. 166
OMC, MS lat. 198
OMC, MS lat. 206
OMC, Archives, MS Additional 99 (Lovell Papers)
OMC, Archives, MS Fastolf Papers 43
Oxford, New College, MS 162
Salisbury, Cathedral Library, MS 113
HEHL, MS Ellesmere 26.A.13
HEHL, MS Ellesmere 34.B.6

Incunables

[Anwykyll], John, *Compendium totius grammatice* ([Oxford: Rood and Hunt, 1483];
    STC 696)
    BodL, classmark Inc.e.E2.1483.1
John [Anwykyll], *Compendium totius grammatice* (Deventer: Pafraet, 4/5/1489;
    STC 696.1)
    BL, classmark IA.47600

[Anwykyll], John, *Compendium totius grammatice* ([London: Wynkyn de Worde, *c*.1517]; STC 696.7)
OMC, classmark Arch. C.I.1.20

[Anwykyll, John], *Vulgaria quedam abs Terencio in Anglicam linguam traducta* ([Oxford: Rood and Hunt, 1483]; *STC* 23904)
CUL, classmark Inc.5.J.2.2 [3585]
BodL, classmark Arch G. e.5

[Anwykyll, John], *Vulgaria quedam abs Terencio in anglicam linguam traducta* ([London: de Machlinia, 1483?]; *STC* 23905)
CUL, classmark Inc.5.J.3.5 [3609]

[Anwykyll, John], *Vulgaria Therentij in anglicanam linguam traducta* (Antwerp: Leeu, 1486; *STC* 23907)
CUL, classmark Inc.5.F.6.2 [3353]

[Anwykyll, John], *Uulgaria Therentij in anglicanam linguam traducta* (London: Faques, [*c*. 1505]; *STC* 23907.3)
CCCC, MS 386

[Burgh, Benedict (trans.)], *Parvus Cato Magnus Cato* (Westminster: Caxton, 1478; *STC* 4850)
CUL, classmark Inc.5.J.1.1 [3483]

[Bruni, Leonardo (trans.)], *Aristotelis ethicorum libri* (Oxford: [Rood], 1479; *STC* 752)
BodL, classmark S. Selden e.2

Caxton, William (trans.), *Caton* (Westminster: Caxton, 1484; *STC* 4853)
CUL, classmark Inc.3.J.1.1 [3505]
GUL, classmark Hunter Bv.2.16
BodL, classmark Arch. G. d.13
Oxford, Exeter College, classmark 9.M.4815

Chaucer, Geoffrey (trans.), *Boece* (Westminster: Caxton, 1478; *STC* 3199)
Leeds, Brotherton Library, classmark Ripon Cathedral XVI.E.20q
LPL, classmark Sion College, arc. L.40.4/72
BodL, classmark Arch. G. d.13
Oxford, Exeter College, classmark 9.M.4815
Oxford, Wadham College, classmark A.6.11
HEHL, classmark 82740
OMC, classmark Arch. B.III.2.12 (2)

Cicero, *De Officiis, etc.* (Mainz: Fust and Schöffer, 4/2/1466–7)
TCC, classmark VI.14.24
CUL, classmark Inc.3.A.1.3a [12]
LPL, classified as MS 765

Cicero, *Epistolae ad familiares* ([Louvain: de Veldener, *c*.1470s])
CUL, classmark Inc.3.F.2.1 [3166]

Cicero, *Orationes* ([Venice]: Valdarfer, 1471)
SJC, classmark Ii.1.6

Cicero, *Tusculanarum quaestionum libri* (Venice: Jenson, 1472)
CUL, classmark Inc.3.B.3.2 [1353]

Cicero, *Epistolae ad familiares* (Milan: de Lavigne, 1478)
  CUL, classmark Inc.2.B.7.2 [4336]
Cicero, *De Oratore* (Venice: Catharensis, 20/8/1478)
  CUL, classmark Inc.3.B.3.27 [1478]
Cicero, *Epistolae ad familiares* ([Venice: printer of the 1480 Martial, *c*.1480])
  CUL, classmark Inc.3.B.3.152 [1857]
Cicero, *Pro Lege Manilia, etc.* ([Paris: Martineau, *c*.1482])
  CUL, classmark Inc.5.D.1.10 [2429]
  BodL, classmark Auct.N.5.8
Cicero, *De Amicitia, De Senectute* (Louvain: de Westfalia, 17/5/1483)
  CUL, classmark Inc.3.F.2.2 [3180]
Cicero, *De Officiis* (Louvain: de Westfalia, [*c*.1483])
  CUL, classmark Inc.3.F.2.2 [3184]
[Cicero, *Oratio pro T. Milone*] ([Oxford: Rood, 1483]; *STC* 5312)
  Oxford, Merton College, classmarks P.3.2 and P.3.3a
Cicero, *De Officiis* (Louvain: de Paderborn, 2nd edn. after 1483)
  CUL, classmark Inc.3.F.2.2 [4088]
Cicero, *Epistolae ad familiares* (Venice: de Tortis, 24/5/1485)
  OMC, classmark Arch. B.III.1.13
Cicero, *De Officiis, etc.* (Lyons: Guillaume Le Roy, *c*.1485)
  OMC, classmark Arch. B.III.2.7
Cicero, *Orator, etc.* (Venice: Locatellus, 17/8/1492)
  TCC, classmark VI.15.21[1]
Cicero, *Epistolae ad familiares* (Venice: Locatellus, 22/9/1494)
  CUL, classmark Inc.2.B.3.85 [1659]
Cicero, *De Officiis, etc.* (Venice: Pincius, 3/3/1496)
  CUL, classmark Inc.3.B.3.104 [1736]
Cicero, *Epistolae ad familiares* (Lyons: de Vingle, 12/3/1496)
  CUL, classmark Inc.2.D.2.25 [2713]
Cicero, *Opera Omnia* (Milan: le Signerre, 1498–9)
  SJC, classmark Ii.2.10
  CUL, classmark Inc.1.B.7.26 [1927]
Dati, Agostino, *Libellus super Tulianis elegantiis* (St Albans: [anon.], [1479]; *STC* 6289)
  CUL, classmark Inc.5.J.4.1 [3632]
Dati, Agostino, *Elegantiole* ([Louvain: de Westfalia, *c*.1485])
  BodL, classmark Auct.N.5.3
Griffolini, Francesco (trans.), *Epistole Phalaridis* (Oxford: Rood and Hunt, 1485; *STC* 19827)
  Oxford, Wadham College, classmark A.4.31
Lactantius, *Divinae institutiones* (Venice: John of Cologne and John Mathem de Chernetsem, 1478)
  Cambridge, Pembroke College, classmark C.28

Cambridge, Pembroke College, classmark C.29

de Pizan, Christine, *Lart de cheualerie selon Vegece* (Paris: Verard, 1488)
    BL, classmark IB.41088

Plutarch, *Virorum illustrium uitae* (Venice: Jensen, 2/1/1478)
    OMC, classmark Arch. B.III.4.4–5

Terence, *Comoediae* (London: Pynson, 1497; *STC* 23885)
    BL, classmark C.4.g.13

Terence, *Andria* (London: Pynson, 1497; part of *STC* 23885)
    BodL, classified as MS Fairfax 18

Traversagni, Lorenzo, *Nova rhetorica* (Westminster: Caxton, [1479]; *STC* 24189)
    CCCC, classmark EP.H.6

Traversagni, Lorenzo, *Nova rhetorica* (St Albans: [anon.], 1480; *STC* 24190)
    BL, classmark C.11.a.29
    JRL, classmark 9114
    BodL, classmark Auct.N.5.8

[Worcester, William] (trans.), *Tullius de senectute* (Westminster: Caxton, 1481; *STC* 5293)
    SJC, classmark A.1.4
    SJC, classmark Ii.1.49
    CUL, classmark Inc.3.J.1.1 [3495]
    CUL, classmark Inc.3.J.1.1 [3496]
    CUL, classmark Inc.3.J.1.1 [3497]
    BL, classmark C.10.b.6
    Oxford, Queen's College Library, classmark Sel.a.111
    HEHL, classmark 82872

Printed Primary Works

Anstey, Henry (ed.), *Epistolae Academicae Oxon.*, Oxford Historical Society, 35–6, 2 vols. (Oxford: Clarendon Press, 1898).

Aristotle, *Politics*, ed. and trans. H. Rackham (Cambridge, MA: Harvard University Press, 1932).

——— *Nicomachean Ethics*, trans. H. Rackham (Cambridge, MA: Harvard University Press, 1934).

Ashby, George, *Poems*, ed. Mary Bateson, EETS es 76 (London: Kegan Paul, Trench, Trübner, 1899).

St Augustine, *The City of God Against the Pagans*, ed. and trans. George E. McCracken and others, 7 vols. (Cambridge, MA: Harvard University Press, 1957–72).

Aulus Gellius, *Noctes Atticae*, ed. P. K. Marshall, 2 vols. (Oxford: Clarendon Press, 1968).

Beadle, Richard, and Richmond, Colin (eds.), *Paston Letters and Papers of the Fifteenth Century: Part III*, EETS ss 22 (Oxford: Oxford University Press, 2005).

Blayney, Margaret S. (ed.), *Fifteenth-Century English Translations of Alain Chartier's* Le Traité de l'Esperance *and* Le Quadrilogue Invectif, EETS os 270, 281, 2 vols. (Oxford: Oxford University Press, 1974–80).

Boccaccio, Giovanni, *Famous Women*, ed. and trans. Virginia Brown (Cambridge, MA: Harvard University Press, 2001).

Boethius, *De Consolatione philosophiae*, in his *De Consolatione philosophiae; Opuscula theologica*, ed. Claudio Moreschini (Munich: Teubner, 2000).

[Bokenham, Osbern], 'This Dialogue betwix a Seculer asking and a Frere answeryng […]', in Osbern Bokenham, *Legenden*, ed. C. Horstmann (Heilbronn: Henninger, 1883), 269–74.

Bokenham, Osbern, *Legendys of Hooly Wummen*, ed. Mary S. Serjeantson, EETS os 206 (London: Oxford University Press, 1938).

Bracciolini, Poggio (trans.), *Diodorus Siculus* (Paris: Petit, 1508).

Brigstocke Sheppard, J. (ed.), *Literæ Cantuarienses: The Letter Books of the Monastery of Christ Church, Canterbury*, RS 85, 3 vols. (London: HMSO, 1887–9).

Rawdon Brown (ed.), *Calendar of State Papers and Manuscripts, Relating to English Affairs, Existing in the Archives and Collections of Venice and in Other Libraries of Northern Italy: Volume I. 1202–1509* (London: HMSO, 1864).

War and Society in Renaissance Florence: The De Militia of Leonardo Bruni, ed. C. C. Bayley (Toronto: University of Toronto Press, 1961).

Bruni, Leonardo, *Vita Ciceronis*, in his *Opere Letterarie e Politiche*, ed. Paolo Viti (Turin: Unione Tipografico-Editrice, 1996), 413–99.

—— *Laudatio Florentine urbis*, ed. Stefano U. Baldassarri (Florence: SISMEL-Edizione del Galluzzo, 2000).

Prose e rime de due Buonaccorsi da Montemagno, ed. G. B Casotti (Florence: Manni, 1718).

Buonaccorso da Montemagno, *De Nobilitate*, in *Prosatori Latini Del Quattrocento*, ed. Eugenio Garin (Milan: Ricciardi, 1952), 141–65.

'Capgrave's Preface Dedicating his Commentary *In Exodum* to Humfrey Duke of Gloucester', ed. Peter J. Lucas and Rita Dalton, *BLR*, 11 (1982), 20–5.

[Carmeliano, Pietro (ed.)], *Sex quamelegantissimæ epistolæ printed by William Caxton in 1483*, facsimile ed. James Hyatt, trans. George Bullen (London: Lawrence and Bullen, 1892).

Caxton, William (trans.), *The Book of Fayttes of Armes and of Chyualrye*, ed. A. T. P. Byles, EETS os 189 (London: Oxford University Press, 1932).

Caxton's Own Prose, ed. N. F. Blake (London: Deutsch, 1973).

Chaplais, Pierre (ed.), *English Medieval Diplomatic Practice*, 2 vols. (London: HMSO, 1982).

Chartier, Alain, *Le Quadrilogue invectif*, ed. E. Droz, 2nd edn. (1923; Paris: Champion, 1950).

—— *Le Livre de l'espérance*, ed. François Rouy, Bibliothèque du XVe siècle, 51 (Paris: Champion, 1989).

Chaucer According to William Caxton: Minor Poems and Boece 1478, ed. Beverly Boyd (Lawrence, KA: Allen Press, 1978).

The Riverside Chaucer, ed. Larry D. Benson (1987; Oxford: Oxford University Press, 1988).

Chaundler, Thomas, *Libellus de laudibus duarum civitatum*, ed. George Williams, *Proceedings of the Somersetshire Archaeological and Natural History Society*, 19 (1873), 99–121.

——*Liber apologeticus de omni statu humanae naturae*, ed. Doris Enright-Clark Shoukri, Publications of the MHRA, 5 (London: MHRA, 1974).

Chrimes, S. B. (ed.), 'The Pretensions of the Duke of Gloucester in 1422', *EHR*, 45 (1930), 101–3.

Cicero, *De Re publica*, ed. K. Ziegler (Leipzig: Teubner, 1969).

——*De Officiis*, ed. and trans. Walter Miller (Cambridge, MA: Harvard University Press, 1913).

——*De Natura deorum*, in his *De Natura deorum; Academica*, ed. and trans. H. Rackham (Harvard, MA: Harvard University Press, 1933).

——*De Inventione*, in his *De Inventione; De optimo genere oratorum; Topica*, ed. and trans. H. M. Hubbell (Harvard, MA: Harvard University Press, 1949).

——*De Oratore*, ed. and trans. E. W. Sutton and H. Rackham, 2 vols. (Harvard, MA: Harvard University Press, 1942).

——*Laelius de Amicitia* in his *Cato Maior. Laelius*, ed. K. Simbeck (Stuttgart: Teubner, 1971).

——*Cato Maior de senectute*, ed. J. G. F. Powell, Cambridge Classical Texts and Commentaries, 28 (Cambridge: Cambridge University Press, 1987).

Clarke, Peter D., with Lovatt, R. (eds.), *The University and College Libraries of Cambridge*, Corpus of British Medieval Library Catalogues, 10 (London: British Academy, 2002).

Claudius Claudianus, *Carmina*, ed. John Barrie Hall (Leipzig: Teubner, 1985).

Colet, John, 'Appendix A: Statutes of St. Paul's School', printed in J. H. Lupton, *A Life of John Colet, D.D.* (1887; repr. London: Bell and Sons, 1909), 271–84.

[John Colet and others], *Rudimenta grammatices et docendi methodus* (Southwark: Peter Treveris, 1529; *STC* 5542.3).

Cope, Anthony (trans.), *Annibal and Scipio* (London: Thomas Berthelet, 1544; *STC* 5718).

Courtecuisse, Jean (trans.), *Sénèque des IIII vertus: La* Formula Honestae Vitae *de Martin de Braga (pseudo-Sénèque)*, ed. Hans Haselbach (Berne: Lang, 1975).

Davis, Norman (ed.), *Paston Letters and Papers of the Fifteenth Century*, 2 vols. (Oxford: Clarendon Press, 1971–6).

Decembrio, Pier Candido, *De Laudibus Mediolanensis urbis panegyricus*, in *Pier Candidi Decembri Opuscula Historica*, ed. A. Buti, F. Forsati, and G. Petraglione, Rerum italicarum scriptores, 2nd series, 20 (Bologna: Zanichelli, 1958), 1013–25.

'Piero del Monte, John Whethamstede, and the Library of St Albans Abbey', ed. R. Weiss, *EHR*, 60 (1945), 399–406.

'Pietro del Monte a Poggio Bracciolini', in Poggio Bracciolini, *Opera Omnia*, ed. Riccardo Fubini, 4 vols. (Turin: Bottega d'Erasmo, 1964–9), IV.615–39.

Dyboski, R., and Arend, Z. M. (eds.), *Knyghthode and Bataile*, EETS os 201 (London: Oxford University Press, 1935).

Eccles, Mark (ed.), *Mankind*, in his *The Macro Plays*, EETS os 262 (London: Oxford University Press, 1969), 153–84.

Elyot, Sir Thomas, *The boke named the Gouernour* (London: Berthelet, 1531; *STC* 7635).

—— (trans.), *The Education or bringinge vp of children* (London: Berthelet, 1532; *STC* 20057).

—— *A Preservative Agaynste deth* (London: Thomas Berthelet, 1545; *STC* 7674).

'The Letters of Sir Thomas Elyot', ed. K. J. Wilson, a special issue of *Studies in Philology*, 73 (1976), separately paginated.

A Critical Edition of Sir Thomas Elyot's The Boke named the Governour, ed. Donald W. Rude (New York: Garland, 1992).

Erasmus, *Antibarbariorum liber*, trans. Margaret Mann Phillips, in *Literary and Educational Writings 1*, ed. Craig R. Thompson, Collected Works of Erasmus, 23 (Toronto: University of Toronto Press, 1978), 1–122.

—— *De Ratione studii ac legendi interpretandique auctores*, trans. Brian McGregor, in *Literary and Educational Writings 2*, ed. Craig R. Thompson, Collected Works of Erasmus, 24 (Toronto: University of Toronto Press, 1978), 661–91.

—— *De Pueris statim ac liberaliter instituendis declamatio*, trans. Beert C. Verstraete, in *Literary and Educational Writings 4*, ed. J. K. Sowards, Collected Works of Erasmus, 26 (Toronto: University of Toronto Press, 1985), 291–346.

Firth Green, Richard (ed.), 'An Epitaph for Richard, Duke of York', *Studies in Bibliography*, 41 (1988), 218–24.

Fletcher, Bradford Y. (ed.), *Manuscript Trinity R.3.19: A Facsimile* (Norman, OK: Pilgrim Books, 1987).

Flügel, Ewald (ed.), 'Kleinere Mitteilungen aus Handschriften', *Anglia*, 14 (1892), 463–501.

—— (ed.), 'Eine Mittelenglische Claudian-Übersetzung (1445)', *Anglia*, 28 (1905), 255–99, 421–38.

Foro-Juliensis, Titi Livii [*i.e.* Tito Livio Frulovisi], *Vita Henrici Quinti, Regis Angliæ*, ed. Thomas Hearne (Oxford: [n. p.], 1716).

Frulovisi, Tito Livio, *Eugenius*, in *Opera hactenus inedita T. Livii de Frulovisiis de Ferraria*, ed. C. W. Previté-Orton (Cambridge: Cambridge University Press, 1932), 223–84.

The Works of Sir John Fortescue, Knight, ed. Thomas (Fortescue) Lord Clermont, 2 vols. (London: privately printed, 1869).

Fortescue, Sir John, *The Governance of England*, ed. Charles Plummer (London: Oxford University Press, 1885).

—— *De Laudibus legum Anglie*, ed. S. B. Chrimes (Cambridge: Cambridge University Press, 1942).

'A Letter Preface of John Free to John Tiptoft Earl of Worcester', ed. R. Weiss, *Bodleian Quarterly Record*, 8 (1935–8), 101–3.

Genêt, Jean-Philippe (ed.), *Tractatus de regimine principum ad regem Henricum Sextum*, in his *Four English Political Tracts of the Later Middle Ages*, Camden Society, 4th series, 18 (London: Royal Historical Society, 1977), 40–173.

Gilson, J. P. (ed.), 'A Defence of the Proscription of the Yorkists in 1459', *EHR*, 26 (1911), 512–25.

Given-Wilson, Chris, and others (eds.), *The Parliament Rolls of Medieval England*, 16 vols. (London: National Archives, 2005).

Gray, Douglas (ed.), *The Oxford Book of Late Medieval Verse and Prose* (Oxford: Clarendon Press, 1985).

Griffiths, R. A. (ed.), 'Duke Richard of York's Intentions in 1450 and the Origins of the Wars of the Roses', *JMH*, 1 (1975), 187–209.

Hardyng, John, *Chronicle*, ed. Henry Ellis (London: Rivington and others, 1812).

Harper-Bill, Christopher (ed.), *The Cartulary of the Augustinian Friars of Clare*, Suffolk Charters, XI (Woodbridge: Boydell, 1991).

—— (ed.), *The Register of John Morton, Archbishop of Canterbury 1486–1500*, Canterbury and York Society, 75, 78–9, 3 vols. (Leeds: Duffield, 1987; Woodbridge: Boydell, 1991–2000).

Hervet, Gentian (trans.), *Xenophons treatise of householde* (London: Berthelet, 1532; STC 26069).

Heywood, John, *The Play of the Wether*, in *The Plays of John Heywood*, ed. Richard Axton and Peter Happé (Cambridge: Brewer, 1991), 183–215.

Holt, John, *Lac puerorum* (London: de Worde, c.1508; STC 13604).

Horman, William, *Vulgaria* (London: Pynson, 1519; STC 13811).

Ingram, R. W. (ed.), *Records of Early English Drama: Coventry* (Toronto: University of Toronto Press, 1981).

St Jérôme, *Lettres*, ed. and trans. Jérôme Labourt, 8 vols. (Paris: Budé, 1949–63).

Kaylor, Noel Harold, Jr, Streed, Jason Edward, and Watts, William H. (eds.), 'The Boke of Coumfort of Bois', *Carmina Philosophiae*, 2 (1993), 55–104.

Kekewich, Margaret Lucille, and others (eds.), *The Politics of Fifteenth-Century England: John Vale's Book* (Stroud: Sutton, 1995).

Lester, Geoffrey (ed.), *The Earliest English Translation of Vegetius' De Re Militari*, Middle English Texts, 21 (Heidelberg: Winter, 1988).

Liddell, Mark (ed.), *The Middle-English Translation of Palladius De Re Rustica* (Berlin: Ebering, 1896).

Lily, William, 'Carmen [...] ad discipulos de moribus', in [John Colet and others], *Rudimenta grammatices et docendi methodus* (Southwark: Treveris, 1529; STC 5542.3).

Livy, *Ab Urbe condita*, ed. and trans. B. O. Foster and others, 14 vols. (Cambridge, MA: Harvard University Press, 1919–59).

Lodge, Barton (ed.), *Palladius On Husbondrie*, EETS os 52, 72 (London: Trübner, 1873–9).

Lombard, Peter, *Sententiae in IV libris distinctae*, Spicilegium Bonaventurianum, IV-V (Rome: Collegium S. Bonaventurae ad Claras Aquas, 1971–81).

Lucan, *De Bello civili*, ed. D. R. Shackleton Bailey (Stuttgart: Teubner, 1988).

The Life and Works of Thomas Lupset, ed. John Archer Gee (New Haven, CT: Yale University Press, 1928).

Lydgate, John, *Reson and Sensuallyte*, ed. Ernst Sieper, EETS es 84, 89, 2 vols. (London: Kegan Paul, Trench, Trübner, 1901–3).

—— *The Serpent of Division*, ed. Henry Noble MacCracken (New Haven, CT: Yale University Press, 1911).

—— *Minor Poems*, ed. Henry Noble MacCracken, EETS es 107, os 192, 2 vols. (London: Kegan Paul, Trench, Trübner, 1911–34).

—— *The Fall of Princes*, ed. Henry Bergen, EETS es 121–4, 4 vols. (London: Oxford University Press, 1924–7).

—— and Burgh, Benedict, *Secrees of Old Philisoffres*, ed. Robert Steele, EETS es 66 (London: Kegan Paul, Trench, Trübner, 1894).

Machan, Tim William (ed.), *Sources of the* Boece (Athens: University of Georgia Press, 2005).

Mancini, Dominic, *The Usurpation of Richard the Third*, ed. C. A. J. Armstrong (Oxford: Oxford University Press, 1969).

Marx, William (ed.), *An English Chronicle 1377–1461: A New Edition* (Woodbridge: Boydell, 2003).

The Plays of Henry Medwall, ed. Alan Nelson (Cambridge: Brewer, 1980).

The Plays of Henry Medwall: A Critical Edition, ed. M. E. Moeslein (New York: Garland, 1981).

de Meun, Jean (trans.), *Li Abregemenz noble honme Vegesce Flave René des establissemenz apartenanz a chevalerie*, ed. Leena Löfstedt, Annales Academiæ Scientiarum Fennicæ, series B, 200 (Helsinki: Suomalainen Tiedeakatemia, 1977).

Mitchell, W. T. (ed.), *Epistolae Academicae 1508–1596*, Oxford Historical Society, 26 (Oxford: Clarendon Press, 1980).

Monro, Cecil (ed.), *Letters of Queen Margaret of Anjou and Bishop Bekington and Others*, Camden Society, os 86 (London: Camden Society, 1863).

More, Thomas, *Utopia*, ed. Edward J. Surtz, S.J., and Hexter, J. H., Complete Works of St. Thomas More, 4 (New Haven, CT: Yale University Press, 1965).

—— *In Defense of Humanism*, ed. Daniel Kinney, Complete Works of St. Thomas More, 15 (New Haven, CT: Yale University Press, 1986).

Myers, A. R. (ed.), *The Household of Edward IV: The Black Book and the Ordinance of 1478* (Manchester: Manchester University Press, 1959).

Nelson, William (ed.), *A Fifteenth Century School Book* (Oxford: Clarendon Press, 1956).

Nicolas, Harris (ed.), *Proceedings and Ordinances of the Privy Council of England*, 7 vols. (London: Commissioners on the Public Records, 1834–7).

Norton-Smith, John (ed.), *Bodleian Library MS Fairfax 16* (London: Scolar Press, 1979).

Orme, Nicholas (ed.), 'An Early-Tudor Oxford Schoolbook', *Renaissance Quarterly*, 34 (1981), 11–39.

—— (ed.), 'The Education of Edward V', in his *Education and Society in Medieval and Renaissance England* (London: Hambledon, 1989), 177–88.

Ovidius Naso, Publius, *Metamorphoses*, ed. William S. Anderson (Stuttgart: Teubner, 1977)

Statutes of the Colleges of Oxford, 3 vols. (Oxford: Parker, 1853).

Palladius Rutilius Taurus Aemilianus, *Opera*, ed. Robert H. Rodgers (Leipzig: Teubner, 1975).

Pantin, W. A. (ed.), *Canterbury College, Oxford*, Oxford Historical Society, new series, 6–8, 3 vols. (Oxford: Clarendon Press, 1946–50).

de Premierfait, Laurent, *Des Cas des Nobles Hommes et Femmes: Book I*, ed. Patricia May Gathercole, Studies in the Romance Languages and Literatures, 74 (Chapel Hill, NC: University of North Carolina Press, 1968).

'Laurus Quirinius, Franciscus Conatrenus, Nicolaus Barbus et socii Petro Thomasio prestantissimo phisico suo S.P.D.', in *Lauro Quirini Umanistà*, ed. Vittorio Branca, Civiltà Veneziana Saggi, 23 (Florence: Olschki, 1977), 67–73.

Rabil, Albert, Jr. (ed.), *Knowledge, Goodness, Power: The Debate over Nobility among Quattrocento Italian Humanists*, Medieval and Renaissance Texts and Studies, 88 (Binghampton, NY: Center for Medieval and Early Renaissance Studies, 1991).

Rawcliffe, Carole (ed.), 'Richard, Duke of York, the King's "obeisant liegeman": A New Source for the Protectorates of 1454 and 1455', *Historical Research*, 60 (1987), 232–39.

Robbins, Rossell Hope (ed.), *Historical Poems of the XIVth and XVth Centuries* (New York, NY: Columbia University Press, 1959).

Rouse Bloxam, John (ed.), *A Register [...] of Saint Mary Magdalen College in the University of Oxford*, 8 vols. (Oxford: Graham, 1853–85).

[de Rovroy (?),Jean (trans.)], 'Aucuns notables extraitz du livre de Vegece', ed. Leena Löfstedt, *Neuphilologische Mitteilungen*, 83 (1982), 297–312.

Russell, John, *The Book of Nurture*, in *The Babees Book*, ed. F. J. Furnivall, EETS os 32 (London: Trübner, 1868), 113–239.

Propositio Johannis Russell printed by William Caxton circa A.D. 1476, ed. Henry Guppy (Manchester: Manchester University Press, 1909).

'Bishop Russell's Parliamentary Sermons in 1483', printed in S. B. Chrimes, *English Constitutional Ideas in the Fifteenth Century* (Cambridge: Cambridge University Press, 1936).

Rymer, Thomas (ed.), *Foedera, conventiones, literæ, Et cujuscunque generis acta publica*, 10 vols. (The Hague: Neaulme, 1739–45).

Sallustius Crispus, Gaius, *Catilina, Iugurtha, Fragmenta Ampliora*, ed. Alphonsus Kurfess (Leipzig: Teubner, 1968).

Coluccio Salutati: Editi e inediti Latini dal Ms. 53 della Biblioteca Comunale di Todi, ed. Enrico Menestò, Res Tudertinæ, 12 (Todi: Tipografica Porziuncola, 1971).

Sammut, Alfonso (ed.), *Unfredo duca di Gloucester e gli umanisti italiani*, Medioevo e Umanesimo, 40 (Padua: Antenore, 1980).

Schleich, Gustav (ed.), *Die mittelenglische Umdichtung von Boccaccios De claris mulieribus*, Palaestra, 144 (Leipzig: Mayer und Müller, 1924).

Scrope, Stephen (trans.), *The Dicts and Sayings of the Philosophers*, ed. Curt F. Bühler, EETS os 211 (London: Oxford University Press, 1941).

Seneca, *Ad Lucilium epistulae morales*, ed. and trans. Richard M. Gummere, 3 vols. (Cambridge, MA: Harvard University Press, 1917–25).

Skelton, John, *The Bibliotheca Historica of Diodorus Siculus*, ed. F. M. Salter and H. L. R. Edwards, EETS os 233, 239, 2 vols. (London: Oxford University Press, 1956–7).

Skelton, John, *The Complete English Poems*, ed. V. J. Scattergood (New Haven, CT: Yale University Press, 1983).

'The Chronicle of John Somer, OFM', ed. Jeremy Catto and Linne Mooney, in *Camden Miscellany XXXIV: Chronology, Conquest and Conflict in Medieval England*, Camden Society 5th series, 10 (Cambridge: Cambridge University Press, 1997), 197–285.

Stevenson, Joseph (ed.), *Letters and Papers Illustrative of the Wars of the English in France during the Reign of Henry the Sixth*, RS, 22, 2 vols. (London: HMSO, 1861–4).

'The Chronicle of John Strecche for the Reign of Henry V (1414–22)', ed. F. Taylor, *BJRL*, 16 (1932), 137–87.

Tait, James (ed.), 'Letters of John Tiptoft, Earl of Worcester, and Archbishop Neville to the University of Oxford', *EHR*, 35 (1920), 570–74.

Taylor, Frank, and Roskell, John S. (ed. and trans.), *Gesta Henrici Quinti* (Oxford: Clarendon Press, 1975).

Terence, *Comedies*, ed. and trans. John Barsby (Cambridge, MA: Harvard University Press, 2001).

Tiptoft, John (trans.), *The Declamacion of Noblesse*, reprinted in R. J. Mitchell, *John Tiptoft (1427–1470)* (London: Methuen, 1938), 215–41.

Traversagni, Lorenzo Guglielmo, *Margarita eloquentiae castigatae*, ed. Giovanni Farris (Savona: Sabatelli, 1978).

'The *Epitoma Margarite Castigate Eloquentie* of Laurentius Gulielmus Traversagni de Saona', ed. and trans. Ronald H. Martin, *Proceedings of the Leeds Philosophical and Literary Society*, 20 (1986), 131–269.

The Governance of Kings and Princes: John Trevisa's Middle English Translation of the De regimine principum *of Aegidius Romanus*, ed. David C. Fowler, Charles F. Briggs, and Paul G. Remley (New York, NY: Garland, 1997).

Vegetius, *Epitoma rei militaris*, ed. M. D. Reeve (Oxford: Clarendon Press, 2004).

Virgil, *Eclogues, Georgics, Aeneid I-VI*, trans. H. Rushton Fairclough (Cambridge, MA: Harvard University Press, 1974).

The Commentary of Geoffrey of Vitry on Claudian 'De Raptu Proserpinae', ed. A. K. Clarke and P. M. Giles, Mittellateinische Studien und Texte, 7 (Leiden: Brill, 1973).

John of Wales, *Breuiloquium de uirtutibus antiquorum principum et philosophorum*, in *Summa Johannis Ualensis de regimine vite humane seu Margarita doctorum ad omne propositum prout patet in tabula*, ed. Johannes Ualentis (Lyons, 1511), ff.cci^v-ccxvii^r.

——— *Communiloquium*, in *Summa Johannis Ualensis de regimine vite humane seu Margarita doctorum ad omne propositum prout patet in tabula*, ed. Johannes Ualentis (Lyons, 1511), ff.i^r-cxxxix^v.

[Walsingham, Thomas], *The St. Albans Chronicle 1406–1420*, ed. V. H. Galbraith (Oxford: Clarendon Press, 1937).

Walton, John (trans.), *Boethius: De Consolatione Philosophiae*, ed. Mark Science, EETS os 170 (London: Oxford University Press, 1927).

[Warkworth, John], *A Chronicle of the First Thirteen Years of the Reign of King Edward the Fourth*, ed. James Orchard Halliwell, Camden Society, o.s. 10 (London: Camden Society, 1839)

'*Warkworth's' Chronicle*, in Lister M. Matheson (ed.), *Death and Dissent: Two Fifteenth-Century Chronicles* (Woodbridge: Boydell, 1999), 61–124.

Registrum Abbatiæ Johannis Whethamstede, ed. Henry Thomas Riley, RS, 28, 2 vols. (London: HMSO, 1872–3).

Williams, George (ed.), *Official Correspondence of Thomas Bekynton*, RS, 56, 2 vols. (London: Longman and Trübner, 1872).

Wilson, Edward, and Fenlon, Iain (eds.), *The Winchester Anthology* (Cambridge: Brewer, 1981).

[Worcester, William], *The Boke of Noblesse*, ed. John Gough Nichols (London: Nichols, 1860).

_____ [(trans.)], *Caxton: Tulle of Olde Age*, ed. Heinz Susebach, Studien zur Englischen Philologie, 75 (Halle: Niemeyer, 1933).

Worcestre [*sic*], William, *Itineraries*, ed. John H. Harvey (Oxford: Clarendon Press, 1969).

_____ *The Topography of Medieval Bristol*, ed. Frances Neale, Bristol Record Society's Publications, 51 (Bristol: Bristol Record Society, 2000).

Wyatt, Thomas (trans.), *The quyete of mynde* (London: Pynson, 1528; *STC* 20058.5).

Unpublished Secondary Works

Rundle, David, 'Of Republics and Tyrants: Aspects of *quattrocento* Humanist Writings and their Reception in England, *c*.1400–*c*.1460' (unpublished D.Phil. thesis, University of Oxford, 1997).

Smith, Anthony Robert, 'Aspects of the Career of Sir John Fastolf (1380–1459)' (unpublished D.Phil. thesis, University of Oxford, 1982).

Databases

Chadwick-Healey, *English Poetry, Second Edition*; <http://collections.chadwyck.co.uk/home/home_ep2.jsp>.

Kurath, Hans, and others (eds.), *The Middle English Dictionary* (Ann Arbor, MI: University of Michigan Press, 1952–2001); <http://ets.umdl.umich.edu/m/med/>.

Matthew, H. C. G., and others (eds.), *The Oxford Dictionary of National Biography*, (Oxford: Oxford University Press, 2004); <http://www.oxforddnb.com/subscribed/>.

Murray, James A. H., and others (eds.), *The Oxford English Dictionary*, ed. John A. Simpson and E. S. C. Weiner, 2nd edn., 20 vols. (Oxford: Clarendon Press, 1989); <http://dictionary.oed.com/entrance.dtl>.

Secondary Works

Adamson, Sylvia, 'Literary Language', in *The Cambridge History of the English Language: Volume III. 1476–1776*, ed. Roger Lass (Cambridge: Cambridge University Press, 1999), 539–653.

Alford, John, "'My Name is Worship": Masquerading Vice in Medwall's *Nature*', in *From Page to Performance: Essays in Early English Drama*, ed. John A. Alford (East Lansing, MI: Michigan State University, 1995), 151–77.

Allmand, C. T., *Lancastrian Normandy 1415–1450: The History of a Mediaeval Occupation* (Oxford: Clarendon Press, 1983).

Allmand, Christopher, 'France-Angleterre à la Fin de la Guerre de Cent Ans: Le 'Boke of Noblesse' de William Worcester', in *La 'France Anglaise' au Moyen Âge* (Paris: CTHS, 1988), 103–11.

_____ 'The *De re militari* of Vegetius in the Middle Ages and the Renaissance', in *Writing War: Medieval Literary Responses to Warfare*, ed. Corinne Saunders, Françoise Le Saux, and Neil Thomas (Cambridge: Brewer, 2004), 15–28.

_____ and Keen, Maurice, 'History and the Literature of War: The *Boke of Noblesse* of William Worcester', in *War, Government and Power in Late Medieval France*, ed. Christopher Allmand (Liverpool: Liverpool University Press, 2000), 92–105.

Altman, Joel B., *The Tudor Play of Mind: Rhetorical Inquiry and the Development of Elizabethan Drama* (Berkeley, CA: University of California Press, 1978).

Anderson, Benedict, *Imagined Communities: Reflections on the Origins and Spread of Nationalism*, rev. edn. (1983; London: Verso, 1991).

Avesani, Rino, 'La professione dell'"umanista" nel Cinquecento', *Italia medioevale e umanistica*, 13 (1970), 205–32.

Baldwin, T. W., *William Shakspere's Small Latine & Lesse Greeke*, 2 vols. (Urbana, IL: University of Illinois Press, 1944).

Balsamo, Luigi, 'The Origins of Printing in Italy and England', in *Journal of the Printing Historical Society*, 11 (1976: special issue *Eight Papers Presented to the Caxton International Congress*), 48–63.

Barker, Nicolas, 'St Albans Press: The First Punch-cutter in England and the First Native Typefounder?', *TCBS*, 7 (1979), 257–78.

Baron, Hans, *The Crisis of the Early Italian Renaissance: Civic Humanism and Republican Liberty in an Age of Classicism and Tyranny*, 2 vols. (Princeton, NJ: Princeton University Press, 1955).

Baswell, Christopher, 'Aeneas in 1381', *NML*, 5 (2002), 7–58.

Beadle, Richard, 'Sir John Fastolf's French Books', in *Medieval Texts in Manuscript Context*, ed. Graham Caie and D. Reveney (London: Longmans, 2007), 163–89.

_____ and Hellinga, Lotte, 'William Paston II and Pynson's *Statutes of War* (1492)', *The Library*, 7th series, 2 (2001), 107–19.

Billanovich, Giuseppe, 'Auctorista, humanista, orator', *Rivista di cultura classica e medioevale*, 7 (1965), 143–63.

Black, Robert, *Humanism and Education in Medieval and Renaissance Italy: Tradition and Innovation in Latin Schools from the Twelfth to the Fifteenth Century* (Cambridge: Cambridge University Press, 2001).

Blackwell, Constance, 'Niccolò Perotti in England, 1: John Anwykyll, Bernard André, John Colet and Luis Vives', *Studi umanistici Piceni*, 2 (1982), 13–28.

Blake, N. F., *Caxton and his World* (London: Deutsch, 1969).

_____ *William Caxton: A Bibliographical Guide* (New York, NY: Garland, 1985).

_____ *William Caxton and English Literary Culture* (London: Hambledon, 1991).

Blayney, Peter W. M., *The Stationers' Company before the Charter, 1403–1557* (London: Worshipful Company of Stationers and Newspaper Makers, 2003).

Blodgett, James E., 'Some Printer's Copy for William Thynne's 1532 Edition of Chaucer', *The Library*, 6th series, 1 (1979), 97–113.

Blythe, James M., '"Civic Humanism" and Medieval Political Thought', in *Renaissance Civic Humanism: Reappraisals and Reflections*, ed. James Hankins (Cambridge: Cambridge University Press, 2000), 30–74.

Bourdieu, Pierre, and Passeron, Jean-Claude, *Reproduction in Education, Society and Culture*, trans. Richard Nice, 2nd edn. (1970; London: Sage, 1990).

Bozzolo, Carla, 'La lecture des classiques par un humaniste français Laurent de Premierfait', in *L'Aube de la Renaissance*, ed. D. Cecchetti, L. Sozzi, and L. Terreaux (Genève: Slatkine, 1991), 67–81.

Brayman Hackel, Heidi, *Reading Material in Early Modern England: Print, Gender, Literacy* (Cambridge: Cambridge University Press, 2005).

Brie, Friedrich, 'Mittelalter und Antike bei Lydgate', *Englische Studien*, 64 (1929), 261–301.

Briggs, Charles F., *Giles of Rome's* De regimine principum: *Reading and Writing Politics at Court and University, c.1275-c.1525* (Cambridge: Cambridge University Press, 1999).

Brodie, Alexander H., 'Anwykyll's *Vulgaria*: A Pre-Erasmian Textbook', *Neuphilologische Mitteilungen*, 75 (1974), 416–27.

Brunner, Karl, 'Continuity and Discontinuity of Roman Agricultural Knowledge in the Early Middle Ages', in *Agriculture in the Middle Ages: Technology, Practice, and Representation*, ed. Del Sweeney (Philadelphia, PA: University of Pennsylvania Press, 1995), 21–40.

Brusendorff, Aage, *The Chaucer Tradition* (Copenhagen: Pio-Branner, 1925).

Bühler, Curt F., 'A Middle-English Stanza on "The Commonwealth and the Need for Wisdom"', *English Language Notes*, 2 (1964), 4–5.

Bushnell, Rebecca W., *A Culture of Teaching: Early Modern Humanism in Theory and Practice* (Ithaca, NY: Cornell University Press, 1996).

Campana, Augusto, 'The Origin of the Word "Humanist"', *Journal of the Warburg and Courtauld Institutes*, 9 (1946), 60–73.

Carlson, David, 'The Occasional Poetry of Pietro Carmeliano', *Aevum*, 61 (1987), 495–502.

_____ 'King Arthur and Court Poems for the Birth of Arthur Tudor in 1486', *HL*, 36 (1987), 147–83.

_____ *English Humanist Books: Writers and Patrons, Manuscript and Print, 1475–1525* (Toronto: University of Toronto Press, 1993).

_____ 'Three Tudor Epigrams', *HL*, 45 (1996), 189–200.

_____ 'The Civic Poetry of Abbot John Whethamstede of St. Albans († 1465)', *Mediaeval Studies*, 61 (1999), 205–42.

Carlson, David, 'A Theory of the Early English Printing Firm: Jobbing, Book Publishing, and the Problem of Productive Capacity in Caxton's Work', in William Kuskin, (ed.), *Caxton's Trace: Studies in the History of English Printing* (Notre Dame, IN: University of Notre Dame Press, 2006), 35–68.

Carpenter, Christine, *The Wars of the Roses: Politics and the Constitution in England, c.1437–1509* (Cambridge: Cambridge University Press, 1997).

Carroll, Clare, 'Humanism and English Literature in the Fifteenth and Sixteenth Centuries', in *The Cambridge Companion to Renaissance Humanism*, ed. Jill Kraye (Cambridge: Cambridge University Press, 1996), 246–68.

Carus-Wilson, E. M., 'Evidences of Industrial Growth on Some Fifteenth-Century Manors', *Economic History Review*, 2nd series, 12 (1959–60), 190–205.

Castor, Helen, *The King, the Crown and the Duchy of Lancaster: Public Authority and Private Power, 1399–1461* (Oxford: Oxford University Press, 2000).

de Certeau, Michel, *The Practice of Everyday Life*, trans. Steven Rendall (Berkeley, CA: University of California Press, 1984).

Clarke, M. L., *Rhetoric at Rome: A Historical Survey*, 3rd edn., rev. D. H. Berry (1953; London: Routledge, 1996).

Clough, Cecil H., 'Thomas Linacre, Cornelio Vitelli, and Humanistic Studies at Oxford', in *Essays on the Life and Work of Thomas Linacre c.1460–1524*, ed. Francis Maddison, Margaret Pelling, and Charles Webster (Oxford: Clarendon Press, 1977), 1–23.

Copeland, Rita, *Rhetoric, Hermeneutics, and Translation in the Middle Ages: Academic Traditions and Vernacular Texts* (Cambridge: Cambridge University Press, 1991).

——— *Pedagogy, Intellectuals and Dissent in the Later Middle Ages: Lollardy and Ideas of Learning* (Cambridge: Cambridge University Press, 2001).

——— 'Lydgate, Hawes and the Science of Rhetoric in the Late Middle Ages', in *John Lydgate: Poetry, Culture, and Lancastrian England*, ed. Larry Scanlon and James Simpson (Notre Dame, IN: University of Notre Dame Press, 2006), 232–58.

Corsten, Severin, 'Caxton in Cologne', *Journal of the Printing Historical Society*, 11 (1976–7: special issue *Eight Papers Presented to the Caxton International Congress*), 1–18.

Cowen, Janet, 'An English Reading of Boccaccio: A Selective Middle English Version of Boccaccio's *De Mulieribus claris* in British Library MS Additional 10304', in *New Perspectives on Middle English Texts: A Festschrift for R. A. Waldron*, ed. Susan Powell and Jeremy J. Smith (Cambridge: Brewer, 2000), 129–40.

Cummings, Brian, *The Literary Culture of the Reformation: Grammar and Grace* (Oxford: Oxford University Press, 2002).

Dane, Joseph A., 'A Note on American Fragments of Grammatical Texts from the Oxford Press of Theodoric Rood (STC 315 and 695)', *The Library*, 6th series, 20 (1998), 59–61.

Darnton, Robert, 'History of Reading', in *New Perspectives on Historical Writing*, ed. Peter Burke (Cambridge: Polity, 1991), 140–67.

Davis, Virginia, *William Waynflete, Bishop and Educationalist* (Woodbridge: Boydell, 1993).

de la Mare, A. C., 'Duke Humfrey's English Palladius (MS. Duke Humfrey d.2)', *BLR*, 12 (1985), 39–51.

____ 'Manuscripts Given to the University of Oxford by Humfrey, Duke of Gloucester', *BLR*, 13 (1988–9), 30–51, 112–21.

____ and Gillam, Stanley], *Duke Humfrey's Library and the Divinity School 1488–1988* (Oxford: Bodleian Library, 1988).

____ and Hellinga, Lotte, 'The First Book Printed in Oxford: The *Expositio Symboli* of Rufinus', *TCBS*, 7 (1978), 184–244.

____ and Hunt, Richard], *Duke Humfrey and English Humanism in the Fifteenth Century* (Oxford: Bodleian Library, 1970).

Delany, Sheila, *Impolitic Bodies: Poetry, Saints, and Society in Fifteenth-Century England* (Oxford: Oxford University Press, 1998).

de Ricci, Seymour, *A Census of Caxtons*, Bibliographical Society Illustrated Monographs, 15 (Oxford: Oxford University Press, 1909).

Dobson, Barrie, 'Henry VI and the University of Cambridge', in *The Lancastrian Court*, ed. Jenny Stratford, Harlaxton Medieval Studies, 13 (Donington: Tyas, 2003), 53–67.

Donaghey, Brian, 'Caxton's Printing of Chaucer's *Boece*', in *Chaucer in Perspective: Middle English Essays in Honour of Norman Blake*, ed. Geoffrey Lester (Sheffield: Sheffield Academic Press, 1999), 73–99.

____ Taavitsainen, Irma, and Miller, Erik, 'Walton's Boethius: From Manuscript to Print', *English Studies*, 80 (1999), 398–407.

Duff, E. Gordon, *Caxton's Tully of Old Age and Friendship 1481 now for the first time collated* ([n. p.]: Pearson, 1912).

Duncan, G. D., 'Public Lectures and Professorial Chairs', in *The History of the University of Oxford, III: The Collegiate University*, ed. James McConica (Oxford: Clarendon Press, 1986), 35–61.

Dwyer, R. A., 'The Newberry's Unknown Revision of Walton's Boethius', *Manuscripta*, 17 (1973), 27–30.

Edwards, A. S. G., 'The McGill Fragment of Lydgate's "Fall of Princes"', *Scriptorium*, 28 (1974), 75–7.

____ 'The Influence of Lydgate's *Fall of Princes c.*1440–1559: A Survey', *Mediaeval Studies*, 39 (1977), 424–39.

____ 'Lydgate Manuscripts: Some Directions for Future Research', in *Manuscripts and Readers in Fifteenth-Century England: The Literary Implications of Manuscript Study*, ed. Derek Pearsall (Cambridge: Brewer, 1983), 15–26.

____ 'The Transmission and Audience of Osbern Bokenham's *Legendys of Hooly Wummen*', in *Late-Medieval Religious Texts and their Transmission: Essays in Honour of A. I. Doyle*, ed. A. J. Minnis (Cambridge: Brewer, 1994), 157–67.

____ 'The Middle English Translation of Claudian's *De Consulatu Stilichonis*', in *Middle English Poetry: Texts and Traditions: Essays in Honour of Derek Pearsall*, ed. A. J. Minnis (York: York Medieval Press, 2001), 267–78.

____ 'Duke Humfrey's Middle English Palladius', in *The Lancastrian Court*, ed. Jenny Stratford, Harlaxton Medieval Studies, 13 (Donington: Tyas, 2003), 68–77.

230   *Works Cited*

Eisenstein, Elizabeth L., *The Printing Press as an Agent of Change: Communications and Cultural Transformations in Early Modern Europe*, 2 vols. (Cambridge: Cambridge University Press, 1979).

Elton, G. R., 'A New Age of Reform?', *Historical Journal*, 30 (1987), 709–16.

Emden, A. B., *A Biographical Register of the University of Oxford to A.D. 1500*, 3 vols. (Oxford: Clarendon Press, 1957–9).

_____ *A Biographical Register of the University of Cambridge to 1500* (Cambridge: Cambridge University Press, 1963).

Farris, Giovanni, *Umanesimo e religione in Lorenzo Guglielmo Traversagni (1425–1505)* (Milan: Mazorati, 1972).

Ferdinand, Christine, 'Magdalen College and the Book Trade: The Provision of Books in Oxford, 1450–1550', in *The Book Trade and its Customers 1450–1900: Historical Essays for Robin Myers*, ed. Arnold Hunt, Giles Mandelbrote, and Alison Shell (Winchester: St Paul's Bibliographies, 1997), 175–87.

Ferguson, Wallace K., *The Renaissance in Historical Thought: Five Centuries of Interpretation* (Boston, MA: Houghton Mifflin, 1948).

Fish, Stanley, *Is There a Text in This Class? The Authority of Interpretive Communities* (Cambridge, MA: Harvard University Press, 1980).

Fitch Lytle, Guy, '"Wykehamist Culture" in Pre-Reformation England', in *Winchester College: Sixth-Centenary Essays*, ed. Roger Custance (Oxford: Oxford University Press, 1982), 129–66.

Fletcher, J. M., 'The Faculty of Arts', in *The History of the University of Oxford, III: The Collegiate University*, ed. James McConica (Oxford: Clarendon Press, 1986), 157–99.

Foucault, Michel, *The Archaeology of Knowledge*, trans. A. M. Sheridan Smith (1969; London: Tavistock, 1972).

Fox, Alistair, and Guy, John, *Reassessing the Henrician Age: Humanism, Politics and Reform 1500–1550* (Oxford: Blackwell, 1986).

Gaita, Raymond, *A Common Humanity: Thinking about Love and Truth and Justice* (1998; London: Routledge, 2002).

Gathercole, Patricia M., 'Lydgate's "Fall of Princes" and the French Version of Boccaccio's "De Casibus"', in *Miscellanea di Studi e Ricerche sul Quattrocento Francese*, ed. Franco Simone (Turin: Giappichelli, 1967), 167–78.

Genêt, Jean-Philippe, 'New Politics or New Language? The Words of Politics in Yorkist and Early Tudor England', in *The End of the Middle Ages? England in the Fifteenth and Sixteenth Centuries*, ed. John L. Watts, Fifteenth Century Series, 6 (Stroud: Sutton, 1998), 23–64.

Gillespie, Alexandra, 'Framing Lydgate's *Fall of Princes*: The Evidence of Book History', *Mediaevalia*, 20 (2001), 153–78.

_____ *Print Culture and the Medieval Author: Chaucer, Lydgate, and their Books 1473–1557* (Oxford: Oxford University Press, 2006).

Giustiniani, Vito R., 'Homo, Humanus, and the meanings of "Humanism"', *Journal of the History of Ideas*, 46 (1985), 167–95.

Goldschmidt, E. Ph., *Medieval Texts and their First Appearance in Print* (1943; New York: Biblo and Tannen, 1969).

Goodman, Anthony, and Morgan, David, 'The Yorkist Claim to the Throne of Castile', *JMH*, 11 (1985), 61–9.

Grafton, Anthony, and Jardine, Lisa, *From Humanism to the Humanities: Education and the Liberal Arts in Fifteenth- and Sixteenth-Century Europe* (London: Duckworth, 1986).

——— ' "Studied for Action": How Gabriel Harvey Read his Livy', *Past and Present*, 129 (1990), 30–78.

Gray, Douglas, 'Some Pre-Elizabethan Examples of an Elizabethan Art', in *England and the Continental Renaissance: Essays in Honour of J. B. Trapp*, ed. Edward Chaney and Peter Mack (Woodbridge: Boydell, 1990), 23–36.

——— 'Humanism and Humanisms in the Literature of Late Medieval England', in *Italy and the English Renaissance*, ed. Sergio Rossi and Dianella Savoia (Milan: Unicopli, 1989), 25–44.

Greene, Thomas M., *The Light in Troy: Imitation and Discovery in Renaissance Poetry* (New Haven, CT: Yale University Press, 1982).

Grendler, Paul F., *The Universities of the Italian Renaissance* (Baltimore, MD: Johns Hopkins University Press, 2002).

Griffin, Miriam, 'From Aristotle to Atticus: Cicero and Matius on Friendship', in *Philosophia Togata II: Plato and Aristotle at Rome*, ed. Jonathan Barnes and Miriam Griffin (Oxford: Clarendon Press, 1997), 86–109.

Griffiths, R. A., 'The Trial of Eleanor Cobham: An Episode in the Fall of Duke Humfrey of Gloucester', *BJRL*, 51 (1969), 381–99.

——— *The Reign of King Henry VI: The Exercise of Royal Authority, 1422–1461* (London: Benn, 1981).

Gross, Anthony, *The Dissolution of the Lancastrian Kingship: Sir John Fortescue and the Crisis of Monarchy in Fifteenth-Century England* (Stamford: Watkins, 1996).

Hall, J. B., *Prolegomena to Claudian*, Bulletin of the Institute of Classical Studies: Supplement, 45 (London: Institute of Classical Studies, 1986).

Halpern, Richard, *The Poetics of Primitive Accumulation: English Renaissance Culture and the Genealogy of Capital* (Ithaca, NY: Cornell University Press, 1991).

Hammond, Eleanor Prescott, 'Poet and Patron in the *Fall of Princes*: Lydgate and Humphrey of Gloucester', *Anglia*, 38 (1914), 121–36.

——— 'The Nine-Syllabled Pentameter Line in Some Post-Chaucerian Manuscripts', *MP*, 23 (1925), 129–52.

——— 'Lydgate and Coluccio Salutati', *MP*, 25 (1927), 49–57.

Hankins, James, *Plato in the Italian Renaissance*, Columbia Studies in the Classical Tradition, 17, 2 vols. (Leiden: Brill, 1990).

Harper-Bill, Christopher, 'The *Familia*, Administrators and Patronage of Archbishop John Morton', *Studies in Religious History*, 10 (1979), 236–52.

Harriss, G. L., 'The Struggle for Calais: An Aspect of the Rivalry between Lancaster and York', *EHR*, 75 (1960), 30–53.

Harvey, I. M. W., *Jack Cade's Rebellion of 1450* (Oxford: Clarendon Press, 1991).

Harvey, Margaret, *England, Rome and the Papacy 1417–1464: The Study of a Relation-ship* (Manchester: Manchester University Press, 1993).

Hay, Denys, 'The Early Renaissance in England' (1965), in his *Renaissance Essays* (London: Hambledon, 1988), 151–67.

—— 'England and the Humanities in the Fifteenth Century' (1975), in his *Renaissance Essays* (London: Hambledon, 1988), 169–231.

Hellinga, Lotte, 'Importation of Books Printed on the Continent into England and Scotland before *c*.1520', in *Printing and the Written Word: The Social History of Books, circa 1450–1520*, ed. Sandra Hindman (Ithaca, NY: Cornell University Press, 1991), 205–24.

—— and Trapp, J. B. (ed.), *The Cambridge History of the Book in Britain. Volume III: 1400–1557* (Cambridge: Cambridge University Press, 1999).

Hicks, Michael, 'From Megaphone to Microscope: The Correspondence of Richard Duke of York with Henry VI in 1450 Revisited', *JMH*, 25 (1999), 243–56.

Hilles, Carroll, 'Gender and Politics in Osbern Bokenham's Legendary', *NML*, 4 (2001), 189–212.

Hogrefe, Pearl, *The Life and Times of Sir Thomas Elyot Englishman* (Ames: Iowa State University Press, 1967).

Horner, Olga, '*Fulgens and Lucres*: An Historical Perspective', *Medieval English Theatre*, 15 (1993), 49–86.

Horobin, Simon, 'The Angle of Oblivioun: A Lost Medieval Manuscript Discovered in Walter Scott's Collection', *Times Literary Supplement*, 11 November 2005, 12–13.

Howlett, D. R., 'The Date and Authorship of the Middle English Verse Translation of Palladius' *De Re Rustica*', *Medium Ævum*, 46 (1977), 245–52.

Hughes, Jonathan, 'Stephen Scrope and the Circle of Sir John Fastolf: Moral and Intellectual Outlooks', in *Medieval Knighthood IV*, ed. Christopher Harper-Bill and Ruth Harvey (Woodbridge: Boydell, 1992), 109–46.

Hutson, Lorna, *The Usurer's Daughter: Male Friendship and Fictions of Women in Sixteenth-Century England* (London: Routledge, 1994).

Jacob, E. F., 'Two Lives of Archbishop Chichele', *BJRL*, 16 (1932), 428–81.

James, M. R., *The Chaundler MSS.* (London: Nichols, 1916).

Jardine, Lisa, *Erasmus, Man of Letters: The Construction of Charisma in Print* (Princeton, NJ: Princeton University Press, 1993).

—— and Sherman, William, 'Pragmatic Readers: Knowledge Transactions and Schol-arly Services in Late Elizabethan England', in *Religion, Culture and Society in Early Modern Britain: Essays in Honour of Patrick Collinson*, ed. Anthony Fletcher and Peter Roberts (Cambridge: Cambridge University Press, 1994), 102–24.

Jed, Stephanie H., *Chaste Thinking: The Rape of Lucretia and the Birth of Humanism* (Bloomington, IN: Indiana University Press, 1989).

Jensen, Kristian, 'Text-books in the Universities: The Evidence from the Books', in *CHBB: III*, 354–79.

Jocelyn, Henry David, 'The Two Comedies of Tito Livio de' Frulovisi Allegedly Written in England', *Studi umanistici Piceni*, 12 (1992), 135–42.

Johns, Adrian, *The Nature of the Book: Print and Knowledge in the Making* (Chicago: University of Chicago Press, 1998).

Johnson, P. A., *Duke Richard of York 1411–60* (Oxford: Clarendon Press, 1988).

Jones, Howard, *Master Tully: Cicero in Tudor England*, Bibliotheca Humanistica et Reformatoria, 58 (Nieuwkoop: De Graaf, 1998).

Jones, Michael, 'John Beaufort, Duke of Somerset and the French Expedition of 1443', in *Patronage, The Crown and The Provinces In Later Medieval England*, ed. Ralph A. Griffiths (Gloucester: Sutton, 1981), 79–102.

⎯⎯ 'The Battle of Verneuil (17 August 1424): Towards a History of Courage', *War in History*, 9 (2002), 375–411.

Jones, Michael K., 'Somerset, York and the Wars of the Roses', *EHR*, 104 (1989), 285–307.

⎯⎯ and Underwood, Malcolm, *The King's Mother: Lady Margaret Beaufort, Countess of Richmond and Derby* (Cambridge: Cambridge University Press, 1992).

Jongkees, A. G., 'Translatio studii: les avatars d'un thème médiéval', in *Miscellanea Mediaevalia in memoriam Jan Frederik Niermeyer*, ed. D. P. Blok and others (Groningen: Wolters, 1967), 41–51.

Kahn, Victoria, 'Humanism and the Resistance to Theory', in *Literary Theory/Renaissance Texts*, ed. Patricia Parker and David Quint (Baltimore, MD: Johns Hopkins University Press, 1986), 373–96.

Kekewich, Margaret, 'The Attainder of the Yorkists in 1459: Two Contemporary Accounts', *Bulletin of the Institute of Historical Research*, 55 (1982), 25–34.

Kempshall, M. S., *The Common Good in Late Medieval Political Thought* (Oxford: Clarendon Press, 1999).

⎯⎯ 'De Re Publica I.39 in Medieval and Renaissance Political Thought', in *Cicero's Republic*, ed. J. G. F. Powell and J. A. North, Bulletin of the Institute of Classical Studies: Supplement, 76 (London: Institute of Classical Studies, 2001), 99–135.

Kintgen, Eugene R., *Reading in Tudor England* (Pittsburgh, PA: University of Pittsburgh Press, 1996).

Koeppel, Emil, *Laurents de Premierfait und John Lydgates Bearbeitungen von Boccaccios De Casibus Virorum Illustrium: Ein Beitrag zur Litteraturgeschichte des 15. Jahrhunderts* (Munich: Oldenbourg, 1885).

Kohl, Benjamin G., 'The Changing Concept of the *studia humanitatis* in the Early Renaissance', *Renaissance Studies*, 6 (1992), 185–209.

Kristeller, Paul Oskar, 'Humanism', in *The Cambridge History of Renaissance Philosophy*, ed. Charles B. Schmitt and others (Cambridge: Cambridge University Press, 1988), 113–37.

⎯⎯ 'Humanism and Scholasticism in the Italian Renaissance', *Byzantion*, 17 (1944–5), 346–74.

Kuskin, William, 'Caxton's Worthies Series: The Production of Literary Culture', *English Literary History*, 66 (1999), 511–51.

⎯⎯ ' "Onely imagined": Vernacular Community and the English Press', in William Kuskin (ed.), *Caxton's Trace: Studies in the History of English Printing* (Notre Dame, IN: University of Notre Dame Press, 2006), 199–240.

Lancashire, Ian, *Dramatic Texts and Records of Britain: A Chronological Topography to 1558* (Toronto: University of Toronto Press, 1984).

Lane Ford, Margaret, 'Importation of Printed Books into England and Scotland', in *CHBB: III*, 179–201.

Latham, R. E., *Revised Medieval Latin Word-List from British and Irish Sources* (London: British Academy, 1965).

Lathrop, H. B., 'The Translations of John Tiptoft', *Modern Language Notes*, 41 (1926), 496–501.

Latour, Bruno, *We Have Never Been Modern*, trans. Catherine Porter (1991; Hemel Hempstead: Harvester Wheatsheaf, 1993).

Leader, D. Riehl, 'John Argentein and Learning in Medieval Cambridge', *HL*, 33 (1984), 71–85.

Lehmberg, Stanford E., *Sir Thomas Elyot: Tudor Humanist* (Austin: University of Texas Press, 1960).

Lerer, Seth, *Chaucer and his Readers: Imagining the Author in Late-Medieval England* (Princeton, NJ: Princeton University Press, 1993).

—— 'William Caxton', in *The Cambridge History of Medieval English Literature*, ed. David Wallace (Cambridge: Cambridge University Press, 1999), 720–38.

Lester, G. A., *Sir John Paston's 'Grete Boke'* (Cambridge: Brewer, 1984).

Lewis, Lucy, 'A Newly Discovered Lyric from Exeter College, Oxford on the Theme of 'know thyself', *Medium Ævum*, 75 (2006), 123–7.

Lewis, P. S., 'Sir John Fastolf's Lawsuit over Titchwell 1448–55', *Historical Journal*, 1 (1958), 1–20 (12–16).

Liddell, J. R., 'The Library of Corpus Christi College, Oxford, in the Sixteenth Century', *The Library*, 4th series, 18 (1937–8), 385–416.

Lowry, Martin, 'Diplomacy and the Spread of Printing', in *Bibliography and the Study of 15th-Century Civilisation*, ed. Lotte Hellinga and John Goldfinch, British Library Occasional Papers, 5 (London: British Library, 1987), 124–46.

—— 'The Arrival and Use of Continental Printed Books in Yorkist England', in *Le Livre dans l'Europe de la Renaissance*, ed. Pierre Aquilon and Henri-Jean Martin (Paris: Promodis, 1988), 449–59.

McConica, James, 'The Rise of the Undergraduate College', in *The History of the University of Oxford: Volume III. The Collegiate University*, ed. James McConica (Oxford: Clarendon Press, 1986), 1–68.

McFarlane, K. B., 'The Investment of Sir John Fastolf's Profits of War', in his *England in the Fifteenth Century: Collected Essays*, ed. G. L. Harriss (London: Hambledon, 1981), 175–97.

—— 'William Worcester: A Preliminary Survey', printed in his *England in the Fifteenth Century: Collected Essays*, ed. G. L. Harriss (London: Hambledon, 1981), 199–224.

Machan, Tim William, 'Scribal Role, Authorial Intention, and Chaucer's *Boece*', *Chaucer Review*, 24 (1989), 150–62.

—— 'Glosses in the Manuscripts of Chaucer's *Boece*', in *The Medieval Boethius: Studies in the Vernacular Translations of* De Consolatione Philosophiae, ed. A. J. Minnis (Cambridge: Brewer, 1987), 125–38.

Mack, Peter, 'Rhetoric, Ethics and Reading in the Renaissance', *Renaissance Studies*, 19 (2005), 1–21.

Mackenzie, W. Roy, 'A Source for Medwall's *Nature*', *PMLA*, 29 (1914), 189–99.

McKitterick, David, *Print, Manuscript and the Search for Order* (Cambridge: Cambridge University Press, 2003).

MacLean, Sally-Beth, and Nelson, Alan H., 'New Light on Henry Medwall', *Leeds Studies in English*, 28 (1997), 77–98.

Major, John M., *Sir Thomas Elyot and Renaissance Humanism* (Lincoln, NE: University of Nebraska Press, 1964).

Marsh, David, *The Quattrocento Dialogue: Classical Tradition and Humanist Tradition* (Cambridge, MA: Harvard University Press, 1980).

Marston, Thomas E., 'A Book Owned by Giovanni Gigli', *Yale University Library Gazette*, 34 (1959), 49.

Martin, Henri-Jean, and Vezin, Jean (eds.), *Mise en page et mise en texte du livre manuscrit* ([Paris]: Éditions du Cercle de la Librairie—Promodis, 1990).

Maurer, Helen, *Margaret of Anjou: Queenship and Power in Late Medieval England* (Woodbridge: Boydell, 2003).

Meyenberg, Regula, *Alain Chartier Prosateur et l'Art de la Parole au XVe Siècle: Études Littéraires et Rhétoriques* (Bern: Francke, 1992).

Minnis, A. J., 'From Medieval to Renaissance? Chaucer's Position on Past Gentility', *Proceedings of the British Academy*, 72 (1986), 205–46.

——— 'Chaucer's Commentator: Nicholas Trevet and the *Boece*', in *Chaucer's* Boece *and the Medieval Tradition of Boethius*, ed. A. J. Minnis (Cambridge: Brewer, 1993), 83–166.

——— and Machan, Tim William, 'The *Boece* as Late-Medieval Translation', in *Chaucer's* Boece *and the Medieval Tradition of Boethius*, ed. A. J. Minnis (Cambridge: Brewer, 1993), 167–88.

Mitchell, R. J., *John Tiptoft (1427–1470)* (London: Methuen, 1938).

——— *John Free: From Bristol to Rome in the Fifteenth Century* (London: Longmans, Green, 1955).

——— 'Italian "nobiltà" and the English Idea of the Gentleman in the XV Century', *English Miscellany*, 9 (1958), 23–37.

Modigliani, Anna, 'Un nuovo manoscritto di Pietro Carmeliano: Le "epistolae" dello Pseudo-Falaride nella Trinity College Library in Dublin', *HL*, 33 (1984), 86–102.

Mombello, Gianni, 'Notizia su due manoscritti contenenti "l'Epistre Othea" di Christine de Pizan ed altre opere non identificate', *Studi francesi*, 31 (1967), 1–23.

Morgan, David, 'The Household Retinue of Henry V and the Ethos of English Public Life', in *Concepts and Patterns of Service in the Later Middle Ages*, ed. Anne Curry and Elizabeth Matthew (Woodbridge: Boydell, 2000), 64–79.

Mortimer, Nigel, *John Lydgate's* Fall of Princes: *Narrative Tragedy in its Literary and Political Contexts* (Oxford: Clarendon Press, 2005).

Murphy, James J., 'Caxton's Two Choices: "Modern" and "Medieval" Rhetoric in Traversagni's *Nova rhetorica* and the Anonymous *Court of Sapience*', *Medievalia et Humanistica*, 3 (1972), 241–55.

Murray, Alexander, *Suicide in the Middle Ages*, 2- vols. (Oxford: Clarendon Press, 1998–2000).

Mynors, R. A. B., *Catalogue of the Manuscripts of Balliol College* (Oxford: Clarendon Press, 1963).

Najemy, John, 'Civic Humanism and Florentine Politics', in *Renaissance Civic Humanism: Reappraisals and Reflections*, ed. James Hankins (Cambridge: Cambridge University Press, 2000), 75–104.

Nelson, Alan H., 'Life Records of Henry Medwall, M.A., Notary Public and Playwright; and John Medwall, Legal Administrator', *Leeds Studies in English*, 11 (1980), 111–55.

Nève, Joseph, *Catonis Disticha: Facsimilés, Notes, Liste des éditions du XVe siècle* (Liège: Vaillant-Carmanne, 1926).

Nolan, Maura, ' "Now Wo, Now Gladnesse": Ovidianism in the *Fall of Princes*', *ELH*, 71 (2004), 531–58.

Norland, Howard B., *Drama in Early Tudor Britain 1485–1558* (Lincoln, NE: University of Nebraska Press, 1995).

Oates, J. C. T., *A Catalogue of the Fifteenth-Century Printed Books in the University Library, Cambridge* (Cambridge: Cambridge University Press, 1954).

——— *Cambridge University Library: A History: From the Beginnings to the Copyright Act of Queen Anne* (Cambridge: Cambridge University Press, 1986).

Orme, Nicholas, *From Childhood to Chivalry: The Education of the English Kings and Aristocracy 1066–1530* (London: Methuen, 1984).

——— 'John Holt (d.1504), Tudor Schoolmaster and Grammarian', *The Library*, 6th series, 18 (1996), 283–305.

——— *Education in Early Tudor England: Magdalen College Oxford and its School 1480–1540*, Magdalen College Occasional Papers, 4 (Oxford: Magdalen College, 1998).

——— 'Schools and School-books', in *CHBB: III*, 449–69.

O'Sullivan, William, 'John Manyngham, an Early Oxford Humanist', *BLR*, 7 (1962–7), 28–39.

Pace, George B., and Voigts, Linda E., 'A "Boece" Fragment', *Studies in the Age of Chaucer*, 1 (1979), 143–50.

Patrides, C. A., 'Renaissance Ideas on Man's Upright Form', *Journal of the History of Ideas*, 19 (1958), 256–8.

Pearsall, Derek, *John Lydgate* (London: Routledge and Kegan Paul, 1970).

——— *Old English and Middle English Poetry* (London: Routledge Kegan Paul, 1977).

——— 'The Ellesmere Chaucer and Contemporary English Literary Manuscripts', in *The Ellesmere Chaucer: Essays in Interpretation*, ed. Daniel Woodward and Martin Stevens (San Marino, CA: Huntington Library, and Tokyo: Yushodo, 1995), 263–80.

——— *John Lydgate (1371–1449): A Bio-Bibliography*, English literary studies monograph series, 71 (Victoria, BC: University of Victoria, 1997).

——— 'The Organization of the Latin Apparatus in Gower's *Confessio Amantis*: The Scribes and their Problems', in *The Medieval Book and a Modern Collector: Essays in Honour of Toshiyuki Takamiya*, ed. Takami Matsuda, Richard A. Linenthal, and John Scahill (Cambridge: Brewer, 2004), 99–112.

Perkins, Nicholas, *Hoccleve's* The Regiment of Princes: *Counsel and Constraint* (Cambridge: Brewer, 2001).

Pernoud, Régine, *Pour en finir avec le Moyen Âge* (Paris: Seuil, 1977).

Petrina, Alessandra, *Cultural Politics in Fifteenth-Century England: The Case of Humphrey Duke of Gloucester* (Leiden: Brill, 2004).

Pollard, A. W., and Redgrave, G. R., *A Short Title Catalogue of Books Printed in England, Scotland, and Ireland, and of English Books Printed Abroad, 1475–1640*, ed. W. A. Jackson, F. S. Ferguson, and Katherine F. Pantzer, 2nd edn., 3 vols. (London: Bibliographical Society, 1976–91).

Pugh, T. B., 'Richard Plantagenet (1411–60), Duke of York, as the King's Lieutenant in France and Ireland', in *Aspects of Late Medieval Government and Society: Essays Presented to J. R. Lander*, ed. J. G. Rowe (Toronto: University of Toronto Press, 1986), 107–41.

Rees Jones, Sarah, 'Thomas More's "Utopia" and Medieval London', in *Pragmatic Utopias: Ideals and Communities, 1200–1630*, ed. Rosemary Horrox and Sarah Rees Jones (Cambridge: Cambridge University Press, 2001), 117–35.

Renoir, Alain, *The Poetry of John Lydgate* (London: Routledge and Kegan Paul, 1967).

Reynolds, Suzanne, *Medieval Reading: Grammar, Rhetoric and the Classical Text* (Cambridge: Cambridge University Press, 1996).

Rhodes, Dennis E., *John Argentine Provost of King's: His Life and his Library* (Amsterdam: Hertzberger, 1967).

Richards, Jennifer, *Rhetoric and Courtliness in Early Modern Literature* (Cambridge: Cambridge University Press, 2003).

Richmond, Colin, *The Paston Family in the Fifteenth Century: Fastolf's Will* (Cambridge: Cambridge University Press, 1996).

—— 'The Earl of Warwick's Domination of the Channel and the Naval Dimension to the Wars of the Roses, 1456–1460', *Southern History*, 20 (1999), 1–19.

Robinson, P. R., *Dated and Datable Manuscripts c.737–1600 in Cambridge Libraries*, 2 vols. (Cambridge: Brewer, 1988).

—— *Catalogue of Dated and Datable Manuscripts c.888–1600 in London Libraries* (London: British Library, 2003).

Rodgers, R. H., *An Introduction to Palladius*, Bulletin of the Institute of Classical Studies: Supplement, 35 (London: Institute of Classical Studies, 1975).

Rosenthal, Joel T., 'Richard, Duke of York: A Fifteenth-Century Layman and the Church', *Catholic Historical Review*, 50 (1964–5), 171–87.

—— 'The Universities and the Medieval English Nobility', *History of Education Quarterly*, 9 (1969), 415–37.

Roskell, J. S., 'Sir William Oldhall, Speaker in the Parliament of 1450–51', in his *Parliament and Politics in Late Medieval England*, 3 vols. (London: Hambledon, 1981–3), II.175–200.

Ross, Charles, *Edward IV*, 2nd edn. (London: Methuen, 1974).

Rossi, Sergio, *Ricerche sull'Umanesimo e sul Rinascimento in Inghilterra* (Milan: Vita e Pensiero, 1969).

Rouy, François, *L'Esthétique du traité moral d'après les œuvres d'Alain Chartier* (Genève: Droz, 1980).

Rowe, B. J. H., 'Discipline in the Norman Garrisons under Bedford, 1422–35', *EHR*, 46 (1931), 194–208.

Rummel, Erika, *The Humanist-Scholastic Debate in the Renaissance & Reformation*, Harvard Historical Studies, 120 (Cambridge, MA: Harvard University Press, 1995).

Rundle, David, 'On the Difference between Virtue and Weiss: Humanist Texts in England during the Fifteenth Century', in *Courts, Counties and the Capital in the Later Middle Ages*, ed. Diana E. S. Dunn, Fifteenth Century Series, 4 (Stroud: Sutton, 1996), 181–203.

—— 'Two Unnoticed Manuscripts from the Collection of Humfrey, Duke of Gloucester', *BLR*, 16 (1998), 211–24, 299–313.

—— 'Was There a Renaissance Style of Politics in Fifteenth-Century England?', in *Authority and Consent in Tudor England: Essays Presented to C. S. L. Davies*, ed. G. W. Bernard and S. J. Gunn (Aldershot: Ashgate, 2002), 15–32.

—— 'Humanism before the Tudors: On Nobility and the Reception of the *studia humanitatis* in Fifteenth-Century England', in *Reassessing Tudor Humanism*, ed. Jonathan Woolfson (Basingstoke: Palgrave Macmillan, 2002), 22–42.

—— 'Carneades' Legacy: The Morality of Eloquence in the Humanist and Papalist Writings of Pietro del Monte', *EHR*, 117 (2002), 284–305.

—— 'Tito Livio Frulovisi and the Place of Comedies in the Formation of a Humanist Career', *Studi Umanistici Piceni*, 24 (2004), 193–202.

—— 'Habits of Manuscript-Collecting: The Dispersals of the Library of Humfrey, Duke of Gloucester', in *Lost Libraries: The Destruction of Great Book Collections since Antiquity*, ed. James Raven (Basingstoke: Palgrave, 2004), 106–24.

Ruysschaert, José, 'Les manuscrits autographes de deux œuvres de Lorenzo Guglielmo Traversagni imprimées chez Caxton', *BJRL*, 36 (1953) 191–7.

Saygin, Susanne, *Humphrey, Duke of Gloucester (1390–1447) and the Italian Humanists* (Leiden: Brill, 2002).

Schibanoff, Susan, 'Avarice and Cerberus in Salutati's *De Laboribus Herculis* and Lydgate's *Fall of Princes*', *MP*, 71 (1974), 390–2.

Schirmer, Walter F., *Der Englische Frühhumanismus: Ein Beitrag zur Englischen Literaturgeschichte des 15. Jahrhunderts*, 2nd edn. (1931; Tübingen: Niemeyer, 1963).

—— *John Lydgate: A Study in the Culture of the XVth Century*, trans. Ann. E. Keep (1952; London: Methuen, 1961).

Schurink, Fred, 'An Elizabethan Grammar School Exercise Book', *BLR*, 18 (2003), 174–96.

Scott, Kathleen L., *Later Gothic Manuscripts, 1390–1490*, 2 vols. (London: Harvey Miller, 1996).

Scrope, G. Poulett, *History of the Manor and Ancient Barony of Castle Combe* (London: privately printed, 1852).

Seymour, M. C., *A Catalogue of Chaucer Manuscripts*, 2 vols. (Aldershot: Scolar, 1995–7).

Sharpe, Kevin, *Reading Revolutions: The Politics of Reading in Early Modern England* (New Haven, CT: Yale University Press, 2000).

Sherman, William H., 'What Did Renaissance Readers Write in their Books?', in *Books and Readers in Early Modern England: Material Studies*, ed. Jennifer Andersen and Elizabeth Sauer (Philadelphia, PA: University of Pennsylvania Press, 2002), 119–37.

Simpson, James, *Sciences and the Self in Medieval Poetry: Alan of Lille's* Anticlaudianus *and John Gower's* Confessio Amantis (Cambridge: Cambridge University Press, 1995).

_____ *The Oxford English Literary History: Volume 2: 1350–1547: Reform and Cultural Revolution* (Oxford: Oxford University Press, 2002).

_____ 'Bonjour Paresse: Literary Waste and Recycling in Book 4 of Gower's *Confessio Amantis*', forthcoming in *Proceedings of the British Academy*.

Skinner, Quentin, *The Foundations of Modern Political Thought*, 2 vols. (Cambridge: Cambridge University Press, 1978).

_____ *Reason and Rhetoric in the Philosophy of Hobbes* (Cambridge: Cambridge University Press, 1996).

Smith, Bruce R., *Ancient Scripts and Modern Experience on the English Stage 1500–1700* (Princeton, NJ: Princeton University Press, 1988).

Southern, R. W., *Medieval Humanism* (New York, NY: Harper and Row, 1970).

Spearing, A. C., *Medieval to Renaissance in English Poetry* (Cambridge: Cambridge University Press, 1985).

Starkey, David, 'Which Age of Reform?', in *Revolution Reassessed: Revisions in the History of Tudor Government and Administration*, ed. Christopher Coleman and David Starkey (Oxford: Clarendon Press, 1986), 13–27.

_____ 'England', in *The Renaissance in National Context*, ed. Roy Porter and Mikuláš Teich (Cambridge: Cambridge University Press, 1992), 146–63.

Stewart, Alan, *Close Readers: Humanism and Sodomy in Early Modern England* (Princeton, NJ: Princeton University Press, 1997).

Stock, Brian, *The Implications of Literacy* (Princeton, NJ: Princeton University Press, 1983).

Stratford, Jenny, 'The Manuscripts of John, Duke of Bedford: Library and Chapel', in *England in the Fifteenth Century: Proceedings of the 1986 Harlaxton Symposium*, ed. Daniel Williams (Woodbridge: Boydell, 1987), 329–50.

Strohm, Paul, *Politique: Languages of Statecraft between Chaucer and Shakespeare* (Notre Dame, IN: University of Notre Dame Press, 2005).

Summit, Jennifer, ' "Stable in study": Lydgate's *Fall of Princes* and Duke Humphrey's Library', in *John Lydgate: Poetry, Culture, and Lancastrian England*, ed. Larry Scanlon and James Simpson (Notre Dame, IN: University of Notre Dame Press, 2006), 207–31.

Sutton, Anne F., and Visser-Fuchs, Livia, 'Richard III's Books: XII. William Worcester's *Boke of Noblesse* and his Collection of Documents on the War in Normandy', *The Ricardian*, 9 (1991), 154–65.

_____ *Richard III's Books: Ideals and Reality in the Life and Library of a Medieval Prince* (Stroud: Sutton, 1997).

Swanson, Jenny, *John of Wales: A Study of the Works and Ideas of a Thirteenth-Century Friar* (Cambridge: Cambridge University Press, 1989).

Swanson, R. N., 'Caxton's Indulgence for Rhodes, 1480–81', *The Library*, 7th series, 5 (2004), 195–201.

Thomson, David, *A Descriptive Catalogue of Middle English Grammatical Texts* (New York: Garland, 1979).

Tilmouth, Christopher, *Passion's Triumph over Reason: A History of the Moral Imagination from Spenser to Rochester* (Oxford: Oxford University Press, 2007).

Tournoy-Thoen, Gilbert and Godelieve, 'Giovanni Gigli and the Renaissance of the Classical Epithalamium in England', in *Myricae: Essays on Neo-Latin Literature in Memory of Jozef IJsewijn*, Supplementa Humanistica Lovaniensia, 16 (Leuven: Leuven University Press, 2000), 133–93.

Trapp, J. B., *Erasmus, Colet and More: The Early Tudor Humanists and their Books* (London: British Library, 1991).

—— 'The Humanist Book', in *CHBB: III*, 285–315.

Tuve, Rosemund, 'Notes on the Virtues and Vices', *Journal of the Warburg and Courtauld Institutes*, 26 (1963), 264–303, 27 (1964), 42–72.

Ullmann, Walter, *Medieval Foundations of Renaissance Humanism* (London: Elek, 1977).

Vale, M. G. A., 'Sir John Fastolf's "Report" of 1435: A New Interpretation Reconsidered', *Nottingham Mediaeval Studies*, 17 (1973), 78–84.

Vanderjagt, Arjo, *Qui sa vertu anoblist: The Concepts of noblesse and chose publique in Burgundian Political Thought* (Groningen: Miélot, [1981]).

—— 'Three Solutions to Buonaccorso's Disputatio de nobilitate', in *Non Nova, Sed Nove: Mélanges de civilisation médiévale dédiés à Willem Noomen*, ed. Martin Gorman and Jaap van Os (Groningen: Bouma, 1984), 247–59.

—— 'Il pubblico dei testi umanistici nell'Italia settentrionale ed in Borgogna: Buonaccorso da Montemagno e Giovanni Aurispa', *Aevum*, 70 (1996), 477–86.

Vickers, Brian, 'Leisure and Idleness in the Renaissance: The Ambivalence of *otium*', *Renaissance Studies*, 4 (1990), 1–37, 107–54.

Vickers, K. H., *Humphrey Duke of Gloucester: A Biography* (London: Constable, 1907).

Waith, Eugene M., 'Controversia in the English Drama: Medwall and Massinger', *PMLA*, 68 (1953), 286–303.

Wakelin, Daniel, 'William Worcester Reads Chaucer's *Boece*', *Journal of the Early Book Society*, 5 (2002), 182–5.

—— 'The Occasion, Author and Readers of *Knyghthode and Bataile*', *Medium Ævum*, 73 (2004), 260–72.

—— 'Scholarly Scribes and the Creation of *Knyghthode and Bataile*', *English Manuscript Studies*, 12 (2005), 26–45.

—— 'William Worcester Writes a History of His Reading', *NML*, 7 (2005), 53–71.

—— 'Possibilities for Reading: Classical Translations in Parallel Texts *c.*1520–1558', forthcoming in *Studies in Philology*, 105 (2008).

Walker, Greg, *Writing Under Tyranny: English Literature and the Henrician Reformation* (Oxford: Oxford University Press, 2005).

Wallace, David, *Chaucerian Polity: Absolutist Lineages and Associational Forms in England and Italy* (Stanford, CA: Stanford University Press, 1997).

——— 'Dante in Somerset: Ghosts, Historiography, Periodization', *NML*, 3 (1999), 9–38.

——— (ed.), *The Cambridge History of Medieval English Literature* (Cambridge: Cambridge University Press, 1999).

Walsham, Alexandra, and Crick, Julia, 'Introduction: Script, Print and History', in their *The Uses of Script and Print, 1300–1700* (Cambridge: Cambridge University Press, 2004), 1–26.

Wang, Yu-Chiao, 'Caxton's Romances and their Early Tudor Readers', *Huntington Library Quarterly*, 67 (2004), 173–88.

Watts, John, '*De Consulatu Stiliconis*: Texts and Politics in the Reign of Henry VI', *JMH*, 16 (1990), 251–66.

——— 'Ideals, Principles and Politics', in *The Wars of the Roses*, ed. A. J. Pollard (London: Macmillan, 1995), 110–33.

——— *Henry VI and the Politics of Kingship* (Cambridge: Cambridge University Press, 1996).

——— '*The Policie in Christen Remes*: Bishop Russell's Parliamentary Sermons of 1483–84', in *Authority and Consent in Tudor England: Essays Presented to C. S. L. Davies*, ed. G. W. Bernard and S. J. Gunn (Aldershot: Ashgate, 2002), 33–59.

——— 'Was there a Lancastrian Court?', in *The Lancastrian Court*, ed. Jenny Stratford, Harlaxton Medieval Studies, 13 (Donington: Tyas, 2003), 253–71.

Weinberg, Carole, 'Thomas More and the Use of English in Early Tudor Education', *Moreana*, 15 (1978), 21–30.

Weiss, Roberto, *Humanism in England During the Fifteenth Century*, 3rd edn. (1941; Oxford: Blackwell, 1967).

Westfall, Suzanne R., *Patrons and Performance: Early Tudor Household Revels* (Oxford: Clarendon Press, 1990).

Wickham, Glynne, *Early English Stages 1300–1600: Volume III. Plays and their Makers to 1576* (London: Routledge and Kegan Paul, 1981).

Wilson, K. J., *Incomplete Fictions: The Formation of English Renaissance Dialogue* (Washington, DC: Catholic University of American Press, 1985).

Wisman, Josette A., 'L'*Epitoma rei militaris* de Végèce et sa fortune au Moyen Âge', *Le Moyen Âge*, 85 (1979), 13–31.

Wolffe, Bertram, *Henry VI* (London: Methuen, 1981).

Workman, Samuel K., *Fifteenth Century Translation as an Influence on English Prose*, Princeton Studies in English, 18 (Princeton, NJ: Princeton University Press, 1940).

——— 'Versions by Skelton, Caxton, and Berners of a Prologue by Diodorus Siculus', *Modern Language Notes*, 56 (1941), 252–8.

Wright, Herbert G., *Boccaccio in England from Chaucer to Tennyson* (London: Athlone, 1957).

Wyatt, Michael, *The Italian Encounter with Tudor England: A Cultural Politics of Translation* (Cambridge: Cambridge University Press, 2005).

Index

Like the list of works cited, the index alphabetizes works under their authors, translations under their translators; however, it alphabetizes works or translations of which the author or translator is anonymous or uncertain under the title (*'Epitoma rei militaris* in English'). Like the list of works cited, the index alphabetizes writers known by a Christian name and a toponym by the toponym ('Rome, Giles of'). It alphabetizes reigning monarchs by Christian name but members of the nobility by toponym ('Worcester, Sir John Tiptoft, Earl of'), if the toponym is commonly used, or surname if not. It lists colleges under the university of which they are part.